The Psychology of Eyewitness Testimony

A. Daniel Yarmey

"...psychology has as much to gain from studying the operation of law as law has to gain from greater appreciation of psychology."
— Riesman, 1951

In recent years, the courtroom has become a frequent setting for the study of human behavior, particularly in the area of eyewitness testimony, where the psychological principles of perception, attention, memory, thought, and language have been increasingly brought to bear on the court's decision-making process.

With this in mind, A. Daniel Yarmey has written an introduction to the psychological and legal aspects of eyewitness identification and testimony. He has done so with the latest material on eyewitness testimony from such normally diverse areas as experimental psychology, social psychology, and justice administration, and throughout the book shows the relevance of the scientific literature to the workings of the criminal justice system.

The Psychology of Eyewitness Testimony highlights various aspects of the ways in which the eyewitness perceives, remembers, and reconstructs his or her experiences. Yarmey first examines the scientific principles and practices employed by psychologists and the methods used by police and the courts to determine truth. Then, introducing the psychological factors involved in memory and person perception, he examines the evidence on facial recognition, criminal identification, and the testimony of the child, the adult, and the aged witness.

(Continued on back flap)

criminologists, and psychologists practicing in the area of psychology and the law.

The Psychology
of
Eyewitness Testimony

The Psychology
of
Eyewitness Testimony

A. Daniel Yarmey

THE FREE PRESS
A Division of Macmillan Publishing Co., Inc.
NEW YORK

Collier Macmillan Publishers
LONDON

To my wife, Judy,
my children, Craig, Linda, and Meagan,
and my mother and late father

The Free Press
A Division of Macmillan Publishing Co., Inc.
866 Third Avenue, New York, N.Y. 10022

Collier Macmillan Canada, Ltd.

Library of Congress Catalog Card Number: 78-20648

Printed in the United States of America

printing number

1 2 3 4 5 6 7 8 9 10

Library of Congress Cataloging in Publication Data

Yarmey, A. Daniel.
  The psychology of eyewitness testimony.

  Bibliography: p.
  Includes indexes.
  1. Witnesses--United States. 2. Evidence,
Criminal--United States. 3. Psychology, Forensic.
4. Memory. I. Title.
KF9672.Y37   347'.73'66019   78-20648
ISBN 0-02-935860-4

Copyright Acknowledgments

CHAPTER 1

Quotation, pp. 5–6. Watson, A. (Ed.), *Adolf Beck's Trial*, Notable British Trials Series. Glasgow: Hodge, 1924. Passage on pp. 118ff. Reprinted by permission.

Quotation, p. 14. Eidlin, F., Symposium on the meaning of science in the social sciences. University of Guelph, Guelph, Ontario, February 1975. Passage on p. 6. Reprinted by permission.

CHAPTER 2

Quotation, p. 34. Fitzsimons, J., Science and law—a lawyer's viewpoint. *Journal of Forensic Science Society*, 1975, *13*, 261–267. Passage on p. 265. Copyright 1975 by the Journal of the Forensic Science Society. Reprinted by permission.

CHAPTER 3

Figure 3.2. Ames. A., Visual perception and the rotating trapezoidal window. *Psychological Monographs*, 1951, *65*, No. 7, Whole No. 324. Figure 1, p. 2. Copyright 1951 by the American Psychological Association. Reprinted by permission.

Quotation, p. 50. Ittleson, W. H., & Kilpatrick, F. P., Experiments in perception. *Scientific American*, 1951, *185*, No. 2. Passage on p. 55. Reprinted by permission.

CHAPTER 4

Quotation, pp. 56–57. Wigmore, J. H., *Evidence* (2nd Ed.). Boston: Little, Brown, 1923. Passage on p. 426. Reprinted by permission.

Figure 4.1. Atkinson, R. C., & Shiffrin, R. M., Human memory: A proposed system and its control processes. In K. W. Spence and J. T. Spence (Eds.),

The psychology of learning and motivation: Advances in research and theory, Vol. 2. New York: Academic Press, 1968. Figure 1, p. 93. Reprinted by permission.

Figure 4.2. Carmichael, L. L., Hogan, H. P., & Walter, A. A., An experimental study of the effect of language on the reproduction of visually perceived form. *Journal of Experimental Psychology*, 1932, *15*, 73–86. Figure 2, p. 80. Copyright 1932 by the American Psychological Association. Reprinted by permission.

Figure 4.3. Collins, A. M., & Quillian, M. R., Retrieval time from semantic memory. *Journal of Verbal Learning and Verbal Behavior*, 1969, *8*, 240–247. Figure 1, p. 241. Reprinted by permission.

Quotation, p. 70. Gardner, D. S., The perception and memory of witnesses. *Cornell Law Quarterly*, 1933, *18*, 391–409. Passage on pp. 391–392. © Copyright 1933 by Cornell University. Reprinted by permission.

Figure 4.4. Yarmey, A. D., Hypermnesia for pictures but not for concrete or abstract words. *Bulletin of the Psychonomic Society*, 1976, *8*, 115–117.

CHAPTER 5

Quotation, p. 83. Kirkham, G. L., From professor to patrolman: A fresh perspective on the police. *Journal of Police Science and Administration*, 1974, *2*, 127–137. Passage on pp. 130–131. Reprinted by special permission of the Journal of Police Science and Administration. © Copyright 1974 by Northwestern University School of Law, Vol. 2, No. 2.

Quotation, p. 83. Culliton, B. J., Edelin trial: Jury not persuaded by scientists for the defense. *Science*, 1975, *187*, 814–816. Passage on p. 187. Copyright 1975 by the American Association for the Advancement of Science. Reprinted by permission.

Figure 5.1. Allport, G. W., *Pattern and growth in personality*. New York: Holt, Rinehart and Winston, 1937, 1961. Figure 5, p. 41. Reprinted by permission.

Table 5.1. Lavrakas, P. J., & Bickman, L., What makes a good witness? Paper presented at the Annual Meeting of the American Psychological Association, Chicago, Illinois, 1975. Table 1. Reprinted by permission.

Table 5.2. Reprinted by permission of author and publisher from Kuehn, L. L., Looking down a gun barrel: Person perception and violent crime. *Perceptual and Motor Skills*, 1974, *39*, 1159–1164. Table 2, p. 1162.

Quotation, p. 106. Jones, E. E., & Nisbett, R. E., The actor and the observer: Divergent perceptions of the causes of behavior. In E. E. Jones, D.

E. Kanouse, H. H. Kelley, R. E. Nisbett, S. Valins, & B. Weiner (Eds.), *Attribution: Perceiving the causes of behavior*. Morristown, N.J.: General Learning Press, 1972. Passage on p. 79. Copyright 1972 by the Silver Burdett Company. Reprinted by permission.

CHAPTER 6

Figure 6.2. Ellis, H., Shepherd, J., & Davies, G., An investigation of the use of the Photo-fit technique for recalling faces. *British Journal of Psychology*, 1975, *66*, 29–37. Reprinted by permission of Cambridge University Press.

Figure 6.3. Fagan, J. F., III, Infant recognition of faces. Paper presented at the Annual Meeting of the Midwestern Psychological Association, Chicago, Illinois, 1975. Figure 1. Reprinted by permission.

CHAPTER 8

Quotation, p. 166. Thomas, E. I., Cross-examination and rehabilitation of witnesses. *Defense Law Journal*, 1965, *15*, 247–263. Reprinted from *Defense Law Journal*, Volume 15 (1965). Published by The Allen Smith Company, Indianapolis, Indiana, U.S.A. Passage on p. 257. Reprinted by permission.

Table 8.1. Rotter, J. B., & Stein, D. K., Public attitudes toward the trustworthiness, competence, and altruism of twenty selected occupations. *Journal of Applied Social Psychology*, 1971, *1*, 334–343. Table 1, p. 339, and Table 2, p. 340. Reprinted by permission.

Quotation, pp. 187–188. Weinberg, A., *Attorney for the damned*. New York. Copyright ©, 1975. Reprinted by permission of Simon & Schuster, A Division of Gulf and Western Corporation.

Quotation, p. 189. Lund, F. H., The psychology of belief: IV. The law of primacy in persuasion. *Journal of Abnormal and Social Psychology*, 1925, *20*, 183–191. Passage on p. 191. Copyright 1925 by the American Psychological Association. Reprinted by permission.

Quotation, p. 196. Moore, C. C., Psychology in the courts. *Law Notes*, 1908, *11*, 186–187. Reprinted by permission.

CHAPTER 9

Quotation, p. 211. Cutts, N. E., & Moseley, N., Notes on photographic memory. *Journal of Psychology*, 1969, *71*, 3–15. Passage on p. 9. Reprinted by permission.

Quotation, p. 213. Rouke, F. L., Psychological research on problems of testimony. *Journal of Social Issues*, 1957, *13*, 50–59. Passage on p. 54. Reprinted by permission.

Quotation, p. 214. Quoted in an article written by Stephen Handelman, *The Toronto Star*, January 12, 1978. Reprinted with permission—The Toronto Star.

Figure 9.1. Wapner, S., Werner, H., & Comalli, P. E. Perception of part-whole relationships in middle and old age. *Journal of Gerontology*, 1960, *15*, 413–418. Figure 1 and Figure 3, p. 413. Reproduced with the permission of the Journal of Gerontology.

Contents

List of Illustrations

List of Tables

Preface

The primary purpose of this book is to present an integrated account of our knowledge of the psychological and legal aspects of eyewitness identification and testimony. Another aim of this book is to show the relevance and implications for the criminal justice community of the scientific literature on memory, perception, and social perception.

The book is intended both as a textbook and as a resource book. Students of law and criminology, as well as professional lawyers wishing to apply psychological theories and supporting evidence to their practices, will find this book useful, I hope. In addition, it is hoped that students of social and cognitive psychology interested in applying their knowledge to the criminal justice system will find some valuable insights and suggestions for further research.

Basic concepts about the psychology of the witness and the assumptions often made by the criminal justice system are introduced in the first chapter and are carefully integrated throughout the remaining nine chapters. The book has three major sections. The first, which consists of chapters 1 and 2, introduces the scientific principles and legalistic practices employed in the pursuit of truth and understanding. The second major section—chapters 3, 4, and 5—presents an overview of the psychological literature on perception, memory, and person perception. The third major section, chapters 6 through 9, examines the evidence on facial memory, criminal identification, and testimony of the adult, the child, and the aged witness. Chapter 10 closes the book with a summary statement of my hopes, my reservations, and my challenges to both psychologists and lawyers for further work in this exciting area.

To reach the diverse audience for whom this book is intended, I have tried to be descriptive at an introductory level of knowledge. I have not assumed that the reader is sophisticated in legal and psychological terminology, theory, or procedures. Nevertheless, I would hope that the more sophisticated scholars will find the book both provocative and challenging.

Acknowledgments

I am indebted for the many comments and suggestions that I have received from several people during the writing of this book. The editorial advice and assistance of Drs. Peter Duda and Howard Pollio is especially appreciated. I thank Drs. Stephen Handel, Michael Johnson, Peyton Todd, and William Verplanck for valuable suggestions and comments on my initial endeavors. Professors Norma Bowen, Fred Eidlin, Wayne Gatehouse, and Thom Herrmann offered valuable comments on various chapters, as did my research assistant, Mrs. Laurie Hogg, and graduate students, Gordon Briscoe, Victor Sartor, and Janet Wright.

I wish to express my gratitude to Dr. William Calhoun, head of the Department of Psychology, University of Tennessee, for his generous support during my sabbatical leave spent at UT, where this book was conceived. It was also my good fortune to have the able assistance of Maury Bull, a senior at Tennessee, during my year in Knoxville.

All of my own research reported in this book has been maintained financially by the National Research Council of Canada (Grant A0228). I thank the Council for its continued support.

I would like to pay my respects to two men in particular who stimulated me and guided my career in its early development—Professor Ralph Dent, one of my first and best undergraduate teachers, who encouraged me to make psychology a career, and Professor Allan Paivio, my dissertation advisor, teacher, and friend, who is a constant source of inspiration.

Completion of this book would have been impossible without the excellent typing services of Mrs. Edna McKinney and Mrs. Ina Hutchings. Mrs.

Hutchings also helped proofread the various drafts and assisted in correcting the references.

Finally, I would like to thank my wife, Judy, for her constant support, editorial advice, and patient assistance throughout the many trials and tribulations of this project.

The Psychology
of
Eyewitness Testimony

Chapter 1

Psychology and the Law

In the last twenty years or so, television has allowed many of us to be policemen and detectives, lawyers and judges. Eyewitness testimony, cross-examination, reasonable doubt, and presumption of innocence are events and concepts which are familiar to anyone who is addicted to "law and order" TV. We have learned how to detect important clues, how to solve hundreds of murder cases, when to stand up to defend our client and yell "Objection" and when to vicariously enjoy the power of answering "Objection overruled." We have become court-wise. In many respects the law and the courthouse have lost their aura of omniscience. Perry Mason and his imitators consistently win their cases and even are able to solve murders for the police during the trial.

Most of us do not suspect that there are major differences between the criminal justice system as it functions in the real world and the system as it is depicted on television. One aspect of that system which is more complex than is generally believed is the practice of eyewitness identification and testimony. My primary purpose in writing this book has been to describe and interpret the psychology behind eyewitness identification and testimony for lawyers, professionals, and others studying and working in the criminal justice system. Implicit in this purpose is the belief that psychology has important contributions to make to some of the legal problems and issues confronting contemporary society.

The relevance of experimental psychology and sociopsychological research needs to be stated in simple straightforward language which can be understood and appreciated by both the criminal justice worker and the academic psychologist. The use of psychological principles and explanations

1

of behavior in the courtroom is growing, but very few individuals in our legal system have had any formal training in this area. At the same time, while many psychologists believe that their scientific training prepares them for the prediction, testing, and understanding of behavior, few of them are prepared to apply their findings to the practical everyday problems of the world we live in. Perhaps this conservative approach is correct, since we are a young science and have few, if any, hard facts to give society. On the other hand, our reluctance to get involved in applying our knowledge in the real world may be a cop-out. By staying in our laboratories and publishing our research in professional journals, we can reward ourselves in our closed system and avoid any accusations from the general public of being irrelevant. However, this posture, in my opinion, is deficient and irresponsible. Thus a second purpose of this book is to present members of the academic psychology community with a summary of how their knowledge and research can be applied to legal proceedings.

These two audiences may be seen by some people as incompatible, since the methods and goals of the lawyer and the academic are so dissimilar. The cynical view of lawyers has it that they are interested only in winning their cases and not in arriving at truth and explanation. Another pessimistic view is that any advice psychologists can offer lawyers must be presented in a cookbook format which can be directly applied to the specific circumstances of a particular trial and can make no pretense to general validity. I do not have any evidence that either supports or opposes these negative and shallow descriptions, but I believe that successful lawyers are interested in the reasons and causes behind normal and deviant behavior and that psychologists can directly and efficiently help them, a great deal in this regard.

I am sure that someday a practical book on psychology and the law will be written in the same fashion as books we now have that have been written by authorities on "How to Parent" or "How to Fix Your Own Car." This volume, however, is not a list of psychological principles packaged for immediate transfer to the courtroom. In writing this book, I have deliberately tried to present the material in such a manner that the reader does not feel he or she is being forced to accept psychological findings and their application to the criminal justice system as absolute truth. I leave it to you to judge whether or not my effort has been successful.

The Psychology of the Witness

When a witness is called to testify in court that he saw "Mr. Brown shoot Mr. Jones," a large number of psychological factors influence his report. In order for the witness to testify meaningfully, we must assume the following conditions. First, the witness must have been able to perceive the event.

Remembered information is based upon observation, but in everyday experience observations are not planned and deliberate. In other words, they are not intentionally studied and stored for subsequent testing and questioning. How complete and accurate the observations made by our witness were is a matter of conjecture. Since his perceptual experiences are private events which are dependent upon the capabilities of his sensory and motor systems, we can never share the experience itself. We can, however, learn about his observations through what he reports. Unfortunately, the report may or may not correspond to the perceptual experience with any degree of accuracy.

The second factor having considerable psychological importance with respect to eyewitness testimony is memory. The witness must be able to recall the events. However, the long delay between the time of observing the critical incident and testifying in court can only interfere with remembering. At one time psychologists conceptualized memory as the records of sensory experiences etched onto the mind, which was regarded as a tabula rasa, or blank tablet. These memory traces were thought to be more or less permanent. This viewpoint no longer prevails. Instead, memory is now explained by some theorists (e.g., Atkinson and Shiffrin, 1968) as a system of structures, or stores, through which information sequentially passes. As information moves through these stores, it is constantly being transformed, or recoded, by later information. Moreover, the traces of these encodings are susceptible to all forms of interference and decay. According to this theory, a witness is continually being subjected to conditions which have a high likelihood of influencing his memory. Being asked questions by the police, reading accounts of the crime in the daily newspaper, engaging in discussions with friends and acquaintances, and all of the everyday experiences of living which normally affect memory are possible sources of bias, distortion, and forgetting. Once the witness is in the courthouse and takes the stand, a new set of events will act to confuse his recall. The testimony that the witness gives is subject to cross-examination, which is intended to determine the reliability of his reports and to separate truth from error. However, the questions of cross-examination also may act to distort memory.

Finally, a third factor of psychological importance is the communications process itself. The witness must be able to tell the court in his own words what he saw and heard. Witnesses must be able to find the correct phrases and sentences which convey most accurately the meanings of their experiences. Memory and language obviously overlap a great deal, and some psychologists are convinced that what we see in the world and what we think about these experiences are dependent upon the language of our culture (Whorf, 1956). In order for the judge and the jury to understand the witness, the words that he chooses must be free of double or multiple meanings. This problem may appear to be simple, but the consequences of different interpretations given to witnesses' statements are profound. Again, the cross-examination will influence the reports of the witness. A good lawyer wants to destroy the credibility of the opposing witness. He wants to show that the knowledge of the witness is doubtful or wrong and therefore untrustworthy.

To illustrate the psychological processes just discussed, suppose that our witness is asked by an attorney to state the color of the face of the person he saw commit a shooting. Most people would agree that the response "Black" is simple, direct, and easily understood. Nevertheless, the reliability of this statement is debatable. We can conclude two things regarding the witness's statement. The first is that he thinks he saw a black face. The second is that he *said* he saw a black face. All that we actually know from his statement of what he observed is this second thing. This may appear to be a trivial distinction, but reports of perceptual experiences must not be confused with the experiences themselves. Further questioning of the witness may reveal that even his answer "Black" is suspicious. How good is his eyesight? How much light was available in the area of the crime? What distance was he from the crime? How many other persons were present when the crime was committed? Were they black, or were there whites also in the general vicinity? What physical features of faces determine whether or not a face is considered black, brown, swarthy, or white? And finally, what are the attitudes of the witness toward blacks, and how familiar in his everyday experiences is he with blacks? The answers to questions such as these help to establish the credibility of witnesses, and courts judge the truth or validity of witnesses' perceptions, memory and accuracy of communication on the basis of them.

Adolf Beck's Trial

A famous example of the dangers inherent in accepting at face value the identification testimony of several eyewitnesses and not substantiating their testimony with other evidence was the case of Adolf Beck. In December 1895 in London, England, Beck was accused of obtaining jewelry and money on false pretenses from loose women. Ten women testified at his trial in March 1896 that Beck committed these crimes and positively identified him. Beck was convicted and sentenced to seven years imprisonment, always claiming his innocence. In 1898 he was able to prove that he was not the guilty party by showing that he had been mistaken for one John Smith and he was released from prison on a "ticket-of-leave." The courts decided that he was not innocent of the 1895 offenses but was innocent of being a second offender. In 1904 while he was visiting London, more crimes of a similar nature were committed. Beck was arrested again and identified by several women (presumably moral women this time, since no reference is made to their being loose), tried, found guilty, and sentenced in April 1904 to five years imprisonment. Fortunately for Beck, in July 1904 another series of the same kind of offenses occurred in London. John Smith, "alias Thomas," was arrested, tried, and found guilty. The court decided that Smith was probably the perpetrator of the crimes of 1895 also. Beck was released in July 1904 and declared innocent of the crimes of 1895 and 1904. To rectify this miscarriage of justice an indemnity fund was bestowed on him (Wigmore, 1931).

Nevertheless, the identity evidence that contributed to the original conviction of Beck is convincing, as shown in the following quotations that appear in the printed record of his case:

> Adolf Beck was indicted for unlawfully obtaining from Fanny Nutt two gold rings; and from other persons other articles by false pretenses with intent to defraud.
>
> The prisoner pleaded Not Guilty. . . .
>
> *Fanny Nutt,* examined—"I am a widow. In December 1894, I was living in Delancey Street, Regent's Park. . . . I went straight into the Court, and found the prisoner standing in the dock; I saw his back; I should know him among a thousand. I recognized him at once; I am quite sure he is the man. . . . I identified him by his back at once at the Police Court. I was quite sure of him, and always have been."
>
> *Marion Taylor,* examined—"In the early part of January, 1895, I was living at Morton Place, Pimlico. . . . I did not see him again till, on 2nd January, 1896, I went to Rochester Row Police Court, in consequence of seeing his case in the paper, and picked the prisoner out of eleven or twelve men without the slightest difficulty. I am quite sure about him." (Cross-examined)—"There was no one there a bit like him. . . . I went to the Police Court for revenge. I had read no description of the man in custody. The prisoner is the living picture of the man I saw."
>
> *Ottilie Meissonier,* examined—"I live at Fulham, and teach music. . . . I noticed when he sat in my room he had some mark just below the right jaw, whether it was from a drawn tooth or not I cannot say. I described it at the station. I next saw him on 16th December; I was coming along Victoria Street from the Army and Navy Stores, and I saw the prisoner standing in the doorway of 135, or 139, Victoria Street. As soon as I passed I recognized him, and I stepped up to him and he smiled. I touched his coat, and said—'Sir, I know you.' As soon as he heard my voice he tried to push past me into the street, and said—'What do you want from me?' I said—'I want my two watches and my rings.' . . . The policeman said, as I charged him, he must take him to the station. . . . I am sure about the scar or something I spoke of on the right side; it might be from a drawn tooth; it was something I could notice; I could not see it quite plainly. I see the mark on the prisoner now. . . ."
>
> *John Watts,* examined—"On 16th December I was at Rochester Row police station shortly after the prisoner was brought in. I told him he answered the description of a man giving the name of Earl Wilton, who was wanted for stealing jewelry. He said, 'It is a mistake.' I sent for Miss Grant, who had given a description; she came, the prisoner was placed, with six other men in the charge-room. She looked at the men and said—'I believe that is the man; if he will take his hat off I shall know.' All the men took their hats off, and then she

said—'That is the man.'. . . I arranged the identification in the first case, when the prisoner was detained at Rochester Row police station; on the next occasion Inspector Waldock arranged it. . . . The fifteen or sixteen women who saw him at the police station include the ten who have sworn to him here; the other five or six did not identify him; one woman was not sure, she would not swear to him. The five or six women who are not here saw him under the same circumstances as the others, three failed to identify him; they said they could not see the man there. Another of them came into the charge-room while he was in the dock being charged, and she said she did not think he was the man. Another of them afterwards said she thought he was the man. All of them but one had lodged complaints, I believe. . . ."

Rose Reece—"In August, 1903, I was living in Marylebone Road. . . . I did not see the prisoner until I picked him out of a number of other men, I believe, at Paddington Green police station, about 23rd April—I gave the police a description of the man who has swindled me." (Cross-examined)—"When I picked him out I believed he was already in custody on Miss Scott's charge—I did not particularly notice the other men when I picked him out—I believe all of them were younger than he is—I cannot remember if any of them had grey mustachios—I caught sight of the prisoner immediately. . . . I do not remember if anything was said when I picked him out—his nose is most peculiar, and is one I could pick out of a thousand—his whole face is different from any other man I ever remember seeing. . . ." [Watson, 1924, pp. 118ff.]

Psychology in Perspective

Psychology has not been a favorite son of the legal profession or law enforcement agencies. In fact, the courts have often been indifferent or even hostile to this relatively young science and profession. This misunderstanding is regrettable but perhaps explainable. Since we all pride ourselves on having "a whole lot of common sense," each of us in a sense is a psychologist. But just coming into contact with people every day of our lives and learning about others through these interactions does not make us experts on human behavior. Such experiences are inadequate foundations for drawing valid conclusions about people. In the search for scientific understanding observations of human behavior usually have to be made under controlled conditions and often have to be verified by replication before we can consider them valid judgments.

Misconceptions about psychology held by lawyers and the general public often are the result of a general tendency to attribute too much to psychology. Some of the popular misconceptions are that it deals with the occult and the supernatural; that psychologists can read your mind or "psychoanalyze you on the spot"; that your personality can be instantly identified and judged to be lacking in this or that; and that all psychologists by definition are experts in mental illness and raising children.

Other misconceptions about psychology result from the failure to distinguish clinical psychology from psychiatry and psychoanalysis. Psychiatrists are medical doctors who have had specialized training in the diagnosis and treatment of personality disorders. The major responsibility of psychiatrists has been the classification and treatment of mental illness. Being trained in medicine, psychiatrists often will prescribe drugs or physical treatments as therapeutic aids. Psychoanalysts usually but not always possess the M.D. degree. They differ from psychiatrists in that their theoretical conceptions of personality and therapeutic treatments of disorders follow the teachings of Sigmund Freud and his followers. Therapeutic practices of psychoanalysts do not include the use of drugs. Clinical psychologists deal with many of the same problems handled by psychiatrists and psychoanalysts. Clinical psychologists usually have a Ph.D. degree and also work primarily in hospitals and mental health centers. They are involved in some medical functions, such as diagnostic testing and psychotherapy, and nonmedical services such as research on psychopathology and teaching of nurses, social workers, and medical interns. In short, the major differences between clinical psychologists, psychiatrists, and psychoanalysts are first, that psychiatrists often use drugs or surgery in their treatment, second, that clinical psychologists receive their basic education in the scientific study of behavior and not in medicine, and third, that psychoanalysts are trained in and follow the teachings of Freud or one of his followers.

Experimental Psychology and the Courts

When court decisions are dependent upon witnesses, the psychology of perception, attention, memory, thought, and language is involved. Both psychology and the courts are concerned with predicting, explaining, and controlling human behavior. Many of the decisions and principles employed by legal investigators are based on common sense, empirically derived explanations, and precedents. Much of modern-day experimental psychology, is unknown to the criminal justice system. Police investigators and officers of the court appear to understand only that portion of psychology concerned with mental illness and the legal concept of insanity. Scientific psychology has reached a point of development, however, at which some of its findings and theoretical explanations are ready for consideration by the legal system. For example:

1. Testimony given in an assertive and positive manner is treated by the courts as probably accurate and truthful (Gardner, 1933). Experimental psychologists, as we will see later, have systematically studied the relationship between emotionality and recall, the development of morality, and the ten-

dency to lie and cheat. Accuracy of recall and confidence of report occasionally are correlated but are not necessarily related in all conditions and psychological states.

2. The courts are aware that we quickly forget a large amount of what we have just learned, and the longer we retain the information the more likely it is to be forgotten. Under certain conditions, judges have allowed memoranda or notes recorded soon after the occurrence of an event to be presented as evidence.[1] Psychology has been interested in scientifically describing the course of forgetting since 1885 (Ebbinghaus, 1964). Most forgetting begins immediately after learning. However, performance will vary as a function of different factors. The courts appear to have a general knowledge regarding the importance of forgetting for testimonial purposes, but the processes involved are not simple and straightforward (Gardner, 1933; Hutchins and Slesinger, 1928).

3. The courts have accepted the assumption that memories of scenes that are vivid, striking, novel, or impressive are retained more readily than routine, common scenes devoid of interest.[2] This assumption, which is true in some respects, is in error if it conceives of memory simply as a passive recorder of events in contrast to an active, constructive process (Neisser, 1967).

4. Retrograde amnesia and anterograde amnesia, which are psychological states involving the loss of memory prior to or following the occurrence of a critical incident, have also been of interest to the law. The law, apparently, is more interested in memory of events just prior to the occurrence of the critical emotional event in question. Furthermore, it assumes that the perceiver is able to automatically isolate causes of events. Because of the excitement surrounding the critical event, recall of succeeding events is considered more likely to be in error.[3] Related to the phenomena of memory for emotional events, the law assumes that someone who is highly aroused is not likely to have had time to construct lies and that his spontaneous declarations immediately after an accident or injury are probably factual and accurate.[4] Recent research on retrograde and anterograde amnesia questions the validity of such assumptions. Furthermore, perception is not as automatic and mechanical as the courts may assume.

5. The courts have noted that concentrated attention and intention to remember improve recall.[5] Most witnesses, however, fail to study a crime in

[1]Wigmore, Evid., Vol. III, § 2118; Dyeing Co. v. Hosiery Co., 126 N.C. 292, 35 S.E. 586 (1900).

[2]23 C.J., Evid., § 1764, notes 82, 86, 93.

[3]23 C.J., Evid., § 1764, notes 92, 93, 95. Giltner v. Gorham, 10 Fed. Cas. 424, 4 McLean 402 (1848); U.S. v. McGlue, 26 Fed. Cas. 1092, 1 Curt. 1 (1851); Williams v. Hall, 1 Curt. Eccl. 597.

[4]Wigmore, Evid., Vol. III, § 1747 (1).

[5]Dean v. Dean, 42 Ore. 290, 296, 70 Pac. 1039, 1041, (1902); 23 C.J. Evid., § 1764, notes 91, 95.

action in the same way that people study verbal and pictorial materials in a laboratory experiment. The nature of attention and the "will to learn" and remember has been studied by psychologists and does have importance for the law. Whether or not this scientific evidence may be generalized to the courtroom, however, is the important question.

6. The courts also distinguish among witnesses who are children, adults, and elderly adults and among groups differing in formal education. McCarty (1960) insists that the better educated a witness, the less reliable is his testimony, because his mind is more apt to be preoccupied with competing thoughts; and that the less the education of the witness, the better his perception and memory.[6] Perceptual development and memory processes among age groups and socioeconomic groups have not been thoroughly researched, but evidence to be discussed later refutes rather than supports McCarty's assertions.

7. Courts are aware of the interaction between memory of events and imagined memory of these events and accepts the statement made by William James in 1890 that "Ere long fiction expels reality from memory and reigns in its stead alone" (James, 1950, p. 373).[7] In the past few years, experimental psychology has witnessed a renewal of interest in imagery and memory processes. Contrary to the old beliefs held by the courts, imagery representations have been shown to facilitate rather than retard memory (Paivio, 1971a).

8. Lawyers and judges are constantly on the alert to rule out hearsay or biasing questions. The power of suggestion has been shown in recent investigations to distort memory and encourage errors even more than has been previously suspected. Research indicates that the wording of questions to witnesses significantly affects their recall. For example, more uncertain or "don't know" responses are given if a witness is asked about an indefinite item (e.g., "Did you see *a* knife?") than occurs when the question contains a definite article ("Did you see *the* knife?") (Loftus and Zanni, 1975).

9. According to the maxim "Falsus in uno, falsus in omnibus," juries may be instructed to ignore all the evidence given by a witness if it can be proved that one of his recalls was inaccurate.[8] This proposition assumes that different types of memory, such as verbal, visual, or motor, are identical and that different memory tests, such as recall and recognition, measure the same kind of behaviors. This is false. For example, witnesses, may be able to recognize a person's face but not able to recall his name even if his name is very familiar. Some years ago, Hutchins and Slesinger (1928) pointed out to lawyers that memory does not operate as a "faculty" or entity in which an all-or-nothing process takes place. Furthermore, memory is understandable only in the context of theory construction and experimental testing. As we

[6]23 C.J. Evid., § 1766.
[7]Cunningham v. Burdell, 4 Bradf. Surr. 343 (N.Y. 1857).
[8]28 R.C.L. *Witnesses* § 244.

know, most lawyers are neither trained in nor familiar with cognitive theory or research design. Nevertheless, this deficiency does not deter lawyers from defining memory for their own purposes, such as establishing the competency of a witness to testify, on the basis of their subjective impressions of cognitive capacities. The law's ignorance of memory could be defended if the legal system acknowledged that it uses a simple layman's level of understanding (Redmount, 1959). But the law does more than this. Lawyers theorize about the nature of the mind, and judges rule out evidence according to their own primitive theoretical conceptions of cognition.

10. The stated (idealistic) purpose of a criminal trial is to discover the truth in order to administer justice. The procedures to reach this goal have varied from the historical trial by ordeal and trial by battle to modern adversary proceedings. In order to tell which side is telling the truth, the court relies on cross-examination of witnesses. Some psychologists and lawyers doubt that this is the most accurate procedure by which to reconstruct memory. As we will see, different performances in recall occur if a subject is allowed to freely narrate his story as opposed to having to answer specific questions.

11. In a paper addressed to his fellow lawyers, Thomas (1965) stated that five basic attributes of memory—(1) primacy, (2) recency, (3) association, (4) vividness, and (5) frequency—influence both the advocate and the cross-examiner in their management of witnesses. He pointed out that the cross-examiner must prepare his attack knowing that his opposition will generally use his best witness first and his next-to-best witness last. Furthermore, he will question each witness in such a way that answers are associatively related to each other and to the whole train of thought, are expressed in vivid and concrete detail, and will be repeated both by the same witness and by other witnesses, so that the jury will not fail to attend to the critical message. Recent research evidence shows that these five memory attributes are of variable importance in determining retention and recall. Memory is much more complex than Thomas (1965) assumes.

Science, Psychology, and the Law

Blom-Cooper and Wegner (1968), in a pessimistic note, claim that the courts have changed very slowly in their attitude toward scientific validation of psychological factors involved in a witness's testimony. What Münsterberg (1908) wrote still appears to be true: "The court would rather listen for whole days to the 'science' of the handwriting experts than allow a witness to be examined with regard to his memory and his power of perception ... with methods ... of experimental psychology. It is so much easier ... to be satisfied with sharp demarcation lines ... ; the man is sane or insane, and if he's sane, he speaks the truth or he lies. The psychologist would upset this satisfaction completely."

If the courts do retain an outdated viewpoint toward science, and in particular toward psychology as a science, we should begin by describing some of the different scientific and philosophical assumptions that form the foundations of modern psychology. In the following discussion, the classical nineteenth-century views about science, still held by many scientists, will be outlined first, followed by some contemporary viewpoints held by other scientists and philosophers.

It has been assumed in the past that:

1. The universe is orderly, uniform, and permanent. If the universe was assumed to be chaotic or random, there would be no sense in attempting to study the nature of events. Since the universe is taken to be uniform and permanent, it is assumed that we can know or discover the orderliness in nature. Some scientists have interpreted the concept of stability and orderliness in nature to mean that nature is governed by a set of laws that are universal, timeless, and unchanging, and it is their purpose to search for these laws. The use of the word "law" in this context may be unfortunate (Kemeny, 1959). The word "law" has the connotation of obedience-disobedience, but nature cannot obey or disobey. Laws of nature do not prescribe; rather, they *describe* what happens. Laws of nature are careful recordings of the observations of scientists of what happens in the present and what has happened in the past, and are predictors of what will happen in the future.

Many scientists now recognize that man-made laws of nature do change and are not universal. Nineteenth-century Newtonian principles of physics are sufficient for explaining much of the behavior of elements in our universe but are inadequate in certain limiting cases, e.g., in explaining light or radiation of energy from black bodies. Other theoretical systems, such as relativity and quantum mechanics, are necessary for such explanations. In contrast to early physics, contemporary theories do not provide an exhaustive explanation of the universe and are seen as only approximations of the truth (Nagel, 1961).

2. Another assumption is that the universe is deterministic, so that each event in the universe is given or defined by its relation to some other event. The assumption is made that if all other events are discoverable, then the event being sought can be logically deduced. Although scientists admit that they cannot get back to ultimate first causes, except in theoretical discussion, many believe in the notion of limited causality. This assumption states that a limited number of events cause or determine the action or movement of any other event.

Strict determinism may be a satisfying belief, particularly to those of us still living in the nineteenth century, but modern physics no longer accepts the notion that the physical world is completely determined (Oppenheimer,

1956). Every event contains within it some degree of uncertainty, something which cannot be solved. Consequently, scientific laws cannot be considered causal, but rather are probabilistic. Although the universe is orderly and reliable, it is not completely causal, and science can be predictive only within limits. Whenever we attempt to measure something—in particular, atomic and subatomic phenomena—our methods of study disturb the system which is being observed (Heisenberg, 1958). The principle of indeterminacy, at least at the level of the atom and subatomic particles, is now accepted as a valid premise of science.

The contemporary viewpoint of science regarding determinism must affect the age-old conflict between a belief in free will and the belief that forces beyond our will determine our behavior. Furthermore, the philosophy of determinism must influence society's conception of criminal law and responsibility. Our decisions to apply a moral judgment to specific behaviors of our fellow man—to assign fault, guilt, and blame—are all based upon the premise that man is free to choose how he acts. But how can free will exist in a world that is still largely conceptualized by many people as more or less deterministic?

In the early part of the present century the famous defense lawyer Clarence Darrow presented to a jury the philosophical argument of determinism for the purpose of defending the criminal behavior of two clients, Loeb and Leopold. The two defendants appeared to be models of success—highly intelligent, sophisticated, students of the prestigious University of Chicago, and sons of wealthy families. The two young men had confessed to murdering a young boy just for the thrill of the experience and to test whether or not they were clever enough to plan and execute the perfect crime.

Darrow argued that Leopold and Loeb, who were said to be legally sane, could not be held morally responsible for the murder because their behavior was the result of their heredity and environment. This argument, which is from a strict deterministic viewpoint, holds that Loeb and Leopold did not have a real choice as to what they did and therefore could not be held responsible for their behavior. Because of certain antecedent events in their home life and society, supposedly, they were forced to commit this murder. Consequently, Darrow argued, society could not hold them responsible for their actions, because these were determined by forces beyond their control. The jury rejected this plea, and Leopold and Loeb were found guilty and sentenced to life imprisonment. This verdict does not surprise many people who understand what Darrow was trying to do. But what is surprising, at least to me, is that many criminologists and other sociologists continue to argue in much the same way as Darrow did. According to some criminologists, crimes are not committed through free choice or willful decision making, but are the products of the hereditary and environmental circumstances in which individuals find themselves. They point to the high-crime-rate sections of any city and the low socioeconomic levels of the people found there—the broken homes and neglected children, poor education, and so on—and claim that these people are destined to act in a criminal manner because of these factors.

These deterministic conclusions are, in my opinion, false. The percentage of individuals raised in poor environments who lead a life of crime is greater than that among persons who live in good neighborhoods, but these poor individuals are in the minority in their own community. Most persons raised in poor environments do not become criminals. The higher statistical correlation between crime and poor background suggests partial determination or probabilistic determination but not causative determination. All of our values and our knowledge of right and wrong are determined by our cultural, religious, educational, and familial backgrounds. When we are faced with the chance to steal or to break any legal or moral code, our values influence us but do not force us to choose one behavior over another. Our behavior then, is responsible, since we do have a choice of outcomes (Silverman, 1969).

Most psychologists would agree that man is determined insofar as the meaning of this term refers to his genetic background and environmental history; we are what we are because of the interaction of our heredity and environment. But this does not mean that our behavior is controlled by these circumstances. Through scientific study it is possible to understand the laws of heredity and the laws of the environment, but these laws, as we learned earlier, are simply descriptions. They do not determine how we choose, and they do not prohibit our freedom of choice (see Immergluck, 1964).

3. Another historical assumption is that science is neutral insofar as value judgments are concerned. This assumption also is false. All sciences, including the social sciences, accept a set of values which limit their activity on the one hand but stimulate inquiry on the other.

Psychology and the natural sciences, with one exception, are based upon the same set of ethical assumptions (LaFave, 1971). These assumptions include the traditional beliefs that scientific theories must be testable, logically consistent, precise, comprehensive, and parsimonious. These beliefs differ, for example, from theological doctrines or eastern philosophies such as Zen Buddhism, which do not view logical inconsistency as undesirable. Scientific researchers select problems for study that are consistent with their own values. Any application of science to solve one problem of society as opposed to another involves a value judgment—e.g., the application of theoretical physics to build atomic plants to provide energy for consumers or to build nuclear bombs for military purposes. Value judgments also affect the design of research projects and interpretations of their results. Even the choice of words to describe and explain results reflects values. The use of technical language acts to minimize potential bias and error, but even technical language may fail to convey the meaning originally intended. The essential difference in assumptions between the natural sciences and psychology springs from the fact that psychology not only must bridge the gap between objectivity (the world out there as it exists) and subjectivity (the phenomenal world in our mind's eye) but also must deal with people, who at the same time may be objects of study by others and also subjects reflecting about themselves and other persons and events. This difference may seem trivial, but without this subjective-objective distinction there would be no fundamental reason for psychologists to study man as man.

In summary, the nineteenth-century spirit and method of Newtonian physics and the logical positivistic movement of the early 1900s have had a strong effect on psychology, which persists in some measure even today. Newtonian physics emphasized objectivity, orderliness, and a mechanical and deterministic conception of the universe. This nineteenth-century structure of science was readily adopted by psychologists, who wished to be accepted as "true scientists." Logical positivists added to this spirit by arguing that knowledge can be achieved only if the proper questions are asked. By asking intelligent questions, we can avoid internal contradictions in logic and reject metaphysical explanations. Furthermore, it was believed that we can know only those things that we can verify through observation.

The outcome of these early-twentieth-century influences on psychology was a rejection of subjective experiences as a part of science, a stress on objectivity, and the construction of general theories and models of human behavior. These philosophical ideas were important at the time, but they have generally outlived their usefulness or have been shown to be wrong. Metaphysical problems cannot simply be labeled pseudo-propositions and banished because they are difficult to measure. Questions about the mind, human experience, and truth must be answered, since they affect the nature of man and society.

Most psychologists now understand "science" in its simplest and most fundamental sense to mean "knowledge" (Deese, 1972). Science is best defined as:

> a quest for theoretical knowledge and [it] has two essential characteristics: first, it seeks general explanatory principles in nature which account for an indeterminate range of phenomena. When a scientist formulates or discovers an explanatory principle, or theory, that principle or theory must explain not only the case before him but an indeterminate number of similar cases—at least help to explain such similar cases. Secondly, the scientist is prepared to subject these explanatory principles, and theories, to the test of experience and to intersubjective criticism. In other words, scientific statements must be able to withstand rational criticism and must not fly in the face of experience. The search for general explanatory principles which can withstand criticism and test is, I believe, the proper focus of science. [Eidlin, 1975, p. 6]

I wish to emphasize the importance of this description of science relative to our more traditional views, since many laymen and participants in the criminal justice system hold incorrect conceptions of what psychology can contribute to their work. Science and psychology do not present truth. Science, being the construction of scientists, brings us only images or representations of truth. Knowledge is almost always the result of both observation and inference (theory), and not of observation alone (Bakan, 1967). To the extent that scientists have vivid and creative imaginations it may be possible to discover more profound knowledge of and more truthful insights into selected aspects of reality.

In chapter 1 I have attempted to place psychology in relationship to law, identify some of the assumptions of science, and give the reader a flavor of what will follow in the remainder of the book. Chapter 2 has been written more to inform psychologists and students than for participants in the criminal justice system. In it I discuss what evidence is in the legal sense and how it is gathered and used in the pursuit of truth in court. This subject is generally unfamiliar to those outside of the criminal justice system, and this is part of what has led to a conflict between science and the law.

Chapter 2

Evidence and Truth in the Criminal Justice System

"We're just interested in the facts, ma'am, nothing but the facts."

This common police expression is familiar to very nearly everyone who watches the late show or reads detective novels. In a vague sort of way most of us know that detectives search for clues, ask questions of eyewitnesses, theorize about a suspect's motives, and so on. We also have a general idea of what takes place and how things are organized once a case gets to court. And this bit of practical knowledge of the law is enough for most laymen. But I wonder if we should not expect more from psychologists, particularly those of us who profess to be experts on just about anything and everything that goes on in society. Perhaps my comment is too mild and I should use more critical terms, such as those offered by Paul Meehl, the eminent clinical psychologist at the University of Minnesota. Meehl (1971) considers many psychologists "ignorant, slightly hostile, ideologically tendentious and often completely uninformed with respect to the law." In another article, Meehl (1970) states that psychologists are prepared to "make very strong evaluative statements—usually negative—about the law . . . but . . . could not even list the four traditional functions of the criminal law." (Fortunately, Meehl does list the four purposes, which allows me to pass them on: (1) incarceration or physical isolation of the guilty person, (2) rehabilitation, (3) a general deterrent effect, and (4) retributive justice.)

I doubt that my efforts in this chapter will make psychologists any less tendentious with respect to the law. However, I hope by focusing on legalis-

16

tic conceptions of evidence and truth, and some selected aspects of how the police and courts operate, as well as discussing the purported conflict between law and psychology, that I can introduce some new material, or at least another organization of some criminal processes, to the nonlegal reader. If any new insights into the legal process are found in this chapter by the legal specialist, that will of course be pleasing to this writer.

Police Work

At the level of the cop on the beat, the police normally look for suspicious actions and crimes in progress and act on calls for help. The deductive or inductive method of reasoning found in Sherlock Holmes is not part of the typical behavioral repertoire of most cops. Quite often the police follow a routine of stopping and questioning "suspicious persons" without any grounds for arrest. If the police believe that the suspect may be armed, they will frisk him for concealed weapons. The question of whether or not field interrogations or the "stop and frisk" procedures are a violation of our privacy as citizens and are unconstitutional is not of concern for our purposes here. The practice does go on, as any long-haired "hippie" college student or "professional" woman of the street can testify.

The police consider field interrogation an important and essential part of their duties. Superintendent O. W. Wilson of the Chicago Police Department in a statement to the United States Senate commented as follows:

> When a policeman encounters someone on the street under circumstances that would lead a reasonably prudent policeman to suspect that something was amiss, he must and should stop the suspect long enough to ask a few pertinent questions. Perhaps the explanation of the person suspected may resolve all grounds for suspicion right then and there, thus terminating the incident.... The incident... may not, on the other hand, terminate with the immdiate release of the suspect. What he says or refuses to say, what the officer observes and what he learns from possible witnesses at the scene, may add to the reasonable grounds for belief sufficient to justify arrest and may provide evidence of the need for wider and more intensive investigation. While the quantum of proof may justify arrest, the officer may still lack the degree of proof needed for prosecution.[1]

Field interrogation is common practice in all large cities (Tiffany, McIntyre, and Rotenberg, 1967). For example, a conservative estimate of the number of field interrogations in Milwaukee, Wisconsin, during a four-month period over the winter months of 1955 was 8,400 reports. Since more people are on the streets at night during the spring, summer, and autumn

[1]Hearings on H.R.7525 and S.486 Before the Committee on the District of Columbia of the United States Senate, 88th Cong., 1st Sess., pt. 1, at 310 (1963).

seasons, the number of annual field contacts in this city alone probably exceeded 40,000. It is important for us to note that this practice may be so common that it assumes a key place in any theoretical model of how legal evidence is gathered.

An obvious limitation of this approach and one that troubles many civil rights observers is the fact that a patrolman's belief may be a self-fulfilling prophecy (Rosenthal, 1966; Rosenthal and Jacobson, 1968). That is, a policeman's prediction of criminal behavior may somehow come to be realized. It is possible that some suspects show criminal behavior because that is what is expected of them, and it also may be that police officers see criminal behavior more often in people of a particular socioeconomic level or skin color because that is what is expected of them. The explanation usually given for the criminal behavior of the poor person or minority-group member may be inadequate. For example, people living in high-density-housing or ghetto conditions often are considered criminalistic because they belong to antisocial groups. The high incidence of deviant behavior found in slums, however, may originate not in the different socioeconomic, ethnic, and cultural background, but in the policeman's and society's response to that background. Police do not stop and question suspects equally often in all neighborhoods, in all age groups, or even as between males and females. Since police will often conduct field interrogations in order to determine whether a crime has been committed, there is a greater probability of finding crime in groups who are more likely to be stopped and questioned.

Several factors which appear to determine whether or not a person will be stopped for interrogation have been summarized by Tiffany et al. (1967):

1. *Sex*. The vast majority of suspects stopped and questioned by the police are male. Except for "red light" districts where prostitution is apparent, male police are reluctant to interrogate women. Fear of being accused of improper conduct or physical and sexual abuse and the knowledge that a male police officer cannot frisk a female suspect act to create a sex difference in field interrogation. It will be interesting to observe whether field interrogation of females increases in the future as the number of female offenders in society increases. In the past, males have committed significantly more crimes than women; consequently, police have reacted and interrogated more men on the street. Unfortunately, the incidence of crime among females has rapidly increased in the last few years (see Adler, 1975).

2. *Age*. Young men, adolescents in particular, are more likely to be stopped and searched than elderly men. The police assume that crimes other than drunkenness and disorderliness are committed predominantly by young men. This assumption is verified (self-fulfilling prophecy) by a visit to any correctional center: the mean age of the male residents is 19 years old.

3. *Race*. Since police concentrate their attention in areas having high crime rates, more blacks and other minority-group members are stopped

and questioned than are whites. However, in racially mixed areas, police give equal scrutiny to all racial groups. The police will stop and question or give advice to a person of one race observed in an area which is considered to be predominantly inhabited by another race.

4. *General appearance.* A well-dressed individual, regardless of his race, is not likely to be stopped by the police in racially mixed areas or predominately white areas. This distinction of relative affluence, however, is disregarded by the police in black areas, which suggests that the police tend to restrict the meaning of "respectability" to white racial groups or to white areas.

5. *Time of day.* As you would expect, most field interrogations occur at night. The police are more likely to stop someone at a very late hour than earlier in the evening or in the daylight hours. It is assumed that "good" people are at home sleeping at night: someone walking the streets at a late hour is likely to be guilty of some crime or planning some criminal offense. The courts have officially recognized and sanctioned the practice of increased field interrogations at night. To give one example, a New York court stated that "the field interrogation need not necessarily be confined to the nighttime but obviously occurrences at night are much more likely to arouse justifiable suspicion."[2]

6. *Crime rate of the location.* Each city has specific locations where the crime rate is particularly high. Consequently, the police are set to look for suspicious persons in these areas and are more likely to infer guilt from a particular behavior if demonstrated in these locations in contrast to other parts of the city. For example, if a person is seen running in a high-crime-rate location, the inference is not often made that he is a jogger out for his daily mile; rather, the police often assume that he is fleeing from the scene of a crime. This suspicious behavior is considered serious enough to justify police action.

In summary, police are more likely to stop and question suspicious persons whenever certain social factors or environmental conditions exist. Officers are guided by their common sense, intuitive guesswork, and their schematic representations of "criminal types" based upon experience in the field. The quality of police decision making can be improved by minimizing the conditions that lead to self-fulfilling prophecies. Many of the criteria such as race, sex, time, and location used for decision making in stopping and questioning, or field interrogation, are experientially valid but are not free of cultural and police bias. It is apparent that research along these lines is needed.

[2]People V. Estrialgo (Sup. Ct. Kings County, 1962).

Solving the Crime

Everyone, especially Canadians, likes to feel that "the Mounties always get their man," but with due respect to the Mounties, it is recognized that many crimes are not solvable. Crimes are often committed which lack any apparent motive. The corpus delicti, or the fact that a crime was committed, is not always obvious. The lack of any eyewitnesses to a crime or, something even more disturbing to the law, ambiguity in the reports of eyewitnesses obstructs an investigation. Even the meaning of the phrase "solving the crime" is not as simple and straightforward as it appears. The police have solved a crime only when three conditions are met: (1) the identity of a suspect is known, (2) he is apprehended, and (3), which is the most important, the elements of proof are presented in court in a manner which can secure a conviction.

SCIENTIFIC APPROACH

Detectives never start their probe from scratch. From the moment they go to work there are certain propositions or assumptions guiding their investigation—though these assumptions are not spelled out and many investigators are not even aware of their logical necessity. The police accept the postulates that each crime is determined or committed for some explainable reason and that a crime has a beginning and, at least theoretically, can be traced to its origin. It is assumed that criminal offenders are rational and so are responsible for their actions. This is not to say that the police are unaware of the bizarre nature of some people and the fact that crimes may be committed also for irrational reasons.

Investigations of crime usually follow an eclectic approach: there is no one correct procedure for arriving at a solution. Initially, detectives attempt to critically frame and delimit conditions of the crime in order to organize available evidence into a meaningful and understandable arrangement (Sanders, 1977). Once the nature of the crime is known, the task of discovering, applying, fitting, modifying, and finally of rejecting or accepting potential solutions begins. Unlike the scientist who selects a particular activity or behavior to observe, the detective at first does not know what critical evidence and clues are needed to find a solution. Consequently, the investigator makes a comprehensive collection of any and all data that in any way appear related to the incident. Witnesses are interviewed, personal observations made, photographs and sketches collected, and reports of laboratory experts recorded. The facts discovered by the investigator are constantly organized and reorganized in an attempt to discover any logical patterns. At the same time, the investigator may construct hypotheses, or tentative post hoc solutions. The more creative or imaginative the hypotheses, the more likely it is that he will be able to accurately reconstruct the possible events that preceded, occurred during, and occurred after the crime. Rigidity or an inability to theorize about the many ways that the event may have taken place will maximize the chance for error. In his attempt to narrow down the list of possible suspects to one or more specific individuals, the detective will speculate or infer possible motives involved. Who stands to gain from the crime? Is there any evidence that desire for revenge, hatred, jealousy, or quarrels existed among the participants? Depending upon the nature of the crime, different types of motivations are considered. Other considerations, such as the physical locations of different suspects at the time of the crime are reviewed. All of these motives or courses of action are considered in an attempt to reduce the universe of uncertainties of the crime into one or only a few patterns which can be fixed to known conditions.

Once a solution is tentatively accepted, the detective will attempt to attack his hypothesis by systematically testing the validity of each bit of evidence and conclusion. The greatest danger at this point is that the detective may bias his interpretation because of an extreme desire to confirm his hypothesis. Bias enters into the problem solving of all investigators through errors in selection of data, errors of interpretation, and errors of inference. O'Hara (1970) in his discourse on criminal investigation states that detectives initially are objective in their general perspective and have no special interest in establishing the guilt of a particular suspect. Objectivity in this sense, however, still does not free the investigator from possible bias entering his data collection, analysis, and interpretation. Bias may be due to inaccurate judgments at any one of the many decision points in the investigation rather than a direct attempt to distort truth.

PHENOMENOLOGICAL APPROACH

Up to this point, I have suggested that the methods of police investigation are similar to the traditional scientific model of theory construction and testing of hypotheses. Criminal investigation, however, in addition to using the scientific model, follows the phenomenological method (Sanders, 1975). This procedure involves describing the way things appear without any theories or hypotheses of how they ought to appear. To illustrate this method, let us suppose that the body of the lord and master of the house is discovered by the butler. A gun is found lying beside the body, and after the crime the only door to the room had to be forced open, since it was locked from the inside. Clearly, we have a case of suicide. The error, however, of assuming suicide if in fact it was murder can lead the detectives to commit further errors of finding other facts (e.g., he was despondent, he was dying of cancer, etc.) to confirm their hypothesis. Instead of theorizing that a suicide took place, detectives often will suspend their interpretations until all of the evidence can be critically examined. (Unlike academic researchers, detectives are not forced to prematurely rush their findings into print because of a "publish or perish" ethic.) Obvious facts may or may not prove to be usable evidence. What are useful facts and what are irrelevant details is often unknown at the beginning of the investigation.

Phenomenologists adhere to the position that we perceive appearances, not real things, that we respond to people, situations, or events not as they are but as they appear to be. The phenomenological approach has the virtue of producing an orderly account of how things look. What is observed and what is reported are seen as legitimate observations without any need to elaborate or analyze the perceptions into elements. The essence of this approach is the suspension of any commitments to biases. In this manner, the detective hopes to build a picture or schema which is an accurate representation of the crime in question. The investigator attempts to observe both detail and generality. Observations of a gun, a shell, and the body in a homicide are insufficient without the additional observations of the exact position of each object, the distance between objects, the distance between objects and the body, and so on. These measurements must be made accurately and recorded carefully. Nothing can be considered to be insignificant.

The phenomenological approach taken by detectives to their work is a pragmatic and necessary step in the criminal justice system. Evidence gathered by the detective eventually will be presented to a judge and jury. The danger in court is not that too much evidence is available for presentation, but that not all the evidence is available. The absence of some of the facts may result in the drawing of inaccurate inferences and conclusions. If the investigator is asked by an attorney to describe what he observed, the omission of reporting a particular object may lead to the inference that the object was not there. Ultimately, what is evidence is for the court to decide, not the detective. His job is to be able to present all of his findings in such a way that they can convince a court that the accused committed an illegal act. Guilt of the accused must be proved beyond all reasonable doubt. If the quantity of proof presented by the detective is indefinite and inaccurate, the court will not convict a suspect, regardless of the personal conviction of the investigator that the suspect is guilty. The criterion of success for the police investigator is ambiguous. Success is not dependent on the decision of the court to find a person guilty; rather, success is dependent on whether the detective has gathered all the available facts of the case. Of course, since it is impossible to prove that there are no more facts available, we must trust the ability and integrity of the detective, as long as he was not vague or inaccurate.

The investigatory techniques of the detective may appear to be contradictory because of the simultaneous use of hypothesis testing, data collecting, analysis, and a phenomenological perspective. Nevertheless, detectives do and must operate this way.

Legal Truth

Primarily for the benefit of the layman and nonlegal specialists, we will now look at the next critical stage of the criminal justice process, which is the presentation of evidence in court. As an aid to understanding the events and proceedings involved in a criminal prosecution, the simple flowchart in figure 2.1 describes by means of a sequence of boxes and arrows the order in which the various events occur.

EVIDENCE

Testimony of witnesses, writings, material objects, recordings, photographs, and visual demonstrations such as diagrams or films presented to the court potentially constitute evidence. Often what is held to be evidence by one of the attorneys will be objected to by the attorney for the other side on the grounds that it is irrelevant or dangerously misleading. Relevant evidence includes testimony which might be seen to be able to prove the truth of the case. To illustrate, in an armed robbery relevant evidence includes the information that the defendant owns a gun, irrelevant evidence includes the knowledge that he owns a cannon.

Objections by lawyers often appear to restrict the free flow of information and seem to the layman to be unnecessary and obstructive. We assume that the jury is composed of intelligent people who can get the gist of the truth from the witnesses' testimony. This assumption, however, is dismissed by the courts. The judicial system considers the jury inexperienced in legal matters and unable to separate facts from fiction. Juries must be told if testimony is immaterial, that is, if the evidence is not related to or has no significance for the issue at hand. For example, if a defendant is being tried for armed robbery, a long discussion of whether the gun was gray or light blue would be considered immaterial.

Another exclusionary rule of the law of evidence is the hearsay rule, which is one of the best-known rules of law. Put simply, the hearsay rule says that a witness must testify only about matters that he has seen, heard, touched, tasted, or smelled. If a witness reports second-hand knowledge of what he has heard others say, his testimony is considered hearsay evidence. For example, if a witness says, "I know that Mr. Smith was at the robbery because Mr. Brown told me he saw him there," his testimony is hearsay. The principal reasons for the hearsay rule are, first, to have the witness physically present in court so that he may be cross-examined, and, second, to minimize error in recall because of omissions and intrusions of information which occur in the repeated telling of stories from person to person.

The last exclusionary rule I want to mention attacks the problem of competency of witnesses. If a witness is unable to see, recall, or verbally express his thoughts, is mentally retarded or mentally defective, or is a

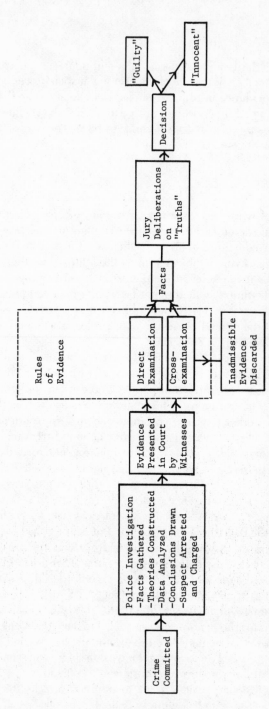

FIGURE 2.1 Major events and proceedings involved in a criminal prosecution

24

young child, his testimony will be considered unreliable. Apart from physical or maturational deficiencies, a witness must be morally competent. He must understand the meaning of truth and the consequences of lying and must be free and able to tell the truth. A communication to a lawyer from his client or to a physician from his patient is considered to be privileged information. Consequently, neither the lawyer nor the medical doctor is competent to testify on such a communication.

Rules of evidence, or exclusionary rules, are the foundations of the modern judicial system. They have been developed over years of the development of precedents to allow the determination of truth about a fact in question. With this long history exclusionary rules are complex, and there are exceptions to these rules which are beyond the scope of this book to explain and discuss. It is the presiding judge who must rule on the admission of evidence. His rulings serve to transform evidence into legal truths.

As figure 2.1 indicates, testimony of witnesses is subjected to both direct examination and cross-examination, one by the prosecutor, the other by defense counsel. When an attorney questions his own witness, he is giving a direct examination, and when he questions witnesses from the opposing side, he is involved in cross-examination. North American and British lawyers view cross-examination as the best method available in the search for truth. Wellman (1958) has stated that "no substitute has ever been found for cross-examination as a means of separating truth from falsehood, and of reducing exaggerated statements to their true dimensions" (p. 438). However, not all jurists agree that the adversary proceeding is necessarily the best method to administer justice (Frank, 1949).

It is apparent that the legal system does not search for reality or truth in the same sense that a scientist does. Evidence is presented to the judge and jury by many witnesses. If the judge accepts the evidence, it becomes part of the court records and is considered legally significant because of its power to influence the results of the proceedings. Evidence from different witnesses may be ambiguous and open to several interpretations and even be false. Ultimately, the judge, in trials without jury, or the jury decides what a fact or legal truth is. The judge or jury in criminal cases then deliberates upon these truths in order to decide guilt beyond any reasonable doubt. Thus judges and juries are faced with the problem of making a decision based upon facts which have emerged through the filtering process of the court proceedings. Beliefs, attitudes, and personal thoughts of the judge or jury toward the defendant are not supposed to influence this decision making. But, of course, they do.

LEGAL TRUTH

As stated earlier, cross-examination is widely viewed as the greatest test of truth in the courtroom. The cross-examination combined with the sanctity of the oath is said to exert great pressure on the witness to say the truth. First, there is the threat of being publicly exposed as a liar or fraud, and second, there is the promise of final judgment by the Creator knowing that a lie was told in His name. Although threat of divine punishment is not as strong a sanction today as it once was, the promise of punishment for perjury is a powerful control. Let us now consider both the merits and the abuses of the adversary procedure in the discovery of truth.

In contrast to the practice of direct examination, where one's own lawyer asks relatively direct questions—such as "Will you please tell the court what happened?" and "What happened next?"—in cross-examination the opposing attorney may ask leading questions. The answer in effect may be suggested by the question. For example, the witness may be asked, "Isn't it true that you were in the house where the murder was committed on the second day of September?" Leading questions are warranted in cross-examination, since the purpose is to probe the truth and accuracy of the witness's memory. If the attorney suspects that the truth is being withheld or the facts are being distorted, any means of questioning seems to be justified. Cross-examination is an art and not a science. Reconstruction of the facts of the case is deliberately managed by the skillful lawyer in such a way that the jury is led to positively interpret the witness's remarks in favor of his client. If it is necessary to destroy the testimony of the witness and make him appear to be a fool, if not a perjurer, the cross-examiner will do so. In an optimistic note, Thomas (1965) feels that most modern-day advocates primarily endorse a more positive approach to cross-examination. He believes that its principal goal "is its use as a tool for securing admissions of facts supportive or corroborative of the cross-examiner's contentions, with the secondary object being that of discrediting the witnesses of the opposition or their stories." Still, it is no wonder that every witness fears the cross-examination.

Frank (1948), who is the best-known critic of the adversary procedure, says that our system of law supports the techniques of cross-examination and that we should not blame lawyers for using this system to their advantage.

Still, because of the primary loyalty of counsel to his client and not to justice, the advocacy procedure prevents the emergence of vital evidence and allows the distortion of testimony so that it is easily misinterpreted. Attorneys are allowed to attack, intimidate, and cajole the witness, and every lawyer knows that these strategies act to impair recall and spoil verbal report. If a witness hesitates and thinks over his answer before responding, or asks that a question be repeated so that he may be sure to give what he thinks is an accurate recollection, the cross-examiner is likely to leave the jury with the thought that the witness was being evasive or was withholding evidence. Young lawyers are taught by countless textbooks that it is their duty as cross-examiners to discredit the witness even if they have no reason to doubt the accuracy and veracity of the testimony.

Lawyers not only try to destroy adverse witnesses but also attempt to hide the defects of witnesses who are going to testify favorably on behalf of their clients. This is done before the trial by teaching a witness how to present a more personable picture to the jury—how to conceal irritability, how not to be sarcastic, aloof, etc. This coaching may prevent the jury from observing the "real" witness as opposed to the actor-witness. In the same vein, lawyers guard against calling a witness to testify, even if his testimony could be vital to their client, if they suspect that on cross-examination he might testify to other facts that would be helpful to their opponent. Distortion of evidence can also occur by a lawyer's failure to point out inaccuracies in a witness's testimony if the inaccuracies are favorable to his client.

Whether or not this practice is dishonest is a matter of opinion. The trial, which is supposedly an inquiry for the discovery of truth, is conducted by officers of the court who deliberately distort evidence to promote their client. In their own defense lawyers acknowledge that justice must be done in the court, but they consider their behavior acceptable insofar as they do not positively mislead the court or introduce evidence or testimony which is known to be false or perjured. Nevertheless, Belli (1954) admonishes us not to be naive: "law and justice are not always synonymous [and law students are not trained] to study justice, [but] are here to study law ... a body of rules formulated for the conduct of society."

FACT, INFERENCE, AND OPINION

The ordinary person involved in a criminal case such as a robbery usually does not question what he or she has witnessed or experienced. Let us assume that a woman is the victim of a holdup. Because of her involvement in the robbery she knows "the actual facts" and is quite prepared to tell the police and other officials exactly what happened. She expects, because of her sense of rightness, that the police and court officials will see that justice is done. When the case comes to court, however, she may find that the judge and jury do not believe the "facts," that is, the evidence as she knows it to be.

The layperson often makes the erroneous assumption that his or her "facts" will automatically be accepted as the truth by the judge or jury. We often act as if facts exist separate from us as individuals in some sort of self-evident, ideal form which can be copied and given to another person. Judges and juries, however, have to look at all the evidence, which may include that from several eyewitnesses, whose testimony often will differ on critical events. In civil cases the judge or jury will accept proof only if the preponderance of evidence is clearly established. Proof in criminal cases must be beyond a reasonable doubt. The criteria of what constitutes preponderance are subjective reactions of the judge or jury. Ideal facts may exist in some Platonic world of forms known to philosopher-kings, but the judge and jury do not have any objective criterion for establishing their proof. In cases in which testimony is in conflict, judges or juries must make their decision on the basis of subjective probability. The theory of statistical probability and its application in the legal process has received considerable attention in the last few years, as we shall see in detail in the next section. Before we turn to issues of statistical probability, however, it is necessary to review the different legal conceptions of "fact," "inference," and "opinion."

Let us return to our example of the woman being robbed and her knowledge of the facts. The court, as we know, is interested in discovering the truth. Assume that she testifies, "First I saw the defendant holding a gun and knew he was going to rob me, so I ran as fast as I ever ran in my life to get away." This statement offered by our witness is seen by her as factual and true, but the court, as she will discover in cross-examination, will be shown that it contains inferences and opinions as well as facts. Remember that the witness is asked to testify to what she saw or what she heard and not what she has concluded from her observations. It may be true (a *fact*) that the witness saw the accused and that the object she saw him carrying was a gun, but the statement that he was about to rob her is an *inference*. It may be true that the defendant was intending to rob the witness, but he can have been holding a gun for any number of reasons. Finally, the witness expressed the *opinion* that she ran away as fast as she ever ran. Whether or not this is so, or she could have run faster when she was younger or could have run more quickly in a pants suit than in a dress, is an academic question which is of little interest to the court.

Facts or evidence may be categorized as direct or circumstantial. Direct evidence refers to testimony of eyewitnesses, that is, persons who saw and heard the criminal act. Circumstantial evidence is indirect evidence. A fact proved by inference from the existence of another factor is circumstantial evidence. For example, consider our robbery victim mentioned earlier. Suppose that she tried to escape by hiding in the back of a parked van. The accused allegedly followed her into the truck and closed the door behind himself. Screams were heard, and the accused was seen running away from the truck. The victim was found lying on the floor, and her purse and jewelry were missing. An eyewitness relating this event to the court would in part be giving circumstantial evidence, since he did not see the accused take the purse and jewelry. The facts, however, appear to be logically related, and it may be reasonable to infer that the defendant did rob the woman. Of course, it is possible that the woman never had a purse or jewelry in the first place and the intention of the defendant was not robbery at all. Other evidence, called real evidence, may have to be provided to prove theft. There would be real evidence, for example, if the accused was found to possess the woman's purse and rings, or the fingerprints of the accused were found on the purse and rings once they were recovered.

In summary, direct evidence is testimony from eyewitnesses which can prove the fact in question without drawing upon any inference or presumption. Circumstantial evidence proves the fact in issue through logical inferences and conclusions from observations. Facts and opinions are difficult to separate for the court, but the court must attempt to do so if it wishes to follow the rules of evidence.[3] *The difference between facts and opinions is not a problem in psychology, since they are seen there as identical.* To the psychologist, all perception is judgmental or inferential and there is no scientific distinction between the two terms. Both statements of opinion and statements of observations are treated as inferences by psychologists. We will examine in more detail the nature of the psychology of perception and decision making in chapter 3.

Statistical Probability of Legal Truth

Lawyers wanting to impress the judge and jury with their objectivity and precision have shown increased interest in the last few years in the use of statistical procedures to aid decision making in the trial process (see Finkelstein and Fairley, 1970; Kingston, 1966; Kingston and Kirk, 1964; and Tribe, 1971). Statistical analysis and research design is an area of expertise claimed by many psychologists, a fact which may not be widely known by the legal profession.

One of the first reported trials based essentially on evidence proved by statistical inference was the 1899 hearing of Alfred Dreyfus, a captain in the French General Staff. Dreyfus was tried for allegedly passing secret documents to the enemy. The documents supposedly were written by Dreyfus in his own handwriting. The court attempted to prove through a statistical technique called frequency analysis the number of times the formation of the letters in the word *intérêt* matched the shape and style of writing of these letters made by Dreyfus in other correspondence. On the basis of this statistical evidence Dreyfus was found guilty by the French judges. Years later, a panel of experts appointed to review the evidence in this case showed that the mathematics on which the decision was based were invalid (Tribe, 1971). The statistical comparisons were found to be improper. In addition, the court and the counsel for Dreyfus told the panel that they did not understand a word of the expert witnesses' testimony regarding mathematical probability and admitted that they had been overly impressed by the appearance of scientific rigor and accuracy.

More recently, a California court was asked to find Malcolm and Janet Collins guilty of second-degree robbery on the basis of evidence which connected the defendants to the crime by probability theory. The victim, Juanita Brooks, an elderly lady, told the police that a young blonde woman

[3]Exceptions to the opinion rule such as the testimony of expert witnesses will not be covered here.

stole her purse containing $35. Another witness, a neighbor of Mrs. Brooks, reported that she saw a young white woman with blonde hair styled in a pony tail run from the scene and get into a yellow car driven by a black man sporting a moustache and beard. The Collinses were arrested several days later, since they matched the descriptions of the two wanted persons. The case against them was weak. Mrs. Brooks, the victim, was unable to identify either defendant, the missing purse was not found, and the trial identification of Malcolm Collins by the neighbor was impeached. In an attempt to bolster his case, the prosecuting attorney called a mathematics professor, an authority on statistical probability, as an expert witness. The prosecutor hoped to show that the defendants were guilty because of the overwhelming unlikelihood of finding another woman and man who duplicated six characteristics observed by the witnesses. The expert witness testified that the probability of seeing (1) a yellow car on a Los Angeles street was one in ten, (2) a man having a moustache, one in four, (3) a girl with a pony tail, one in ten, (4) a girl with blonde hair, one in three, (5) a black man with a beard, one in ten, and (6) a white woman with a black man in a car, one in a thousand. The probability of the joint occurrence of these six allegedly mutually independent events was calculated by multiplying these ratios and was found to be one chance in twelve million. The prosecutor argued that on the basis of this statistical evidence, the chance that any other couple chosen at random would possess the characteristics in question would only be one in twelve million. Furthermore, the jury was told by the prosecutor to draw the conclusion that the probability of this couple being innocent was only one in twelve million. The jury, convinced beyond reasonable doubt, convicted the two defendants. Subsequently, the California Supreme Court reversed this decision, stating that the mathematical testimony and the prosecutor's argument were inadmissible for four separate reasons:

1. The prosecutor failed to show any empirical evidence to support the assumed individual probability of any of the six characteristics.

2. The procedures employed to determine the ratio of one in twelve million were found to be invalid. The principle of conjunctive probability assumes that each factor is causally independent, but no proof was presented by the prosecutor that this was so. Furthermore, it is obvious that factor 6, the probability of an interracial couple being in a car, is dependent upon all five of the other factors.

3. Proof by statistical probability, even if valid, does not rule out the possibility that the defendants were misidentified by the witnesses through honest error or perjury, and does not govern the possibility that the guilty couple were somehow disguised.

4. The prosecutor erred in estimating the probability that a randomly chosen couple possessing all six characteristics would be innocent in only one out of twelve million chances without also giving the size of the suspect

population. Different sizes of suspect populations would alter the probability of how many couples having all six characteristics could be found, and therefore would alter the probability that any given couple possessing the six characteristics would be innocent.

The California Supreme Court concluded that few defense attorneys or jurors could discriminate the errors in the prosecution's analysis and that this trial by mathematics distorted the jury's role and so disadvantaged the defense counsel as to constitute a miscarriage of justice.[4] However, the court saw "no inherent incompatability between the disciplines of law and mathematics and intend[ed] no general disapproval... of the latter as an auxiliary in the fact-finding processes of the former."[5] If science or any branch of knowledge can contribute to truth seeking, the legal system will welcome the benefits of its expertise. Specialized techniques of science and technology must, however, be understood by the courts to be fair and be open to cross-examination.

Trial by mathematical proof someday may be developed into a more valid technique for trial court deliberations. In the meantime, certain objections to the procedure must be noted. First, the courts are asked to determine the truth about a specific case in question. The use of statistical probability measures in criminal cases requires a transformation of evidence about the generality of cases to evidence which is specific to the case in question. Many critics suggest that the task demands of statistical probability are so different from those of the legal system that such transformations of evidence are impossible. Second, statistical proof is expressed by a decimal figure ranging from 0 (certain negative) to 1 (certain positive). If "beyond reasonable doubt" can include a statement of probability of anything less than certainty, a probability of .99 will mean that an innocent person would be convicted one time in one hundred. Quite simply, as in the Collins case, "no mathematical equation can prove beyond a reasonable doubt (1) that the guilty [party] *in fact* possessed the characteristics described by the People's witnesses, or even (2) that only *one* [party] possessing those characteristics could be found in the [relevant] area."[6]

Mathematical evidence does have a place in the legal system. If statistical probability evidence is combined with other more conventional evidence, it can be a useful tool in assisting court decision making. Nevertheless, any combination of statistical evidence and conventional evidence ultimately will be reduced by the judge or jury to "truths," which are subjective probabilities based upon experience, intuition, rational beliefs, and facts.

[4]People v Collins (1968).
[5]68 Cal. 2d at 320, 438, P. 2d at 33, 66 Cal. Rptr. at 497.
[6]People v Collins (1968).

Law and Psychology: Conflict or Rapprochement?

Since the turn of the century psychologists have attempted to show the courts that the knowledge of psychology and its procedures have practical applications. Freud (1906), Münsterberg (1908), and Watson (1913), among others, have discussed the application of psychology to the testing of truth, the reliability and validity of eyewitness testimony, and jury decision making. But a working interaction between psychology and law, although reasonable and logical and one which can promote both science and justice (see Riesman, 1951; Tapp, 1976), has not been the rule over the years. It is evident that a conflict or mutual distrust has existed between the two disciplines. This conflict can be traced back to at least 1908 when Münsterberg, a Harvard psychologist, attacked the law profession as backward and ignorant of any contributions to criminal justice made by scholars from outside the legal profession. He chastised lawyers for their disinterest in his word association test, a reaction-time measure designed to detect lying.

Although Münsterberg's intentions were honorable, he should have known that the worst possible way to get people to change their attitudes is to attack them directly. The immediate response to an attack is to defend one's existing beliefs and attitudes either through counterattack or withdrawal. Münsterberg's criticism did not go unnoticed. Wigmore (1909), a professor of law at Northwestern University, answered Münsterberg satirically. He showed that Münsterberg's suggestions were merely hypothetical proposals. Münsterberg had presented an experimental program and not a valid test that the courts could accept with confidence. Since the courts deal with property, liberty, and life, caution and healthy skepticism about psychological generalizations claiming to have relevance for the law are necessary.

Just what do lawyers object to when scientists enter the courthouse? It is likely that lawyers consider the court their territory and subconsciously resent the entry of experts from any specialty outside of the legal area (Fitzsimons, 1973). Questioning of ordinary witnesses is not a problem, since the lawyer is in control of the situation. However, examination of an expert witness whose knowledge of a particular subject that has relevance to the law is greater than the knowledge of the lawyer may cause resentment, since the lawyer is no longer totally in command in his own habitat. Furthermore, expert witnesses, unlike ordinary witnesses, have the right to offer opinions based on facts, which also may create anxiety among lawyers. Anxiety about the role of expert witnesses also affects most scientists. Very few psychologists are prepared to state that the principles established in the laboratory adequately predict outcomes in the social environment. Expert witnesses are expected to tell the court the meaning of their findings and to generalize their laboratory evidence to life situations. This is always hazardous, since the controlled laboratory situation and the "real-world" environment often are very different. Scientists know this is the case; the public, however, does not necessarily appreciate the problem. Consequently, psychologists are aware that if they appear as expert witnesses, they can easily fall into traps which show their limitations or, even worse, their ignorance. Very few of us relish going through such an ordeal.

Another reason for the strife between lawyers and scientists, and one which Fitzsimons (1973) believes is more fundamental than those given above, is the communication gap that exists between the two disciplines. Scientific investigation and the legal process are striving toward the same goal, the discovery of truth, through their particular techniques and methodologies. However, each side fails to appreciate the other's strengths and weaknesses (see Walls, 1971). Scientists, in general, do not appreciate how the courts work and how legal truth is determined (Levine, 1974). Lawyers, on the other hand, think that science is interested in gathering data as an end in itself and often view this pursuit as an inconsequential one having only academic relevance and no practical applicability. Very few scientists are as myopic and narrow as this viewpoint suggests. First, facts are never gathered without some theoretical purpose, and second, there is nothing so practical as a good theory. Theoretical models are tested empirically, and many findings are applicable for both scientific and nonscientific uses. Scientific fact finding and application to societies' needs are interrelated goals. Scientists do not know before they do their research which of their findings, if any, will prove someday to have practical relevance, but most scientists hope that this will be the case.

A second false impression that lawyers have of science is that scientists measure with absolute accuracy the data they collect. The scientific trappings with respect to quantification, statistical treatment, and the use of the precise tools of laboratory sciences have created a myth about science. In actual fact, the scientific method and its associated statistical paraphernalia do not insure a precise test of quantitative hypotheses, but rather allow the scientist some bases for stating whether or not the evidence found supports the hypothesis he was testing (see Levine, 1974). What is reported is the significant p value, which is a statement of the level of confidence that the experimenter has in the confirmation of his hypothesis. Most typically, psychologists report statistical probabilities at the .05 and .01 levels of confidence, which means that they are sure ninety-five times out of a hundred or ninety-nine times out of a hundred that their prediction is confirmed. Notice that by chance alone they will always be wrong at least one time in a hundred. Decision making in both science and law is based on the balance of probabilities, but the word "probability" does not mean the same in each context. Scientific probability is based on statistical probability or replication, but legal probability is a subjective conclusion based on experience and intuition that one set of events is more likely to have occurred than another.

In civil law the courts require proof on the balance of probabilities, but in the criminal sphere the law goes one step higher on the ladder of probabilities and requires proof beyond reasonable doubt. The law is not infallible and does not claim to be so; when a court finds a man guilty, it is not necessarily saying he is guilty—it is saying that it has been proved beyond reasonable doubt, on the evidence presented to it, that he committed the crime. The two are not necessarily synonymous. Probability in this sense is a degree of rational belief but it is not necessarily measurable or quantifiable. In the same way, the scientist does not prove everything with certainty—he also hopes to establish facts beyond reasonable doubt; the difference between the scientific and the legal situation is that the scientist is able to calculate the probability of the doubt. . . . [Fitzsimons, 1975, p. 265]

Nothing I have said should be interpreted to mean I believe that the aim of science is statistical prediction. Following Polanyi (1964), I believe that the goal of science is explanation through understanding. Prediction is a means to this goal and not an end in itself, since it is possible to predict an event without understanding the mechanisms underlying the action. For example, I can predict with accuracy that if I eat a certain mushroom I will be very ill, but I cannot explain why I will be ill.

Science is the construction of the scientist (Polyani, 1968) in the same sense that justice is the creation of the judge or jury. Both disciplines approach reality but never bring us into touch with absolute truth. The major contribution of science is not to teach us the absolutely true nature of things or attempt to present an exact copy of reality, but rather to give us an organized coherent knowledge of the world. In a similar fashion, the law does not claim to be equal to absolutely true justice; the only standard for the sufficiency of evidence in criminal court is a feeling of certainty that the issue has been proved beyond reasonable doubt.

The frequently cited discord between science and law, with the former's emphasis on experiment and observation and the latter's on precedent, is not so basic as it appears. Lawyers are and must be conservative, and in the interest of justice the law changes slowly. This does not mean that the criminal justice system is antagonistic to new developments in science. The courts gradually adopt scientific truths after they have been fully accepted by the scientific community. Nevertheless, it is also true that the courts are not inclined to accept empirical information as the definitive criteria in deciding crucial issues such as corporal punishment, the death penalty, and sex discrimination. Other considerations referred to as "normative philosophy"— constitutional history, philosophy, and precedent—overshadow the scientific data presented by the psychologist (Bersoff and Prasse, 1978).

A genuine interest in the rapprochement between law and psychology has begun. The positive interaction has been heralded by the appearance of conferences such as "The First Annual Convention of the American Psychology-Law Society" in June 1974; the Battelle Institute conference on

"Psychological Factors in Legal Processes" held in June 1975; and "The First Bi-Annual Law-Psychology Conference" held in October 1975 at the University of Nebraska. In addition, an ever-increasing number of articles on perception, memory, and testimony related directly to legal concerns are appearing in traditional cognitive journals.

Psychology has contributed and will continue to assist the criminal justice system by scientifically investigating the principles of cognitive and behavioral processes as they stand in relation to specific legal situations (Squires, 1931). The most important contribution that psychology can make to legal decision making is to provide scientific information that would not ordinarily be available to the law (Morse, 1978).

Chapter 3

Perception: An Overview

The identification of criminal suspects is based upon the accuracy of perception and the memory of witnesses. Witnessing a crime, whether as a bystander or victim, involves the acquisition, storage, and retrieval of selected information. When a witness answers police questions, memory processes become the focus of psychological interest. On the other hand, when a witness is asked to identify the alleged criminal in a lineup, perception and memory interact to permit decision making and judgments of recognition.

The purpose of this chapter is to outline those perceptual processes which have theoretical and empirical importance for how we come to know our world. Research findings of relevance to eyewitness testimony can best be explained when the basic principles of perception are understood.

To illustrate some of the factors that a lawyer might consider in assessing the perceptual skills of witnesses or in questioning expert witnesses about perception, three hypothetical cases are presented below:

Case 1. Company A is being sued by one of its employees for negligence. The claimant states that the company failed to provide proper lighting in a stairwell, which resulted in a fall that broke his back. In considering this case, a lawyer might want to obtain answers to such questions as: What are the general standards and regulations regarding lighting for stairwells? Was the amount of illumination available sufficient in terms of safety considerations for those people who would normally be in the area? (Illumination levels might differ if young people and the aged were normal users of this space.) What is the visual acuity of the injured employee? Does he have normal vision or is he nearsighted or farsighted? And did he enter the stairwell from a lighted room or a dark room?

The relevance of these questions will be apparent from discussion presented later in this chapter.

Case 2.   Company B finds itself in a product liability litigation suit over a fire resulting from a piece of equipment it manufactured. The jury is asked to consider whether the fire was caused by human error or faulty design of the safety signal light. Several questions of perceptual importance could be asked here. What was the clarity of the signal light, its size, luminance, and the exposure time? What was its position in relation to other lights and the general background? Questions of color blindness, eye fixation, and movement of the observer could also be asked.

Case 3.   A child is killed in a hit-and-run car car accident. Questions put to eyewitnesses in this type of case must recognize the effects of stress on perception. Estimations of time, speed, and size of the car will be affected by the shock involved in such circumstances. Furthermore, the nature of the environment at the time of the accident must be clarified in any assessment of the clarity of perception.

These three examples illustrate some of the perceptual factors that the courts ought to take into account when testimony is given. The examples do not, of course, sample the entire scope of perceptual variables that should be considered, nor will this chapter attempt to be comprehensive. Instead, its central purpose is to sensitize nonpsychologists to some basic sensory and perceptual mechanisms. And, where possible, to encourage psychologists to consider and investigate the human-factor issues related to the law. Whenever man interacts with machines or with the products of our social environment, legal questions of rights and responsibilities have to be considered. However, these legal considerations should be linked in a systematic manner with the knowledge of the related human sensory, information-processing, and decision making factors that play a role in such a man-machine interactions.

The Witness Says He Has "Good" Vision

In most cases the court accepts the testimony of witnesses, made in good faith, without checking the efficiency of the instruments of perception, that is, the sensory system of the witness. The administrative burden that would be entailed in testing each individual for sight and hearing acuity of course makes this impractical, but the implications of wide individual differences in sensation and perception on testimony are profound. The courts want to know what the witness has seen and heard. We will restrict our attention mainly to the visual system in this chapter, excluding the other sensory systems only because of space limitations and not because of any less importance to the law.

VISUAL DEFECTS

Deficiencies in vision are common, and witnesses often suffer from some visual handicap. One of these is depth perception. Depending upon the refraction of light as it passes through the lens of the eye, a witness may be farsighted (hyperopia) or nearsighted (myopia), which may make his or her testimony regarding close and distant events unreliable. Normally, depth perception requires two eyes, but it is possible to achieve visual depth perception even with one eye because of the effects of various monocular cues. The ability to perceive depth will be influenced by such cues as *interposition*—the object partially covering another is seen as closer; *relative size*—the larger of two objects is seen as closer; *relative height*—the lower of two objects is seen as closer; *relative clearness*—the more detailed and salient the features of an object, the closer it appears to be; *linear perspective*—the greater the convergence of lines such as two railway tracks, the greater the phenomenon of distance; *light and shadows*—patterns of shadows on edges and curves promote the appearance of depth; and *movement parallax*, or relative movement—as the head moves to one side, close objects are displaced in the opposite direction, whereas distant objects appear to move in the same direction the head turns.

Problems in depth perception can seriously influence driving behaviors or other such visual-motor skill performances. Drivers may misjudge their distance from an approaching car or a curve in the road as a result of misreading any one or more of the above mentioned monocular cues.

COLOR BLINDNESS

Identification of suspects is often based in part on the color of clothes, the color of the getaway car, and so on. Color blindness is a relative matter, since everyone is color-weak to some degree. Normal-seeing individuals vary in their ability to discriminate one red and another, although they can accurately tell red from green, yellow, or blue. In rare instances a person may be completely color-blind and able to see only varying shades of gray ranging from white to black. Partial color blindness is more common, and different combinations are found. Some people are red-green–blind but can perceive blues and yellows, while others can perceive reds and greens but not blues and yellows.

An interesting question is how color-blind persons cope in a world in which color plays such an important role, as with traffic signal lights and even color combinations of dress apparel. Some persons who are color-blind are not aware of their deficiency. They operate by discriminating brightness differences between lights. Often the color-blind person will talk about colors in the same way others do and give the appearance that he experiences similar sensations, but his reports are based upon inferences and logical conclusions.

DARK ADAPTATION

When an individual walks from sunlight into a semidarkened room, he experiences immediate difficulty in finding his way. Similarly at dusk as evening approaches, motorists find driving difficult and hazardous. Both of these examples indicate that the eyes go through a short period of change (approximately thirty minutes) before they become accustomed to the dark. Dark adaptation is a function of differences in the chemical activity of the rods and cones of the retina. At dusk both rods and cones are operating but with different levels of effectiveness. Cones are active in daylight vision, while rods function mainly in night vision. A sudden change from light to dark or dark to light requires an adjustment in chemical action between the rods and cones which creates the momentary experience of "blindness." It takes a few minutes for the eye to shift from dim light to brightness, and even longer to adapt from bright light to darkness. Thus it is highly improbable that a witness could make an accurate identification of a person or object immediately after a change in the conditions of illumination. However, the longer a person is in a dark room, the more sensitive his eyes become to light.

VISUAL ACUITY

People said to have good vision or poor vision are described in terms of their visual acuity, that is, their ability to make fine discriminations among differences in the size and shape of objects. Someone with 20-20 vision measured on the conventional eye chart is able to identify stimuli at 20 feet as well as people with average vision. In contrast, someone with 20-40 vision must be as close to the chart as 20 feet in order to identify what the person with average vision can identify at 40 feet.

Visual acuity is highly variable and will change as a function of the visual angle of viewing, changes in intensity of illumination, the relationship of an object with its background, and the presence of eye defects such as near-sightedness and farsightedness.

CONTRAST AND CONSTANCY

The problem of understanding the perceptual processes of detection and recognition involves not only the characteristics of a single target stimulus but also the interrelations among the target and surrounding background stimuli. Objects, events, and people are perceived always as part of some environmental context. Knowledge of an object may be influenced by the effects of perceptual contrast and perceptual constancy. In perceptual contrast a particular stimulus may appear small next to large objects and large in the company of small objects. A sound can seem loud if preceded by total stillness but appear soft if it follows very loud noises or crashes. Perceptual constancy, on the other hand, refers to percepts that remain the same even though the stimulation has changed. For example, we perceive a person as having the same size and brightness of color if he or she is walking toward us from a shaded area or away from us even though the information hitting our visual receptors has changed considerably. Although perceptual constancy is not perfect, our estimates of size, for example, are quite accurate for moderate distances; they are less accurate at greater distances. For example, adults are able to estimate sizes of familiar objects quite easily up to distances of a mile or so (Gibson, 1950).

PERCEPTION OF MOVEMENT

Perception of movement is often of primary importance in eyewitness testimony. Did the witness see the defendant raise his hand, turn his head, jump away, and so on?

The simplest explanation of the perception of movement involves two signals to the brain: (1) the image of a moving object stimulates cells on one side of the retina of the eye and runs along these receptors stimulating other cells, and (2) the movement of the eyes and head follows the moving object. Some of the brain cells receiving input from the visual sensory system are specialized as movement detectors. The information on relative timing of stimulation at different retinal positions and the stimulation of receptors in the muscles of the eyes, head, and neck providing kinesthetic information are integrated by the brain to produce the experience of movement.

How fast an object appears to be moving is a relative matter. It is difficult for us to judge speed in an absolute sense; rather, we perceive speed in terms of how fast other things in the context are moving.

The naive view that perception of movement involves actual motion of an object is sometimes wrong, since it is impossible to perceive apparent motion without a successive pattern of stimulation of adjacent cells of the retina. One kind of apparent motion is called the autokinetic effect. If a room is completely dark except for a single stationary spot of light, the light will appear to move about in a random manner. The lack of a frame of reference against which to judge the light is the best interpretation of this effect. Another type of apparent motion is the phi phenomenon. When lights sequentially are turned on and off, we see movement though nothing is moving. The illusion of movement is created by the apparent displacement of a single light moving from one position to the next and is best seen in the neon light displays of advertising in urban centers.

The perception of movement also involves the notion of causality. It is obvious, for example, that when one billiard ball strikes another billiard ball, the movement of the first causes the movement of the second. Not all sequential movement of two objects, however, results in perceptions of causality. Michotte (1963) has shown that movement of two simple geometric figures on a screen can be interpreted as causally related if the figures are initially stationary and one figure moves to the right until it comes to rest next to the second figure which in turn moves to the right. The perception of causality will be destroyed, however, if the second figure is made to move faster than the first, if the second figure delays moving for one-half second after the first figure's motion stops, or if the direction of movement of the second figure is erratic or unusual. In addition, the movement of two simple geometric figures often receives an anthropomorphic interpretation. A triangle may be seen as pushing a circle, or chasing and catching it as it tries to escape, or the two may be seen as attracted to one another, dancing or fighting. Apparently there is a similarity in patterns underlying the movement of cartoon-like objects which reminds observers of other similar patterns experienced in the movement of real-world objects and even interpersonal events.

PERCEPTUAL ORGANIZATION

When someone witnesses a crime in action, certain things become selected and focused upon. Our attention is drawn to intense stimuli, the loud noise, the bright color, the quick movement, and so on. These stimuli stand out from their background because of the definite contrast involved.

A fundamental question in perception is how different elements, objects, and persons are perceived as belonging together as a unified whole or as elements of a group. Most of our knowledge of the principles of perceptual organization has its origin in the early-twentieth-century school of Gestalt psychology. Gestaltists maintained that our perceptions of elements or parts are affected by the properties of wholes. We tend to structure whatever we see into organized configurations. For example, parts of a stimulus pattern that are "similar" to each other or occur close together in "proximity" tend to be perceived as belonging together. If we see an incomplete or unfinished piece of work, we automatically fill in the missing piece ourselves, demonstrating the Gestalt principle of "closure." Parts of a stimulus array that move together or get brighter or duller at the same time are seen as having "a common fate." In sum, perception is organized, and its organization tends to be as good as the stimulus conditions permit.

Gestalt principles of perceptual grouping are useful in explaining observations made about individuals and groups. For example, a person who is similar in physical appearance to a gang of delinquents, or is seen in the company of troublemakers, may be perceived by the police as a member of that group. We often make the error of disregarding individual differences among people and classifying them into categories simply because they seem to be similar or appear to belong together.

How Long Was the Robber in the Store?

TIME PERCEPTION

Time is an important dimension of our interpersonal activities. We perceive time both as "background," in which persons, objects, and events are organized, and as "figure" in which time itself is the salient feature of the situation. In this second meaning we perceive the flow of time; time is said to "fly," to "drag," or even to stand still." Perceived time in contrast to physical or chronological time is best understood as the interaction between a person and the happenings or events of the situation. For instance, to the robbed shopkeeper the minutes between calling the police and their arrival may seem like hours; to the escaping thief the sudden arrival of police may seem instantaneous.

Short intervals of time such as three or four seconds can be experienced directly. On the other hand, long intervals of time such as ten seconds or more must be judged or retrospected from long-term memory rather than perceived. If someone is asked to estimate the length of an interval of time, short time intervals of less than a second are usually overestimated and intervals of more than one second are underestimated (Fraisse, 1963). Accuracy in judgment of long time intervals depends upon two kinds of cues, events in the external environment and events defined by an internal "biological clock" within the person. External events refer to such things as the position of the sun in the sky, the appearance of certain programs on radio or television, or even the chimes of the grandfather clock. Internal physiological events are more difficult to specify, but it is clear that man has considerable accuracy in time orientation in the absence of external cues (Hoagland, 1933).

Large individual differences also are apparent in judgments of length of time intervals. Time appears to pass slowly for children but much too quickly for their parents and grandparents (Cohen, 1964). Mental and physiological states of the individual affect the perception of time. For depressed patients time passes slowly, as it does for persons experiencing frustrations and failure. Stimulant drugs such as coffee and nicotine lengthen duration experience, and sedative and hypnotic drugs shorten it. Energizers or mood-elevating drugs such as amphetamines or pep pills lengthen duration experience (Goldstone, Boardman, and Lhamon, 1958). The psychedelic drugs such as LSD and marijuana also act to lengthen the experience of duration (Fischer, 1967). Individuals experiencing an LSD trip usually report an overwhelming sense of immediacy or "nowness" which diminishes their normal ability to evaluate perspectives of past and future.

The discussion presented so far has listed a number of perceptual variables—visual defects, color blindness, etc.—which often have relevance in the courtroom. I would now like to discuss what psychologists try to accomplish in studying perception, which as we have already seen is not simply an automatic, mechanical process.

The Perceptual World

The goal of the study of perception is to explain why things or events appear or seem as they do. The diagram in figure 3.1 shows that perceptual events can be understood at different levels of explanation.

Perceiving begins with some form of physical energy in the real world meeting the sensory receptors of the body such as the eyes or ears. These receptors are sensitive to that energy and transform it into electrochemical impulses which are carried along sensory pathways of the peripheral nervous system. These nerve impulses are transmitted to the brain, where they are interpreted in the form of subjective experiences of sight or sound. Psychologists interested in perception have attempted to explain perceptual phenomena in terms of how the sensory systems function and more recently in terms of central brain mechanisms that ultimately receive and decode environmental information from the senses. Since our primary aim is to outline human perception and memory in terms of their relevance to practices in the criminal justice system, sensory-oriented topics and neurophysiological mechanisms of perception will be given only limited attention.

Sensory Capacities

Sensory responses of detection, recognition, and identification of stimuli are some of the most fundamental acts that man performs. The first step in the perceptual process involves detection of the stimulus or physical energy that comes into contact with a sense organ and excites it into action. In order for a person to detect a stimulus, the physical intensity of energy must be above some fixed or absolute threshold. That is, it must be strong enough to excite the sensory system and send impulses to the brain. For example, a spot of light on a radar screen must reach some measurable intensity before it can be distinguished from other competing signals called "noise."

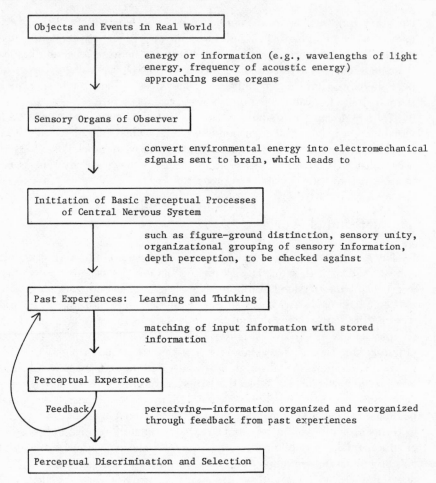

FIGURE 3.1   Levels of perceptual events

Detection or nondetection of weak stimuli which are not clearly distinguishable from the background context is not as simple a matter as it may seem, since among other things humans vary in their ability to detect weak signals. The particular intensity value beyond which a stimulus will be detected varies from one observer to the next. Furthermore, the absolute threshold for a given individual will vary from time to time depending on his motivational state, his physical condition, and the environmental context under which the observations are made. Consequently, psychologists define the absolute threshold as that value of stimulus intensity at which it is detected 50% of the time by the observer (Galanter, 1962).

There are serious limitations to using the fixed-threshold models in detecting very weak stimulus energies, since they ignore motivation and other factors that contribute to an observer's decision of whether a stimulus is present. A relatively recent approach is to regard detection as a statistical process of decision making; this approach involves what is referred to as the theory of signal detection (Green and Swets, 1966). According to this theory, perception or recognition is a process of decision making. An observer reports that he saw, heard, or felt some change in a stimulus as a function, in part, of his sensory capabilities and in part as a result of his attitude or motivation to commit himself. To illustrate, two witnesses might both "see" a suggestion of a gun in the hand of a thief. An impulsive subject might report that he definitely saw a gun, whereas a cautious person would report that he did not see a weapon. The application of signal detection theory in the research situation permits us to determine the extent to which the attitude or motivation of an observer influences his decision to report a perceptual experience in the face of a weak, unclear stimulus signal. A theoretical and mathematical description of signal detection procedures, however, is beyond the scope of this book and will not be presented here.

Pattern Recognition

WHAT IS OUT THERE?

Most of us have been in situations where we have had to decide whether or not our eyes were playing tricks on us. Did we really see what we thought we saw? Is that a man standing in the alley, or is it simply a shadow? These questions suggest that perception is a process of hypothesizing the meaning of sensations received by our receptors (Bruner, 1957). When stimuli are not clearly distinguishable from a background, the observer has to decide what the objects or things mean and organize his perceptions accordingly.

The perceiver creates his percepts from the interaction of external sensory information entering his perceptual system and his stored internal knowledge. This constructive act emphasizes the active nature of the perceptual system. In most situations we are given consistent and clear sensory information, the interpretation is done easily, and the construction of a percept is quick and sure. Under other situations, and especially in emotionally heightened circumstances such as witnessing a crime in action, the hypothesis-testing nature of perception is more apparent, since the situation is unusual and often ambiguous.

WHO IS THAT?

In chapter 1 excerpts of the trial records of Adam Beck were presented. Testimony of several witnesses refers to specific features they apparently noticed in their recognition of the defendant. For example, one witness reported that "I saw his back; I should know him among a thousand. I recognized him at once." Another witness said, "I noticed when he sat in my room he had some mark just below the right jaw . . ." while another witness reported, "his nose is most peculiar, and is one I could pick out of a thousand—his whole face is different from any other man I ever remember seeing. . . ."

Whether or not human perception of faces operates through feature detection or in some other fashion is of theoretical and practical concern, as will be explained in chapter 6. Current conceptualizations of recognition and identification involve three major theoretical approaches: template matching, feature analysis, and schema matching.

TEMPLATE MATCHING

This hypothesis dates back to man's first recorded writings. Plato (Jowett translation, 1892) spoke of recognition in the following way:

> . . . when knowing you and Theodorus, and having on the waxen block the impression of both of you given as by a seal, but seeing you imperfectly and at a distance, I try to assign the right impression of memory to the right visual impression, and to fit this into its own print: If I succeed, recognition will take place. . . . [p. 257]

Plato was suggesting that his sensory experiences of his two colleagues were represented in his memory store as a template, or image. Later, on seeing the two again, he compared his present visual information with the template. If the stimulus and template fit and a match occurred, then Plato would report that the two were familiar and that he recognized them.

Although this theory has intuitive appeal, it does have a theoretical shortcoming. If the form of the stimulus changes in size or orientation from its original template, we should have trouble in matching the stimulus to the template. Nevertheless, we are able to recognize stimuli of altered shape or size. For example, we recognize old friends over the years even though their faces often have changed with aging and cosmetic styles. Since we are able to recognize an almost endless number of changing patterns, which would require an infinite number of templates, template matching is not a good model for human pattern recognition.

FEATURE ANALYSIS

Most of our knowledge of feature detectors has come from studies on lower animals, where it has been shown that particular cells in the brain serve as angle detectors, horizontal line detectors (a straight line boundary between light and dark regions), vertical line detectors, and so on. Examination and extraction of parts of patterns such as horizontal lines, vertical lines, and areas of circles and the combination of features to characterize a pattern typifies the method of feature analysis (Gibson, 1969). Thus in the recognition of a simple stimulus like the letter A, distinctive features might be two oblique lines converging at their tops and joined somewhere between top and bottom by a horizontal line. These features, in contrast to a template representation, are stored in memory. At the recognition test the list of stored features can include A's that are large or small, fat or thin and even slightly off angle. As long as these features are stored and match the test stimulus, the stimulus will be recognized. If man's nervous system has feature detectors, then in theory these detectors form the basis of form recognition. Whether it does or does not, the strategy of feature analysis is suggestive of how the human recognition memory system works.

SCHEMA MATCHING

In some respects psychologists understand perception to be similar to historical reconstruction of the past or the work of a paleontologist (Hebb, 1949). Paleontologists are able to "reconstruct" the image of a dinosaur merely from extractions of a few critical bone fragments separated from a background of irrelevant rubble. In the understanding of perception, this approach assumes that the observer constructs and builds his percept rather than simply reacting reflexively to sensory inputs. The construction of percepts must, of course, be done in some systematic manner and, at some time or other, be compared to some model, referred to as a "schema" or "prototype."

Schemas are developed through repeated experiences and, once established, serve as a guide to behavior (Bartlett, 1932). The resulting representations or maps are abstractions of a person's world and how he fits into that environment. According to the schema hypothesis, perceptual recognition involves matching what you are looking at with an abstract mental representation. The schema is conceptualized as a genuine perceptual abstraction or image which contains all of the essential identifying characteristics of a class of objects without comprising the stimulus properties of any of them (Attneave, 1957). This conceptualization of a schema differs from template matching and feature analysis, since the latter two involve the storing in memory of particular characteristics of each stimulus.

It is likely that schema matching and feature analysis are combined in some fashion to produce perceptual recognition. Schemas may be composed in part of subsets of features in common with the representations of a class of patterns. Those features which are common with the schema may be considered the class-defining features of a stimulus. Accordingly, recognition may consist of matching a subset of features of a stimulus to a generalized pattern of abstraction.

Perception and Learning

If a witness expects people with certain skin color or facial appearances to behave in particular ways, will his expectations influence what he sees? That is, will he anticipate visually on the basis of his prior experiences and present knowledge? Results of studies on perceptual organization, movement, the perceptual constancies, and other perceptual phenomena allow us to understand generally what it is that an observer perceives. However, these studies do not solve our problem of explaining how perception occurs. One of the persistent problems in philosophy and psychology is the question of whether or not some of our perceptual responses occur independently of past experiences and are innate, or are learned and modified by practice and experience. According to the philosophical theory of nativism (Descartes, Kant), man is born with the ability to perceive as he does; in particular, perceptions of space and motion are considered innate characteristics. In contrast to this view, we will examine in this section some of the evidence which shows that perception is influenced by the individual's past experiences.

EFFECT OF DEVELOPMENTAL CHANGES ON PERCEPTION

What an individual perceives will to a great extent be dependent upon his development. Since the visual sensory system is physiologically and anatomically fully developed at a very young age, it is reasonable to argue that changes in perception are a consequence of learning. Evidence of such changes in perception has been revealed in studies of perceptual constancy and spatial illusions. Studies of young children between the ages of 2 and 10 on their perceptions of apparent size, brightness, and shape of objects reveal that perceptual judgments became more veridical with maturation. That is, the older the individual, the better his capacity to perceive objects in terms of their actual physical properties. Consistent with this finding is additional evidence showing that spatial illusions have less influence in distorting true perceptions as individuals increase in age (Brunswik, 1956.)

EFFECT OF PAST EXPERIENCE ON PERCEPTION

The clearest examples showing that what is perceived is not what exists, but, rather, what one believes through experience to exist are the so-called

Ames (1951) demonstrations such as the rotating trapezoidal window, which is illustrated in figure 3.2.

> By means of a piece of apparatus called the "rotating trapezoidal window" it has been possible to extend the investigation to complex perceptual situations involving movement. This device consists of a trapezoidal surface with panes cut in it and shadows painted on it to give the appearance of a window. It is mounted on a rod connected to a motor so that it rotates at a slow constant speed in an upright position about its own axis. When an observer views the rotating surface with one eye from about 10 feet or more or with both eyes from about 25 feet or more, he sees not a rotating trapezoid but an oscillating rectangle. Its speed of movement and its shape appear to vary markedly as it turns. If a small cube is attached by a short rod to the upper part of the short side of the trapezoid, it seems to become detached, sail freely around the front of the trapezoid and attach itself again as the apparatus rotates.... [Ittelson and Kilpatrick, 1951, p. 55]

What is seen is what fits our past experiences. The rotating trapezoid is perceived as an oscillating rectangle, partly because it is perceived as a window and partly from our knowledge that windows are usually rectangular. The assumption that the window is rectangular determines the apparently reversed motion of the window-like object.

It has been hypothesized that language has a direct effect on the way the individual perceives the world (Whorf, 1956). According to this hypothesis our language predisposes us to perceive and to interpret real-world events in certain ways. Thus the Eskimo, who has seven separate words in his language for "snow," would be more set for differences in varieties of snow than a speaker of English, who has only one word for snow and, consequently, may make less accurate discrimination.

It may be concluded that what we select to perceive and how we organize it are determined in part by our expectations. Our past experiences prepare us or give us a "set" to see what we expect to see. No two people perceive the world in exactly the same way. The implication of this conclusion is that witnesses will interpret their observations as a function of what they have learned in the past and what they expect will happen in the future. This tendency to perceive the world in meaningful representations based on past experience rather than what exists is, of course, the dilemma that the courts constantly face. So-called credible witnesses often report what they believed must have happened rather than what they actually observed (Buckhout, 1974).

The Effects of Motivation on Perception

Although much of our perception accurately corresponds with real-world events, particularly when these events are well above our sensory thresholds and highly discriminable and meaningful, some of our perceptions are am-

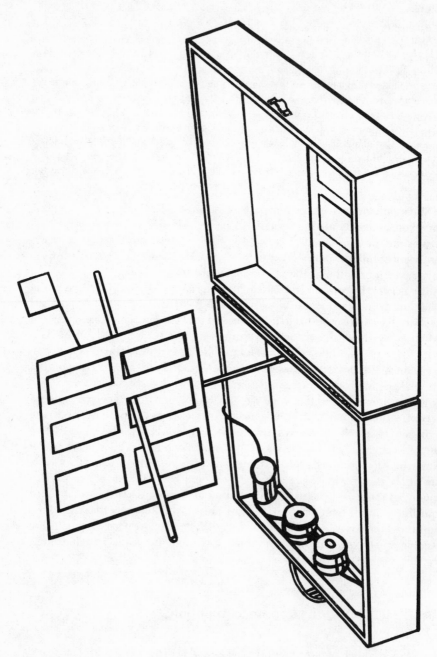

FIGURE 3.2   The rotating trapezoid demonstration *(from Ames, 1951)*

biguous. When this is the case, perception may be interpreted as a function of our wishes, desires, feelings, interests, and values.

The effects of motivation on perception have been investigated in terms of (1) primary drives, such as hunger and thirst, (2) acquired or social drives, such as need for achievement and prestige, and (3) motives deriving from fear and anxiety. Food, for example, is more readily noticed and appears more appetizing to the hungry man than to the satiated (Levine, Chein, and Murphy, 1942). The effects of social drives on perception are shown in studies of children from poorer homes who tend to overestimate the size of coins more than children from well-to-do homes (Bruner and Goodman, 1947). Since the experience of fear and anxiety is common to many witnesses observing an accident or crime in action, we will examine in some detail some evidence concerning the effects of these variables on perception.

Several theories, especially the psychoanalytic theories of Freud, suggest that some subjects use a "perceptual defense" when confronted with threatening or emotionally disturbing stimuli. There is some question whether individuals literally do not perceive threatening stimuli or whether they fail to report them, or think about them, because of their anxiety or embarrassment. For example, words which are not commonly used in conversations in "polite society," such as "whore" and "penis," may go unrecognized not because we are unfamiliar with them, but because we have learned that these words are not proper in social contexts and should not be uttered, particularly to members of the opposite sex (Howes and Solomon, 1950; McGinnies, 1949). In addition, an idea following Freud's lead again, stimuli which signal immediate danger promote a "perceptual vigilance" in which dangerous stimuli are selected for processing and less dangerous stimuli are perceptually avoided.

Recent research by Suedfeld, Erdelyi, and Corcoran (1975) suggests that observers engage in multiple levels of perceptual processing. When viewing a stressful scene, subjects allocate attention to this visual input which persists in time even past the termination of the unpleasant information. Consequently, there is a relative rejection and lack of attention given to other visual input following the termination of the unpleasant stimulation. On the other hand, observers often tend to physically defend themselves in viewing negative scenes by turning away, which, of course, causes them to miss any new information. According to Erdelyi (1974), an observer may stop looking at a target if he considers it irrelevant or if he finds it stressful or upsetting. If a stimulus is considered potentially dangerous, we process it rapidly and make any necessary adjustments such as perceptual defense or vigilance.

Any threat to a person demands attention and may produce a narrowing of selection in the perceptual field. Behavioral reactions to such stimuli may take the form of inattentiveness, such as hoping the danger will go away if you avoid thinking about it; aggression toward the instigator of the threat;

defensive reactions such as leaving the area through escape; and rigidity, an inability to change directions in spite of altered information. Rigidity resulting from threat and fear, in particular, produces decreased efficiency on intellectual and visual search tasks (Beier, 1951). Studies also show that the amount of time perceived as going by is overestimated under conditions of danger and that the overestimation tends to increase as the stress increases (Langer, Wapner, and Werner, 1961). Furthermore, individuals perceive distances differently when threatened. People overestimate the distance they have traveled when they are in danger. As threat and fear increase, individuals perceive themselves as traveling farther and taking longer to complete the distances (Werner and Wapner, 1955).

Witnesses of crimes in action, either as bystanders or, more often, as victims, often fail to recognize their assailants. We know that perceptions under stress in laboratory situations are reckless, premature, nonsensical, and inaccurate (Postman and Bruner, 1948). What is surprising, however, is how good perceptions can be in the real world, realizing all of the various limitations and difficulties involved in knowing and understanding what we perceive.

In this chapter I have tried to show how the perceiver constructs the world that he sees. In the next chapter we will look at what he remembers of what was seen and how he remembers it.

Chapter 4

Memory: An Overview

The memory of individual witnesses, as it is reported in the courtroom, is the largest fact-substance of juridical decisions. It is frequently intended as the vehicle for the accurate reconstruction of past events which form the subject matter of litigation. . . . [Redmount, 1959, p. 249]

Obviously, the courts are interested in how accurately a witness remembers testimonial events from his past. Since jurors are not allowed to take notes during trials, the courts also have to be concerned with the ability of jurors to remember the testimony of witnesses, the closing arguments of both attorneys, and the instructions of the judge. The complexity of court proceedings and their effects on jurors are dramatized by empirical findings which show that individual jurors remember and understand only approximately two-thirds of the judge's instructions. And when questioned about the nature of evidence presented in court, 80% of deliberating jurors cannot answer correctly one or more questions (Forston, 1970). The consequences of misunderstanding a judge's instructions and forgetting the evidence presented during a trial can include the defendant being found guilty when the jury intended to free him, or just the reverse, finding the defendant innocent when the jury really meant to convict him (see Elwork, Sales, and Alfini, in press, and Sales, Elwork, and Alfini, 1978, for thorough discussion of these issues).

We will see in this chapter that the psychology of memory is a theoretical and empirical area of knowledge which cannot be understood simply in commonsense terms. Police, lawyers, and judges who fail to appreciate the limitations of memory and sensitive differences between such cognitive operations as recall, recognition, and reconstruction seriously undermine the operations of their own proceedings.

In the next section a brief review of different kinds of remembering is presented; then follows a discussion of the memory processes which make these kinds of remembering possible. This chapter has been written as a basic overview of some of the fundamental processes and principles of memory. More intensive and in-depth coverage of memory is available in several contemporary texts, such as Adams, 1976; Baddeley, 1976; Horton and Turnage, 1976; Kausler, 1976; Klatzky, 1975; Loftus and Loftus, 1976; Norman, 1976; Wickelgren, 1977.

Kinds of Remembering

RECALL

A laboratory subject asked to reproduce a specific list of words or sentences without using explicit cues to facilitate his recitation is performing a test of free recall. In more realistic settings, a student writing an essay examination, an actor reciting a poem on stage, and a witness giving a free narration of his experiences are utilizing recall memory. We will look at the factors which facilitate or disrupt this process later in this chapter.

RECOGNITION

It is generally believed that recognition is simpler than recall. When presented a test item, the individual must decide whether the item is or is not the item presented earlier. Thus, for students taking a multiple-choice test or for witnesses looking at suspects in a police lineup, recognition involves the correct identification of the target item or target person and the rejection of the alternative choices. Errors in recognition usually occur because of a similarity between the target and the distractors.

A common experience of faulty recognition for most people is the deceiving sense of familiarity or *déjà vu* sometimes aroused by strange and totally new surroundings. People sometimes have the feeling that they have been somewhere before or have seen a particular room or building before but know that this is impossible. This experience can be explained by suggesting, as Plato did, that the experience "proves" your previous existence in an earlier life. A more rational explanation is that the stimuli of the present situation are similar in some way or other to those of other situations you have been in. The similarity of the two situations creates a sense of familiarity which can be very convincing (see Weimer, 1973).

Recognition memory often is impressively accurate and tends to be better for visual than for verbal memory. For example, Shepard (1967) presented subjects with 612 color pictures for a few seconds each and found that 98% of the old stimuli were correctly identified in a two-alternative recognition test. When words were used as stimuli, recognition performance was still high but dropped to 90% accuracy. Other studies testing the large capacity of visual memory have confirmed these findings. For example, Standing, Conezio, and Haber (1970) showed 2,560 photographs for 10 seconds each and found that subjects accurately recognized over 90% of the stimuli even after a 3-day retention interval. The amount of time spent looking at the photographs does not seem to determine performance, since recognition accuracy is still high when viewing time is reduced to 1 second per picture. More recently, Standing (1973) increased the number of test pictures to 10,000 and concluded on the basis of his findings that the capacity of recognition memory for pictures may be limitless.

REDINTEGRATION

Witnesses asked to tell the court in their own words what they saw at a particular time, day, and place will often answer by recollecting a flood of details. Recollections will focus on the sought-after event but in addition will arouse other details of events and circumstances that occurred prior to and following the critical incident. Although such recollections are common in our everyday experiences, few psychologists apart from clinical psychologists have given much attention to the study of personal memories. The major limitation to the scientific investigations of redintegrative memory is the difficulty in knowing what originally was stored in memory compared to the materials reconstructed or refabricated in an individual's recall. A person's redintegration of events from his or her past will contain factual truth, inferences, and conclusions of what "probably" must have happened. Thus the difficulty facing investigators is to distinguish between true facts and "facts" that are refabrications.

FACULTY PSYCHOLOGY

In the nineteenth century a popular theory, referred to as faculty psychology, conceptualized the mind as being composed of separate areas of power such as memory, perception, personality, and so on. Memory in itself was considered a unitary factor and the individual either had a good memory, average memory, or poor memory.

The law has acted in the past and even very recently (see Graham, 1978) as if this hypothesis were true. If a witness under cross-examination was able to remember the material fact but was shown to have a poor memory of events entirely unconnected with the event in question, the court assumed

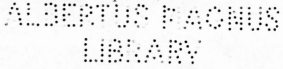

the right to doubt the correctness of the material fact (Wigmore, 1923). A famous example of this practice occurred during the trial of Queen Caroline.

> Among the various charges of adultery and improper intimacy between the Queen (the Princess) and her servant Bergami during her tour in Germany, Austria, Italy, and the Mediterranean, one charge was made of adultery on board a polacca during a sea-voyage to Palestine; the witness Majocchi, a servant in her suite during most of her journeys, had testified specifically to this charge under the following questions from Mr. Solicitor-General Copley: "Did the Princess sleep under that tent (placed on deck) generally on the voyage from Jaffa Home?"
>
> Majocchi: "She slept always under that tent during the whole voyage from Jaffa to the time she landed."
>
> Mr. Sol. Gen.: "Did anybody sleep under the same tent?"
>
> Majocchi: "Bartolomo Bergami."
>
> Mr. Sol. Gen.: "Did this take place every night?"
>
> Majocchi: "Every night."
>
> On cross-examination Mr. Brougham sought to test his trustworthiness by inquiring as to other details of the sleeping arrangements of the suite: "(On this voyage) where did Hieronimus sleep in general?"
>
> Majocchi: "I do not recollect (Non mi ricordo)."
>
> Mr. Brougham: "Where did Mr. Howman sleep?"
>
> Majocchi: "I do not recollect."
>
> Mr. Brougham: "Where did William Austin sleep?"
>
> Majocchi: "I do not remember."
>
> Mr. Brougham: "Where did the Countess Oldi sleep?"
>
> Majocchi: "I do not remember."
>
> Mr. Brougham: "Where did Camera sleep?"
>
> Majocchi: "I do not know where he slept."
>
> Mr. Brougham: "Where did the maids sleep?"
>
> Majocchi: "I do not know."
>
> Mr. Brougham: "Where did Captain Flynn sleep?"
>
> Majocchi: "I do not know."
>
> Mr. Brougham: "Did you not, when you were ill during the voyage, sleep below (in the hold) under the deck?"
>
> Majocchi: "Under the deck."
>
> Mr. Brougham: "Did those excellent sailors always remain below in the hold with you?"
>
> Majocchi: "This I cannot remember if they slept in the hold during the night-time or went up."
>
> Mr. Brougham: "Who slept in the place where you used to sleep down below in the hold?"

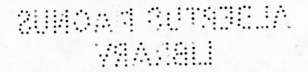

Majocchi: "I know very well that I slept there, but I do not remember who else."

Mr. Brougham: "Where did the livery servants of the suite sleep?"

Majocchi: "This I do not remember."

Mr. Brougham: "Were you not yourself a livery servant?"

Majocchi: "Yes."

Mr. Brougham: "Where did the Padroni of the vessel sleep?"

Majocchi: "I do not know."

Mr. Brougham: "When her Royal Highness was going by sea on her voyage (at another time) from Sicily to Tunis, where did she sleep?"

Majocchi: "This I cannot remember."

Mr. Brougham: "When she was afterwards going from Tunis to Constantinople on board the ship, where did her Royal Highness sleep?"

Majocchi: "This I do not remember."

Mr. Brougham: "When she was going from Constantinople to the Holy Land on board the ship, where did she sleep then?"

Majocchi: "I do not remember."

Mr. Brougham: "Where did Bergami sleep on these three voyages of which you have just been speaking?"

Majocchi: "This I do not know." [Wigmore, 1923, p. 426]

Clearly, the trustworthiness of this testimony was suspect, but there is no justification in psychology to assume that an inability to recall some information means that other information could not be accurately recalled. Contemporary theorists do not assume that memory is a unitary factor and, as you would expect, the theory of faculty psychology has lost its scientific credibility.

Memory Processes

When asked to remember past experiences and events, we are conscious of particular facts which seem to pop into our awareness, but the mechanisms by which we remember these facts are beyond our personal inspection. This everyday experience tells us that the contents of memory can be made available in our consciousness but not the processes of memory. The scientific study of memory is concentrated on the identification and knowledge of the contents of memory and the processes by which information gets into and out of memory. These processes are generally referred to as encoding, storage, and retrieval, and are the three basic phases of information processing by a human observer.

ENCODING

In technical terms, encoding is the process of transforming physical stimulus energies impinging upon the senses of an observer into memory codes. The registration processes of perception are necessarily involved in the memory process of encoding. Looking at any physical object or event may result in the registration of information on the sensory receptors of the eyes. This information is encoded in terms of neuronal excitations and conveyed as electrical signals to the brain for further processing. Subsequent encodings in the brain may be in the form of phonetic codes such as sounds, or coded in terms of words or mental images which represent the stimuli in visual or picture-like representations. These encodings may be either selective or elaborative. When a witness claims he saw a "big man," he may remember that he was a white man but not that he was bald. Thus in this case attention selected some information and not other information. In addition, the coding may be elaborated by remembering whom the man resembled. Thus the "big man" may be remembered as a person who resembled a wrestler or football player.

STORAGE

Once an event is encoded, it is stored in memory in some systematic, organized network. The form of storage will depend upon the nature of the material to be remembered and the particular coding techniques employed by the individual. For example, material that is meaningful usually leads to efficient storage, since it can be grouped, classified, or organized into smaller chunks of information. The words "north," "south," "east," and "west," for example, are easily remembered and stored as "directions." Coding techniques vary from simplistic rote repetition to sophisticated mnemonic strategies such as those used by professional "memory experts." Mnemonic strategies are defined as plans to remember. Through the use of such plans, individuals can build elaborate associative networks which organize both meaningful and nonsensical materials into readily recalled structures.

RETRIEVAL

Information stored in memory is not of much use unless it is accessible for recall. However, many experiences may be stored in memory even though they are not at the moment retrievable. To illustrate this point, think back to the last time you saw an old friend but couldn't remember his name. You might say to yourself, "Is it Sam? Dan? Craig? no, it's Peter. I remember last seeing him at. . . ." This experience is referred to as the tip-of-the-tongue phenomenon. It occurs whenever a person attempts to recall a name or word and has the feeling that he knows it and is on the verge of producing it but, for the moment, cannot find it.

Brown and McNeill (1966), in their study of the tip-of-the-tongue (TOT) state, demonstrated that words are frequently available in memory but, at least temporarily, not accessible for retrieval. Subjects in the TOT state often are able to identify a number of characteristics or attributes of the to-be-recalled word, such as its number of syllables, its beginning letter, and even which syllable is accented in pronunciation. In their search for the proper word, individuals often evoke similar-sounding words as well as words similar in meaning to the target word. The closer the subject is to recall without actual success, the more accurate is his knowledge.

A major interpretation of this research is that memory is the storage of features or attributes of verbal meaning. The more features that a person is able to locate, the more likely that a word will be remembered. Retrieval of similar-sounding words and words similar in meaning to the target words, referred to as "generic recall," progressively arouses more and more common features unique to the to-be-remembered word, which usually leads to its retrieval.

Retrieval of words from storage does not depend, however, solely upon generic recall. Subjects attempting to verbally identify visual scenes such as photographs of well-known celebrities also use imagery and verbal associations to facilitate their recall (Yarmey, 1973). For example, a subject given the photograph of Muhammad Ali might report, "I remember seeing that face in the newspapers and television a few years ago—didn't he have something to do with boxing? I can picture him in my mind 'dancing like a butterfly.' Yes, it's the former world champion, Muhammad Ali."

Stages of Memory Storage

The nature of memory reflects a complex system of processes and stages. For ease of communication we will conceptualize memory at this point as consisting of three hypothetical stages: (1) sensory memory, (2) short-term memory, and (3) long-term memory. The most influential stage theory of verbal memory which distinguishes among these three phases of memory is the Atkinson and Shiffrin (1968) model shown in figure 4.1.

To follow the stream of information through this system, let us take a hypothetical example and imagine that you are in a restaurant and want to order a special wine from the restaurant's wine menu. Since the names of the wines must be read, the input is visual and enters the system through the eyes. Memory at this point is a sensory representation of letters and words, which in effect is a fairly literal or graphic display of the items. Information is

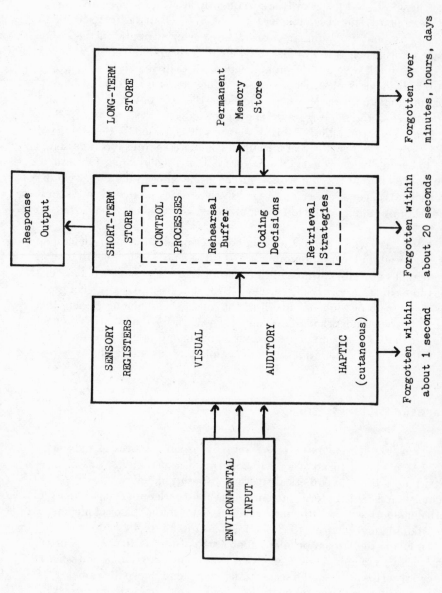

FIGURE 4.1 A schematic view of memory *(from Atkinson and Shiffrin, 1968)*

analyzed and coded immediately in terms of its physical characteristics such as lines, curves, and figure-ground relationships. The initial processing of such information is said to be very rapid and superficial, and the information is lost quickly through either decay or being bumped out of the system as the page is scanned for other names. Eventually, we will make contact with one or two names which we have selected for further processing, which takes us to the short-term memory stage.

Short-term memory is characterized by its limited capacity and use of a predominantly verbal-linguistic coding strategy. Only so much information can be held in this temporary store with accuracy. Generally, five plus or minus two bits of information can be stored in short-term memory at any one time. Thus, in our hypothetical example, we can hold the names of approximately five different wines in our short-term store for a few seconds before they fade away. If the waiter is tardy and our kids grab the wine list from our hands, we will be forced to hold the names in memory by rehearsing the labels. Rehearsal prevents the memory traces from decaying at least for the time being. If we get the wine list back and begin to review the list again, the old items may be displaced from the store through interference from new items entering the system. If we need to retain these names for future reference, we will code them for transfer to long-term storage.

Long-term memory is identified by an apparent infinite capacity to store information in a relatively permanent fashion. The phrase "relatively permanent" is emphasized, since information is not necessarily stored forever; some of our experiences are always accessible, and information from other experiences is accessible only some of the time.

To get back to our example, we will eventually choose a wine. If the wine turns out to be good, we will probably want to remember its name for future occasions. Consequently, we will rehearse its name or use other coding strategies to promote its long-term storage. Long-term memory is an active reconstructive process which is constantly manipulating its contents and transforming incoming information and stored experiences into more organized units. This process of reconstruction characterizes long-term memory as much as its more familiar property of being a storehouse of experiences. Retrieval of information is basically a search of the long-term store and the transfer of this information to the short-term store for utilization.

Levels-of-Processing View of Memory

In the last few years a number of researchers have argued that the stage model of memory is cumbersome and unable to handle a number of recent research findings. Memory, they suggest, should not be conceptualized as a discrete series of phases, but, rather, in terms of multiple levels of information processing. The levels-of-processing hypothesis, as proposed by Craik and Lockhart (1972), conceptualizes memory as a hierarchy of processing levels through which new information is passed. The first level is a preliminary stage of analysis where physical and structural features of the stimulus such as angles, lines, brightness, and pitch are examined. The stimulus is then processed at progressively deeper levels of analysis, such as pattern recognition, and finally at the semantic and associative level. At this point meaning is extracted and associations such as images and verbal processes based upon the individual's past experiences with the stimulus are aroused.

Retention of stimuli depends upon the depth of processing; the greater the depth, the less forgetting. Information which is progressively processed to deeper levels in the hierarchy results in stronger and more durable memory traces. The depth to which material is processed is determined largely by the demands of the situation or task. Meaningful and important demands lead to deep processing, whereas demands of little consequence result in material being maintained only temporarily through rehearsal at shallow levels of analysis. Forgetting, then, is understood in terms of levels of analysis; if processing is interrupted at any point in time, the individual will remember the stimulus only to the depth to which it had been processed.

According to this theory, recognition of an event depends upon two factors: (1) the depth of the initial encoding and (2) the similarity of perceptual and memory encodings (Lockhart, Craik, and Jacoby, 1976). On the initial presentation of a stimulus, the semantic memory system interprets input information through a series of analyzing and encoding operations. The product of this analysis is a memory trace, which will be as rich and as detailed as the depth and elaboration of encoding performed.

When a stimulus pattern such as a human face is recognized, the individual experiences a feeling of familiarity. Recognition is the product of reconstructive/retrieval processes. If the reconstruction is derived from rich, unique, and distinctive encodings then recognition is highly probable, since one or more of the encoded memory attributes of the target face will be common to the encodings of the initial perception. Recognition also is facilitated by a "set to recognize." If an individual knows that he wants to remember a particular face for later recall, he will encode the face in such ways that the recognition decision is relatively easy.

Organization and Coding in Memory

RECONSTRUCTION OF EVENTS

Witnesses asked to tell the court in their own words what they saw and heard cannot provide an exact replication or reproduction of the event, but instead will remember certain general features of their experience. Nevertheless, reconstructions of memories usually are organized and logical. People never simply retain information they want to remember. According to one theory (Bartlett, 1932), we start with some schematized representation of what we wish to remember. Our schemas reflect our individual understanding of phenomena and are based upon our own personalities, values, attitudes, and general plans of thought.

This hypothesis about memory is based upon the following type of evidence. Students were given an American Indian folk tale to read. Fifteen minutes later they were asked to reproduce the story. Several other reproductions were obtained hours and days later. Analyses of results showed that subjects made an active effort to mold the material into a reasonable and more coherent picture. Reconstructions became increasingly shorter with repetition (referred to as leveling), and certain features of the story became dominant or salient (sharpening). Also the language of the story changed as subjects used their own more familiar words to recall the "core" meaning of the story. In effect, an individual's personality, expectancies, and general knowledge all contributed to what he or she remembered.

Another type of distortion is "assimilation,"which is the alteration of memory to fit expectations. A good example of this memory process is provided by the research of Carmichael, Hogan, and Walter (1932). Subjects were asked to look at ambiguous drawings such as those shown in the center of figure 4.2. During the inspection period the experimenters gave separate groups of subjects the labels from word list 1 or word list 2 to associate to each stimulus. Following a short retention period, subjects were asked to draw from memory each of the stimulus figures. Samples of the subjects' drawings are shown in the left and right columns of the figure. It is clear that the drawings made from memory were distorted in the direction of the verbal labels. Although Bartlett and others thought that memory distortions took place during the attempt to reconstruct the story, it is impossible to determine whether these results are attributable to labeling during the inspection period or to distortions introduced at the time of reproduction, or both.

Clearly, this research has implications for the law. Witnesses may distort their memory at the time of their original observations of an incident, or distortions may occur later at the time of the trial, or both. In any event, memory is not an exact replica of the original perceptions and is influenced by a number of factors.

CATEGORY CLUSTERING

As a rule, the more effective the storage of items, the better the recall. Since long-term memory is said to have an unlimited capacity, there must be

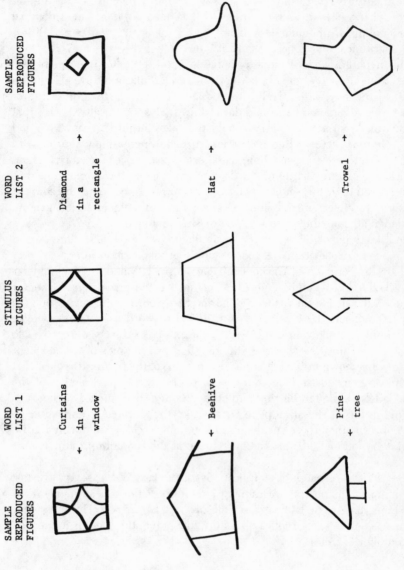

FIGURE 4.2 Examples of the effects of verbal labels on the reproduction of ambiguous figures *(from Carmichael, Hogan, and Walter, 1932)*

rules and principles of organization which govern the input and output of information. One principle of memory organization is clustering. Laboratory studies show that subjects do not free recall words in the order in which they heard them, but instead remember them in catogory clusters. Proper names, for example, although presented randomly throughout a list, often are recalled together as a group; then another category cluster of words is recalled, and so on. By the grouping of words into clusters the names of the categories can serve as cues for retrieval (Bousfield, 1953).

The tendency to organize items into clusters is relatively strong. When individuals are asked to remember unrelated words, rather than a categorized word list, they will impose their own subjective organization upon the list. For example, when a list of unrelated words is presented repeatedly, each time in a different order, subjects tend to recall the words in the same order from trial to trial (Tulving, 1962). Thus recall is facilitated by subjects' arranging the to-be-recalled material according to their own sense of relationships and associations. Organization in memory, however, involves more than mere grouping of related and unrelated information. Information also is woven into narrative chains or thematic organizations which facilitates retrieval (Bower and Clark, 1969).

MNEMONIC TECHNIQUES

One of the oldest systems of systematic memory organization is the mnemonic technique used by the early Greek philosophers. Simonides, the Greek poet, is considered the inventor (circa 500 B.C.) of the mnemonic system which encourages the learner to associate things to be remembered with highly familiar places, or "loci," in his environment. Simonides discovered this memory technique through a tragic personal experience. Being a poet, he was asked to give a recital at a public banquet. After chanting his poem he was called away from the banquet hall by a messenger. While he was away, the roof of the building collapsed, killing all of the guests. The corpses were so mangled that personal identification seemed impossible. Simonides was able to assist family members in identifying each of the bodies by remembering where each guest had been sitting during his recital.

This experience prompted Simonides to formulate the method of loci, a memory technique in which items to be remembered are assigned to particularly well-known and orderly locations in space. When an individual wishes to remember specific items, he can retrieve them by taking a mental walk past these geographical places and finding each item in sequence. In effect, the method of loci forces the learner to use stored items in an orderly fashion. Several laboratory investigations have confirmed the validity of these ancient Greek mnemonic techniques (see Bower, 1970).

Professional mnemonists perform their fantastic tricks of memory by utilizing elaborate plans or mediative aids. An example of such a mnemonic plan is the familiar nursery rhyme "One-bun, two-shoe, three-tree, four-door, five-hive, six-sticks, seven-heaven, eight-gate, nine-wine, ten-hen." The learner is instructed to construct bizarre mental pictures of the words in the rhyme. Thus for "bun" we might imagine a big hamburger bun; for shoe, the shoe made famous in the child's rhyme "The old lady who lived in a shoe," and so on. Once the individual has learned the number-picture rhyme, the system is used to organize what has to be remembered. The individual attaches the first to-be-recalled item in some imaginal interaction with the first number-picture cue, then the second is associated to the second imaginary cue, and so on. Recall presumably is facilitated by the organized store of information. The learner recalls the words to be remembered by calling out the number-picture rhyme, which cues the compound image, which leads to the decoding of the appropriate verbal response (Bugelski, 1968; Bugelski, Kidd, and Segmen, 1968; Paivio, 1968). This mnemonic rhyme technique has been shown also to facilitate the storage and retrieval of human faces and names (Yarmey, 1970).

Countless studies show that mnemonic imagery both mediates the associative process and organizes information for storage and retrieval. In simple terms, subjects form interacting mental pictures of the items they wish to remember, and the more vivid and bizarre the association, the better the retention (Andreoff and Yarmey, 1976). Imagery has been found to facilitate memory performance in a variety of tasks including associative recall, free recall, recognition, and reconstruction (Paivio, 1971a).

The Dual-Coding Theory of Memory

The courts accept the hypothesis that vivid images are better retained than memories devoid of interest. Research support for this common belief has been provided by the theoretical and experimental studies of Allan Paivio and others.

Paivio (1969, 1971a) assumes that memory is based on two distinct systems, an imagery system and a verbal system. The two systems are said to be functionally independent but at the same time partially interconnected for the encoding, storage, and retrieval of information. They are differentiated by the quality of symbolic information that they process. Imagery is said to be specialized for the pictorial representations of concrete objects, situations, and scenes, while the verbal system is characterized by its ability to deal with more abstract concepts such as language. The functional distinctions between the two systems include their manner of organizing information. Imagery is distinguished for its spatial organization of memory contents much as visual perception handles objects in space, whereas the verbal system is specialized for processing verbal information sequentially or in a linear way.

For an illustration of this theory imagine that a witness is asked to report his observations of being held up. According to the dual-coding approach, the witness may have had one or more of the following kinds of sensory information hitting his receptors: *visual,* the physical appearance of the robber including facial impressions; *auditory,* the verbal commands, e.g., "Stick 'em up"; *tactual,* the robber feeling his breast pocket for a wallet; and *kinesthetic,* his attempt to maintain balance and posture after being jostled.

It is assumed that these sensory inputs are represented and processed by the two independent but interconnected imaginal and verbal symbolic codes. Accordingly, the witness may store images of the assailant's face and physique and also may covertly talk to himself, e.g., "He is big and ugly and is probably crazy." The witness also may store the verbal threats of the robber. It is possible that these verbal threats may arouse in the witness such a related imagery as the mental visual image of himself lying on the ground, bleeding and rolling in pain. Verbal coding of the sequence of steps the robber takes in finding the witness's wallet, watch, jewelry, etc., may be stored, as well as the nonverbal codes of texture and roughness of his hands on the witness's body. Finally, the motor feedback from talking to himself may be stored by the witness, as well as the nonverbal motor feedback involved in regaining balance and searching through pockets to prove to the assailant that they contain no more hidden valuables. Other sensory inputs with corresponding symbolic representations are possible also, such as the smell of the individual.

The importance of such codings for remembering is that multiple-encoded information is likely to be more available for retrieval (recall or recognition) than information stored only in one code or the other. However, it is possible also to retrieve information from one system without involving the other. For example, it is impossible for a witness to verbally code all of the physical attributes of the environment that are present during a robbery. Thus recall in this instance would rely on visualizing the robbery scene. Similarly, it is unlikely that a witness would imagine the abstract meanings of such words as "bad luck," "why me," and "bastard" that may have been considered during the holdup. These words are coded first as linguistic units and only secondarily as associative images. Memory in this case would rely primarily on linguistic coding strategies.

Although the availability of one or both codes often will facilitate recall, there is also the chance of error when one symbolic code is transformed into the other. This is particularly true when a witness must verbally describe his assailant from a memory image. Verbal descriptions of a memory image involve the transformation of mental images into words and sentences, which increases the chance of error in recall. We will come back to this point later in our discussion of police drawings made from eyewitness reports.

The Semantic Theory of Memory

The point has been made repeatedly in this chapter that memory is an organized store from which information is reconstructed. Much of what is stored is episodic information, that is, memory for specific events, objects, and persons. In addition, memory also contains nonepisodic information, for example, the knowledge that a canary can sing, an ostrich can't fly, and so on. This type of nonepisodic information is referred to as semantic memory, which, as we will see shortly, can influence the testimony of an observer.

Some cognitive psychologists have proposed that the computer can be used as a metaphorical model to suggest how the human mind may represent information. Accordingly, in this approach, man's memory does not consist of words and images, but instead consists of codes connected to each other through the mediation of propositions, or abstract descriptions. This process is assumed to operate in the same way that a computer uses abstract mathematical languages to connect symbolic information. Memory is theorized to consist of two parts, a data base representing a person's skills and knowledge, and processes that operate on this data base, such as encoding, storage, and retrieval. The data base consists of a network of nodes, or concepts which are linked to each other by their relative association. To illustrate this structure, figure 4.3 presents part of the semantic network proposed by Collins and Quillian (1969).

The figure shows that a person's knowledge about a canary, ostrich, shark, and salmon is organized as a hierarchical network of interconnected relations. Each word is defined in terms of other words. Thus the meaning of *canary*, in part, refers to features that distinguish it; for instance, canaries can sing and are yellow. Canaries also are birds, and we know that birds are characterized as having wings and feathers, and can fly. These features are true of all birds and not just canaries and therefore are stored with the node *bird*. Basic to this model is the assumption that information about a particular concept is stored only at the level of the hierarchy for that category. If a person is asked, "Does a canary have skin?" he starts at the node for *canary* and searches for the feature *skin*. Discovering that the information is not there, he goes to the next highest node, *bird*, and looks for the necessary property. Not finding the answer there, he must move up to the general node for *animal*, where he will locate the property *has skin*.

Collins and Quillian's semantic memory model is only one of several models now available which describe the meaning of memory through prop-

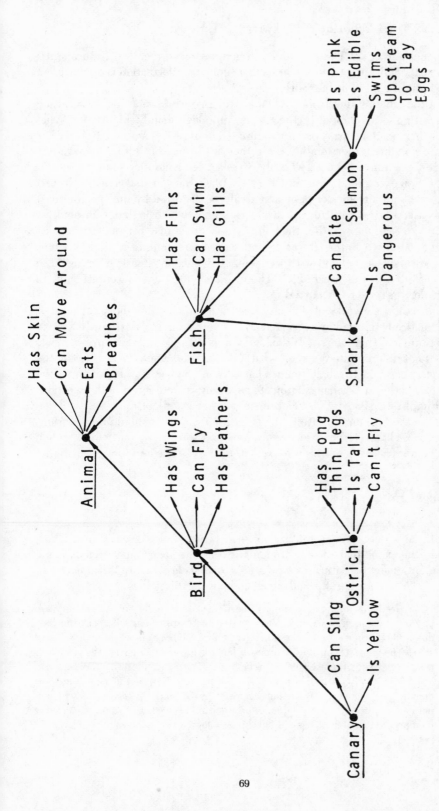

FIGURE 4.3 A portion of a semantic network *(from Collins and Quillian, 1969)*

69

ositional networks. These models, in general, have received experimental support, confirming the hypothesis that semantic information is organized in the form of a memory network.

Although this description of how memory works may be intrinsically interesting to psychologists, the lawyer quite legitimately might ask, "What does this mean in terms of courtroom testimony?" The answer, I think, lies in the possible understanding these theories provide in telling us what we can expect from a witness when he is asked to remember some important facts. For example, Loftus and Palmer (1974) showed that eyewitness testimony about a traffic accident may easily be distorted by the type of questions asked. If an interrogator uses a sentence which includes an emotive word like "smashed" rather than "hit," the witness may remember the accident as being worse than it was. Witnesses may "remember" different details that are more associated with the semantic concept "smashed" than those associated with the word "hit." These details often are inaccurate and, in fact, may never have occurred.

Semantic networks of memory may also influence memory for what is pragmatically implied or suggested as if it were a direct assertion. In a study of a simulated trial, Harris, Teske, and Ginns (1975) found that juror-subjects could not differentiate between what was stated testimony, e.g., "I rang the burglar alarm in the hall," and what was implied, e.g., "I ran up to the burglar alarm in the hall." Subjects generally remembered both assertions and implications as definite fact, even when warned not to do so.

The implication of these findings for the courtroom should be apparent. Jurors are likely to confuse implications and assertions, particularly when long intervals occur between presentation of evidence and jury evaluations.

Forgetting

In an article written for his fellow lawyers, Dillard S. Gardner (1933) made the point that most testimonial errors are made unconsciously and unintentionally by witnesses who are "*subjectively* accurate but *objectively* false." Gardner asked his colleagues to consider the following:

> What are the factors determining the accuracy and reliability of the memory of a particular witness? . . . Memory is a matter for the psychologists, yet even they differ among themselves—the objectivists use "memory" in a strained technical sense, the imagists consider it almost solely a question of imagery, the gestaltists are fairly losing themselves in metaphysics. Little wonder that lawyers and jurists, generally, have been unable to learn anything of the true nature of memory. Upon what bases shall we test the reliability of testimony which is neither perjured nor the product of unsound minds? What of value, concerning memory, can the infant science, legal psychology, today present to trial lawyers? [pp. 391-392]

Gardner answered his own questions with a discussion of memory which emphasized the Aristotelian notion of remembering ideas as a function of their similarity, contrast, and contiguity. Many psychologists would dismiss Gardner's essay as being out of date even for the 1930s and certainly for today. In the following section some of the more popular approaches to the problems of forgetting are outlined and discussed.

FREUDIAN VIEW

Freud's (1900, 1906, 1938) theory of forgetting is based on the concept of repression, which is an unconscious resistance and defense against painful, threatening, or anxiety-arousing memories. According to Freud, if painful events are remembered, they endanger the emotional survival of the individual. Repressed memories and traumatic conflicts form the foundation of the psychoanalytic view of psychopathology, but Freud did not intend to limit his theory of repression solely to clinical instances of forgetting. Freud regarded the processes of memory as permanent and felt that all forgetting is intentional or motivated. Proof of such forgetting is revealed in everyday life by lapses of memory or slips of the tongue or pen. Slips of the tongue such as calling a woman a "bitch" when you meant to say "rich" were interpreted by Freud as revealing the underlying true feelings and intentions of the speaker. Law enforcement officers and lawyers often are quick to pounce on such slips, inferring that lapses of memory indicate that the "truth" is being withheld and testimony is fraudulent.

How does contemporary psychology evaluate the Freudian hypothesis of forgetting? Before commenting on this question let me return to an earlier observation. Gardner (1933) suggested that lawyers want psychologists to tell them the true nature of memory. If only psychologists would stop squabbling among themselves, the courts could get on with their job of tending to law and not have to be concerned with interpreting another discipline's business. Unfortunately this modest appeal cannot be easily resolved because it runs counter to the purpose and nature of scientific theory.

Psychoanalysts are convinced of the validity of the repression hypothesis of forgetting. Their confidence is based upon daily clinical observations which from their point of view give them all the evidence they need. Furthermore, there is no doubt that certain types of motivated forgetting such as amnesia, a pathology in which a person under extreme emotional stress may forget his personal identity, can and do occur. Since this condition usually is temporary and the individual regains his past memory, his inability to retrieve personal information may be attribuutd to repression.

Experimental psychologists, on the other hand, do not accept the hypothesis that repression is a useful explanation of normal forgetting. Laboratory experiments testing the Freudian view of forgetting have in most

cases failed to support the theory (see Holmes, 1974). Whether or not laboratory studies can ever find support for the repression hypothesis is debatable.
Perhaps as Baddeley (1976) concludes, the concept of repression is more an
article of faith than a scientific testable hypothesis. Supporters of the
psychoanalytic view, however, insist that the concept of repression is only
meaningful in a clinical sense and can be tested only by clinical methods and
not by artificial, laboratory-type studies.

What validity do slips of the tongue and other lapses of memory have as
indicators of repressed truths? Very little, in my opinion. Slips of the tongue
are amusing and embarrassing but are little more than intrusion errors from
our store of networks of word associations. Words that are similar in sound or
meaning often interfere with and are substituted for each other in both
memory and testimony. Contemporary experimental psychology has rejected the Freudian hypothesis of repression as an adequate explanation of
normal forgetting.

TRACE DECAY HYPOTHESIS

Whenever we perceive an event, physiological correlates of this experience called memory traces are said to be formed in the nervous system. The
nature of these traces, their number, their quality of enrichment, and so on
are open to scientific dispute, but it is agreed that some sorts of physical
representations exist in the brain which correspond to psychological events.
A popular notion of forgetting and one with intuitive appeal is that these
brain traces spontaneously decay and disintegrate over time. This hypothesis
is attractive, since it emphasizes both physiological changes in the brain and
the passage of time. Evidence to test this theory, however, is difficult to
attain. In order to show that trace decay and not some other agent or activity
occurring during the retention interval, causes forgetting, it is necessary to
insure that the retention interval is truly neutral. One way to minimize
activity between learning and the retention test is to test subjects after sleep
in contrast to an equivalent waking period. Such studies indicate greater
retention following sleep than following awake activity, suggesting that
forgetting is a function of interference and not mere passage of time
(Ekstrand, 1972). Nonetheless, to demonstrate that interference can be a
cause of forgetting does not prove that trace decay is absent.

GESTALT TRACE TRANSFORMATION HYPOTHESIS

The influential German school of Gestalt psychology which contributed
much to our understanding of perceptual organization also has give us a
theory of retention and forgetting. The Gestaltist's position is that memory
traces do not weaken over time; rather, they change their configuration in

specific ways. Memory for shapes changes progressively over time toward more symmetrical, more perfect figures. These changes are a result of spontaneous internal influences inherent in the brain which transform the memory trace of a figure toward the good "Gestalt," or ideal prototype shape for its class. According to this hypothesis, because the memory trace consistently changes toward a good Gestalt, individual qualities of the form must be forgotten—in effect, we lose memory of the original figure.

This hypothesis has been studied extensively since the 1920s when it was first proposed. Although some investigators have reported evidence supporting the Gestalt theory of forgetting (e.g., Brown, 1956; Crumbaugh, 1954; Irwin and Seidenfeld, 1937), their studies have been criticized for one or more research design flaws. The most recent conclusion drawn by investigators testing this theory (e.g., Baddeley, 1968, 1976; Riley, 1962) is that the Gestalt hypothesis of memory has lost its usefulness.

INTERFERENCE HYPOTHESIS

According to this hypothesis, forgetting occurs because of the interference between memory traces from old learning and memory traces of new learning. Two specific types of interference have been distinguished, retroactive inhibition and proactive inhibition. The first type refers to the situation in which an event learned after the learning of the original target material interferes with the remembering of the target. The second type refers to forgetting occurring because an event learned prior to the learning of a target stimulus interferes with the remembering of the target. Experimentalists have devoted a great deal of effort in an attempt to specify precisely what it is about stimuli and the contextual conditions in which learning occurs which causes interference. Although the contribution of this hypothesis to the workings of memory is large, the problem remains that we do not know how to predict in any given situation how much, if any, interference will occur. The basic nature of the mechanism by which interference is produced remains unresolved. An even greater limitation of this hypothesis is that most of the evidence testing this theory is restricted to a laboratory understanding of verbal materials (see Duncan, Sechrest, and Melton, 1972). It is not yet clear how these principles apply to everyday conditions of life where, for example, I have to remember such things as whether my class was at 9:00 or 10:00 a.m. or where I left my hat and gloves.

At this point let me say a few words about the role of contextual stimuli and state-dependent learning on recall, since these types of interference conditions are related to the police practice of taking witnesses back to the scene of the crime to jog their memory for further details.

Several studies have shown that recall is facilitated if recall is attempted in the environment where the original learning took place. In an investigation examining the role of the immediate environment on retroactive inhibition, Greenspoon and Ranyard (1957) had subjects learn a list of syllables, followed by a second list, then gave them a recall test for the original list. Comparison of different learning and test groups showed best recall for subjects who learned and recalled the original materials in the same room but learned list 2 in a different room. Poorest recall occurred for a group which learned the first two lists in the same room but was tested for recall of list 1 in a different context.

A novel study by Godden and Baddeley (1975) confirmed the effects of context-dependent memory in dramatic fashion. Sixteen deep-sea divers learned word lists on land or 4 meters under water and were subsequently asked to recall the words in either the same or the alternative condition. Recall performance was best when the test conditions were identical to the learning conditions for both land and sea groups.

Finally, evidence indicating that material acquired while an individual is in a drug state is best recalled under the same physiological state could lead to interesting implications for law enforcement officers and the courts. Goodwin, Powell, Bremer, Hoine, and Stern (1969) found that for rote learning and avoidance learning performance was best when subjects given alcohol during acquisition were also given alcohol at test. This finding, however, was not true for recognition memory.

CUE-DEPENDENT FORGETTING

The discussion above on trace decay and interference theory has little to say about a very common type of forgetting in which a person knows what he wants to report but for the moment at least has forgotten it. When you give the person a cue or reminder of the sought-after information, he often is able to recall the lost material. What this suggests is that recall does not depend solely upon information being available in the memory store, but depends also on the quality and quantity of retrieval cues available to guide the search for the to-be-remembered information (Tulving and Pearlstone, 1966).

The courts recognize that memory is imperfect, and they will allow a witness to refresh his recollection by consulting a memorandum made immediately after observing the event. Whether or not the memorandum is an effective retrieval cue depends upon how long after the event in question it was made and whether the observation was accurate in the first place.

From common experience we know that some cues are more effective than others in helping us remember. One hypothesis which has received experimental support suggests that to be effective at recall, a retrieval cue must be stored along with the to-be-remembered information during learning (Tulving and Thomson, 1973). Retrieval cues do not have to be perceptually or semantically similar to the cues present during encoding, but the closer the association between retrieval cues at the test and the contextual cues present during learning, the greater the probability of recall (Light, 1972).

To recapitulate, retrieval cues that are encoded with the information to be remembered facilitate the recall of this material if they are presented as prompts at the time of test. However, recent research by Anderson and Pichert (1978) shows that the retrieval process is not necessarily related to encoding processes. These investigators found that material that was previously forgotten is recalled on a second attempt when subjects adopt a different phenomenological perspective. For example, if subjects are asked to remember a story about a house and its contents, they will recall additional information, which was previously unrecallable, following a shift in their viewpoint from that of a prospective homebuyer to one of a burglar.

AMNESIA

Earlier in our discussion of the Freudian approach toward forgetting it was suggested that amnesia may be a type of repression in which a person suffering from an emotional trauma forgets both the conflict he faces and his own identity. In this section a more complete description of amnesia is presented, which introduces clinical conceptions of the phenomenon as well as some of the experimental evidence and theoretical explanations of its occurrence.

Two types of amnesia are possible, retrograde and anterograde amnesia. Retrograde amnesia is defined as the loss of memory for events immediately *prior* to a trauma, shock, head injury, or illness, while anterograde amnesia is defined as the inability to remember events immediately *following* the occurrence of the amnesic agent. According to Williams (1975), the principle causes of retrograde amnesia include (1) a sudden loss of consciousness due to a concussional blow to the head or seizure—head injuries that do not result in a loss of consciousness very seldom produce retrograde amnesia (Russell and Nathan, 1946)—(2) illness involving specific sites of the brain, especially the limbic system, as found in some postalcoholic Korsakov conditions or tuberculous meningitis; and (3) degenerative changes of the brain found in senility.

Most of our evidence on forgetting of recent and remote events in amnesic patients is based upon anecdote and clinical observations. Clinicians have generally accepted, without any experimental support, Ribot's (1882) hypothesis of amnesia. Supposedly, memories increasingly distant from the present get lost as brain lesions enlarge, but when the amnesia begins to subside, remote memories are the first to return.

One study investigating Ribot's hypothesis compared the long-term memory of a group of normal individuals with the performance of five amnesic patients (Sanders and Warrington, 1971). Subjects were given a questionnaire which inquired about specific news events between 1930 and 1968. A recall and recognition memory test for names of faces of public celebrities of the late 1940s through the early 1960s also was given. The results showed that normal subjects were superior in recalling recent news events over more remote events, whereas amnesic subjects had poor recall for all of the time periods sampled. On the recall and recognition tests of famous persons, normal subjects showed a gradual decrease in recall of names over time. In contrast, amnesic subjects could not do better than recall names at a chance level of guessing over all of the time spans tested. When subjects were provided with multiple-choice selections of the names of these celebrities, performance was facilitated in both groups, although more errors occurred over time. Two of the five amnesic patients were able to identify the names of contemporary personalities at a better than chance level of responding, but even these patients were unable to reliably identify names of famous people who were prominent only seven or eight years past. Sanders and Warrington concluded that Ribot's law of forgetting "that the dissolution of memory is inversely related to the recency of the event was unsupported."

Research psychologists interested in the experimental investigation of the amnesic effect have derived several interesting hypotheses. One explanation emphasizes the concept of *consolidation*. This theory suggests that information recently put into memory is encoded in a temporary form. Time is needed for the consolidation of the memory trace from a transient state into a more permanent representation. The amnesic agent somehow disrupts the consolidation by blocking the encoding or storage process, or both. This disruption creates a "gap" in which information becomes lost and unavailable for later recall. A second hypothesis emphasizes the concept of *rehearsal*. The occurrence of an amnesic agent presumably diverts attention away from the encoding of other events. Consequently, the lack of repetition or verbal rehearsal in the encoding of surrounding events leads to their poor retention and recall. A third hypothesis attributes amnesia to difficulties in *retrieval* rather than to consolidation or rehearsal processes. This theory is based upon the observation (see Ervin and Anders, 1970) that retrograde amnesia is not permanent. Patients often remember pockets of intact information which were presumed lost because of the amnesic agent. According to the consolidation and rehearsal hypotheses, amnesia should be permanent. However, if patients can remember these so-called lost events with the passage of time or can remember when cued with appropriate mnemonics, amnesia must reflect a temporary inaccessibility of information rather than a loss.

In an attempt to simulate the amnesia resulting from head injuries, investigators have studied the effects of electroconvulsive shock given to patients for therapeutic purposes. Electroconvulsive shock produces a cerebral seizure and temporary loss of consciousness. Most typically, patients have poor memory for events immediately prior to the shock and better memory for more remote events. Although these investigations produce results similar to those found in clinical cases of amnesia, the results of such studies provide limited explanation. The inability to adequately control the many interfering variables from the therapeutic context minimizes the theoretical and empirical contributions of such investigations (see Squire, 1975). However, more controlled laboratory procedures are now available, which eliminates the need to study ammnesia only in the clinical context with amnesic patients.

Several experimental investigations of *induced* laboratory-created amnesia have been conducted in the past few years (see Ellis, Detterman, Runcie, McCarver, and Craig, 1971; Saufley and Winograd, 1970; Schulz and Straub, 1972; Tulving, 1969). Controversy over the theoretical explanations for these memory effects continues to persist. Nevertheless, a comprehensive study by Detterman and Ellis (1972) suggests that retrograde amnesia (loss of memory for events prior to a shock) probably is best accounted for by retrieval failures, whereas anterograde amnesia (loss of memory for events immediately after shock) probably results from a disruption in the perceptual and memory encodings.

This discussion has particular relevance to this writer because of a personal incident which happened a few years ago. One Sunday morning my wife and I were having coffee and were reading the weekend newspaper when we heard a loud banging on our front door. Our neighbor told us that our son had just been hit by a car in front of his house. Although I spent over thirty minutes talking with the driver and witnesses at the scene of the accident, I was unable to recognize the driver of the car on the following day, though I could remember and identify the police officer and witnesses. Luckily, our son was more scared than hurt from the accident. Thinking back on the accident now as I sit in my office writing, I remember quite vividly what I was doing moments before the accident and can reconstruct many of the subsequent events, but I have difficulty in describing or imaging the face of the driver. Whatever the proper explanation of this effect may turn out to be, the complexity of the principles and mechanisms involved in the perception of and memory for people is enormous, as we shall see in the next chapter.

HYPERMNESIA

Typical descriptions of forgetting indicate that subjects show a sudden decrease in memory soon after learning and gradually level out their recall performance over time. However, recent evidence by Erdelyi and his associates illustrates that some memories do not necessarily get poorer over time, but instead may improve with passing time and with repeated attempts at retrieval. This "negative forgetting" phenomenon, however, is limited specifically to memory for pictures and not for words. Erdelyi and Becker (1974) discovered that subjects given only a single visual presentation of a list of pictures or a list of words were significantly better in recalling the pictures over the three consecutive free recall trials. But more importantly, subjects recalled a greater number of pictures, but not words, with each additional attempt. In a subsequent study, Shapiro and Erdelyi (1974) showed that the hypermnesia effect for pictures was not simply a matter of several recall attempts. Picture recall improved over time with better performance after an interval of 5 minutes compared to a 30-second retention period, whereas word recall showed a slight decline over time. Most recently, Erdelyi and Kleinbard (1978) have shown that memory can substantially improve over periods of days.

What accounts for these effects? One possible interpretation is that pictures unlike words easily evoke memory images which serve to mediate the improved performance (Yarmey, 1976). The hypermnesic effect for pictures but not for concrete nouns or abstract nouns is illustrated in figure 4.4.

These results raise interesting implications for both theories of forgetting and the reliability of eyewitness testimony. Memories for visual materials

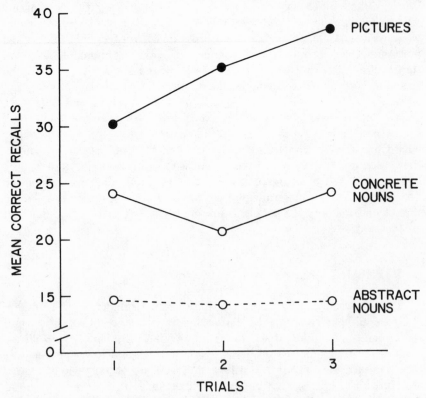

FIGURE 4.4   Hypermnesia: Mean number of correct recalls over successive trials *(from Yarmey, 1976)*

which are inaccessible for immediate recall may become accessible with repeated recalls or with the passage of time. Police investigators and the courts must be cautious in rejecting the testimony of witnesses who claim they cannot remember who or what they saw soon after its occurrence, but can remember it minutes, hours, or perhaps even days later. Memory does not necessarily get poorer over time, but instead may improve, decline, or stay constant.

Motivational Factors in Memory

Motivation influences memory in a number of ways, not all of which are obvious. Motivation to learn and remember depends upon the attentional processes and coding activities of the learner and not, as often thought, upon desire, will, or intent. Thus if someone attends to the proper cues and performs the appropriate coding activities, he will learn and remember the information without any intention to deliberately store the material (Postman, 1964). These effects are found in adults (Yarmey and Ure, 1971) and in normal and educable retarded children (Yarmey and Bowen, 1972).

Psychological stress or tension affects learning and memory by restricting the individual's attention to the most salient factors of an event. Accordingly, a corresponding loss occurs in the utilization of other less obvious but often important factors. High-anxiety subjects are generally less organized in their recall (Mueller and Goulet, 1973), and low-anxiety subjects recall a greater number of words (Mueller, Carlomusto, and Marler, 1977), In the identification of faces, research also shows that low-anxiety subjects (as determined by test anxiety scores) are better in performance than high-anxiety subjects (Mueller, Bailis, and Goldstein, in press).

On occasion police will interview witnesses minutes after a traumatic event and find they are unable to remember much of what happened, but an hour or so later they show a dramatic improvement in recall. Several laboratory studies of generalized arousal at the time of learning confirm the hypothesis that high emotional arousal promotes long-term recall but hinders short-term recall (e.g., Butter, 1970; Kleinsmith and Kaplan, 1963). Arousal may be manipulated in a number of ways including being watched by observers. Two studies show that observed subjects recall fewer items immediately after learning but have superior recall an hour later (Deffenbacher, Platt, and Williams, 1974; Geen, 1973).

Finally, research on the relationship between attitudes and memory shows that a person's frame of reference influences what he remembers. In a classical study by Allport and Postman (1945), subjects were shown a picture of a white man holding a razor while arguing with a black man. Of the subjects questioned, 50% later remembered the black man as holding the razor, and some subjects reported that he was "brandishing it widely" while others remembered him as "threatening" the white man. It is easy to attribute these results to prejudiced whites, but Allport and Postman report that the distortion may occur even in subjects who have no antiblack bias. In our culture, the stereotype of blacks includes hot tempers and quick reactions to violence, which promotes a motivated type of memory distortion. More will be said about the relationship between attitudes and memory for people in chapter 6.

Personality and Memory

Differences among individuals in terms of personality variables and their relationship to cognitive functioning have been of interest to psychologists for some time. Several dimensions of personality such as cognitive style, extraversion-introversion, rigidity, need achievement, and psychopathology have been extensively studied and shown to influence memory (see Johnson, 1974). In this section, however, I want to restrict our review to the effects of the authoritarian personality and recall of evidence.

Authoritarianism may be defined as "a personality type characterized by individuals high in rigidity, prejudice, political and economic conservatism, and fascistic traits" (Zimbardo and Ruch, 1977). An interesting question is whether or not high- and low-authoritarian jurors differ in their selection and recall of testimony about criminal behavior. Earlier research by Marshall (1966) found that subjects who were classified as high-punitive (who are likely to be authoritarian) were more accurate than low-punitive subjects in recall of evidence.

Building from this research, Berg and Vidmar (1975) conducted a simulated criminal trial in which the subject-jurors were either high or low in authoritarianism as measured by Boehm's (1968) Legal Attitudes Questionnaire. Subjects were given a transcript of a criminal case accompanied with a description of the defendant's character. A recall test given seven to ten days later showed that high-authoritarian subjects recalled more information about the character of the defendent than did the low authoritarians. In contrast, low-authoritarian subjects recalled more situational evidence relating to the details of the crime.

Following on the heels of this research Garcia and Griffitt (1978) further explored the relationship between the authoritarian personality and recall of evidence. These investigators hypothesized that high and low authoritarians would differ in their attention given to evidence presented by the prosecution and evidence presented by the defense. It was predicted that high authoritarians with their greater respect for and submission to constituted authority would recall more evidence presented by the prosecution. Results from two experiments supported the prediction. High authoritarians were found to focus more on prosecution evidence than on defense evidence. High authoritarians also showed a greater tendency to draw more direct inferences from incriminating evidence than did low authoritarians.

These results suggest that personality factors of jurors influence what is remembered in courtroom proceedings. It is likely that lawyers' formulations of strategies for presentation of evidence and argument and the selection of potential members for juries might benefit from these research insights.

We have seen in the last two chapters how psychologists understand the basic principles of perception and memory. On occasion, generalizations of these processes to the workings of the court have been made. In the next chapter, we will see that basic principles of perception have to be modified when people, as opposed to more simple environmental stimuli, are observed.

Chapter 5

Perceiving People

Solely on the basis of immediate appearance—a glimpse at a face across the room, a look at a family phtograph, a verbal description uttered by a newscaster—we often draw conclusions about others. Whether or not these impressions are accurate is debatable, as we will see later in this chapter, but the fact remains that people generally do make such judgments, which guide their thinking and possible interactions with people. In chapter 3 the focus of discussion was on how we discover and know physical events and objects in the world. Although the empirical findings on and interpretations of such problems are important for a general understanding of perception, they cannot be considered basic to an understanding of person perception. Our reactions to people as stimuli are based upon an initial assessment of complex physical characteristics which include actions, physical appearance, style of clothing, manner of speech, and facial expression. These first impressions allow us to infer certain personality traits, emotional states, and even intentions and dispositions for future behaviors. To exemplify these points consider the following observation:

> A murder trial hinges on the testimony of one witness. The jury's belief in this witness, which will determine their decision, depends almost entirely on the impression they form of him in his brief time on the witness stand. They examine his face, his features, his clothes, the quality of his voice, and his answers and try to decide what kind of person he is. . . . [Freedman, Carlsmith, and Sears, 1974, p. 30]

The study of person perception also involves the relationship of the perceiver and his situational context. Kirkham (1974), a former correction counselor and presently a professor of criminology and part-time police officer, vividly illustrates the importance of contextual differences on perception as follows:

> I found that there was a world of difference between encountering individuals, as I had, in mental health or correctional settings, and facing them as the patrolman must: when they are violent, hysterical, desperate.... Now, as a police officer, I began to encounter the offender for the first time as a very real menace to my personal safety and the security of our society. The felon was no longer a harmless figure sitting in blue demins across my prison desk, a "victim" of society, to be treated with compassion and leniency. He became an armed robber fleeing from the scene of a crime; a crazed maniac threatening his family with a gun; someone who might become my killer crouched behind the wheel of a car on a dark street.... [pp. 130-131]

Finally, person perception can involve attribution of personality traits, feelings of attraction or avoidance, and perceptions of causality, intent, and justifiability to photographs, or other representations of people. This characteristic of person perception occurs in the courtroom when the judge permits counsel to introduce photographs of victims as evidence. In the recent trial of Dr. Kenneth C. Eidelin, a physician charged with manslaughter during the course of a legal abortion at Boston's City Hospital, the prosecution was allowed to introduce a photograph of the dead fetus in evidence. The photograph showed a normally developed fetus, but its face was distorted.

> The district attorney asked the jury:
> Is this just a subject? Is this just a specimen? Look at the picture. Show it to anybody. What would they tell you it was? Use your common sense when you go to your jury deliberation room and humanize that. Are you speaking about a blob, a big bunch of mucus, or what are we talking about here? I respectfully submit we are talking about an independent human being that the Commonwealth of Massachusetts must protect as well as anybody else in this courtroom.... [Culliton, 1975, p. 187]

Edelin was found guilty and give a sentence of one year's probation. The conviction has been appealed and recently was granted.

These three examples show clearly that people form rapid and vivid impressions of others on the basis of very little information. Jurors in the Edelin case reported that it looked like a baby.... the picture helped people draw their own conclusions. Everybody in the room made up their minds that the fetus was a person... (Culliton, 1975, p. 187). The jury must have resolved that the fetus was a person who could have developed with proper nurturing conditions into an honest, intelligent, warm, and valuable member of society. These attributes are recognized and judged quickly by observers, practically without hesitation. Our purpose in this chapter is to describe and understand the various processes that facilitate categorization, description, and impression formation of people.

CATEGORIZATION AND DIFFERENTIATION

It is impossible to perceive everything about a person in his or her full complexity. Somehow, we become sensitive to certain features or attributes and ignore others. Attributes are defined as any characteristics differentiating any two things. When there is a similarity among attributes, we can group them together as a class and respond to them in terms of their class membership rather than their individuality.

Perhaps the most extensive study on the nature of categorization in human thinking is the treatise by Bruner, Goodnow, and Austin (1956). Since their discussion of categorizing is relevant to the study of person perceptions, some of their conclusions deserve emphasizing. Categorization occurs at two levels of inquiry, the perceptual level and the conceptual level. Perceptual categorization consists of "the process of identification, literally an act of placing a stimulus input by virtue of its defining attributes into a certain class. An object of a certain color, size, shape, and texture is seen as an apple . . ." (Bruner et al., 1956, p. 9). Conceptual categorization consists of searching for attributes of a more abstract nature, such as "beliefs" or "attitudes," before placing the set of stimuli in a specific category. With practice, people short-circuit conceptual categorization and utilize immediate perceptual cues which earlier would have been considered insufficient information for such classification.

Bruner and his colleagues state that categorization has five purposes: (1) it reduces the complexity of the environment; (2) it is the means by which the objects of the world about us are identified; (3) it minimizes the need for constant learning—if appropriate attributes of an object are present, we can identify it even though we have never encountered this particular object before; (4) it gives direction for our responses—that is, we can anticipate how we should respond; and (5) it allows for restructuring of our knowledge of the world by linking new categories to old ones.

The development of perceptual sensitivity and differentiation begins early in life. We learn first by recognizing then practicing various sensory-motor connections of our experiences. Initially, these percepts are massed into wholes, or undifferentiated cognition or thoughts. Gradually, the child learns to perceive and organize information about his world and the people around him into increasingly more differentiated and abstract categories. Because certain attribute properties are particularly important to the person, they take preference or become salient in his perceptions. As you would expect, stimulus attributes vary in their saliency for different people. This phenomena was shown in a skillful study by Dornbush, Hastorf, Richardson, Muzzy, and Vreeland (1965). Children in a summer camp for the underprivileged were asked to give free descriptions of one another. The analysis of reports revealed that children tended to use the same terms in describing different persons. For example, if a child described one person in terms of his generosity, cooperation, and trust, he was likely to choose these same terms in describing other children. When two children described the same other child, slightly less than half of their descriptions overlapped. And finally, when two children described two different children, their overlap in terms used was just greater than 33%. These results suggest that categorization of people depends upon attributes that are salient and relevant to the perceiver and is not something that is highly shared over all persons. Furthermore, asking someone to describe another person gives us more information about the testifier than about the person being described.

The ability to make fine distinctions among people and perceive them as different from one another has been related to certain personality dimensions. People can be described in terms of their concreteness or abstractness in conceptualization of the world and how they see people (Harvey, Hunt, and Schroder, 1961). The concrete person makes clear-cut, concise definitions: good-bad, right-wrong, black-white, etc. He is relatively willing to accept the authoritarian viewpoint, the traditional way of doing things; he has a low tolerance for ambiguity and uncertainty, and cannot adopt the subjective viewpoint of someone else. In contrast, the more complex and abstract the person, the greater the likelihood that he will demonstrate directly opposite reactions in his perceptions and thinking. Abstract persons make fewer evaluations and fewer extreme judgments (Ware and Harvey, 1967), are better problem solvers (Harvey, 1966), and are more concerned with cognitive consistency and integration of the impressions they form of another person (Harvey and Schroder, 1963).

CONSISTENCY AND CENTRALITY

When we are introduced to a person for the first time, we judge him or her in many ways, and our impressions usually are consistent with one another. The individual may be attractive, kind, and honest, or awkward, embarrassing, and gauche. These impressions, unlike our descriptions of objects and events, which can be inconsistent with each other (a car can be small but roomy, ostentatious but attractive), usually are organized on the basis of a central evaluative dimension. This categorization is persistent over time and will help determine our evaluation of this person in different settings and circumstances.

The classic investigation showing the importance of centrality of traits in impression formation was conducted by Solomon Asch (1946). One group of subjects was given a description of an individual as intelligent, skillful, industrious, warm, determined, practical, and cautious. A second group was given the identical list of adjectives except that "cold" was substituted for "warm." Both groups were then asked to describe the person and to indicate which of the experimenter-provided traits best fit his personality. Asch found that subjects receiving the "warm" list felt positive toward the individual; the other group described him negatively. The warm-cold dimension was shown to be a central trait which markedly affected the subjects' impression of the imagined person.

A later study by Kelley (1950) showed that Asch's findings were replicable in more realistic settings. Students in psychology courses were prepared for a guest lecturer by hearing a resumé which described him in one of the two ways listed by Asch. The students who expected the lecturer to be warm in contrast to cold described him after the talk as more sociable, popular, and humorous, and showed a greater tendency to interact with him following the presentation.

More recent investigations on impression formation reveal a number of important qualifications and extensions of Asch's and Kelley's findings. First, the centrality of traits such as warmth and coldness depends to some degree on the context in which these words are buried. Warmth will not act as a central trait if "warm" is included in a list of adjectives—such as conceited, shallow, stupid—which have little relation to each other. Second, the subject's purpose in categorization is important in determining whether a trait is perceived as central or peripheral. Thus warmth could be a central trait even if "warm" was located in a list of unrelated adjectives providing the purpose of the description was to relate how sociable or popular the individual was. And third, when people have a great amount of information about a person, they form their impression by averaging all of the facts (Anderson, 1965). Hence a subject who evaluates someone very positively on two traits but recognizes that he has one shortcoming will average the negative trait with the two positive traits and perceive him as a moderately attractive person.

Selectivity of Perception

PRIMACY AND RECENCY EFFECTS

Lawyers often present their most credible witness first under the assumption that first impressions have a strong impact on judges and juries. Experimental demonstrations substantiating this belief were originally carried out by Asch (1946). When subjects are given sequential information about a person, their impressions are more readily influenced by information detailed earlier in the list (primacy) than later (recency). Luchins (1957) has replicated these effects in dramatic fashion. When subjects are given two one-paragraph descriptions of the same person, one paragraph describing him as friendly and extraverted and the other as shy and introverted, recency-primacy effects are shown to determine the evaluation. Subjects categorize the person as friendly if the information is presented in a positive-negative order; the person is seen as shy and less friendly if the negative-positive order is used.

The greater influence of primacy may be due to the subjects' decreased attention to information presented late in the sequence (Anderson and Hubert, 1963). It is possible that individuals assume that traits mentioned first are most important and thereby discount information that comes last as less valid. Primacy effects, however, can be eliminated if subjects are warned to resist forming their impressions until they have heard all of the information. In the Luchins (1957) study recency, not primacy effects, were found when subjects were required to form an impression of personality after hearing the first block of information (positive or negative) and again after hearing the second block (the opposite direction). Presumably, separation of information into two blocks heightens the importance of the second block and the subject gives it more attention relative to the first block, thereby promoting the recency phenomenon.

VIVIDNESS OF STIMULI

Stimulus attributes that are striking or conspicuous are readily detected and remembered. Once a person describes someone with words such as "attractive," "energetic," "wealthy," or "athletic," there are such strong imaginal properties involved (see Kirby and Gardner, 1972) that impression formation is immediate and persistent.

FREQUENCY

The more often we see a person, the more likely it is that we will notice him or her. Frequency of repeated appearance of a person also determines how we feel toward that person. In one study a string of photographs of faces were shown to subjects, some of which were presented only once or twice while others were shown up to twenty-five times. Following the inspection trials, subjects were asked how much they liked each face and how much they thought they would like the person pictured. The results showed that familiarity leads to positive reactions. The more often the subjects saw a face, the greater their liking of it and the more they thought they would like the person photographed (Zajonc, 1968).

Implicit Personality Theory and Stereotypes

If I asked you to describe in your own words a friend and a mere acquaintance, it is likely that your two lists of trait descriptions would be highly

o each other. Similarly, if asked to describe a third person, and a
nd so on, it is probable that many of your judgments of these
people would overlap and would yield high correlations over all
stimulus persons. This tendency to use a relatively fixed set of traits in
describing others is called the "implicit personality theory" of the perceiver
(Bruner and Tagiuri, 1954). It appears that each of us judge others from our
own implicit theory of what people are like, and we do this often without
regard for the actual characteristics of the person being observed. This performance tells us once again that we may learn more about the perceiver
than about the person being described in any investigation of person perception.

The study of implicit personality theory allows us to make predictions of
how someone will perceive another person, providing we know at least some
of the attitudes that he or she has toward this other person. We know, for
example, that trait relationships are organized in terms of their distance from
each other along conceptual dimensions of semantic space (Rosenberg, Nelson, and Vivekananthan, 1968). Thus trait words such as "stern" and "critical" are closely related and are considered "good" along an intellectual dimension of traits but are considered "bad" along a social dimension. Since
trait relationships generally lie along some sort of evaluative dimension,
investigators are able to predict the final impression formation constructed
by a perceiver from a knowledge of simple trait relationships.

An interesting puzzle is the question of how a perceiver resolves the
apparent contradiction of a stimulus person possessing two traits that may be
seen as incompatible. For example, skillful people are perceived as intelligent, whereas unintelligent people are considered frivolous. How do we
understand the skillful frivolous person? We often perceive such a person as
being somewhat intelligent because both words elicit the trait word "intelligence" as a word associate. Although the relationship between traits obviously has a semantic overlap, it is also true that individuals experience in
their normal everyday activities certain relationships between traits in the
people they interact with. Thus it is not unusual to know someone who is
bright and frivolous, skillful and clumsy.

Implicit personality theory also includes the tendency to bias impression
formation into all-good or all-bad assessments. Sometimes a particular quality or attribute of a stimulus person is so salient that it creates a "halo" effect
which influences our judgments of other attributes of the person. For example, people considered to be physically attractive are also considered to be
socially desirable, to hold high occupational status, and to be good marriage
partners (Dion, Berscheid, and Walster, 1972).

The development of impressions based on implicit personality theories
ultimately can be understood as a kind of stereotype. A stereotype may be
defined as "a set of characteristics which is assumed to fit a category of
people" (Hastorf, Schneider, and Polefka, 1970). People are very ready to

infer that older men are distinguished, responsible, refined, and conscientious (Secord, Dukes, and Bevan, 1954), that Jews are clannish, that professors are impractical, and that bearded students are radical (Hastorf et al., 1970).

Although stereotypes can be misleading in that they ignore the wide variety of individual differences which exist among people, they are functional in some respects. Stereotypes are employed because they reduce the tremendous amount of information we have about others into more manageable units. Furthermore, stereotypes are not necessarily negative attributions about others. Stereotypes of Germans as hard-working, Americans as ambitious, and Italians as romantic may be regarded by members of these nationalities as accurate and positive representations. Nevertheless, stereotypes do not necessarily yield high agreement among all observers or among people of the same age and education. For example, college students disagree among themselves on the definition of physical characteristics describing blacks and show even greater disagreement in their assignment of personality traits characteristic of blacks (Secord and Backman, 1974).

Physical Attractiveness and Impression Formation

When an individual meets someone for the first time, he seeks to acquire as much information as he can about this person in order to know what to expect of him and how to act toward him. Recent research evidence indicates that the stereotype we hold about physical attractiveness often determines what we expect of others. Without the availability of other information, we are prepared to attribute positive traits to high-attractive people and to relate negative traits to low-attractive individuals (Miller, 1970).

A "beauty is good" stereotype appears to exist which mediates much of our behavior. People within a particular culture at a particular time show a high consensus as to what constitutes beauty in both men and women (Berscheid and Walster, 1974a, 1974b). Investigations of the effects of physical attractiveness on social interaction have demonstrated that the physically attractive are given several advantages over their unattractive counterparts. The attractive person is seen as being more desirable as a date (Walster, Aronson, Abrahams, and Rottman, 1966) and held to be more socially desirable, to achieve greater vocational success, and to lead a more fulfilling life (Dion, Berscheid, and Walster, 1972). These results were consistent for both males and females as perceivers and as stimulus persons. However, one study suggests that there may be important differences in the way in which physical attractiveness is related to males and females. The "beauty is good" stereotype may be true only if restricted to females. Physically attractive females in contrast to their unattractive counterparts were perceived as significantly happier and more intelligent. Males, however, did not show reliable differences as a function of their attractiveness level (Hill and Lando, 1975; Kaplan, 1978).

It is clear that attractive people are perceived differently from unattractive people and are better liked. In addition, they are treated differently. When a child has committed a transgression, adults interpret the action differentially as a function of the child's attractiveness (Dion, 1972). Unattractive children were perceived to have an antisocial disposition and to be more dishonest. Furthermore, when the transgression was severe, adult women predicted that unattractive children were more likely to commit future transgressions.

Research on decision making of simulated juries shows that the attractiveness of the defendant influences juridic judgment. The courts may be more lenient toward beautiful women than toward their unattractive counterparts (Monahan, 1941). In a recent study, simulated jurors presented with an attractive victim and unattractive victim favored sentencing the defendant to a longer prison term when he violated the attractive person. Furthermore, when the defendant himself is unattractive, he is likely to receive a longer sentence (Landy and Aronson, 1969). These results are consistent with the findings of Efran (1974), who found subjects more lenient in assignment of punishment to attractive as opposed to unattractive defendants accused of cheating on an exam or committing a burglary.

However, an interesting qualification to juridic judgments based upon the attractiveness stereotype of offenders has been found. When the misbehavior or felony is related to attractiveness, such as a beautiful girl using her charms to swindle a victim, as opposed to an offense such as burglary which is not attractiveness-related, the attractive defendant is treated more harshly. On the other hand, the unattractive defendant is more severely punished in non-attractiveness-related offenses such as burglary (Sigall and Ostrove, 1975).

Once an offender is in prison, the physical attractiveness stereotype continues to operate in a predictable manner. Unattractive female youth prisoners receive more negative behavior reports from the correctional staff and win fewer privileges to visit a nearby town (Cavior, Hayes, and Cavior, 1974).

Sex and Age Differences in Person Perception

It is widely believed that girls are more interested than boys in observing people and social activity. However, Maccoby and Jacklin (1974) dispute this hypothesis, claiming that their review of the literature fails to substantiate such a belief. Sex differences do not occur among newborns in their attention to any of the social and nonsocial visual stimuli presented to them. Testing during the first year of life also has failed to detect consistent differences between the sexes in social perception. Differences between the sexes in social sensitivity, however, do occur with increasing maturity. In an investigation of the tendency of 700 boys and girls between the ages of 10 and 16 to draw inferences of "good" and "bad" behavior of a boy presented on film, reliable sex differences were found. A steady increase in the percentages of subjects making inferential judgments was found over age levels, and girls at all ages exceeded their male counterparts (Gollin, 1958).

Clearly, by the time that individuals reach adulthood, females and males differ in their observations of others (Allport, 1961; Mazanec and McCall, 1975; McCall, Mazanec, Erickson, and Smith, 1974; Smith, 1966). Males tend to attend more to what others say and slightly more to their physical appearance, while females allocate their attention more to actions and verbal style (Mazanec and McCall, 1976).

Impression Formation and Nonverbal Information

People differ in their facial features, body build, height, and other structural ways as well as in their expressive movements, gestures, and muscle tension. All of these nonverbal cues contribute to our formation of impressions. In this section we will review some of the major characteristics of such cues and show how they may be important in person perception.

PHYSIOGNOMY

The discovery or judgments of personality traits solely through observation of the human face is an old enterprise which can be traced back to the writings of Aristotle. The ancient Greeks differentiated, as figure 5.1 indicates, four personality temperaments from particular physiognomic representations (Allport, 1961). Most people (80%) identify the traditional lovesick poet as "melancholic." Supposedly, the slender and delicately textured face is given by nature, but this person acquires the habits of withdrawal and unpleasant thoughts, which are reflected by his downcast eyes and furrowed brow. The "choleric" face shows inherent strength of physique and natural power, which is associated with the acquired habits of openness, curiosity, and intensity of feeling. The "phlegmatic" face suggests an innate drowsiness and apathy which is supplemented by inattentive habits. Finally, the Greeks considered the "sanguine" face to be normal in bone structure but the lack of lines indicated insensitivity in emotional experiences. The interest in physiognomy was so great in the seventeenth and eighteenth centuries that the British Parliament was forced to control its abuses from quacks and charlatans by outlawing its practice. Although the exercise of physiognomy continues to be popular, particularly in slick magazines and popular literature, it scientific usefulness has not been proved.

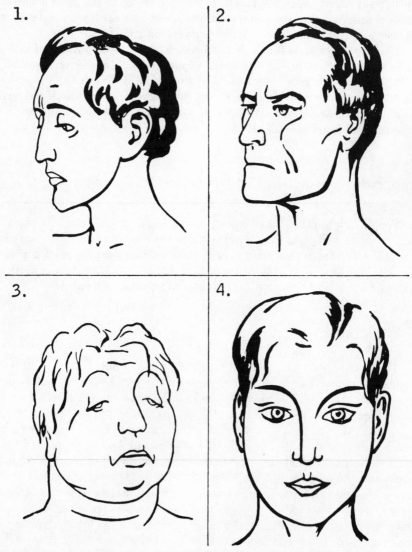

FIGURE 5.1   **Physiognomic representations of the four temperaments: 1. melancholic, 2. choleric, 3. phlegmatic, 4. sanguine** *(from Allport, 1961)*

PHYSIOGNOMY AND CRIME

At one time physiognomy was of interest to sociologists and criminologists in their attempt to show a biological connection between crime and anthropological types. In the nineteenth century an Italian surgeon, Cesare Lombroso, published the thesis that the criminal was a close descendant of primitive man controlled by wild and irresponsible instincts, which made him lawless in modern society. Lombroso formulated this hypothesis following a post mortem examination of an infamous criminal of the time.

To prove his theory, Lombroso measured with a caliper and tape the body sizes of Italian prisoners and Italian soldiers. He found that the prisoners had a greater number of anomalies in the size and shape of the head, chin, and eyes. These diferences were used as an argument for a biological causation of crime. At the time, this theory was taken seriously, and people believed that they could detect the criminal by his small eyes, receding chin, and so on.

Contemporary research on face perception is not directed to identifying the true "reality" or meaning of the face per se, but rather consists of determining what impressions are made on observers by particular facial stimuli. Some of the major findings of this research may be summarized as follows:

1. Judges of personality show a high consensus of agreement in attributing certain personality impressions to faces with particular physiognomic cues. This finding indicates that the wider culture in which a person lives determines how an individual responds to persons possessing certain physiognomic facial features (Secord, 1958).

2. Women who wear heavy lipstick and have narrow eyes, a relaxed full mouth, and smooth skin are perceived as sexually attractive. In contrast, bowed lips indicate conceit, demandingness, and immoral behavior (Secord, 1958).

3. Men with dark complexions are perceived as hostile, boorish, conceited, dishonest, unfriendly, sly, and lacking in a sense of humor (Secord, 1958).

4. Blondeness and light skin are associated with heroes, while villains are associated with darkness and swarthiness (Berelson and Salter, 1946).

5. Observers' expectations of what people are likely to do are reliably influenced by their facial appearance (Hochberg and Galper, 1974).

APPEARANCE, BODY BUILD, AND HEIGHT

Does the size and shape of a person's body determine the structure of his personality? Shakespeare thought so and so do many others, including some scientists. Probably the best known theory of "body types" is the work of Sheldon (1942). Sheldon hypothesized that there were three major body types: endomorphs—characterized by extended stomachs and soft, plump bodies; mesomorphs—persons having hard, muscular, bony bodies; and ectomorphs—people with tall, thin, and fragile bodies. These body types, according to Sheldon, are genetically determined and are related to the development of distinctive personalities or temperaments. Thus the endomorph is highly sociable, content, relaxed, talkative, a lover of the easy and good life. The mesomorph is energetic, assertive, competitive, powerful, courageous, and confident. And finally, the ectomorph is introverted, shy, quiet, intellectual, and inhibited.

Sheldon's theory was tested through ratings of college males to see if their personality traits and body types were correlated. The correlations turned out to be highly positive, but critics argue that these findings are invalid because the ratings were not done on two independent factors. Sheldon's research design and statistical analyses were faulty. However, his research is important since it suggests that impression formations based upon body builds develop from a kind of reasoning by analogy. We infer that fat people, for example, have difficulty in movement or physical exertion; therefore, they must be relaxed, easygoing, and lazy in their temperament.

Just as a stereotype exists about body builds, false impressions exist about tall, medium, and short persons. Children, asked to estimate the heights of adults, judge those adults who are perceived as more important also as taller (Shaffer, 1964). The perceived relationship between height and importance is not restricted to children. Nursing students asked to estimate the heights of persons differing in authority and status also overestimated height in relation to the judged importance of the stimulus persons (Dannenmaier and Thumin, 1964). Because height is perceived to be valuable in our society, discriminatory behavior often occurs. Height has been found to be correlated with success in business (Kurtz, 1969), social life (Ward, 1967), and politics (Kassarjian, 1963).

CLOTHING

How accurately can people predict the personality of an individual from the clothing he or she wears and prefers? In one study 400 college women were categorized into four groups: high-fashion dressers, low-fashion, out-of-date, and counter-fashion. After determining the women's values, attitudes, and personality traits, it was possible to successfully match or predict 72% of these women with their appropriate clothing category. These results suggest that clothing is an outward symbol of personality (Reed, 1974).

NAMES

Evidence indicates that first names of people arouse definite stereotypes of personality. Subjects consistently agree in their matching of masculine-judged names and feminine-related names to photographs of males that vary in their degree of masculine and feminine appearance (Bruning and Albott, 1974). Names are differentially important to males and females, with males preferring to be called with common first names while women dislike their own first names only if they are very uncommon or very common (West and Shults, 1976).

Age differences also are apparent in preferences for names, with older people favoring formal given names while the young prefer shortened names or nicknames. Names are not simply verbal labels which differentiate people for identification and communication purposes. Instead, they have a deeper significance which carries a wide range of connotative meanings. These differences in meaning affect how easily they are remembered. A disliked name is more salient and learned more quickly than neutral or liked names. Names are also remembered more easily when they are presented with an associated face. Apparently, people discriminate some feature of the photograph which is associated with the name, thereby facilitating its recall (Bruning, 1972).

As you might expect, people with unusual or disliked names are discriminated against by others. A study by Harari and McDavid (1973) showed that experienced elementary school teachers gave higher scores to the same essays when supposedly written by David, Michael, Adelle, Lisa, or Karen in contrast to Elmer, Hubert, or Bertha. Furthermore, children with attractive first names are perceived as more popular by their peers than children with unattractive first names (McDavid and Harari, 1966).

BODY POSTURE AND MOVEMENT

Many nonverbal behaviors in everyday situations are read and judged by observers separately from other information. Often these conclusions are false and would not be made if the observer and stimulus person verbally interacted. For example, Geidt (1955) found that subjects make different interpretations of behavior when they observe actors on a silent film in contrast to hearing their verbal interactions. People also interpret attitudes differently as a function of the actors' posture and movement. For example, observers of a videotaped conversation between a man and a woman concluded that the female actor liked the man when she displayed certain positive postures, i.e., sat directly facing him, leaned forward, and nodded her head in agreement. However, when she looked at the ceiling, shook her head in disagreement, attended to her fingernails, and played with the ends of her hair, observers inferred that she did not like the man (Clore, Wiggins, and Itkin, 1975).

Accuracy in Judgments of Others

Potential victims of an attack quickly must judge the thinking and emotional balance of their assailant if they are to mount a successful defense. Should they fight back or should they try to escape? Can he be reasoned with, can he be talked down, does his face suggest fear or hate? Since we cannot read the mind of a potential attacker, we must judge his intentions from his physical appearance, facial expressions, manner of speech, posture, and other body language cues.

The emotional and cognitive states of witnesses are routinely evaluated by judges and jurors. These judgments are not, of course, based on technical or scientific tests, but instead consist of "reading" certain expressions and behaviors shown by the witness. Is the witness credible? Does she have a trusting face? Does she stutter because of fear of the courtroom and cross-examination, or are her language and general nervousness a sign of lying?

Accuracy in the judgment of others is normally divided into two areas of interest, the recognition of emotions of others and the identification of their predisposing personality traits. We have already reviewed some of the literature on impression formation of personality characteristics. In this section the discussion will be restricted to studies and hypotheses concerning identification of emotions, particularly emotions in the human face. Can individuals accurately judge facial behavior? Do people differ in their ability to control or disguise their emotions? How do people react to others if they judge their facial expressions to be appropriate or inappropriate? Interest in the emotions displayed in the human face is a contemporary concern for both the law and psychology, and as we shall see, scientists such as Charles Darwin, had this interest over a hundred years ago. Incidentally, the discussion of truthfulness of testimony and the review of techniques such as the polygraph and other physiological tests to detect deception will be covered in chapter 8. We will also leave to then comments and analysis of why certain people appear to be deceitful even when they are not, whereas others can avoid detection when in fact they are liars.

Darwin (1872) hypothesized from his theory of evolution that facial expressions in man are biological derivatives of complex animal movements which once had important functions for our early ancestors. For example, drawing back the lips for biting evolved over time to mean "prepare for attack." Many mammals including man show this grin-like response when startled. Darwin assumed that facial expressions were related to underlying internal states; people smile when they are happy and frown when they are disturbed. Furthermore, it was suggested that observers are able to perceive accurately which expressions are associated with which particular emotions; if people behave in a joyful, playful way, observers know they are happy.

Since the early part of the present century investigators have studied whether or not subjects can make accurate inferences about emotional states. Common sense and everyday experiences tell us that we can judge the emotions of others fairly accurately, but, in general, laboratory studies have not supported this conclusion. Until recently, investigations of emotions were conducted in artificial settings with subjects asked to make judgments about emotions by looking at photographs of faces. It is doubtful that these types of laboratory tests can approximate our everyday experiences, which force us to be aware of situational conditions and multidimensional inputs of information. Nevertheless, laboratory studies, in spite of their methodological limitations, have yielded some interesting findings. One study, for example, showed that subjects can discriminate among six broad categories of emotions which can be plotted along a single scale of (1) love, happiness, and mirth; (2) surprise; (3) fear and suffering; (4) anger and determination; (5) disgust, and (6) contempt (Woodworth, 1938). If subjects are told about the situational context in which the emotions are evoked, accuracy of identification is improved (Munn, 1940).

A series of studies by Buck and his colleagues (Buck, 1975; Buck, Miller, and Caul, 1974) indicates that people differ to a great extent in the amount of emotionality they express. Buck found that subjects may be divided into two groups of different emotional expressiveness, internalizers and externalizers. Internalizers show very little outward signs of emotionality but have high levels of internal physiological arousal as measured by heart rate and galvanic skin response scores. Externalizers produce a high amount of facial expressiveness when excited but show low scores of physiological arousal. These differences in expressive behaviors were found to be correlated with personality traits. Internalizers were significantly lower than externalizers in self-confidence, openness, and extroversion. As you would expect, observers are much more accurate in perceiving the emotions of externalizers than internalizers. Buck also found that observers were more successful in judging the emotions of women than men. Apparently, in our society adult males learn to inhibit their emotional behavior, since it is considered weak or improper to show grief or pain. In contrast, young boys who have not yet learned these cultural expectations show similar public displays of emotion to girls.

Research shows that the situation and the choice of expression that a person employs in expressing his feelings influence the perceptions of observers and their consequent behavior toward this person (Savitsky, Izard, Kotsch, and Christy, 1974). Experimental confederates who showed mock anger, fear, joy, or lack of emotion in response to punishment (electric shock) administered by observers were perceived and treated differently as a function of the emotion they expressed. When a victim suggested that he enjoyed the punishment by having a smile on his face, subjects increased the amount of shock they delivered. The expression of anger, however, decreased the aggression shown by observers. The expressions of fear and neutrality did not differ from each other in discriminability, nor did they affect the amount of shock administered by the judges.

Researchers continue to investigate the recognition of emotions (see the review by Frijda, 1969), and a few general conclusions can be made at this time. Darwin's hypothesis that facial expressions are universally recognizable in conveying particular emotions has received support. Ekman and his associates (e.g., Ekman, 1972; Ekman, Sorenson, and Friesen, 1969) found that college-educated subjects from such different cultures as Brazil, the United States, Argentina, Chile, and Japan labeled the same faces with the same emotional words. This result is not restricted to highly educated people, since Ekman and Friesen (1971) also found similar results in comparing subjects from primitive tribal groups of New Guinea with American college-educated subjects. Both cultural groups gave equivalent identification responses to picutres of emotional behaviors as depicted in photographs of American whites.

Individuals vary in their ability to transmit recognizable facial cues (Thompson and Meltzer, 1964) and in their ability to judge accurately the cues sent by others (Rosenthal, Archer, DiMatteo, Koivumaki, and Rogers, 1976). Females are significantly better interpreters but not reliably better transmitters of emotional cues than are males (Zuckerman, Hall, DeFrank, and Rosenthal, 1976).

It has been estimated by Mehrabian (1968) that facial expression contributes 55% of the emotional meaning of a message while verbal language and vocal characteristics of speech add 7% and 38%, respectively. These scores suggest that feelings are communicated much more through nonverbal means than through language. Other investigators have shown that if conflicting messages are being sent, observers rely more upon facial expressions than on either verbal content or style of speech (Bugental, Kaswan, and Love, 1970). People indicate their liking of one another by leaning toward them, standing close to each other, and gazing for long time periods directly into each other's eyes (Mehrabian, 1972).

Studies of eye contact, gazing, and staring as indicators of emotionality indicate that we judge the affective state of others by the frequency with which they look us in the eye. It is assumed that the more often eye contact is made, the more likely people are in a good mood (Exline, 1971). In contrast, avoidance of eye contact leads to the interpretation that a person is feeling poor, depressed, guilty, or hostile (Knapp, 1972). Too much eye contact, as in staring, however, is perceived as threatening in both animals (Exline, 1971) and man (Ellsworth, Carlsmith, and Henson, 1972).

The importance of facial expressions and other nonverbal cues as sources of communication between the defendant and the jury is well understood. Lawyers are being advised by their colleagues (e.g., Van Camp, 1978) to use videotapes with their clients before the trial begins in order to rehearse "proper" facial expressions and minimize or eliminate troublesome mannerisms. Whether or not these manipulations are ethical or desirable is debatable. As we shall see in chapter 8 jurors tend to identify deceit and truth more by what a testifier says as opposed to how she or he looks. But this is not to say that the visual element of a defendant's or witness's testimony is unimportant.

The Good Judge of Personality

An old question in social psychology asks what characteristics distinguish good judges from bad judges of personality. A second question asks how accurate people are in their assessments of personality characteristics of others.

One authority described the "good judge" as a person having breadth of personal experience, intelligence, cognitive complexity, self-insight, social skill and adjustment, and detachment (Allport, 1961). This description is general and nonspecific, but as researchers have found, it is difficult to specify what accuracy in judgment of personality entails. Judges of others differ in their accuracy as a function of the different types of interpersonal judgments to be made. Thus it may be more or less difficult to describe others if we have to evaluate personality dimensions as opposed to socioeconomic background, or work skills, or athletic excellence, etc. Furthermore, what are the criteria of accurate perception? If we compare the ratings of ordinary people with the ratings of experts (i.e., psychiatrists, clinical psychologists), there is no guarantee that the authorities themselves are accurate. Such comparisons may tell us more about our judges' ability to guess or stereotype the responses of experts than accuracy of perception.

In 1955, Cronbach published an article which showed that most of the earlier research in this area was invalid because of methodological problems. Accuracy of perception does not reflect just one skill, but rather involves several independent skills. As a consequence of Cronbach's critique, researchers have stopped trying to identify the "good judge," and have turned their attentions to more specific questions, such as what types of information are necessary in order to make judgments of personality (Cline, 1964), and what events and processes (e.g., halo effect) distort impression formation—questions which were reviewed earlier in this chapter.

Although investigators shifted their research interests, this does not mean that all individuals are regarded as equivalent in their judgments of others. Individual differences do exist, and some people are better judges of personality than others (Taguiri, 1969). But until the methodological problems in this area are resolved, scientific explanations for this ability will have to be postponed. Furthermore, reliance on experts, such as psychiatrists or psychologists, to determine "good" and "bad" personality should be made with caution. Recent evidence shows that psychiatrists as a group are not particularly effective in spotting "dangerous" defendants. In a study of inmates labeled dangerous and not dangerous by psychiatric assessment no reliable differences were found between the two groups in subsequent violent behavior over a three-year period (Cocozza and Steadman, 1978).

The Good Witness

Although psychology has not been able to establish scientifically the differences between good and poor judges of personality, it does have something to offer to the criminal justice system regarding characteristics of the good witness. Melvin Belli (1954), the celebrated criminal lawyer, suggests that jurists can classify witnesses as to "types." Drawing from practical experience, Belli classifies witnesses into the following categories: the loquacious witness, the hesitant witness, the evasive witness, the flippant witness, the romancing or prepared-story witness, the dishonest witness, and the stupid witness. Although these role categories may be useful, the simplification suggested by such coding procedures misrepresents the complexity involved in describing the "good" witness.

Instead of relying on commonsense notions, Lavrakas and Bickman (1975) questioned fifty-four prosecutors regarding their perceptions of the "good" witness. A "good" witness may be defined in two complementary ways. First, he can give accurate testimony, and second, provided he has certain personality characteristics, he can be perceived as more credible by others in the criminal justice system. Both of these features are important in influencing the key actors in the courtroom, specifically the prosecutor, the defense attorney, the jurors and/or judge.

Lavrakas and Bickman asked their subjects to consider the effect thirty-two different witness attributes would have on the outcome of four major areas of prosecution: (1) felony review; (2) preliminary hearing; (3) plea bargaining; and (4) trial. Subjects rated the importance of each attribute at the stages they had experience with on a 5-point scale.

Table 5.1 shows the rank order of importance for each attribute averaged over the four different stages of prosecution. Of interest to the focus of this book is the high importance placed on witnesses' memories for faces and clarity of recall. Subject variables such as age and intelligence of the witness were considered moderately important, whereas attributes such as

TABLE 5.1. **Rank-ordering of the effect of witness attributes on the outcome of prosecution of criminal cases.** *(Lavrakas and Bickman, 1975)*

(*N* = 180 ratings for each mean.)

ATTRIBUTE	MEAN RATING
1. Is the victim available for testimony?	4.534
2. Is there a witness with a good memory of the defendant's face?	4.435
3. Is there a witness in addition to the victim who will testify?	4.405
4. Does the victim remember the incident clearly?	4.370
5. Did the victim contribute to the crime in some way?	4.300
6. Did a witness contribute to the crime in some way?	4.095
7. Was the victim intoxicated at the time of the crime?	4.023
8. Has the witness been adequately prepped by the prosecutor?	3.972
9. Was the victim physically harmed by the defendant?	3.875
10. Was there a police officer who witnessed the incident?	3.861
11. Did the victim know the defendant prior to the incident?	3.791
12. Is the victim an addict?	3.652
13. Did the witness know the defendant prior to the incident?	3.628
14. The age of the witness.	3.617
15. Is the victim currently a defendant in another case?	3.608
16. Is a witness currently a defendant in another case?	3.581
17. Will the witness be cooperative with the prosecutor?	3.561
18. Is a witness an addict?	3.548
19. The intelligence of the witness.	3.464
20. Does a witness have a prior arrest record?	3.407
21. Does the victim have a prior arrest record?	3.233
22. Is the victim vengeful toward the defendant?	2.961
23. Did a witness know the victim prior to the incident?	2.771
24. Will the witness be in control of her/his emotions in court?	2.744
25. Does the witness speak English?	2.695
26. Will the victim be anxious while testifying?	2.620
27. Is the witness motivated to testify by a desire to serve justice?	2.531
28. The socioeconomic status of the witness.	1.899
29. Is the witness the same race as the defendant?	1.878
30. Does the witness have any procedural knowledge of the criminal justice system?	1.660
31. Is the victim the same sex as the defendant?	1.592
32. The race of the witness.	1.589

Scale Employed

1. This attribute is totally unrelated to the outcome of this stage.
2. This attribute is usually unrelated to the outcome of this stage.
3. This attribute is somewhat related to the outcome of this stage.
4. This attribute is usually related to the outcome of this stage.
5. This attribute is very related to the outcome of this stage.

socioeconomic status, race, and sex were only of minor consideration. Although these ratings were collapsed over the four different stages of prosecution, further analyses showed that in general the relative importance of an attribute remained constant in each of the four stages.

PERCEPTIONS OF CRIMINAL ASSAILANTS

Laboratory studies of social cognition allow us to test the effects of particular variables under controlled conditions. The results of these studies may be examined for their validity and reliability and, if confirmed, may be accepted with high confidence as accurate measures of behavior. An obvious limitation, however, is the inability of laboratory investigations to reflect real-life situations in which the observer is under extreme stress. For example, a victim of a violent crime such as forcible rape, or aggravated assault, or armed robbery often encounters the assailant face to face and has to provide a description of the thug to the police.

The capabilities of victims of such crimes to provide complete verbal descriptions on their assailants have recently been investigated (Kuehn, 1974). Data for this study were taken from 100 police reports completed within minutes after the investigators arrived at the scene of the crime. In all cases the victims were unacquainted with their assailants. Victims were able to describe up to nine physical characteristics: race, sex, age, height, weight, build, complexion, hair color, and eye color. Over 85% of the victims could describe six or more traits, while only four victims were unable to provide any descriptions. Sex of the assailant was most frequently identified (93%) while eye color was the least cited characteristic (23%). Age, height, build, race, weight, complexion, and hair color in that rank order were identified in over 70% of the cases. Descriptions tended to cluster so that if a victim mentioned height he would also describe build, or age and sex together.

Kuehn also tested whether certain circumstances of the crime or the victim's social characteristics were related to the perceptual recall. The threat of a weapon and intoxication of the victim were not related to completeness of description. Notice that Kuehn was not attempting to judge the accuracy of description, but, rather, limited his attention to completeness. Table 5.2 shows the percentage of victims able to provide complete descriptions as a function of certain selected variables. It is apparent, for example, that victims provide reliably more complete descriptions during the day and night than at twilight. Additional information not shown in the table indicated that age and race of the suspect were the two characteristics most frequently identified by injured victims, but were ranked fourth and eighth, respectively, by noninjured victims. This result suggests that injured victims attend to or remember different perceptual cues than do noninjured victims.

TABLE 5.2.   Completeness of victim's description of suspect by selected variables. *(Kuehn, 1974)*

VARIABLES	% COMPLETE DESCRIPTIONS	N
Time of offense		
Daytime	64	39
Twilight	21*	14
Night	61	54
Type of crime		
Robbery	61	61
Assault	33**	15
Rape	45	22
Victim injury		
Injured	40*	38
Not injured	61	62
Sex of victim		
Male	66	52
Female	43***	44
Race of victim		
White	58	74
Black	36***	11
Interracial crimes		
White victim, white suspect	83	18
White victim, black suspect	68	38
Black victim, black suspect	33**	6
Black victim, white suspect	none	none

*$p = .01$ **$p = .05$ ***$p = .10$

Furthermore, injury to victims was found generally to lower the completeness of description in each of the different types of crimes studied.

PSYCHOLOGICAL PROFILES: INTERESTING BUT FAULTY

The final type of application of knowledge about people to predicting criminal behavior to be considered at this point is the construction of personality profiles. Police often ask psychologists and psychiatrists to prepare psychological profiles of unapprehended killers in the belief that these descriptions can predict the future actions of the assailant and, perhaps, when publicized provoke him to reveal himself.

Psychological profiles usually describe the type of home life that the wanted person probably came from, his level and type of education, his physical and racial characteristics, social and work skills, sexual preferences, and the psychodynamics which compel him to act.

How accurate are such sketches? Not very, according to critics (e.g., Campbell, 1976). For example, in January of 1976 a grand jury indicted Vaughn Orrin Greenwood, 33 years old, the man Los Angeles police believed was the "Skid Row Slasher," responsible for nine killings. The last murder occurred three days before Greenwood was arrested for a burglary assault escapade through the Hollywood Hills. A letter containing Greenwood's name and address found in the vicinity of the slayings led to the charges of murder. Greenwood was found guilty in December of 1976 of nine counts of murder, including eight of the "Skid Row Slasher" killings, and was sentenced in January of 1977 to life imprisonment (*New York Times,* January 20, 1977).

Before his capture and indictment a psychological profile of the suspect was constructed. This profile drawn by several psychiatrists and psychologists working with the Los Angeles police was correct in four respects: age, sexual inclinations, identification with drifters, and alienation from people. But it was incorrect for race, potency, deformity, and alcoholic father. Other parts of the profile were so vague that is difficult to perceive their usefulness in tracking down or pointing out the killer when apprehended. The inadequacy of this profile is typical of psychological profiles that have been used over the years. Basically, these sketches are no better than commonsense guesses requiring no formal psychological training whatsoever. Except for one or two famous cases of psychiatrists being correct in their profiles, these predictions are usually wrong, irrelevant, and pretentious.

If one type of criminal profile can be called a success in recent years, it is the description given to the skyjacker. These profiles often are effective, since they are systematically constructed from the knowledge of every past skyjacking. Such data are not available for descriptions of mass murderers, which makes their psychological profiles much less reliable.

The danger of psychological profiles, besides the possibility that they may stimulate the villain and his admirers to act out the descriptions, is the possibility that the wrong man could be identified, harrassed, arrested, and even convicted.

Perceiving the Causes of Behavior and Responsibility

Suppose while out for a walk late one evening you witness a man beating up a woman. The man is white, approximately 25 years old, 185 pounds, 6' in height, wearing a sweater and blue jeans. The woman is also white, approximately 22 years old, 115 pounds, 5' 4" tall, and dressed in a blouse and skirt. It is obvious to you that the woman is in pain, yet the man continues to strike her. You are upset and even scared and wish that there were something you could do, but you decide that you are powerless to intervene.

The first and most obvious interpretation of the criminal act is that the man is vicious, depraved, evil, or crazy. Your attitude toward the girl will probably be concern and compassion for her plight. But is it the right attitude? Perhaps after thinking about it, you might start wondering why the girl was out walking by herself late in the evening. Maybe she isn't blameless after all, and maybe she got just what she deserved. It has been widely reported that police officers and the courts have treated rape victims as the criminal, harassing them and disbelieving their claims that they had been sexually assaulted. Officers often have assumed that the attack was encouraged by the complainant through her provocative actions and dress. Finally, what about your own behavior as a witness? You were aware that the situation upset you and frightened you, yet you decided not to intervene even though you recognized that the girl was suffering. How do you explain your behavior?

Understanding the causes of others' behavior and one's own behavior has been theoretically and empirically analyzed in recent years by the attributional approach in social psychology. This perspective attempts to answer such questions as: Under what conditions will an observer be confident that he knows what caused his own and others' behavior? How do we attach responsibility to a person's actions? What factors allow us to know what another person is like? Attribution theory deals with discovering the underlying cause of events and attempts to attribute the cause to the correct source. By discovering which conditions are consistently associated with actions or behavior, we can attribute causal properties to a condition if that condition is present whenever the event is present and absent whenever the event is absent.

Fritz Heider (1958) proposed that people's behavior is determined by two classes of forces: structured dispositions within a person and the environmental situation in which the person finds himself. It is very easy in our imagined situation given above to interpret the aggressive acts of the man as an expression of his viciousness. The situational and circumstantial factors that led to this act, however, are more difficult to understand. Most people are very quick to attribute causality to the individual and fail to recognize also the situational and social forces that determine the behavior of the person being judged. Experimental and empirical evidence is now available that accounts for the basic processes involved in perceiving the self, other persons, and the social situations in which people act. This literature is important to our general focus in this book, since people frequently draw erroneous inferences about the causes of everyday behavior and criminal activity. Attribution theory is particularly relevant to criminal justice theory, since it also assumes a reality orientation to the world and a need to understand causes of observed behavior.

SITUATIONAL FORCES AND PERSONAL DISPOSITIONS

Consider the following two examples given by Jones and Nisbett (1972):

When a student who is doing poorly in school discusses his problem with a faculty adviser, there is often a fundamental difference of opinion between the two. The student, in attempting to understand and explain his inadequate performance, is usually able to point to environmental obstacles such as a particularly onerous course load, to temporary emotional stress such as worry about his draft status, or to a transitory confusion about life goals that is now resolved. The faculty adviser may nod and may wish to believe, but in his heart of hearts he usually disagrees. The adviser is convinced that the poor performance is due neither to the student's environment nor to transient emotional states. He believes instead that the failure is due to enduring qualities of the student—to lack of ability, to irremediable laziness, to neurotic ineptitude.

When Kitty Genovese was murdered (March 13, 1964) in view of thirty-nine witnesses in Queens, social scientists, the press, and the public marvelled at the apathy of the residents of New York and, by extension, of urban America. Yet it seems unlikely that the witnesses themselves felt that their failure to intercede on the woman's behalf was due to apathy. At any rate, interviewers were unable to elicit comments from the witnesses on the order of "I really didn't care if she lived or died." Instead, the eyewitnesses reported that they had been upset, but felt that there was nothing they could or needed to do about a situation that in any case was ambiguous to them. . . . [p. 79]

In both examples, the observers and the actors perceive differently the causes of the actors' behavior. The actor attributes his behavior to the environmental conditions at the time of the action, while the observer attributes the behavior to stable personal dispositions of the actor. The view that actors attribute the cause of their own behavior to the environment while the observer attributes the cause to personality dispositions or traits has received empirical support in a study by Nisbett, Caputo, Legant, and Maracek (1973). They found that college students asked to judge how a set of traits (e.g., neat-messy, strong-weak) described themselves, their best friend, their father, an age peer who was liked but not known well, and a prominant newscaster were willing to assign traits to others but not to themselves. When asked to judge themselves they favored the response "Depends on the situation." This finding confirms the hypothesis that people interpret the behavior of others in terms of their predisposing personalities but see their own behavior as being flexible in response to the current situation.

Another question tested by social psychologists is how people assign responsibility for another person's actions when things just seem to happen to them. Do people get what they deserve, and do they cause their own misfortunes?

One hypothesis suggests that people assign more or less blame to the person potentially responsible for an accident as a function of the seriousness of the consequences of the accident (Walster, 1966). Subjects were given one of four stories describing an auto accident and the precautions that the young man causing the accident had taken. His behavior was identical in each situation, but the consequences of the accident ranged from slight to critical. The results showed that subjects perceived the young man to be more responsible for the outcome if the consequences of the accident were serious than if they were insignificant. Responsibility for the accident was not associated with general carelessness; instead, it was related only to severity of the consequences of the incident.

Several subsequent experiments on attribution of responsibility have failed to replicate Walster's (1966) results and have even shown the opposite (e.g., Shaver, 1970; Vidmar and Crinklaw, 1975). The failure to replicate does not deny the validity of the original finding, but it does suggest that different operational measures and their relevancy for blame, guilt, and legal responsibility need further investigation.

Another important question is whether or not observers judge innocent victims responsible for their fate. Lerner and Simmons (1966) have theorized that people assume that the world is just and orderly and will act and control their behavior in order to maintain this belief. By working hard and avoiding dangerous situations, people assume they will be rewarded eventually and will receive what they deserve. If they see someone suffering, there may be a tendency to attribute this misfortune to the person rather than to fate or to the situation. Furthermore, observers will reject a suffering victim in order to maintain their belief in a just world.

To test their hypotheses, Lerner and Simmons designed an investigation in which subjects believed they were observing an innocent victim being punished for making errors in a learning experiment. Actually, the "victim" was a confederate of the experimenters and did not suffer. The subjects were asked to describe the troubled victim at different points in time during their observations. The results showed that observers rejected and devalued the personal characteristics of the victim when they believed she would continue being punished and continue suffering. However, if an observer believed he or she could assist the victim by having the punishment stopped, less rejection occurred. Rejection and depersonalization of the victim were strongest when the victim was considered to be a martyr—that is, when she accepted the suffering for altruistic motives. These results suggest that people want to believe in a just and orderly world and will blame and mistreat innocent victims if they are powerless to alter the victims' situation.

Finally, recent evidence (e.g., Feldman-Summers and Lindner, 1976; Jones and Aronson, 1973) indicates that the respectability of the victim influences judgments about his or her responsibility for a crime. Feldman-Summers and Lindner asked male and female subjects to make judgments about a female victim and an accused male assailant in criminal cases which varied in the type of crime committed (rape, attempted rape, and nonsexual assault) and the respectability of the victim (married woman; single, nonvirgin; single, virgin; divorced; and prostitute). One of the many findings reported was that characteristics of the victim clearly influenced judgments about her responsibility for the rape. The prostitute was regarded as more responsible for the rape than any of the other victims. This result suggests that people strive to maintain a balance between their perceptions and beliefs. If "respectable" women are raped, they cannot be blamed for their misfortunes because respectable people do not lie or provoke such actions. On the other hand, if prostitutes are raped, the thinking is that they probably took an active role in the incident, which would be consistent with their lack of respectability.

If the findings of this study can be generalized to the legal system, the perception of a crime by the police, the prosecuting attorney, the judge, and jury will be influenced by the characteristics of the victim. If certain characteristics of rape victims, such as her sexual history, are allowed to be introduced in the courtroom, judgments about the seriousness of the crime and the type of punishment to be prescribed will be selectively biased.

SELF-PERCEPTION

How does the individual understand the causes of his own behavior? If we accept the solipsism theory of knowledge that the only reality is myself and that of which I am aware, propounded by Bishop Berkeley (1685–1753), the question may be rhetorical. We may assume that we understand the causes of our own behavior because we believe we are aware of why we do things. This belief, however, is an illusion. We are unaware of many of the things that we do (Bem, 1967).

People often ask themselves, much as they would ask someone else, "Why did I do that?" It is likely that people infer their beliefs and feelings from observations both of their own overt behavior and their own autonomic behavior. Just as we can learn about the attitudes and behavioral tendencies of others from observing them, we can apply the techniques of self-observation to explain our own behavior (Nisbett and Valins, 1972).

Knowledge of my own feelings depends upon a complex interaction of my interpretation of the environment that I am in, the emotions that are aroused in me, and the labels that I have learned to attach to these emotions. The labeling-of-arousal hypothesis states that when I experience a generalized physiological reaction of emotion that I cannot explain, I will interpret my feelings in terms of my particular environmental surroundings.

A classic experiment by Schacter and Singer (1962) supports this hypothesis. Subjects were given injections of adrenalin or an injection of a placebo under the guise that they were participating in a study designed to measure how a vitamin supplement affects vision. The volunteers were divided into four groups, and experimental conditions were manipulated by giving different explanations to each group. Subjects in the informed adrenalin group were told to expect their hands to shake, their heart to pound, and their face to get warm and flushed. Subjects in the misinformed adrenalin group were told that they would feel numb and itch. Those in the ignorant adrenalin group were not told anything about side effects. The last group was a control group which did not receive an injection of adrenalin, but rather was given a placebo—a saline solution which produces no side effects. Hence subjects in the informed group were set for physiological arousal and could easily explain their feelings. Subjects in the misinformed and ignorant groups were also physiologically aroused, but they did not have a readily available explanation and would have to justify their feelings somehow. The placebo group was not physiologically aroused at all.

Following the injections and the different types of instructions, each subject was left in a waiting room in order to let the injection compound take effect. In the room was a stooge, a member of the experimental team, who was introduced as a fellow subject in the experiment. It was the task of the stooge to create one of two conditions, euphoria or anger. Either he would engage in euphoric behavior, playing basketball with crumpled paper and a wastebasket, flying paper airplanes, or he would act in an angry manner, becoming more and more obnoxious and insulting, asking personal and rude questions, and eventually leaving the room in anger because of an offending questionnaire they were asked to fill out, e.g., "Write the name of a family member who does not bathe or wash regularly."

Subjects were observed through a one-way mirror during their stay in the waiting room and completed a quesionnaire on how they felt following their interaction with the stooge. As might be supposed, the purpose of this study was to observe the behavior of subjects during their waiting-room experience with the stooge as a function of being physiologically aroused through the adrenalin injection or not, whether they could explain their feelings of arousal, and what environmental-cognitive cues were salient to explain their emotions.

Schacter and Singer found that when subjects had no simple explanation for their experience—specifically, the subjects in the misinformed and ignorant groups—they behaved in a manner consistent with the condition created by the stooge. They acted more happily and reported more happy emotions in the context of the euphoric stooge, and they behaved more angrily and reported greater anger with the angry stooge than both the informed and placebo subjects.

These results clearly support the hypothesis that emotional states which are ambiguous will be explained by the environmental-cognitive information available at the time. The two factors, physiological arousal and cognitive cues, are relatively independent but interconnected. Both factors are important for our verbal understanding of emotions. When someone is not physiologically aroused, his emotions are relatively flat and unlabeled. However, when a person is physiologically aroused, with no readily available explanation for his feelings, he will label his happiness or his anger in a manner consistent with his interpretations of situational events. Finally, if a person does have a completely satisfactory explanation, he will not label his arousal in terms of the environment.

The Attribution of Causality and Responsibility Through Hindsight

Judges and juries, like historians, always enter the picture after the fact. They know the final outcome of a particular sequence of events, such as "The bank was robbed of $10,000" or "The man was killed by a knife wound," but do not necessarily know, we presume, the events leading to the robbery or death. Their task, in part, is to reconstruct the past which led to the occurrence of the event. Upon hearing evidence regarding how the incident transpired, judges, juries, or any individual may take the position that the occurrence of the events was inevitable. The historian Georges Florovsky (1969) states:

> The tendency toward determinism is somehow implied in the method of retrospection itself. In retrospect, we seem to perceive the logic of the events which unfold themselves in a regular or linear fashion according to a recognizable pattern with an alleged inner necessity. So that we get the impression that it really could not have happened otherwise.... [p. 369]

Fischhoff (1975) has given this phenomena the metaphorical label "creeping determinism," which suggests that people have the tendency to perceive knowledge of results as having been more or less inevitable. Creeping determinism differs from philosophical determinism, which is the belief that some force deliberately created the world of events to happen as they do.

More important, however, is the finding that observers are unaware of the effects that knowledge of results has on their perceptions. People appear to believe that their excellent hindsight is identical to their foresight. According to Fischhoff, "creeping determinism not only biases people's impressions of what they would have known without outcome knowledge, but also their impressions of what they themselves and others actually *did* know in foresight" (p. 297).

Creeping determinism in perception and thought may be interpreted in terms of an assimilation hypothesis. When we retrospect, we attempt to put the outcome and its antecedents into an organized whole. Once it fits into a coherent whole, it is difficult to imagine how things could have been anything else. The danger of such thinking, however, apart from giving us a feeling of omniscience, is the possibility that we will be unable to accurately judge the past or learn from it.

As you would expect, it is my opinion that most if not all the information on person perception covered in this chapter is indirectly relevant to eyewitness accounts. Hopefully, future research will take these socio-psychological principles and test them directly against legal customs and legal practices used in the courtroom. This chapter has tried to show that many of the principles of perception covered in chapter 3 have to be expanded and accommodated when the object being perceived is a person. In chapter 6 we will see that the basic theories of memory, which were reviewed in chapter 4, are relevant to the study of face recognition. But in addition, explanations of memory for faces must acknowledge the important influence of the social context and personal biases of the witness.

Chapter 6

Memory for Faces

Faces As Social Objects

The human face is one of the most interesting and complex stimuli in our natural world. Man photographs, paints, and sculptures the face to capture for posterity the essence of a person. Parents routinely photograph their children so that they can remember them as they once were.

Psychologists have been interested in the study of faces for two major reasons: one, their communicative value, and two, their importance for identification. Faces may carry messages about the emotional states of persons, they sometimes signal intentions and behavioral dispositions, and they often communicate evaluative reactions. Chapter 5 reviewed some of the literature on the importance of faces in person perception. This chapter will focus upon experimental studies of faces as a source of identification. In contrast to person perception, where personality impressions may be verbalized quickly and often without effort, memory of faces usually is difficult to verbalize, although faces are not, it seems, difficult to recognize.

Obviously, recognition and verbal description of people are important for the criminal justice system. Testimony of eyewitnesses is considered by the police and the courts as a central element in any prosecution. However, eyewitnesses can be wrong either by identifying an innocent person as guilty or by failing to identify a guilty person as guilty. The consequences of such errors for society and for specific individuals who are in fact innocent are obvious.

This chapter will introduce the scientific evidence on memory for faces. We will leave the discussion and criticisms of practical applications of this material to chapter 7. The importance of this literature review for everyday behavior, if not for police practice, is evident in the following anecdote: A swinging middle-aged man asked his young friend, following their lovemaking, "Am I your first?" The young girl rolled over, looked at him carefully, and answered, "Your face looks familiar."

Imagining the Faces of Others

How well can people imagine the faces of others? In an investigation of personality characteristics of police officers, McKellar (1968) found that fifteen out of the nineteen policemen he sampled reported having good visual and auditory imagery of others and claimed to be able to generate life-like three-dimensional representations of target persons. A comment from one of his subjects is of interest: "A police officer has a great advantage if he can imagine what someone looks like from a written description, or if he can form a picture in his mind from a plan or a sketch..." (p. 113).

Imagining the faces of others is not as easy as it seems. Historically, psychology has had difficulty in reaching a consensus on the meaning of the word "imagination" (see Cardno, 1967). I will not try to resolve this dispute, but will yield to William James (1950, original 1890) as our authority. According to James:

> Fantasy, or Imagination, are the names given to the faculty of reproducing copies of originals once felt. The imagination is called "reproductive" when the copies are literal; "productive" when elements from different originals are recombined so as to make new wholes. [1950, Vol. ii, p. 44]

It is highly implausible that images are literal copies of original sensations, but most psychologists agree with James regarding the productive aspect of imagination. That is, images, such as dream-like states or fantasies, are acceptable products of consciousness. And many people report being able to produce such experiences. How accurate and true to life these images actually are, however, is debatable.

Over a hundred years ago, Sir Francis Galton (1883) observed that people with poor imagery ability complained that they could visualize the faces of mere acquaintances, but when they tried to image the face of a departed loved one, they were unable to arouse the proper memory. This imagery experience has happened to me and to many of my friends. However, when I tested Galton's observations by sampling over 500 college students, I found that both good and poor imagers reported their clearest and most vivid facial images to be of friends and relatives, in contrast to their images of mere acquaintances (Yarmey, 1975a). Similar findings have been made by Read and Peterson (1975).

To answer our question of how well people can imagine the faces of others, the results suggest that facial images are aroused relatively easily by many people. Individuals having a high ability to image will also have a superior ability to visualize faces. However, the practical importance of this ability, as suggested by McKellar's (1968) report that policemen often image faces of wanted persons, is doubtful. Facial images are more likely to be easily aroused and vivid in quality for loved persons and not mere acquaintances or strangers. Furthermore, as we will see in the next chapter, the ability to match a mental image of a face with a verbal description of the person whose face it is is not an easy task.

Stimulus Factors in Recognition

Over the last few years a number of different stimulus factors have been shown to influence recognition memory of faces. Our review begins with a look at the importance of individual facial features. Researchers working in this area have attempted to resolve the following types of questions: Is it easier to identify someone if his eyes are covered or if his nose and mouth are masked? Which parts of the face are attended to first or most often for identification?

FACIAL FEATURES

In one of the earliest laboratory studies of face recognition, Howells (1938) discovered that faces were more difficult to recognize when the lower parts of the face, in contrast to the upper parts, were covered. Subjects questioned regarding their strategies for remembering faces failed to specify any particular facial features as being most salient. Also, subjects who were most accurate in the recognition test were the poorest in verbally recalling details of the faces. An interesting secondary finding was the suggestion that social learning can influence face recognition. Howells found that salespeople from retail stores were superior to both farmers and college students as subjects. Whether or not these salespersons were superior in all cognitive tasks or just in face recognition is not known, since Howells did not test these types of control conditions.

DISCRIMINATION OF FACIAL FEATURES BY CHILDREN

Problems related to the calling of children as witnesses in court are presented in a systematic fashion in chapter 9. However, I shall anticipate this discussion with additional references to child studies when the flow of topics permits such inclusion. Can young children recognize faces when given only part of the faces to inspect? This question was investigated by Goldstein and Mackenberg (1966). Children having a median age of 4.5, 6.5 and 10.5 years were shown facial photographs of their own classmates. Stimuli were masked to show only partial portions of the face, and the subject's task was to name the child in the masked picture. As you would expect, the younger children performed significantly more poorly than both older groups of subjects, which suggests that the ability to identify wholes from parts is a developmental process. More important to the present discussion, however, was the finding that various parts of the face differed in their relative contribution to recognition. Upper portions of the face were significantly better cues for identification than the lower portions. These results, which contradict the earlier findings of Howells (1938), have been confirmed with college-age subjects (Sword, 1970).

RELATIVE IMPORTANCE OF FEATURES FOR RECOGNITION

Although most studies show the top part of the face to be more important than the bottom part for identification, the empirical evidence on the relative importance of individual features is difficult to evaluate. Ambiguity exists since some studies (e.g., Friedman, Reid, and Carterette, 1971) have used schematic drawings of faces, such as those shown in figure 6.1, while others have used Photo-Fit[1] constructions of faces (e.g., Ellis, Shepherd, and Davies, 1975), as illustrated in figure 6.2, while still others have used photographs of real faces. These differences in methodology are important, as we will see in chapter 7, since police officers use artists' sketches, Photo-Fit constructions, and photographs in their attempts to identify suspects. Investigators also differ in their reasons for studying facial features. For example, researchers interested in nonverbal communication and emotion (e.g., Argyle, 1967; Ekman, Friesen, and Ellsworth, 1972; Izard, 1971) emphasize the importance of the moving parts of the face (eyes, nose, mouth) as carriers of information, while other investigators have studied the relative importance of one feature over another for identification purposes (e.g., Fisher and Cox, 1975; McKelvie, 1973, 1976).

The difficulty in isolating the importance of individual facial features for recognition is apparent in the following examples. One study of schematic faces found recognition best, in increasing order of importance, when subjects focused on the mouth, the eyes and forehead, and the nose (Friedman et al., 1971). In contrast, McKelvie (1973) found the eyebrows and the mouth most important for recognition. Using Photo-Fit constructions, Ellis et

---

[1]The Photo-Fit system was designed by Jacques Perry and is marketed by John Waddington of Kirkstall Ltd., Leeds, England. It is distributed in Canada and the United States through Sirchie Finger Print Laboratories, Moorestown, N.J. 08057. A complete description of the system is given in chapter 7.

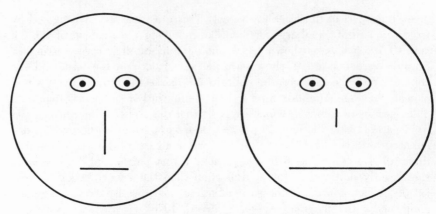

FIGURE 6.1   Examples of schematic faces

al. (1975) found that subjects attended most to the hair and forehead and least to the nose and chin. In a subsequent investigation, testing the relative saliency of different parts of the Photo-Fit face, Davies, Ellis, and Shepherd (1977) discovered that the upper features of the face were most often attended to. The order of saliency for the various features was forehead > eyes > mouth > chin > nose. The forehead seems to be a high-information area, whereas the nose is a low-value cue for Photo-Fit recognition. Other research indicates that subjects attend more to the right half of the face than to the left (Gilbert and Bakan, 1973; Liggett, 1974).

In sum, these results suggest that subjects focus primarily on upper features of faces, particularly the forehead, hairline, and eyes, in making decisions of recognition. However, faces are not recognized solely by an analysis of individual features. Some faces, for reasons which are still uncertain, are simply more difficult to discriminate than others and evoke more misidentifications. Goldstein, Stephenson, and Chance (1977) in a series of six experiments demonstrated that certain faces serving as distractors were either *never* mistaken or were *often* mistaken for a target face. The implication of this finding for the criminal justice system is that an innocent person standing in a lineup may be consistently identified as the guilty person by several witnesses. In addition, Patterson and Baddeley (1977) found that we remember a face best when we make decisions about the person's personality. These decisions presumably force us to encode the whole face at a deep level of cognitive analysis in contrast to attending solely to surface features.

DISTINCTIVENESS

Since faces differ in their uniqueness and distinctiveness, it would seem logical that high-distinctive faces are more easily recognized than low-

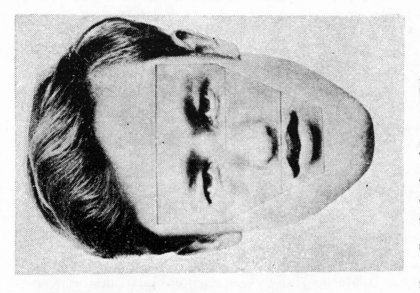

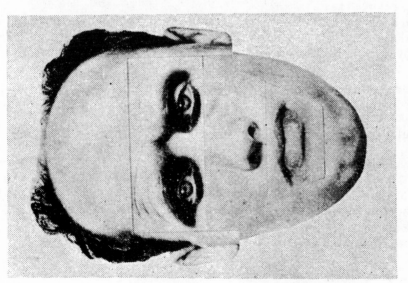

FIGURE 6.2 Examples of Photo-Fit faces *(from Ellis, Shepherd, and Davies, 1975)*

117

distinctive faces. This hypothesis has been confirmed in a number of studies. For example, Going and Read (1974) had an initial group of subjects rate the distinctiveness of each face in a set of 140 full-face photographs of college students. Later, 28 low-distinctive faces and 28 high-distinctive faces along with 56 photographs of faces of intermediate uniqueness were given to a second group of subjects for a recognition test. The results showed that highly unique faces were significantly better recognized than low-unique faces.

Two other investigators (Cohen and Carr, 1975) also studied the influence of distinctiveness on face recognition, but in addition they looked at the kind of errors committed in recognition. They found that low-distinctive faces not only were more difficult to recognize but also were more easily misidentified as the target face when, in fact, they were distractors.

PHYSICAL ATTRACTIVENESS

In chapter 5 it was mentioned that physical attractiveness is related to social acceptance (e.g., Dion, Berscheid, and Walster, 1972; Walster, Aronson, Abrahams, and Rottmann, 1966), judgments of guilt (Efran, 1974), and other variables involved in the process of interpersonal attraction. It is not surprising, then, to learn that physical attractiveness also influences recognition memory of faces.

In a complex study involving blacks and whites, males and females, and four different age groups, Cross, Cross, and Daly (1971) found that perceived beauty in a face significantly facilitates recognition. For example, 36% of all male faces were correctly recognized, but 57% of the male faces initially categorized as "attractive" were correctly identified. These differences in recognition accuracy were consistent for both male faces and female faces viewed by both black subjects and white subjects.

Attractiveness of a female face depends in part on whether or not the pupils of her eyes are dilated (Hess, 1965). Men are much more interested, without knowing why, in photographs of the same female model when her eyes are dilated rather than constricted.

Since physical attractiveness is highly valued in our cosmetically oriented society, it is not unusual that beautiful people are easily remembered. But results of an investigation by Shepherd and Ellis (1973) demonstrate that faces which are high or low in attractiveness compared to faces considered to be of medium attractiveness are easiest to identify. It should be noted, however, that these differences were reliable only when tested after a five-week delay. It is possible that memory for faces may improve with the passage of time in contrast to immediate recognition (see also Milner, 1968; Wallace, Coltheart, and Forster, 1970).

As we know, people are more likely to be attracted to the physically attractive than the physically unattractive (Cook and McHenry, 1978). An interesting question is whether or not we remember physically attractive faces more readily than faces that are likable or faces that are highly distinctive? These questions were tested in two studies by this writer.

In an investigation of memory for first impressions (Yarmey, 1975b), subjects were asked to rate pictures of 200 faces on seven-point scales for one of three stimulus conditions: attractiveness, distinctiveness, and liking. A fourth group, the control, rated these same pictures for their photographic quality. Subjects were instructed also to remember the faces for a recognition test to be given the next day. In the test condition, 15 male faces and 15 female faces were selected from the 200 faces as targets and were randomly mixed with 170 unfamiliar male and female faces. The 15 target faces for each sex were high, medium, and low in terms of the subjects' ratings. Subjects in the attractiveness condition, for example, saw 5 highly attractive males and 5 highly attractive female target faces, 5 medium-attractive males and females, and 5 low-attractive males and females.

The results showed that attractive, distinctive, and likable faces were recognized equally well over a twenty-four-hour retention interval (mean proportion correct was .44). All of these faces were recognized more easily than faces in the control condition (.35 correct) which suggests that attention to these dimensions facilitates memory. Faces which were high or low in the three stimulus conditions, but not in the control condition, were reliably better recognized than faces rated at the medium level. Male faces were as easily identified as female faces, but female subjects were superior to males. In particular, females were able to discriminate most easily among faces that differed in their distinctiveness characteristics as opposed to attractiveness and liking. The results also suggested that males attend to and remember best faces which are encoded for their physical attractiveness.

In a sequel to the above experiment, I again tested the relative effect of physical attractiveness, feature distinctiveness, and liking of faces on recognition memory, but in this study the major focus of interest was whether recognition performance is consistent over a one-month retention period (Yarmey, 1978a). Thirty photographs of male and female faces differing in their level of physical attractiveness, distinctiveness, and likability were selected from my earlier investigation (Yarmey, 1975b) and were studied for two seconds each. During this inspection time subjects were required to judge each face's level of attractiveness or distinctiveness or likability and to encode it for a later memory test. The recognition test was given to one-third of the subjects immediately following the inspection trial; one-third were tested one week later, and the rest of the subjects were tested one month later.

The results proved to be reliably consistent over the three testing periods. First, recognition was best for faces encoded for their liking, followed by those encoded for their physical attractiveness, and poorest for those considered for feature distinctiveness. However, the differences in percentage scores among these three stimulus conditions were quite small, although they were statistically significant. Recognition performance, as you would expect, did get poorer over time (89%, 83%, and 68% correct for the three test periods), but the decrease in accuracy was at a similar rate for each of the three stimulus encoding conditions. Faces rated as medium in attractiveness, likability, and distinctiveness were most difficult to recognize. In contrast to the first study, male and female subjects did not differ in their performance. Male and female faces were recognized equally well. However, the interaction effects showed that when males and females encode faces for their attractiveness, high-attractive females and low-attractive males are most easily identified. When faces are inspected for their distinctiveness, female faces low in distinctiveness and male faces high in distinctiveness are best remembered. And finally, subjects recognize most easily female faces that are high in liking but remember best male faces that are low in liking.

These results show that stimulus properties of faces are not brief and transient phenomena, but are maintained and stored in memory over intervals of weeks. What is even more surprising is the fact that these effects were so strong in spite of subjects' being given only two seconds to encode each face and make a decision regarding its facial attribute.

Expressions and Meaningfulness

The perception and memory of a human face are never determined solely by the sensory information hitting the eye, but in addition are influenced by the attributed meanings an observer gives to a facial percept. This hypothesis was verified in a clever experiment by Smith (1953). Smith predicted that subjects shown faces which differed only in their assumed expressions, two being friendly and pleasant and two expressing anger and scorn, would be perceived differently in terms of their size and distance from an observer. The hypothesis was tested in a series of experiments involving size-distance judgments of photographed faces projected on a screen. Faces perceived as friendly or pleasant were seen as "closer" (larger) than those regarded as unfriendly or unpleasant. Smith interpreted these results as supporting a theory of perception which states that perceptions of faces emerge from an observer's reference to his own self-concept and the assumptions, attitudes, expectations, purposes, and special sensitizations that people acquire through experience with others.

It has been speculated that the fundamental property of faces which distinguishes them from other classes of visual stimuli and which influences what is remembered is their emotional expressions (Bassili, 1978; Galper, 1970). Several studies support this hypothesis. First of all, facial expressions themselves are perceived and stored in memory (Galper and Hochberg,

1971). When photographs of faces are experimentally manipulated so that their expressions are lost or changed on the second viewing relative to the first time they were seen, they become difficult to recognize (Galper, 1970; Sorce and Campos, 1974).

Interference Effects

Photographs of faces, like many other visual stimuli, are difficult to discriminate and remember when they are mixed up with photos of other faces which are similar in shape, size, color, and sexual characteristics (Yarmey, 1974). Furthermore, faces seen first affect the recognition accuracy of faces seen later (Forbes, 1977; Yarmey, 1974). When witnesses are asked to identify criminals from a large set of mug shots, it is possible that their performance is influenced also by the total number of faces to be considered. Two studies have been conducted by Laughery and his colleagues which provide experimental evidence on these types of problems.

In the first investigation, Laughery, Alexander, and Lane (1971) presented four sequentially projected slides of one white male face, each slide showing a different candid position. Following the inspection trial, 150 test faces were presented, all of which were front bust views, and subjects were asked to recognize the target face. The results from two of three experiments produced accuracy scores of 81% and 84%. The longer time that subjects had to inspect the target face and the earlier the occurrence of the target in the list of test faces, the better the recognition. Laughery et al. suggest that the latter finding should be applied in the use of mug shots for criminal identification. If photographic files are organized so that witnesses have only a few alternatives (e.g., 40 vs. 140) to search through, higher accuracy in recognition should occur. The results also showed that neither pose position in the test series (front view, profile of the left side, right portrait at an angle of 45 degrees from the front, and left portrait) nor type of photograph (color vs. black-and-white) affected recognition performance.

In a second investigation, Laughery, Fessler, Lenorovitz, and Yoblick (1974) studied the effects of the time delay between seeing a target face and being tested for recognition memory. The results showed that performance was not affected by delaying the test from four minutes to one week after the inspection trial. This finding suggests that forgetting of faces is not simply a function of delay in testing. Time, at least over a one-week period, in itself is not the crucial factor in the visual identification of people. Experiments 2, 3, and 4 in this investigation strongly confirmed the hypothesis that the greater the similarity of features between the target person and the distractor faces, the poorer the recognition performance. Similarity in these studies was defined in different ways. First, it was defined empirically on the basis of faces which were mistaken for the target face in experiment 1; second, it was defined in terms of nine physical characteristics (hair color, hair length, age, build, eye color, glasses, moustache, beard, and length and shape of sideburns); and third, it was defined by a direct similarity rating given by the subjects. Laughery et al. concluded that the important variables in facial recognition are the number of faces to search through and the homogeneity of the stimuli, and not the delay in time between observation and search. If obviously discrepant facial photographs are eliminated from a search list, leaving only a set of homogeneous faces, the errors in identification because of high similarity among stimuli would be offset by the reduction in inter-ference from a smaller number of alternatives.

Perceptual Organization

The research reviewed to this point strongly confirms the hypothesis that recognition memory for faces depends upon a number of stimulus factors and the heterogeneity and amount of stimuli. An investigation by Wiseman and Neisser (1974) indicates that memory for faces depends also on the observer's ability to construct a coherent organization of the stimulus pattern. Subjects were shown a set of pictures which could be viewed as photographs of human faces or alternatively could be viewed as ambiguous displays of black and white parts. This procedure required the subject himself to determine if the same stimulus object was meaningful or meaningless. The investigators found that recognition memory was better for stimuli seen previously as faces than the same stimuli not seen earlier as faces. Wiseman and Neisser concluded that recognition performance does not depend primarily on the nature of the stimulus, but rather on the perceptual ability of the individual to construct an organized coherent representation of the stimulus. These results have been replicated and shown to be reliable over a three-day delay period (Freedman and Haber, 1974).

Is Recognition of Faces a Special Process?

As you would expect, recognition memory for photographs of faces is reliably better when faces are presented in their normal upright position than in an inverted orientation (Brooks and Goldstein, 1963; Hochberg and Galper, 1967; Yin, 1969). This finding is not surprising and is not new. Köhler (1940), several decades ago, accounted for this difference by attribut-ing it to the loss of facial expression in the inverted photograph. What is more interesting, however, is the finding that photographs of human faces are disproportionately more difficult to recognize than are those of other objects (e.g., buildings, airplanes, dog faces) presented in inverted orientation (Scapinello and Yarmey, 1970; Yarmey, 1971; Yin, 1969). Normally, all of these stimuli including faces are viewed in an upright orientation. The question of importance, then, is whether recognition of human faces is dependent, as Yin (1969) suggests, upon some unspecified factor unique to these stimuli.

In her doctoral dissertation, Toyama (1975) concluded that face recognition is not a special process, although it cannot be denied that inverted faces are more difficult to recognize than normal oriented faces. In a series of studies designed specifically to test the replicability of Yin's findings, inversion of houses and faces resulted in similar and not disproportionate difficulties in recognition. It was suggested that recognition of inverted faces may differ from memory of upright faces for one or more of the following reasons. First, perception of inverted faces is difficult because of an absence of depth cues. Second, there is a difference in the amount and type of coding for the two perceptual orientations. And finally, more time is needed to search through the memory stores for inverted representations.

Although the results of this inversion study do not support a theory that face identification is a special perceptual process, other evidence on early infant development of facial recognition and clinical evidence of brain damage in the right hemisphere may support such an argument. In the clinical condition called "prosopagnosia" patients have difficulty in recognizing faces, even of close relatives, but the ability to recognize other objects is relatively unimpaired. We will look at these types of evidence later in this chapter.

Subject Factors in Recognizing Faces

RECOGNITION MEMORY IN THE YOUNG

A body of experimental literature shows that very young children are able to recognize pictures but, in contrast to recall memory, show little or no improvement in recognition with age (Brown and Campione, 1972; Brown and Scott, 1971; Kagan, Klein, Haith, and Morrison, 1973; Nelson, 1971). Other studies, however, have found improvement in recognition performance with age (Dirks and Neisser, 1977; Mandler and Stein, 1974; Rogoff, Newcombe, and Kagan, 1974; Stein and Mandler, 1975). To take one study as an example, ninety-six subjects from four different age levels (first, third, and sixth grade and adults) were tested on their ability to recognize and recall complex scenes. Subjects viewed crowded, three-dimensional scenes with realistic settings (e.g., canoe scene, gas station scene, railroad scene) and then attempted to identify added, moved, or deleted items. The results showed that recognition memory for added items was superior to recognition of moved items and recall of deleted items, and all three scores improved with age. The results also demonstrated that false alarms (calling a "new" item "old") decreased markedly with age (Dirks and Neisser, 1977).

The literature on developmental changes in the accuracy of recognition of human faces also shows conflicting results. One of the first studies testing age differences found a definite improvement with increasing age for subjects 5 to 14 years old (Goldstein and Chance, 1964). Similarly, 17-year-olds have been found superior to 12-year-olds in remembering faces (Ellis, Shepherd, and Bruce, 1973). Cross, Cross, and Daly (1971) found no differences in recognition memory for faces among subjects aged 7, 12, and 17 years and adults (mean age of 36). An analysis of misidentifications of faces revealed, however, that subjects made fewer false identifications with increasing age.

Developmental differences in recognition memory for faces appear to be dependent upon the different skills and cognitive strategies used by subjects at different age levels. For example, older children (10 years of age) are superior to 6- and 8-year-olds in face recognition because of their ability to use spatial cues to encode meaningful arrangements of facial features, whereas 6- and 8-year-olds focus on isolated features in identifying people (Carey and Diamond, 1977). In addition, Diamond and Carey (1977) found that 6- and 8-year-olds are especially likely to misidentify faces when certain disguises (clothing, eyeglasses, and wigs) are used. However, young children are not fooled by a disguise if the person to be identified is highly familiar.

Although Diamond and Carey have established the ages from 10 to 12 as the critical period for a change in the cognitive processes involved in face recognition, Goldstein (1975) found 14 years of age to be a critical year for one aspect of facial memory. Subjects ranging in age from 3 to 20 years were asked to identify inverted photographs of faces of very familiar peers. Performance was found to improve with age up to approximately 14 years (95% correct) but declined after this age, with college-age subjects doing no better than preschool subjects (60% correct). This result was interpreted as reflecting the prolonged overlearning that adults have done in viewing normal upright faces. Consequently, recognition of distorted faces, such as inversion, becomes very difficult for persons 14 years and older.

These investigations indicate that recognition memory for faces is less for children than adults in both what is discriminated and how accurately. This conclusion is not surprising since it agrees with the principle that cognitive abilities in general are superior for older age groups. However, adults develop a perceptual rigidity in viewing normal upright faces, and deviations from this overlearned ability disrupt performance (Goldstein, 1975). Memory for faces increases with development from childhood to maturity and declines in old age (Blaney and Winograd, 1978; Smith and Winograd, 1978).

INFANT'S RECOGNITION MEMORY FOR FACES

Although the courts usually deal with adolescents and adults rather than children as witnesses, an understanding of the development of facial recognition in children can help us appreciate the difficulties involved in adult facial memory. In this section I want to trace the development of face recognition back to the infancy period.

All parents can remember the fascination of their baby's gazes into their face. Exactly how well young infants can discriminate one face from another or a face from another class of visual objects was originally investigated by Fantz (1956). Fantz assumed that an infant who gazes at one stimulus longer than at another must be able to perceive and differentiate between them. By measuring the amount of time that a baby spends making a visual preference by looking directly at one of two stimuli, it is possible to assess selective attention and make inferences about the underlying cognitive processes determining these fixations. Several studies show that human infants seek out novel stimuli when the opportunity is available. Following exposure to one target, they will shift their attention to a new and different stimulus (e.g., Fantz, 1964; Saayman, Ames, and Moffett, 1964; Fagan, 1970). This change in selective attention tells us that the two targets are discriminable and that the child remembers that one stimulus has been seen before.

The results of several studies testing the infant's developing ability over the first six months to discriminate faces from other stimuli have been summarized by Fagan (1975). Figure 6.3 shows the possible discriminations that infants can make at ages 2, 16, and 20 weeks. At 2 weeks of age the infant can discriminate a face-like pattern from circular nonface patterns (Stechler, 1964; Fantz, 1966), but cannot discriminate between two patterns (face and nonface) which differ in their spatial arrangement of internal features. By 16 weeks, however, the scrambled pattern, which could not be discriminated at 2 weeks of age, can be differentiated from a normal arrangement of facial elements (Fantz and Nevis, 1967), although two normal faces differing in age cannot be differentiated (Fagan, 1972). By 20 weeks of age the child can discriminate two normal upright faces from each other (Fagan, 1972).

Other work by Fagan (1972) demonstrates that infants 5 to 6 months old are able to discriminate between faces of a man and a woman, a man and a baby, and a woman and a baby. In addition, representations of faces can be stored in memory of infants 5 to 6 months of age for at least fourteen days (Fagan, 1973).

Differences between the sexes in recognition of faces first appears during infancy. To give one example, Lewis (1969) presented four photographs of faces varying in realism to male and female infants ranging from 12 weeks of age to 57 weeks of age. Sex differences were observed in response to the facial stimuli. Boys looked longer at the stimuli than girls, but girls indicated greater ability to differentiate among the four types of faces. Whether or not

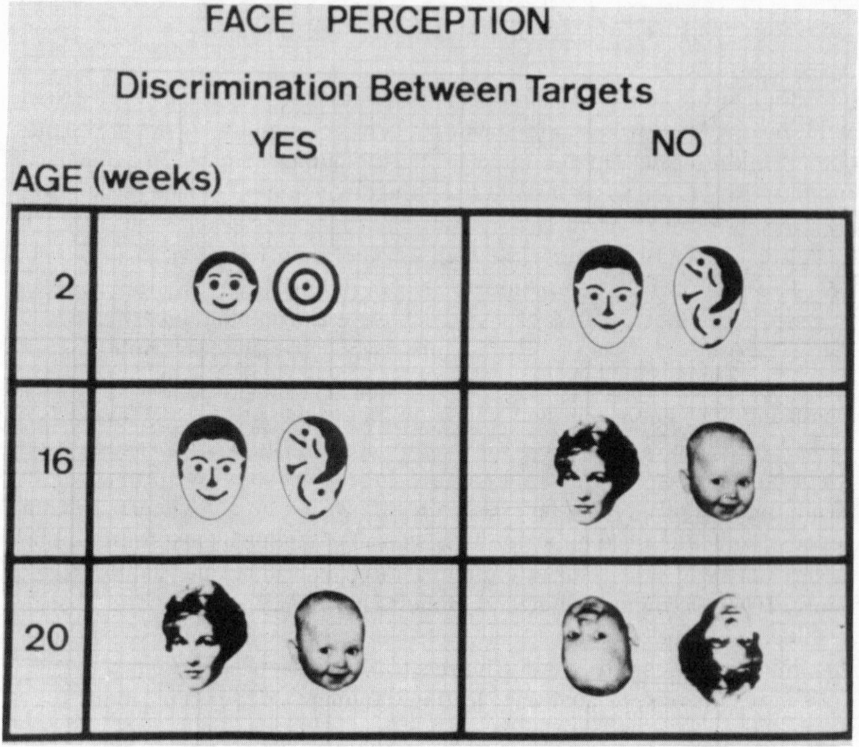

FIGURE 6.3   Discrimination between face targets at different ages
(from Fagon, 1975)

these differences are a result of differential learning experiences or are a
function of innate differences is unknown.

Most studies confirm the finding that infant boys look more at faces than
do infant girls (e.g., Kagan, Henker, Hen-Tov, Levine, and Lewis, 1966)
and, in general, show more interest in visual patterns (Hutt, 1972). This
difference in attentional behavior, however, has not been found by all investigators (e.g., Haaf, 1974). Furthermore, greater visual attention does not
mean a superiority of retention. Fagan (1972) discovered that 5-
to-6-month-old girls compared to boys of the same age had superior immediate recognition memory for photographs of faces. He suggests that
these differences may result from parents' differential treatment of the sexes
beginning in the first days of life. However, in another study a year later,
Fagan (1973) failed to replicate his earlier findings. Subjects showed similar
recognition performance when tested both immediately after inspection and
after a delay (three hours, twenty-four hours, forty-eight hours, one week,
and two weeks). Only further investigations will reveal whether or not the
results of Fagan's 1972 study are an ephemeral effect.

DIFFERENCES BETWEEN MALES AND FEMALES IN FACIAL MEMORY

Whenever a psychologist says that males and females differ in some cognitive ability, such as recognition memory, critics are quick to point to several studies which either show no differences or show conflicting results. This inconsistency in findings is not unusual in science and can be attributed to a number of factors such as differences in time, place, culture, etc. In the case of recognition memory for faces differences in accuracy seem to lean toward females over males, but the differences in absolute percentage scores are very small and have little practical importance. The following studies are reported only for their academic interest.

In 1965, Alvin Goldstein investigated the ability of children from grades two and three and adults to learn paired associates of faces and common proper names. Although Goldstein was interested in testing comparative differences between adults and children in learning of inverted and normally oriented faces, he also compared the performance of boys and girls. The results showed that children, in contrast to adults, had less difficulty in learning inverted faces, which confirmed Goldstein's hypothesis, but girls had more difficulty with the inverted stimulus faces than their male peers. In effect, the girls showed more mature, adult-like performance on the face-name learning task.

Sex differences in retention of faces have also been found in 12-year-olds and 17-year-olds. Ellis, Shepherd, and Bruce (1973) found that girls were significantly better than boys (81% vs. 70% accuracy) in recognizing color slides of faces and were particularly better in remembering other female faces (82% vs. 67%). Girls were only slightly better than boys in recognizing male faces (80% vs. 74%).

Recognition memory for faces in adults also demonstrates differences between males and females. Some studies have shown clear differences favoring females over males (Going and Read, 1974; Goldstein and Chance, 1978a; Witryol and Kaess, 1957; Yarmey, 1974, 1975b, 1978b), while other studies show that accuracy of performance depends upon the sex of the subject and the sex of the face being observed.

Cross, Cross, and Daly (1971) showed that female subjects are reliably better in recognizing other female faces, whereas male subjects recognize male and female faces equally well. This result has been replicated by Going and Read (1974), but Witryol and Kaess (1957) found that males are better in identifying male faces and females are superior in remembering female faces. The complexity of recognition memory for own-sex and other-sex faces extends to an interaction of sex of subjects, sex of stimulus faces, and the attractiveness, distinctiveness, and likability of the faces (Yarmey, 1978a). This interaction effect was discussed earlier in this chapter.

Finally, some investigators have failed to find any reliable differences in face recognition between the sexes (e.g., Laughery and Fowler, 1977; Shepherd and Ellis, 1973). Furthermore, one investigation comprising three different experiments found women slightly better than men, men significantly better than women, and no difference between the sexes in recognition performance (Laughery et al., 1971). As Laughery et al. noted, ". . . the conflicting results of subject sex in these experiments is currently a mystery. Perhaps further research will define which sex, if either, makes the better witness" (p. 483).

INTELLIGENCE AND EDUCATION

Except for an early study by Howells (1938) and two more recent investigations by Feinman and Entwisle (1976) and by Kaess and Witryol (1955), little empirical information is available on the relationship between intelligence and/or educational background and facial identification. Howells found that face recognition correlated with intelligence scores (r = .27, N = 91) and with grades (r = .33, N = 112). Obviously, these correlations are low and account for very little of the variance in recognition performance. Similarly, both Kaess and Witryol (1955), in an investigation using adults as subjects, and Feinman and Entwisle (1976), who used children as subjects, found negligible correlations between IQ and facial recognition ability.

Although the above research suggests that the relationship between IQ and facial recognition ability is minimal, the limits of this independence are unclear. For example, are highly educated and poorly educated observers equally accurate in recognizing ambiguous faces or in recognizing faces in anxiety-arousing situations?

Reserach is needed in this area since, as McCarty (1960) reports, the law places more faith in the accuracy of perception and memory of less educated than highly educated witnesses. The courts assume that educated persons think and speculate too much about their perceptions and fail to fully attend to the situation in question. The less educated, on the other hand, are said to be more open and free from cognitive distractions; consequently, they are said to be superior witnesses. It is hoped that these hypotheses will be tested under controlled laboratory situations before long.

PERSONALITY DIFFERENCES AND RECOGNITION
OF FACES

Several studies suggest that personality differences are related to a given cognitive style. For example, persons described as field-dependent by objective tests are more likely to perceive an object in relation to its surrounding context, whereas persons classified as field-independent are said to be able to escape the influence of the surrounding context and to deal with the object as a more or less independent unit (Witkin, Dyk, Faterson, Goodenough, and Karp, 1962). Field-dependent and field-independent subjects have been found to differ in a number of ways. Field-dependent subjects are more passive, lack initiative, and impose less structure on ambiguous situations (Witkin, Lewis, Hertzman, Machover, Meissner, and Wapner, 1954). In addition, field-dependent and field-independent individuals have been shown to differ in their learning and remembering (Witkin et al., 1962). In particular, field-dependent persons are said to be superior in their memory of human faces (Ellis, 1975; Oltman, Goodenough, Witkin, Freedman, and Friedman, 1975; Ramirez and Castaneda, 1974). This conclusion follows the theory of Witkin et al. (1962) which states that field-dependent people, being in need of support and guidance from others, are particularly attentive to facial cues and expressions which provide ready clues to other people's moods and attitudes.

Two studies are commonly cited to support this hypothesis. The first study used ninety Air Force captains as subjects and found field-dependent persons significantly better than field-independent subjects in recognizing photographs of fellow officers (Crutchfield, Woodworth, and Albrecht, 1958). A second study, conducted by Messick and Damarin (1964), investigated the ability of forty male and ten female subjects to recognize photographed faces. The recognition test was actually a test for incidental memory, since subjects were not warned that they would be tested for the memory of faces. Subjects were led to believe that they were participating in a perception experiment dealing with guessing of age. The results showed that accuracy of recognition memory for faces was significantly correlated with field dependence.

In the last few years a number of studies have been published (see Witkin and Goodenough, 1977) which have explored further the relationship between field independence-dependence and social behaviors, including one study specifically focused on facial recognition (Hoffman and Kagan, 1977). In contrast to the older studies described above, Hoffman and Kagan found field-independent males significantly more accurate in face recognition of photographed faces. Field-independent females were also superior to field-dependent females, but this difference was not statistically significant. Hoffman and Kagan support their argument that field-independent persons, and not field-dependent persons as previously thought, remember faces better by citing three other studies which have also found this result but have been generally overlooked in the literature (Adcock and Webberley, 1971; Baker, 1967; Beijk-Docter and Elshout, 1969). In view of this discrepant and opposite evidence it is difficult to draw a firm conclusion regarding the relationship of cognitive types and facial recognition. Certainly, more research focusing upon personality dimensions, including the field-dependent dimension and memory for faces, must be done.

Two personality dimensions which have been shown to be related to recognition of faces are the affiliation motive (concern for friendship) and the approval motive. People having a high need for affiliation identify faces, in contrast to neutral stimuli (e.g., a lamp or a plate about the size of a face), significantly sooner in a perceptual sensitivity task than subjects low in need for affiliation (Atkinson and Walker, 1956). Another study investigating the relationship between face recognition and personality factors showed that subjects with a high need for approval recognized faces more accurately than subjects with a low need for approval on an incidental memory task. When approval was withheld, the two groups did not differ in performance (Schill, 1966).

These studies indicate that personality differences are related to memory for people. Nevertheless, more research needs to be done to clarify the salient social cues and personality dimensions which determine the social orientations of people and their identification of each other.

Race Membership and Recognition of Own- and Other-Race Faces

Wall (1965) has noted that the courts are sensitive to possible biases and appeals to prejudice when color and racial origins of prosecution witnesses and defendants become key elements in determining the truth of testimony. As Wall correctly states, it is illogical and divisive to judge the veracity of a witness solely by his membership in a particular race. But, at the same time, it is important to emphasize that membership in a race may be related to accuracy in identification of other members of that same race or misidentification of members of other races. Perceptual and memorial abilities of witnesses are psychological attributes and are not democratic and logical principles which can be desensitized by rational argument or emotional debate. The evidence, as we will see, indicates that accuracy of recognition is a function of the interaction between race of observer and race of face. In particular, the differential recognition of black faces by white and black observers is a highly probable event, and more likely to result in error if the observer is white (Malpass, 1974). The term "race" is defined here in a sociological as opposed to a biological sense since in a strict definition the term "race" refers to all human beings.

Malpass and Kravitz (1969) were the first experimenters to show that black faces are identified less accurately by white (58% correct) than by black observers (68% correct). These findings were replicated in part by Cross,

Cross, and Daly (1971), who found that whites were more accurate in recognizing other white faces (45% correct) than black faces (27% correct) but black subjects performed equally well with photographs of black (39% correct) and white (40% correct) faces. Both of these investigations were conducted in the United States. Subsequently, Shepherd, Deregowski, and Ellis (1974) repeated this study in a cross-cultural experiment involving thirty-two black Africans (Rhodesia) and thirty-two white Europeans (Britain). Their results indicated that the other-race recognition effect is not restricted to the U.S.A. (where the majority of the population is white and where a vast majority of persons shown in the mass media are white). European subjects were superior to African subjects in recognizing European faces, whereas African subjects were more accurate in recognizing African faces.

Differences in ability of one race to recognize the faces of another race also have been investigated with children as subjects (Feinman and Entwisle, 1976). Two hundred and eighty-eight black and white children from first, second, third, and sixth grades served as subjects. The results showed that both races recognized photographs of faces of their own race better than the other race (white 72% correct, black 74% correct). However, black children were better at recognizing faces of white children (68%) than white children were at recognizing faces of blacks (65%).

Several variables have been suggested as possibly determinant of the other-race recognition effect. The two most popular explanations are the racial attitudes hypothesis and the differential experience hypothesis, which, of course, may not be mutually exclusive. A third hypothesis, but one which has not been extensively explored, is that the differences in personality or the cognitive styles of the observers are determinant. And finally, a fourth theory, referred to as the perceptual defect hypothesis, suggests that blacks differ from whites and are less accurate in their visual perceptions of the world because of early environmental impoverishment or sensory deprivations. We will look at each of these viewpoints, starting with the racial attitudes hypothesis.

RACIAL ATTITUDES HYPOTHESIS

Since the 1940s, social psychologists have studied the prejudiced person and his sensitivity to subtle cues of racial identity. According to Allport and Kramer (1946), racial identity is important to the bigot, since he must be quick to tell friends from foes. In general, the results of early studies, which focused mainly upon the identifiability of Jews and non-Jews, have been contradictory (see, for example, Allport and Kramer, 1946; Carter, 1948; Elliott and Wittenberg, 1955; Lindzey and Rogolsky, 1950). However, two studies by Elliott and Wittenberg (1955) and by Himmelfarb (1966) showed that high-prejudiced subjects tend to have a differential response bias toward Jews in that they perceive or judge more faces to be Jewish than non-Jewish.

One theory suggests that we remember faces as a function of our attitudes toward people. According to Bartlett (1932):

> Faces seem peculiarly liable to set up attitudes and consequent reactions which are largely coloured by feeling. They are very rarely, by the ordinary person, discriminated or analyzed in much detail. We rely rather upon a general impression, obtained at the first glance, and issuing in immediate attitudes of like or dislike, of confidence or suspicion, of amusement or gravity. . . . [p. 53]

This hypothesis recently was tested by myself and one of my students (Yarmey and Beihl, 1977). Black-and-white photographs of attractive and unattractive male and female faces were shown to eighty female subjects. Half of the subjects were instructed to generate attitudes toward the faces during the study trial. Following inspection, all subjects completed an interpersonal judgment test (i.e., questions regarding probable level of intelligence, sociability, workability, etc.) on the last face they had viewed. One week later a recognition test for faces and a recall test of their previous judgments were given. Results showed that faces encoded with a set to form attitudes were remembered more easily than faces not coded in this manner, and female faces were more easily recognized than male faces. Recall of what subjects thought of target persons was not related to their accuracy of memory for these faces. These results confirm earlier studies which indicated that recognition and verbal recall are independent of each other and appear to involve two different ways of retrieving information (Bahrick and Boucher, 1968). This research demonstrates that attitudes (or deep levels of processing) influence recognition memory for faces; another question is whether attitudes influence identification of other-race faces.

One of the first studies testing the influence of attitudes on the recognition of black and white faces was reported by Seeleman (1940). She found that white subjects with "anti-Negro" attitudes recognized fewer black faces than subjects with "pro-Negro" attitudes. In contrast, Pulos and Spilka (1961) in an investigation of antisemitism found better recognition memory by prejudiced subjects for facial photographs of Jews. Both of these studies failed to control for response bias, which may have inflated the importance of the recognition scores. However, in a study purposefully designed to control response bias, Dowdle and Settler (1970) found that prejudice was not related to accuracy for recognition of black and white faces.

Before proceeding, I would like to return to the study of Shepherd, Deregowski, and Ellis (1974) once again. This investigation showed that white Europeans failed to differentiate among blacks and had a strong tendency to see "all Africans as looking alike." This strong response bias to see all blacks as the same could be related to stereotypic beliefs about Africans.

Other evidence suggests that it is the quality of the attitude which influences other-race identification. Galper (1973) proposed that positive attitudes toward another race influence the remembering of other-race faces. She found that white students enrolled in a black studies course were superior in recognizing black faces in contrast to white students not choosing this course, who were more accurate in recognizing white faces. Galper interpreted this result as suggesting that white subjects choosing to be with blacks have a "functional race membership" in that group. This motivation supposedly leads whites to perceptually orient themselves to blacks as other blacks do to each other. Consequently, whites holding pro-black attitudes respond to faces of blacks in a manner corresponding more to blacks than to other whites. Whether or not these results support the hypothesis that attitudes influence recognition memory for other-race faces is unclear, since it is possible that whites choosing to be class members of black students in black studies courses also have more contact or differential experience with blacks than do other whites.

DIFFERENTIAL EXPERIENCE HYPOTHESIS

A simple but straightforward explanation for the superiority for recognition of own-race faces over other-race faces is the greater familiarity or exposure that a person typically has with members of his own race. This hypothesis has been supported by a number of studies (e.g., Chance, Goldstein, and McBride, 1975; Elliott, Wills, and Goldstein, 1973; Luce, 1974). The first study to question this hypothesis, however, failed to support this assumption (Malpass and Kravitz, 1969). Information gathered from a questionnaire found no relation between stated experience with the other race and the accuracy of recognition performance for faces. Instead of giving subjects a questionnaire, Elliott, Wills, and Goldstein (1973) experimentally tested this hypothesis. Recognition memory for unfamiliar Japanese faces was significantly facilitated by giving white subjects a prior training session on other Japanese faces. In contrast, subjects who were given prior training with white faces did not show a significant improvement when tested later for recognition of Japanese faces, which suggests that the differential experience mediated this performance.

In two experiments using photographs of black, white, and Japanese faces as stimuli, Chance, Goldstein, and McBride (1975) found that whites were superior in recognizing white faces (68% correct), followed by black faces (55%), and poorest with Japanese faces (45%). In contrast, blacks performed best with black faces (60%), next best with white faces (50%), and poorest with Japanese faces (43%). Since black Americans and white Americans both interact more frequently with members of their own race, and more with each other than with Japanese, their differential performances are consistent with their experiences with members of each of these races.

Although the differential experience hypothesis has been supported, other evidence indicates that "experience" should not be defined simply as amount of contact or exposure to the other race. "Experience" should include, as well, the nature or quality of that experience. White subjects who report having black friends have been found to have superior recognition memory for photographs of black faces over white subjects who merely grew up in an integrated neighborhood or simply went to school with blacks (Lavrakas, Buri, and Mayzner, 1976). Similarly, Feinman and Entwisle (1976) found that children attending an integrated school and also living in mixed-race neighborhoods were equally able to recognize both black and white faces. In contrast, children living in segregated neighborhoods or attending segregated schools remembered own-race faces best.

The influence of the quality of differential experiences on the recognition of members of other races may be related to more than physical interactions if the results of an investigation by Luce (1974) are valid. Luce found that black, white, Chinese, and Japanese college students, all of whom were American-raised, recognized best own-race faces but differed widely in recognition of other-race faces. Black subjects performed poorly in recognition of each of the other races in contrast to photographs of other blacks. White subjects—all of whom had lived all their lives in the Southwest, had gone to school with blacks, had reported specific blacks to be personal friends, and reported no previous interaction with Chinese or Japanese persons— recognized Chinese and Japanese faces almost as well as white faces, but performed poorly on recognition of black faces. The performance of Chinese and Japanese subjects was almost identical to each other. Both oriental-American groups recognized each other best, recognized blacks next best, and were poorest in performance with whites.

Luce interpreted these findings as suggesting that political activism in the early seventies on the part of proximal ethnic groups influenced their ability to recognize other races. If whites, for example, perceived blacks as an enemy, they may have inhibited or "blanked out" their recognition of black faces. If future research supports the conclusion that differential experience and its relation to personal identification have political overtones, then we must conclude that eyewitness identification is even more complex than previously suspected.

Before leaving this discussion, a criticism of the differential experience hypothesis should be mentioned. It is possible that differences in recognition between white faces and other-race faces such as Japanese (or blacks) is not a matter of frequency of contact at all. Instead, differences may result from a greater similarity or homogeneity among Japanese faces which makes them more difficult to discriminate as opposed to white faces. Although this is a valid proposal, Goldstein and Chance (1976) found that perceptual discriminations of Japanese faces are no more difficult than discriminations of white faces. Thus the theory that Japanese faces are more homogeneous (i.e., "All Orientals look alike") than white faces and thereby more difficult to recognize is not supported. These results have been replicated in four additional experiments conducted by Goldstein and Chance (1978b).

PERCEPTUAL DEFECT HYPOTHESIS

This hypothesis states that blacks differ and are inferior to whites in their perceptual functioning because of some perceptual defect resulting from early sensory deprivation (Tyler, 1956). Although this theory has some importance in research on individual differences, little significance is attached to it for our purposes. First, studies already reviewed in this chapter indicate that blacks and whites differ in their recognition of other-race faces, but there is no suggestion that these differences suggest an inferiority or deficit in perception. In fact, the performance of black children has been found to be significantly better than white children in recognizing faces of both blacks and whites (Feinman and Entwisle, 1976). Second, a critical review of the literature by Mandler and Stein (1977) shows that the perceptual defect hypothesis is totally unfounded, although racial differences in perception do occur.

COGNITIVE STYLE HYPOTHESIS

The reader should not get the impression that all whites do poorly in identification of black faces. The results of a study by Lavrakas, Buri, and Mayzner (1976) can be added to the growing literature which shows that field-independent subjects are superior to field-dependent subjects in the recognition of faces. The most important finding in this study, however, is the greater probability that field-independent persons are not just superior in recognizing own-race faces but also better in recognizing faces of another race. The authors of this study draw the meaningful conclusion that white police officers working in black communities should be screened for personality variables such as, field-independency traits. The person who complains that "all blacks look alike" may in fact perceive them as similar because of his field-dependent cognitive style, i.e., the tendency to perceive objects or people only in relation to their surrounding environment rather than as independent units.

TRAINING IN FACE RECOGNITION

Since many police officers share with the general population the perceptual difficulty of recognizing other-race faces, an interesting proposal is to train the officers in this cognitive ability. Research by several investigators (Elliott, Wills, and Goldstein, 1973; Lavrakas, Buri, and Mayzner, 1976) demonstrates that facial recognition of other races can be improved with training.

A complete theoretical explanation of how training in face recognition facilitates performance is impossible at this time, since we still lack a strong theoretical explanation of what occurs during face recognition in general. One move in this direction, however, has been made by Malpass (1975). He suggests that observers viewing other-race faces probably attend to features which are relatively uninformative for making within-group discriminations but are informative for differentiating between racial groups. Thus a person's skin color, for example, may be salient and quickly coded for discriminating between members of different races, but would not be helpful in discriminating a particular face from other faces who also have that facial characteristic. Training programs in recognition of faces may be beneficial by showing the observer how to discriminate specific but subtle features in faces as opposed to merely encoding more salient characteristics for the other-race face.

Support for this suggestion is shown by the findings of Ellis, Deregowski, and Shepherd (1975). Significant differences were found between black and white subjects in their attention to physiognomic details of faces. White subjects looking at white faces were found to attend to and to describe such features as hair color and texture and color of the eyes (iris). In contrast, black subjects looking at black faces concentrated upon other features, such as the facial outline, hair style, eye size, the whites of eyes, eyebrows, ears, and chin. These results demonstrate that blacks and whites focus upon different facial features when looking at members of their own race. Furthermore, the same perceptual strategies used to facilitate viewing members of one's own race interfere in observing faces of another race. The use of training sessions for face recognition by the police and other social agencies would seem to be a valuable application of these research findings.

Codability of Faces: The Influence of Verbal Descriptions

It is acknowledged that language helps thinking, but it is not indispensable to thought (see Arnheim, 1970), The questions we wish to explore at this time are the following: in general, what effects does language have on memory, and more specifically, do verbal descriptions facilitate recognition of faces? These questions have applied importance, as we shall see in the next chapter, for police artists who must draw the face of a suspect from the verbal descriptions of a witness and police who must search for wanted persons only having heard a verbal description of their appearance.

Evidence gathered by Russian psychologists demonstrates that recall memory in very young children is increased over seven times in strength when the experimenters name the stimuli to be remembered (Luria, 1961). The influences of naming on reproductive memory was summarized briefly in chapter 4 when we considered the classic work of Carmichael, Hogan, and Walter (1932). In brief, these investigators showed that word labels influence the perception and reproduction of stimulus objects. If an object is presented to a subject and is called by a particular name, the subject tends to reproduce (draw) that object in a manner that is consistent with all objects given that particular label.

The relationship between recognition memory and verbal codability was initially studied by Brown and Lenneberg (1954). They showed that the "codability" of a color, operationally defined as a composite measure of agreement in naming, length of name, and response latency in naming, is related to recognition accuracy of colored objects. Similarly, recognition of facial expressions correlates with their ease of codability (Frijda and Van de Geer, 1961).

The assumption that language has a determining influence on recognition memory was developed further by Glanzer and Clark (1963a) with their "verbal loop" hypothesis. They theorized that subjects given a perceptual recall task, such as remembering a visual display, encode the information verbally and respond on the recall test by transforming the verbalizations into a final response. Test performance is hypothesized to be a function of the length of verbalization required to describe the stimulus. Thus the shorter the verbal description given to the visual scene, the better the accuracy of recall. Support for this hypothesis has been demonstrated, indicating that efficient verbal coding leads to superior memory (Glanzer and Clark, 1963b, 1964).

Communication accuracy also influences memory. Lantz and Stefflre (1964) showed that the degree to which one group of subjects reliably describes a set of objects will influence the accuracy with which another group of subjects using three descriptions can recognize those objects. This index also was shown to be a better predictor of recognition than was codability. In accord with this research, Cohen and Granström (1968) found that communication accuracy is a better predictor of recall than is the verbal loop hypothesis, particularly when subjects give descriptions based upon analogy as opposed to literal descriptions. In summary, the results of these studies confirm the hypothesis that language is correlated with effects of memory. Having established proof of a relationship between language and memory, investigators next set out to study the cause and effect of interactions between language variables and memory.

A large literature is now available which shows that labeling visually presented objects enhances recognition memory for those objects (Ellis and Daniel, 1971; Ellis and Muller, 1964), particularly when there are a large number of stimuli to be remembered (Santa and Ranken, 1972) and when the labels are in some way representative of the visual stimuli (Ellis, 1968). These experiments suggest that verbal labels are facilitative for memory when they properly direct the subject to focus his attention on the salient features of the object. However, these investigations have been conducted primarily on relatively ambiguous or meaningless stimuli. With more meaningful material such as pictures of familiar objects, labeling at the time of inspection has not been found to facilitate recognition memory (Davies, 1969, 1971; Kurtz and Hovland, 1953), and may even lower performance (Bahrick and Boucher, 1968).

Finally, some researchers have shown that memory for visual objects and scenes utilizes both verbal and nonverbal pictorial codes (Frost, 1971, 1972; Paivio, 1971). Furthermore, Tversky (1974) found that for long-term memory, subjects given a stimulus consisting of a picture of an object and its name remember names better than pictures if they expect to be given a recall test and remember pictures better than the verbal labels if they expect a recognition test. Thus visual and verbal coding processes and the verbal and pictorial representations to be remembered interact to produce differential performances in expectancy of either a recall test or recognition memory test.

Now that we have completed a general overview of the influence of language on memory, we can turn our attention to the more specific question of the relationship between verbal coding and face recognition. Few studies have been conducted on the relationship between facial recognition and linguistic variables, but the results that are available are consistent. Goldstein and Chance (1970) found that although faces easily evoke verbal labels as word associates, ease of labeling was not related to accuracy of facial recognition. Following this experiment, Chance and Goldstein (1976) speculated that facial recognition may be facilitated if the verbalizations are face-specific rather than simple word associations. Consequently, they designed an experiment to test whether the use of two kinds of subject-generated descriptions for faces is related to subjects' recognition for the faces one week later. Four groups of subjects were employed, each receiving different learning instructions. Group A was told to look at each face for three seconds and then write down "some one thing about the face which you believe will help you recognize it when you see it again." Group B was told to write "some one thing which the face reminds you of or looks like to you." Subjects in group C were the control. They were told simply to study each face in preparation for the recognition test. Group D subjects, unlike the other three, were an incidental learning group, since they were not informed of the true nature of the task. These subjects were told that they were participating in a small-group decision-making experiment. In addition, they were asked to make age judgments of the target faces but were not informed of the recognition test to follow. The results showed that verbalization only slightly improved recognition accuracy (82%), and only for group A, which "described" the stimuli. Subjects in the three other groups showed similar recognition performance (71%, 74%, and 74%, respectively). These findings indicate that verbalizations did little more than insure that subjects paid close attention to the stimuli and had only a weak effect on recognition memory over a one-week retention interval. A second question in this study asked how well subjects could spontaneously recall their original verbal responses to faces which were successfully recognized. The results showed that only 35% of the verbal responses were correctly recalled, even though these responses were elicited while the subjects were shown the target faces. Evidently, verbal descriptions, at least of the type gathered in this experiment, are not a strong part of the memory trace for faces.

Another group of investigators also failed to show any relationship between face recognition and verbal encoding. Malpass, Lavigueur, and Weldon (1973) trained subjects in three different ways to encode faces: (1) descriptions of faces—i.e., subjects were asked to "describe stimulus faces so that a friend could correctly identify the face from a group of others on the basis of the descriptions alone . . ."; (2) subjects were asked to recognize faces from verbal descriptions (communication accuracy); and (3) subjects were asked to describe similarities and differences in triads of faces. Training in face recognition resulted in subjects having greater facility in describing faces, but this ability did not facilitate their accuracy in identifying faces.

The only investigation to show a link between language and recognition memory for faces is McKelvie (in press). Using schematic faces as stimuli, McKelvie found that hard-to-label faces were recognized better after labeling than after mere observing, whereas easy-to-label faces did not show any improvement in performance when labels were provided. Labeling faces may facilitate their recognition by focusing attention to specific features during inspection. However, labels which focus attention to irrelevant features also may retard performance. Since this study was conducted with schematic faces rather than with photographs of real faces, it is difficult to state that a relationship between language and face recognition has been demonstrated. Instead, it can be concluded that accuracy of facial recognition is decidedly more dependent upon visual encoding than upon verbal processes of memory. In addition, observers' ability to verbally describe faces is not predictive of their ability to recognize these faces (Goldstein, Johnson, and Chance, 1977).

MEMORY FOR NAMES AND FACES

Few people have gone to a party or class reunion and not heard at least one person say, "I can remember your face but I can't remember your name." This experience illustrates once again the common finding that recognition memory is usually superior to recall memory (MacDougall, 1904; Postman, 1950).

In an investigation of the differences between recognition and recall of faces and names, Clarke (1934) found that recognition was superior to recall for both faces and names but names were slightly easier to recognize (97%) than were faces (91%). I have replicated the greater accuracy in recognizing names than faces (Yarmey, 1970). This result is interesting since it contradicts the general conclusion that recognition memory for pictures of objects is superior to the recognition of their word labels (Jenkins, Neale, and Deno, 1967). Whether or not this result is another indication that memory for faces is unique and different from other types of visual memory is debatable (see Yin, 1969). More likely, evidence showing that names are easier to identify than faces occurs because names used in research studies are common and familiar labels, whereas photographs of faces are relatively homogeneous and unfamiliar stimuli.

In a study of short-term memory for faces and for surnames Warrington and Taylor (1973) found that subjects were 100% perfect in immediate recognition of a *single* face, whereas *two* surnames could be recognized without error. When memory span for two faces (faces presented successively) was examined, subjects dropped 10% in accuracy, and they lost 30% accuracy with a string of three faces. These results demonstrate that scanning and remembering even only three faces in succession is a difficult task. In contrast, memory for three faces presented simultaneously was as good thirty seconds after input as it was immediately after viewing (80% accuracy in both cases). However, recognition of three surnames declined from a 90% accuracy level on an immediate test to a 70% performance level after a thirty-second delay. These findings must be a consolation to partygoers who cannot remember whom they were introduced to, or which name goes with which face.

Long-term memory for names is related to our knowledge about that person (Yarmey, 1973). For example, we know that celebrities are associated with specific contexts—the arts, politics, sports, etc.—and when we try to remember their names, we search our memory for certain situational cues which help to characterize these persons. A subject trying to remember the name of a particular celebrity may remember first that he is a movie star, may then remember the name of the movie he was last seen in, imagine scenes from the film, and so on. Imagery is a useful mechanism for remembering names and countless other information in our everyday world (see Lorayne and Lucas, 1976; Morris, Jones, and Hampson, 1978; Yarmey, 1970).

Perhaps the most ambitious and comprehensive investigation of memory for names and faces is the study by Bahrick, Bahrick, and Wittlinger (1975). They found that recent high school graduates and people who had been away from high school for thirty-five years could correctly identify 90% of their classmates' photographs. A drop in identification of high school friends occurred only for those who had left school more than forty years earlier, but even these people, who were now in their 50s and 60s, identified 75% of their classmates. Fifteen years after graduation, 90% of the faces and names of classmates were correctly matched, and no decline in matching performance occurred until twenty years after graduation. Only those people who had been out of school for forty-eight years or more showed a significant drop in both recognition and matching tests.

These high performance scores cannot be accounted for by the suggestion that high school classes are relatively small and that the memory load is minimal. This investigation failed to find any significant differences in recognition memory for names and faces between people who graduated in classes of 800 and those in classes of 100. Although the results for recognition memory were impressive, the free recall of names was much less so. Very recent high school graduates could recall only about forty-seven names regardless of the size of their graduation class (900 vs. 90). Individuals who had been out of school for forty years or more could recall approximately nineteen names of their classmates.

A comparison of performances between men and women in remembering names and faces found women considerably superior with one exception. Men who had been out of school for forty or more years were superior to their female counterparts in recognition of faces and matching names with faces, but not in free recall of names. Men also showed a definite sex bias in their recall of names, remembering twice as many names of boys as girls, whereas women recalled nearly as many names of boys as girls.

This study confirms the hypothesis that long-term memory can retain vast amounts of information. The major problem in memory is to retrieve information efficiently and accurately.

Memory Strength for Photographs of Faces

When a subject recognizes a face, he must make a decision based upon some sort of stored internal representation of that person. Gordon and Hayward (1973) have shown that mental images of the actual shapes of faces form one of the bases of subjects' judgments. How well or how strong these internal representations are depends upon the depth of processing of the face (Craik and Lockhart, 1972; Mueller, 1978).

Recent studies by Bower and Karlin (1974) and by Warrington and Ackroyd (1975) have demonstrated that subjects required to inspect faces and make judgments of their honesty and pleasantness, in contrast to more surface-level judgments of sex or size, are superior on a recognition test. These results have been replicated by Strnad and Mueller (1977) and by Winograd (1976). Surprisingly, Winograd (1976) showed that memory for faces is not affected by positive as opposed to negative classifications when they are initially inspected. Thus, noting that a face does or does not have a particular feature leads to similar recognition performance. However, memory for faces improves as increasing numbers of factors are examined. It may be concluded that memory is enhanced when subjects process photographs at a deep level of analysis by examining, encoding, and making decisions about more and more facial features.

Prosopagnosia and Hemispheric Asymmetry in Face Recognition

It is well documented that for right-handers the right hemisphere of the brain specializes in processing visual information including the recognition of faces, whereas the left hemisphere is usually dominant for processing verbal and linguistic information (Duda, 1978; Hilliard, 1973; Kimura and Durnford, 1974; Milner, 1971; Rizzolatti, Umilta, and Berlucchi, 1971). These differences in function between the left and right hemispheres may be related to the clinical condition called prosopagnosia. Hécaen and Angelergues (1962) suggest that patients failing to recognize even very familiar faces may suffer from right-hemisphere damage. Prosopagnosia is a relatively rare clinical defect (Beyn and Knyazeva, 1962) but one which should be of interest for its implications for eyewitness behavior.

Patients suffering from prosopagnosia often have other agnosia defects .ch as color agnosia (a failure to discriminate among colors); object agnosia (a failure to recognize two objects together which can be identified if separated); or spatial agnosia (a topographical disorientation). These concomitant disturbances sometimes withdraw after a few months, but prosopagnosia patients persist in being severely impaired in recognizing faces of their spouses, children, relatives, friends, and even photographs of themselves (Bay, 1953; Beyn and Knyazeva, 1962; Cole and Perez-Cruet, 1964). The impairment in face identification includes the failure to determine sex (Bay, 1953) and race (Cole and Perez-Cruet, 1964), and an inability to recognize a person from his photograph even when the person depicted is standing in front of him (Hécaen and Angelergues, 1962). Prosopagnosia patients are aware of their defect. They know that a face is a face and can even describe some of the facial features, but the general configuration is distorted and unclear. In order to compensate for their disturbance, identification is made from other cues such as voice, movements, clothes, distinguishing marks such as moles, and hair length and hair texture.

It is tempting to draw the conclusion that the damage shown in patients handicapped from prosopagnosia proves the existence of a special site for face-specific analyzers. This conclusion, however, is invalid in light of a number of weaknesses (see Ellis, 1975). First, damage from different and quite disparate cerebral areas has resulted in prosopagnosia, including damage to the left frontal lobe as well as damage to the right hemisphere (Cole and Perez-Cruet, 1964; Hécaen and Angelergues, 1962). Second, patients often suffer from other agnosias as well as from prosopagnosia. Consequently, not only facial recognition but recognition of other objects such as food (Pallis, 1955) and animals (Macrae and Trolle, 1956) may suffer. And finally, prosopagnosia may be associated with a general perceptual deficit (Bay, 1953; Faust, 1947), which would argue against a hypothesis of face-specific feature analyzers.

What can be said unequivocally is that right-hemisphere damage produces more impairment in face recognition than does left-hemisphere damage (Benton and Van Allen, 1968; De Renzi and Spinnler, 1966; Milner, 1968; Warrington and James, 1967; Yin, 1970). This conclusion suggests that witnesses asked to identify a particular face should be screened for possible brain damage and, more specifically, for right-hemisphere deterioration.

Failure To Recognize Faces

Common sense tells us that a person disguising his face is likely to escape detection. Just how greatly a face can be altered before we fail to recognize it is a testable question. Faces never look the same; they are constantly changing in appearance—from slight changes in expressions, hair styles, complexion and cosmetics, to major alterations from growth and maturation. A police suspect whose face is already in the mug shot file may look quite different over the years as he ages, or if he grows a beard, or gains or loses weight. Two investigations have recently been conducted to test recognition memory of pictures of faces when the appearance of the face was altered from original inspection to the test.

Laughery and Fowler (1977) investigated the effects of changing the facial appearance of males by the addition or removal of glasses, addition or removal of beards, and change of hair style. Results showed that the magnitude of recognition loss is equivalent when an accessory is added or removed. A change in wearing of glasses produced the least amount of recognition loss, greater losses were found with a change in hair style, and the greatest loss occurred with a change in facial hair (beards and moustaches). In one condition, for example, a face originally shown with a beard and then tested with a shaven face decreased 42% in accuracy in contrast to seeing of the face with a beard on both occasions (92.5% correct recognition). The analysis of misidentifications on decoy faces revealed that most errors occurred to faces with long hair and faces having a beard and moustache.

Two researchers from England (Patterson and Baddeley, 1977) have found similar results. Major changes in appearance produced significant decreases in recognition accuracy (a drop from 98% to 45% in correct scores), even though subjects had a relatively long time to encode each face on the original inspection trial (twenty-eight seconds each). This study also showed that disguises, to be effective, need not depend upon a complex change in appearance. Simple addition or removal of accessories substantially alters the recognition of a face.

As I stated at the beginning of this chapter would be the case, its focus has been the scientific or fundamental aspects of research on memory for faces. Not all of the information presented, such as the review of studies on infant behavior, could be said to be crucial to the criminal justice worker. Furthermore, much of this research is still in its early stages of development, and theoretical explanations are still being sought. Nevertheless, this information forms the psychological foundations for courtroom practices of eyewitness identification and testimony. Gaps and omissions in our present knowledge of facial memory will only be resolved by further work by scientific psychologists.

Chapter 7

Criminal Identification: Verbal and Visual Descriptions

Human beings have been involved in the art of self-identification and identification of others since the earliest days of civilization. All of us carry some sort of identification at most times, such as our driver's license, credit cards, business cards, and so on. Classifications of people by photography, fingerprinting, footprints, and even computerized systems of identification are common practices used by federal agencies and others. This chapter will deal primarily with the verbal and visual procedures used by the police and the courts to identify wanted persons. Other methods of identification such as voiceprints, skeletal identification, and fingerprints will not be reviewed since they are beyond the scope of this book. The interested reader is directed to Allison (1973) for such information.

Early records of man's history reveal that branding was used by authorities to identify persons who had been banished from the group. Branding, or mutilation, continues to be practiced in primitive cultures, although it has been dropped by most civilized peoples.

Personal identification and membership in groups has been reflected from early times in style of dress such as the Scottish tartan, school crests, and ties; in caste marks on the face and arms; and in the use of given names and surnames. Surnames were first used in England in the eleventh century and were passed from father to son in the fourteenth century. Surnames or nicknames often originated from a personal trait or mannerism, e.g., Strong, Swift; color or complexion, e.g., Black, White; or dwelling, e.g., Gatehouse, Wood. One writer has facetiously speculated that names may even be responsible for determining one's profession (Davis, 1974). For example, a review of names of animal behaviorists reveals that Wolfe (1936) investigated a system of token rewards for chimpanzees; Fox (1973) published a study of social behavior in the wolf; and Wigglesworth (1964) is the author of a book on *The Life of Insects*.

Police distribution of verbal descriptions of wanted persons is an old practice dating back to the Egyptian Ptolemies and Romans in the second century B.C.; however, their descriptions were highly subjective and non-systematic. Not until the nineteenth century did Alphonse Bertillon in Paris, France develop a scientific method for the classification of wanted persons. Bertillon (1896) devised a procedure called *anthropometrical signalment* which systematically described each criminal by measurement of his or her head, arms, torso, legs, and feet. This system, however, proved cumbersome and inefficient.

A second technique created by Bertillon for identifying suspects was the more useful system called *portrait parlé*. This technique won worldwide acceptance by police forces, and some aspects of this procedure are still used today. In simple terms, the officer is trained in the art of developing a mental image of the wanted person based upon verbal descriptions of the size and shape of different features of the face. Lessons in *portrait parlé* start with lectures describing the various types of facial features paired with visual displays of the characteristic described. It is assumed that policemen learning the technique of matching facial features with their verbal descriptions will be able later to recognize the suspect solely by hearing and then imaging the list of features. Although this technique appears sound, its validity must be questioned in light of the evidence reviewed in the last chapter. Little relationship has been found between verbal labeling and recognition memory for faces. Furthermore, recognition memory cannot depend solely on the identification of separate facial features (Harmon, 1973).

An interesting historical note concerning Alphonse Bertillon is that Bertillon was the expert witness on handwriting whose testimony helped convict Captain Alfred Dreyfus of treason, in a case discussed briefly in chapter 2. Dreyfus, after four years of imprisonment in solitary confinement, finally was declared innocent.

Another significant historical advancement in criminal identification was the application of photography to the legal system. Photography was invented by Daguerre in 1839. Belgium, in 1843, was the first country to develop and display mug shots of arrested persons. These early photographs were called daguerreotypes and presented the frontal image of the criminal on metal plates (see Moenssens, 1962). Photography was not used by the police in the U.S. until 1867, when the Cleveland, Ohio, Police Department introduced mug shots to America. Only full-face photographs were taken initially, accompanied by an identification number. Profile photographs were added to the file in 1898. Black-and-white photographs were used exclusively at one time, but recently some police departments have introduced color photography. The benefit of color prints over black-and-white prints for recognition memory is unresolved, since some researchers have not found any reliable differences (Laughery et al., 1971), whereas others have found that color facilitates performance (Tickner and Poulton, 1975).

Composites

ARTISTS' DRAWINGS

Anyone familiar with the cartoon strip *Dick Tracy* knows the invaluable importance that Junior, the police artist, has in the eventual capture of wicked villains. Police artists are used to construct sketches of suspects from witnesses' descriptions. Usually suspects are not criminals with previous records, which means that mug shots are not available. The composite image of a fugitive is drawn from and based upon the communication accuracy between the witness and artist. Eventually, after several reconstructions, a final likeness is constructed and confirmed by the witness. Several authorities (e.g., Belli, 1954; Turner, 1968) cite concrete examples of the accuracy of artists' sketches leading to the apprehension of wanted persons.

In spite of their reputed value artists' sketches do have limitations. One concern is the risk of error from suggestion. It is possible that repeated constructions can bias the witness's memory such that he or she cannot discriminate between the pictures created by the artist and his or her constantly changing memory image of the suspect's face. Another possible limitation is the skill in which witnesses can accurately describe the face of a suspect (or anyone for that matter).

The difficulty involved in eliciting the kind of information necessary to produce useful sketches is evident in a study by Harmon (1973). Harmon assumed that if anyone could be described as an expert in communicating the memory image of a suspect's face to an artist, it would be another artist familiar with the police practice of drawing suspects' portraits. A test of this hypothesis showed that subjects were accurate only 50% of the time in identifying an artist's sketches, made from the descriptions given by another artist, of people they knew well. In contrast, in a control condition using drawings made from photographs of the "suspects," 93% of the sketches were correctly identified. The difference in accuracy of identification between drawings made from verbal descriptions and drawings made from photographs indicates that even an experienced artist has difficulty in verbally describing faces. An interesting incidental finding was the observation that several of the sketched faces were almost always correctly identified. It seems that some faces for some unknown reason lead to more accurate verbal descriptions and more accurately drawn sketches than other faces.

Sketches and composite pictures drawn by police artists based upon descriptions given by witnesses are generally regarded as hearsay evidence and therefore not allowed as support for eyewitnesses' testimony on the issue of identity (Moenssens, Moses, and Inbau, 1973). However, an exception to this practice occurred in a case in which a witness's testimony was attacked as a recent fabrication. A facial sketch drawn by a police officer shortly after the crime based upon the description given by the witness was considered admissible, since it corroborated the testimony of identity (People v. Coffey, 1962) (Moenssens, Moses, and Inbau, 1973).

COMMERCIAL COMPOSITES

Most police departments, especially those of small cities and towns, are unable to find artists available to provide sketches precisely when needed. Also, few artists are able to draw portraits from description alone, and very few are willing to train themselves in this specialty unless they are employed full-time by the police department. To overcome this difficulty, commercially prepared kits of composites are often used, which minimizes the need for experienced artists. These commercial kits are constructed on the theory that "all faces can be reduced to a small number of parts and each of these parts can be found to be made up of only a limited number of general types..." (Allison, 1973, p. 45). In theory, the combination and recombination of the various parts of these composites should produce any given face.

The theoretical development of composite portraiture can be traced back to Sir Francis Galton (1883), who proposed a method for discovering the central physiognomic type of any group or race including the class of criminal. Galton's method was relatively simple but ingenious. After collecting a large number of facial photographs of different persons all coming from the same representative category, such as criminals, Galton superimposed the portraits one upon the other. He then photographed each portrait onto one plate, blending each of the different faces into a final product. The effect of the composite portrait was to generalize all traits which were similar to each other into one strong image while at the same time minimizing the trace of individual peculiarities. Blending photographs of murderers with men convicted for violent assault and for robbery produced:

...... faces of a mean description, with no villainy written on them. The individual faces are villainous enough, but they are villainous in different ways, and when they are combined, the individual peculiarities disappear, and the common humanity of a low type is all that is left.... [Galton, 1883, p. 11]

In the next section, a look at some of the commercial composites available to police forces and research centers is presented, followed by an evaluation of their effectiveness in identification.

IDENTI-KIT

Hugh C. McDonald of the Los Angeles County Sheriff's Office developed the Identi-Kit more than twenty years ago. The kit consists of 544 transparent celluloid sheets of different facial features originally drawn from 50,000 photographs of whites, blacks, and orientals. An operator is able to select—from hundreds of different hairlines, eyes, noses, chins, lips and ears, beards, moustaches, eyebrows, eyeglasses, hats, scars, wrinkles and age lines—those transparencies which best match the verbal description of the face given by a witness. If the match does not appear to fit, the witness can instruct the operator to try another overlay. Eventually, a final likeness is constructed and confirmed by the witness. Since each facial characteristic is numbered, the composite's code numbers can be communicated to other police forces for duplication.

MULTIPLE IMAGE MAKER AND IDENTIFICATION COMPOSITER (MIMIC)

The MIMIC is a method of film projection using six separate films of different styles or shapes of hair, chin, eyes, nose, mouth, and accessories. The witness describes the suspect to an operator, who codes the description and then selects appropriate films to form a test image. The operator and witness then combine forces to make any necessary changes of the test configuration. Once the witness is satisfied with the final likeness, the image and code number is photographed by a Polaroid camera and distributed to other police forces.

PHOTO-FIT

This system of facial identification was developed by Jacques Penry, a Canadian, working with the British police. The Photo-Fit method divides the face into five facial zones (forehead and hairline, eyes, nose, mouth and chin). Several photographs depict each zone. The witness is asked to inspect the various representations and select those photographs which best reconstruct the suspect's face. The selected features are then mounted on a card-like board. If the composite image is unsatisfactory, the witness can change any of the photo parts by pulling out the troublesome features and inserting other more appropriate matches.

EVALUATION OF FACIAL COMPOSITES

Users of composite kits acknowledge that none of the composites will produce an image that exactly fits the wanted person (Allison, 1973). Nevertheless, supporters point to numerous examples of criminal cases the solution of which was facilitated by the identification provided by composites. Apart from the personal opinions of users who value this technique (King, 1971), relatively little empirical research judging its effectiveness is available. Experimental psychologists have used the Identi-Kit to learn how subjects perceive human faces (e.g., Bradshaw and Wallace, 1971; Matthews, 1978), but these types of studies do not answer the question of eyewitness reliability and validity (see Cohen, 1973).

A series of studies by Hadyn Ellis and his colleagues at Aberdeen University, Scotland, cast serious doubt on the efficiency of the Photo-Fit system for reconstructing faces (see Davies, Ellis, and Shepherd, 1978; Ellis, Shepherd, and Davies, 1975; Ellis, Davies, and Shepherd, 1978; Shepherd, Ellis, McMurran, and Davies, 1978). These studies found that subjects required to reconstruct a stimulus face were able to construct a more accurate copy when they viewed the face as opposed to constructing it from memory. However, neither of the two reconstructions were very accurate. No feature was reliably reconstructed from memory, although on one test the forehead and eyes were selected correctly. Matching a face with its reconstructed Photo-Fit face is a perceptually difficult task. When subjects have to do it from memory, it is even more unreliable. However, individual differences are found, with some subjects clearly being superior to others.

The likeness of the Photo-Fit constructions to real faces or photographs of faces was generally so imprecise as to seriously question their continued use by police forces. Memory performance, as we know, typically declines over time. For example, recall of verbal descriptions of faces is relatively good after a one-day delay in testing but is much poorer after a one-week interval. Nevertheless, this research found that Photo-Fit constructions showed no decline in accuracy for up to three weeks. It is tempting to suggest that this result confirms the effectiveness of Photo-Fit constructions. On the contrary, a better interpretation is that the system itself is so inherently weak or insensitive that it fails to detect changes in memory performance over time.

The Photo-Fit system also failed to differentiate between people who were instructed to try hard to remember faces and do well on the following construction test and subjects who were not told to pay special attention to the original face. Interestingly, those subjects claiming high confidence in their ability to use Photo-Fit faces did not show high performance. This result confirms studies by Buckhout (1974), and by Yarmey (1978b), who also failed to find a relationship between subjects' confidence level and their ability to recognize faces.

Consistent with the research on cross-racial identifications, whites were better at constructing white faces than black faces. The Aberdeen research group also confirmed previous findings which show some people superior to others in constructing Photo-Fit faces. These differences in ability are difficult to explain, since they are not related to subject differences in ability to image, or to differences in field dependency, or to a general ability to recognize faces.

Since Photo-Fit constructions are influenced by the attitudes and biases held by witnesses toward the suspect and are little better than witness-produced sketches of suspects, their continued use at this time without significant improvement in design must be challenged.

Systematic research on the use of sketch artists and the Identi-Kit as procedures for generating faces is currently being conducted in the U.S. at the University of Houston by Kenneth Laughery and his colleagues (Laughery and Fowler, 1978; Laughery, Duval, and Fowler, 1977). The major findings of this research, which in the main confirms the conclusions of Ellis and his colleagues, may be summarized as follows:

1. Artist sketches are better representations of real faces than Identi-Kit composites.

2. The limiting factor in the use of Identi-Kits is not the skill of the technician, but the inherent weakness of the composite technique itself. Witnesses may have accurate memories and good communication skills, but these assets may be lost because of the deficiencies of the Identi-Kit technique.

3. The quality of images generated by witnesses is best for faces of the same race than for faces of another race.

4. Image generation of faces, either through helping a sketch artist or helping a technician generate an Identi-Kit composite, acts to "stamp in" the long-term memory of the target face. Witnesses are able to make almost perfect identifications of a target face from a set of photographs, six to twelve months after doing the original image generation (Laughery and Fowler, 1977).

Very recent research by the Aberdeen group (Davies, Ellis, and Shepherd, 1978) shows that photographs of celebrities are significantly easier to identify than drawings of these same people. Accuracy of identification increased geometrically with an increase in the amount of detail present in the face. Subjects identified 23% of the faces in simple line outlines, 47% of those in detailed line drawings, and 90% of those in photographs. Similar results also were found with faces of strangers. It may be concluded that line drawings are not equivalent to photographs for identification purposes.

Photographs of faces contain extra information which facilitates identification and is not available in drawings of these same people.

In the last year or two a great amount of publicity has been given to police artist representations of the "Skid Row Slasher" and "Son of Sam." The capture by the New York police in August, 1977 of David Berkowitz, the self-confessed "Son of Sam," was not the result of facial composites (which in retrospect were very poor) or of any brilliant flash of deduction. Instead, Berkowitz, who killed six women in a year-long period of horror, was captured through routine, dull, but meticulous police investigation. A woman tipped off the police that she had seen a man get into a ticketed car the night of the last shooting near the scene of the crime. By searching through parking ticket records, the police eventually found their way to David Berkowitz.

The Lineup

The inaccuracy and injustice of many eyewitness identifications have been documented by numerous jurists and social scientists (see Borchard, 1961; Gilligan, 1972; Levine and Tapp, 1973; Wall, 1965; Williams, 1958). According to the Supreme Court of the United States, "Miscarriages of justice are related to the degree of suggestion inherent in the manner in which the prosecution presents the suspect to the witness for pretrial identification."[1]

In 1967 the Supreme Court dealt with the famous trilogy of cases *United States v. Wade, Gilbert v. California,* and *Stovall v. Denno,* which had to do with the unlikelihood of having a fair trial because of prejudicial witness identification. In *United States v. Wade* the Court ruled that a courtroom identification by a witness who had earlier identified the accused in a lineup without notice to, and in the absence of, counsel was out of order since it violated the accused's Sixth Amendment right to the assistance of counsel.

The cases of *Gilbert v. California* and *Stovall v. Denno* raised similar suggestions of prejudice and the unlikelihood of guaranteeing the right to a fair trial. In *Gilbert v. California,* the Court decided that the lineup was unnecessarily suggestive. Gilbert was identified in a large auditorium by 100 witnesses to different alleged state and federal robberies. In each other's presence, all of the witnesses agreed that he was the man they saw at the scene of their respective crimes. Because of the high possibility of mistaken identification through group suggestion, Gilbert was deemed to have been denied due process of law.

Prejudicial suggestion was also apparent in *Stovall.* The accused, a black, was brought handcuffed to a police officer to a hospital room containing four

---

[1]U.S. v. Wade, 338 U.S. 218 (1967).

other white police officers, two white attendants, and the female victim. In asking the victim to identify the accused in that context, due process may have been denied because the entire situation could have been unnecessarily suggestive and may have led to irreparable misidentification. However, the Court decided that there was no denial of due process in this case. Since the victim was critically hurt and was the sole witness, the necessity for an identification was seen to outweigh the importance of suggestive circumstances.

The *Wade–Gilbert–Stovall* trilogy initiated legislative reform which recognized the lineup as a critical stage in the proceedings against an accused. In addition, the Court stated that the accused has the right to the presence of counsel at such times. This legislation is consistent with established practices of many other nations which also consider the lineup to be a principle point in criminal proceedings. For example, the suspect must be allowed the presence of a solicitor or friend in England and allowed the presence of retained counsel in Germany and France, while in Spain, Mexico, and Italy a judicial officer oversees all identification proceedings and records the proceedings for presentation to the court at trial (Murray, 1966). The operational practices of U.S. state and federal courts since 1967 with respect to the interpretation of this legislation have been a focus of lively comment, but this debate is beyond our scope of interest here (for further discussion see Levine and Tapp, 1973). What still needs emphasis and discussion, however, is the unwarranted trust that police officers, jurors, and the courts persist in giving to lineups and eyewitness identifications (Goldstein, 1977).

A lineup usually consists of a suspect standing among a group of five to nine persons out of whom witnesses attempt to pick the guilty individual. This procedure differs from the showup, which occurred in *Stovall*, in which the witness confronts the suspect in a one-to-one situation. Clearly, the showup has to be the most biased and suggestive procedure for guilt yet devised by the police. The lineup procedure was constructed to overcome gross suggestion, but as we will see, it is not a panacea to be accepted without scrutiny. Following are examples of some of the more obvious abuses that have been committed by the police in conducting unnecessarily suggestive lineups: placing an oriental suspect in a lineup containing only whites; having a suspect in a lineup obviously different in hair color, or height, or weight, or age, or clothing, etc., from all other members of the group; conducting a showup after the witness failed to identify the suspect in a lineup, followed by another lineup before the witness could positively identify the suspect; drawing attention to a particular person by stating, "Look closely at the man on the extreme right"; and allowing a suspect to be verbally identified by one witness in the presence of other witnesses.

The different sources of bias conducive to misidentification in lineups can be classified into four categories: police bias, witness bias, situational bias, and response bias. In the last few years psychologists have become very interested in experimenter bias and subject bias, since these variables can influence the interpretation of results made from scientific experimental studies of human behavior. Valid conclusions and inferences about the causes and effects of behavior cannot be drawn if it is suspected that one or the other bias has contaminated the experiment. Similarly, bias in the conducting of lineup identifications is of concern to the criminal justice system. As Wall (1965) has noted, "A line-up may appear quite reliable to a jury, simply because it was obtained by a procedure which is supposed to be fair" (p. 41).

POLICE BIAS

Lineups are conducted by police officers to test their hypothesis that the arrested suspect can be identified by witnesses. Often the police have the expectation that a witness will be able to confirm their suspicions and spot the guilty party. Although it is the duty of police officers to obtain evidence to convict the guilty, this zeal for duty may act to influence witnesses' decisions in favor of the officers' expectations of guilt. Psychologists refer to this influence as the "Rosenthal effect." The expectations or hypotheses of an authority can influence the behavior of others (see Rosenthal, 1966). Although the effects of such expectations are unintentional, and it may be that neither the police nor witnesses are aware of them, this type of bias may be inherent in eyewitness identifications. Police officers command respect and are authority figures for most persons, and it is likely that the Rosenthal effect can occur. It would be related to the differences in relative status between the police and witnesses as a function of power, prestige, sex, age, and race (see Kintz, Delprado, Mettee, Persons, and Schapee, 1965).

Police bias can also occur when fellow officers participate as decoys in the lineup (Williams and Hammelman, 1963). If the suspect is inserted in the middle of a line of detectives all of whom turn their eyes slightly in the direction of the accused (because they suspect he is guilty) instead of following the normal practice of gazing straight ahead, witnesses cannot help but attend to the suspect (Gilligan, 1972).

A possible solution to this type of bias is the use of double-blind techniques, where neither the officer conducting the lineup nor the witness knows if the suspect actually is in the line. Identification parades in England are conducted by officers who are not part of the investigating team. It is assumed that officers who have no immediate stake in the case are more objective than are the arresting police. Finally, the presence of counsel at the lineup insures that the defense counsel can observe the behavior of his client and the police. The fact that lineups are under observation should act to minimize gross suggestions of any kind. Furthermore, counsel can bring examples of improper influence to the attention of the court.

WITNESS BIAS

Eyewitnesses are generally aware that their testimony is crucial for determination of either guilt or innocence, and most witnesses want to be good citizens by showing the authorities that they can do their duty. Duty may take the form of a witness reacting to the demand characteristics of the situation by being "good" (Orne, 1962) so as to please the officers in charge. Other witnesses may behave in whatever way they feel makes them look bright and attentive (Riecken, 1962). And some witnesses will "faithfully" do whatever is asked of them without questioning any ambiguities in procedure (Fillenbaum, 1966). On occasion, individuals who are both witnesses and victims of attack may feel so angry and upset that they approach the identification as involving a moral obligation to rid society of its depravity. Other victims, however, may be so frightened of the suspect and his friends that they may resist the identification process for fear of reprisal (see Cannavale and Falcon, 1976). None of the witnesses in any of these examples is apt to be aware of the circumstances prejudicial to the alleged criminal. Police officials and the courts cannot prevent witnesses from adopting the various behaviors mentioned above, but defense counsel can at least take them into account in questioning the witness.

SITUATIONAL BIAS

The physical characteristics of the lineup as well as the lighting and noise level of the room can contribute to the biased selection of one of the suspects. Some of the more obvious situational biases, such as the suspect being grossly dissimilar in salient features from other participants, have already been mentioned. Other factors, which may contribute to prejudicial suggestion, are differences in facial expressions, posture, and gait between persons volunteering as distractors in the lineup on the one hand and the accused on the other.

RESPONSE BIAS

A witness may tend to consistently respond to some people in certain ways, such as perceiving them as dangerous, evil, or even guilty; this is response bias. Obviously, participants in a lineup show individual differences in a number of ways and should in theory elicit varied interpersonal reactions from observers. However, some observers will make judgments of guilt or innocence solely on the basis of the facial stereotype that a suspect arouses. A negative facial stereotype is highly correlated with judgments of guilt, and male observers make more of these stereotyped judgments than do female witnesses (Shoemaker, South, and Lowe, 1973). Thus some suspects may just look more like a criminal than others and will be judged so by certain witnesses.

Experimental Investigations of Eyewitness Identification

Many of the hypothesized claims of suggestibility and bias introduced in this chapter have been experimentally validated. The importance of these experiments cannot be understated in view of the present custom of certain countries (e.g., Canada, United States, England and Wales but not Scotland) to convict defendants on the uncorroborated testimony of a single eyewitness.

In one study (Buckhout, Alper, Chern, Silverberg, and Slomovits, 1974), only fourteen of fifty-two witnesses to a staged crime accurately identified a suspect in a lineup held three weeks after the incident. A test for witnesses' ability to verbally describe the suspect immediately after the "crime" showed little difference in verbal recall between witnesses who were successful and those who were unsuccessful in their recognition performance in the lineup.

This experiment required the subjects to view two videotaped lineups of five persons each, one containing the suspect and the other without the suspect. The "blank lineup" showed a look-alike who closely resembled the culprit. Of the fourteen "successful" witnesses who picked the suspect out of the bona fide lineup, seven impeached their performance by also picking a suspect out of the blank lineup (five picked the look-alike). Other results were that 19% of the witnesses failed to make any identification, and 44% identified an innocent person. Even more disconcerting was the finding that the witnesses who impeached themselves had the greatest amount of confidence in their accuracy of identification.

Reportedly, witnesses experience a great deal of stress during lineups. This anxiety could result in misidentification of innocent persons. However, if witnesses were told that the suspect might not be in the lineup, there should be less pressure to choose just any suspect and identifications should be more accurate. To test this hypothesis, Hall and Ostrom (1975) told half of their subjects that the "suspect" they had seen and listened to twenty-four to fifty-six hours earlier in a classroom was present in the lineup (high bias) and told the remaining subjects that he might or might not be present (low bias). The two lineups consisted of six persons, one containing the suspect and the other not showing him. Witnesses were asked to mark a certain box on an identification form if they recognized him; otherwise they were to mark another box labeled "none." Reliable differences in performance were found as a function of the high- and low-bias instructions. Of the witnesses told that the suspect was present, 28% made false identifications, in contrast to only 4% of the unbiased group. High-biased instructions also led to subjects being less accurate when the suspect actually was in the lineup. Overall, witnesses given low-biased instructions were incorrect on only 4% of their selections, in contrast to witnesses given biased instructions, who were inaccurate on 38% of their choices. These results suggest that witnesses are more accurate in making identifications when they are led to believe that the suspect may or may not be present in the lineup.

It is obvious that bias and suggestion can enter the criminal proceedings at many points. For example, in the Edelin trial (see chapter 5) photographs of the dead fetus were introduced and allowed as evidence over the protest of defense counsel. Recent experimental studies confirm the hypothesis that observers (juries) are unduly influenced by such techniques (Garcia and Griffitt, 1978; Oliver and Griffitt, 1976). Experimental evidence also shows that bias can influence identification in mug shot lineups. Subjects witnessed a staged assault and seven weeks later attempted to identify the suspect from a photospread of mug shots. Half of the witnesses were told that the suspect was in the photospread (high-bias instruction), while the remaining subjects were asked if they could recognize any of the facial photographs (low-bias instruction). Half of the witnesses also were given a high-biased condition in which the suspect's photograph was tilted to a slight angle and showed him wearing a different expression relative to the other five facial photographs. The low-bias photospread condition did not show varied expressions or tilt of photographs. The analysis of recognition scores demonstrated that the high-biased instruction–high-biased photospread condition resulted in 61.3% of the witnesses selecting the suspect in contrast to an average of 40% selection for subjects in the other three experimental conditions, i.e., low-biased instruction–high-biased photospread, low-biased photospread–high-biased instruction, and low-biased photospread–low-biased instruction. In addition, 25% of all witnesses mistakenly selected a photograph of an innocent bystander who happened to be in the room at the time of the assault. The effects of bias are so persuasive in this task that even nonwitnesses, who merely heard a description of the crime, picked the suspect from the photospread at a better than chance level of accuracy. These results question the validity of identifications made from memory when social influences can be so powerful (Buckhout, Figueroa, and Hoff, 1975).

Bias can be introduced to the lineup simply by drawing attention to particular physical features such as announcing that the suspect was "good-looking." In one experimental study, this type of instruction produced a significant number of selections of one particular attractive suspect, even by nonwitnesses (Doob and Kirshenbaum, 1973). These biased effects will be even further accentuated if a witness publicly reports to the press or to the police that he remembers certain salient features. A witness is more likely in this case to actively look for an offender who fits the remembered verbal descriptions, such as "good-looking" (Doob and Kirshenbaum, 1973).

MEMORY FOR OTHERS AND THEIR CIRCUMSTANCES

Chapter 6 described a great amount of experimental evidence showing that memory for faces is quite good. But how good is our memory for people and the situational contexts in which they are viewed? Furthermore, does repeatedly viewing a face in different criminal-type circumstances make for a stronger memory trace of that person? These questions have been answered by Deffenbacher, Brown, and Sturgill (1975). Subjects were given a set of faces to study in one room and two hours later in a markedly different room were given a second set of faces. Recognition memory was tested two days later. Subjects were able to correctly identify 96% of the faces but were correct in only 58% (chance performance level was 50%) of their responses in remembering in which room they had viewed each face. The implication of this finding for criminal identification is that witnesses may remember a particular person but not remember whether they saw his picture in the paper, on television, or elsewhere as opposed to seeing him at the scene of the crime.

In a second study Deffenbacher and his colleagues attempted to answer the question given above. Are repeated instances of viewing a particular face in different criminal contexts likely to lead to attaching a greater association of guilt to that person? More specifically, is the identification of a suspect in a lineup differentially influenced by having seen him earlier in a display of mug shots? An experimental test of this hypothesis indicated that indictment rates of criminals viewed in lineups is far from perfect but suspects previously inspected in mug shots are easier to identify than accused people not seen in mug shots. However, suspects who in fact are innocent but are seen in mug shots are much more likely to be falsely identified than persons only viewed in a lineup.

NO SAFETY IN NUMBERS

Just as there is uncertainty about the identification of a suspect based upon the testimony of only one witness, errors can occur in group identification (Williams, 1958). In a recent study, witnesses first gave individual eyewitness reports of a simulated crime and then were put into groups to arrive at a "group recall." The results showed that groups remembered reliably more details of the crime than did individuals (47% vs. 30% accuracy of description), but groups also made more errors of commission. That is, they agreed on and reported 40% more errors in descriptive detail (Alper, Buckhout, Chern, Harwood, and Slomovits, 1976). In a subsequent study (Rupp, Warmbrand, Karash, and Buckhout, 1976), it was shown that witnesses who discuss the crime among themselves do not benefit in making lineup identifications. In fact, discussions have the negative effect of influencing some witnesses to change their descriptions to fit innocent decoys present in the lineup.

It may be concluded on the basis of experimental evidence that mistaken identity from lineups is often the rule and not the exception.

Police as Eyewitnesses

Are policemen more reliable as witnesses than the ordinary man on the street? Apparently not, according to a series of studies conducted in Britain and the U.S. Although the police themselves believe that their training and practical experiences develop a superior ability to observe and remember details, experimental evidence fails to confirm this claim (Clifford, 1976). And, experiments suggest that policemen are more prone to committing interpretive errors in their perceptions of people and activities.

First of all, the capacity of memory of police, or more specifically the amount of information that a policeman can attend to and remember at any one time, is not different from that of nonpolice. In an experiment testing how much policemen and policewomen can retain from face-to-face and TV briefing sessions, six or seven bits of information were remembered (Bull and Reid, 1975). This performance is typical of the memory capacity of most people.

Since the police are set to look for actions of a particular sort—traffic violations, break-ins, theft, and so on—it is possible that they are superior to ordinary citizens in memory for people and events. Although this hypothesis has intuitive appeal, it has not been confirmed (Tickner and Poulton, 1975). Twenty-four police officers and 156 civilians were shown films of a street scene for one, two, or four hours. Their task was to watch for various wanted people and certain kinds of actions, i.e., theft, normal exchange of goods, and general antisocial actions, which had been inserted into the film. Photographs of the wanted persons were displayed continuously beneath the screen. In one condition, the observers were shown a warning film on the wanted persons before being shown the main film.

The results showed that only 31% of the wanted persons could be detected even though their photographs were displayed continuously under the screen. Preparing the witnesses for the wanted persons by showing them a preliminary film of the relevant people only raised the detection level to 41%. No significant differences were found between police and civilian observers in their ability to identify suspects. More important, however, was the significantly greater tendency for police officers to report more *alleged* thefts than did the civilian observers. In true detection of people and actions, there was no reliable difference between the police and nonpolice.

In a second investigation, a sequel to the above study, identification of people at night proved to be more difficult, as you would expect. Although the percentages of identifications at night and in daylight were comparable, at night witnesses had to be twice as close to the suspects to make accurate identifications (Simmonds, Poulton, and Tickner, 1975).

The theoretical view that perception and memory processes are selective and reflect what the observer attends to and what he expects to perceive helps to explain errors of omission and commission. Policemen are especially prone, it seems, to see suspicious behavior as intent to commit crime and may justify these perceptions by remembering events that have not happened (Marshall, 1966). The police are much more likely than civilians to misinterpret events because of their training and past experiences.

The biasing influence of expectations which can result in misinterpretations by the police is shown in a study by Verinis and Walker (1970). Ten policemen and ten schoolteachers were shown eleven photographs for ten seconds each. After each photograph was removed, subjects were asked to report all the details that they had seen and to interpret each scene. Eight of these photographs had "criminal" details built into them, such as "a car parked in a back alley with bent-up license plates, with the bent license plates being the 'criminal' detail." The criminal details had been categorized *a priori* by a panel of three policemen as situations which would arouse suspicion of possible crime. Results showed that policemen and teachers recalled the same number of "criminal" details, but the police gave more criminal interpretations to the pictures. For example, a man walking round a corner carrying a can was interpreted by civilians as having run out of gas and looking for a gas station. The police perceived the man as an arson suspect.

Not all policemen, however, were so quick to interpret activities as criminalistic. This finding deserves emphasis, since it argues against the notion of a "paranoid" police force. Only some, not all, policemen are "set" to perceive crime in the street and community. Moreover, the more cautious officer, who made fewer interpretations, was evaluated more favorably by his immediate superior.

In summary, it may be concluded that the police are not better than ordinary citizens at perceiving and remembering people and real-life events. Second, police are more likely to misinterpret events and see criminal behavior where it does not exist. As policemen are frequent witnesses in the courtroom, the quality of their testimony must be evaluated as closely as that of nonpolice witnesses, especially since they are held in such high esteem by the public and jurors.

We can see that the verbal and visual descriptions of eyewitnesses depend upon a large number of factors which have not been fully appreciated in criminal identifications to date. Obviously, further research is needed to clarify all the issues of eyewitness identification. Our work has just begun.

Chapter 8

On the Witness Stand: Truth and Credibility

Since the turn of the century psychology has attempted to assist the courts in the evaluation of testimony. One man in particular, Hugo Munsterberg, can be cited for his outstanding contributions to this end, and this chapter is addressed in part to his early work, which is now only being rediscovered.

Very few students of criminal justice have not experienced or at least heard about staged murders in which the class is asked to describe the victim and the assailant. Münsterberg (1908) described one of the first of these demonstrations:

> There was, for instance, two years ago in Gottingen a meeting of a scientific association, made up of jurists, psychologists, and physicians—all, therefore, men well trained in careful observation. Somewhere in the same street there was that evening a public festivity of the carnival. Suddenly, in the midst of the scholarly meeting, the doors open, a clown in highly colored costume rushes in in mad excitement, and a Negro with a revolver in hand follows him. In the middle of the hall first the one, then the other, shouts wild phrases; then the one falls to the ground, the other jumps on him; then a shot, and suddenly both are out of the room. The whole affair took less than twenty seconds. All were completely taken by surprise, and no one, with the exception of the President, had the slightest idea that every word and reaction had been rehearsed beforehand, or that photographs had been taken of the scene. It seemed most natural that the President should beg the members to write down individually an exact report, inasmuch as he felt sure that the matter would come before the courts. Of the forty reports handed in, there was only one whose omissions were calculated as amounting to less than 20 percent of the characteristic acts; fourteen had 20 to 40 percent of the facts omitted; twelve omitted 40 to 50 percent, and thirteen more than 50 per-

cent. But besides the omissions there were only six among the forty which did not contain positively wrong statements; in twenty-four papers up to 10 percent of the statements were free inventions, and in ten answers—that is, in one fourth of the papers more than 10 percent of the statements were absolutely false, in spite of the fact that they all came from scientifically trained observers . . . [pp. 51–53]

This study and its many replications in hundreds of college classrooms show that much of witnesses' testimony is faulty. The inaccuracy often occurs through misperceptions, distortions of memory, or even failure to adequately communicate. Witnesses reputed to be honest and truthful often vary widely from each other in the testimony they give. It was Münsterberg's hope that psychologists could assist the courts by testing the perceptual and memory capabilities of eyewitnesses and even the truth of their statements and thereby facilitate the evaluation of testimony.

The courts did not readily open their doors to Münsterberg or to other experimental psychologists as expert witnesses, in contrast to the trust they put in psychiatrists and, more recently, in clinical psychologists. Nevertheless, experimental research on such matters as truth and lying, credibility, and other matters of importance to the criminal justice system has continued since Münsterberg and does have an indirect but delayed influence on the system.

What Is Truth?

Before introducing the discussion of psychological procedures to detect witness deception, I would like to address briefly some of the different philosophical interpretations of the meaning of truth.

Starting with early Greek philosophy, we find Plato arguing that absolute truth is innately available in all of us. Nativism is the philosophical label given to this theory. Plato suggests that by freeing ourselves from the distortions created by sensory experiences and accepting only knowledge gained through introspection and self-analysis, we can recollect the inherent truths or *a priori* ideas that the mind possesses (see Baumrin, 1975).

In contrast to this rationalistic approach empiricists, such as Bacon in the seventeenth century, argued that truth could only be found through direct sensory observation, collection, and verification of facts. By the careful arrangement of facts into tables, it was believed, laws and even universal truths could be revealed. Apparently, Bacon never realized that observations (facts) in themselves are not pure elements, but instead are always selected by the observer according to his needs and interests. That is, the act of perception is an ongoing, selective process which is markedly influenced by the perceiver's past social history and his motivations and feelings at the time of perception.

Another problem that philosophers throughout history have grappled with is the issue of absolute truth and relative truth. "Absolute truth" refers to the belief in a final explanation which cannot be wrong. For some people "absolute truth" represents a faith in an omniscient God who would not deceive us with mere illusions. For others, "absolute truth" refers to the belief that science will ultimately reveal all of the mysteries of the universe.

In contrast to this position, naturalists (e.g., John Dewey) and dialectical materialists (e.g., Karl Marx) claim that all truth is relative to specific situations. According to Dewey, ideas are plans of action to test a specific problem in a specific situation. Insofar as an idea solves a problem, the knowledge gained is true for that specific situation. Thus truth is relative to specific problems, and there are as many truths as there are correct solutions to problems.

Marxists, on the other hand, insist that truth emerges from nature only when people control their environment well enough to produce predictable consequences. Since nature or matter is constantly changing, truth must by necessity also change accordingly. Those persons who control matter or production must also control what is true. Thus truth in this philosophical theory is a practical problem concerned with action.

When ordinary citizens enter the courtroom, there is an expectation that truth and justice will prevail. Most people, I believe, share the philosophical positions of naive realism and objective idealism. We are realists to the extent that we believe that what we see, touch, or hear is real and is not some philosophical mystery. If sensory information is ambiguous, we trust the reports of others. Thus public consensus guides our behavior when we are in doubt. At the same time, we are idealists and accept the fact that truth is concerned with ideas. For ideas to be true, they must have some kind of utility and some kind of consequences for behavior (Attneave, 1974). We believe or "know" that the physical world is real. Objective idealism is the interpretation we give of reality. Truth enters the picture to the extent that the interpretation is consistent and comprehensive.

As a group most psychologists and other social scientists make do with naive and simple views of the meaning of truth. Truth is rational and empirically derived. Other scientists, such as nuclear physicists, have abandoned the notion that truth must be rationally justified. They feel that truth deals with the description of an invisible theoretical world.

In the tradition of Karl Popper's (1959, 1963, 1972) philosophy, the law searches for truth from the problems presented in the courtroom. Possible solutions are proposed and refutations attempted. If the charges withstand criticism and all reasonable doubts are removed, then the courts require a decision of guilt. This approach does not prove that truth exists; instead, the law admits that man is prone to error and strives to approach objective truth by challenging and cross-examining each testifier.

The implication of this discussion for the criminal justice system is the realization that the meaning of truth can be analyzed and appreciated from different viewpoints. For the individual, truth is acquired from both sensory information and the different ways that the human nervous system has been genetically determined to deal with sensory experiences. Individuals are also parts of groups, societies, and cultures. Truth must operate and emerge both within and between all of these separate levels. It is little wonder, then, that the concept "truth" is seldom understood and equally shared by all people.

Detection of Truth and Lying

Historically, private justice between two parties was reached through fighting. Later, man decided to find justice through trial by battle, trial by ordeal, and trial by oath. Trial by jury did not appear until the eleventh century in England. Gradually, over time, witnesses became part of the trial procedure. The problem then, as it is now, was to determine the truth and credibility of testimony (see Curtis, 1958).

Most lawyers and jurists appear to subscribe to the belief that "cross-examination is the greatest touchstone of truth ever devised" (Thomas, 1965, p. 247). While the power of cross-examination to reveal truth is to be acknowledged, faulty cross-examination is dangerous and can lead to miscarriage of justice (Thomas, 1965).

The search for truth, however, can be carried on by several means. One relatively recent practice is the calling of psychiatrists and psychologists as expert witnesses to assist in the appraisal of the competency of witnesses (Davidson, 1954). No doubt the use of clinical opinion lends an air of authority and expertise to the courtroom. Furthermore, in the evaluation of certain phenomena such as Freud's concept of "psychological denial," the knowledge and experience of clinicians would be superior to mere intuitions of judges in deciding whether a witness is telling the truth. But psychological diagnoses are often inaccurate, and as Rosenhan (1973) so critically demonstrated, psychiatrists do not have any clear criteria for distinguishing the psychotic from the normal (let alone determining truth from falsehood). Unfortunately, experimental psychology cannot step into the breach and offer any substantive instruments either to force people to speak the truth or to let us all know exactly when they are lying. Nevertheless, some recent investigations are worthy of consideration, since they indicate that deception may be detected by experimental procedures.

Before turning to this evidence, it is important to emphasize the qualitative differences among types of lies. Except for pathological liars and other emotionally disturbed persons who have lost contact with reality, normal persons may be honestly mistaken, ignorant, or prejudiced rather than deliberate perjurors. Most of this book has in some way or other described the "honest" witness. In this section the focus of attention will be on the person who deliberately lies and distorts evidence.

Thomas (1965), a criminal lawyer, states that the earmarks of perjury are evident when witnesses exhibit two or more of the following signs:

> . . .when the witness (1) manifests much zeal on behalf of the party calling him; (2) is forgetful of facts as to which he knows that he is open to contradictions; (3) "balloons" or exaggerates circumstances; (4) proceeds with his answers without waiting to hear the question; (5) remembers facts very minutely as to which he knows that he is not open to contradictions; (6) reluctantly gives adverse testimony; (7) replies flippantly or evasively; (8) seeks additional time to consider the effect of his answer by using such devices as pretending not to hear the question; (9) affects indifference; (10) often protests his honesty, vows before God, and the like. . . . [p. 257]

Whether or not these signs are guidelines to detect the perjurer clearly or are manifestations of honest but misdirected and overly passionate citizens cannot be judged as a general principle. Instead, let us look at some of the evidence gathered by psychologists.

The Effects of Social Influences

Jurisprudence assumes that witnesses, judges, and juries can recognize the truth without being unduly influenced by social pressures to ignore or distort evidence. This assumption, however, runs counter to scores of experimental studies on the effects of social influences on judgment and perception. The classical studies in this field belong to Solomon Asch (1956) and to Muzafer Sherif (1935). In the Asch study subjects were given the relatively easy task of judging the similarity of lengths of lines. However, the task didn't appear so easy to subjects who had to give their decision immediately after hearing four other individuals (all of whom were confederates of the experimenter) give patently incorrect and indefensible responses. The subjects found themselves in the dilemma of trusting their own perceptions of reality or conforming to social pressure and choosing the line the others had chosen. Asch found that approximately one-third of the subjects yielded to group pressures on approximately one-third of all trials. Interviews with subjects who conformed to pressure indicated that half of them were aware of the perceptual discrepancy but confessed that they couldn't stand the pressure. The other half of the conformers claimed not to have noticed any perceptual discrepancies. Whether or not these subjects actually saw what they reported is unknown, but their behavior suggests that some people are influenced by and will conform to the subtle pressures of group norms.

In a similar vein, Sherif (1935) demonstrated that when individuals interact with one another, particularly in ambiguous situations, they tend to develop mutually accepted standards of beliefs, attitudes, and perceptions. Such adopted standards tend to persist and direct behavior when the individual is alone and in another ambiguous situation.

It could be argued that experimental studies represent artificial conditions which may have little direct relevance for courtroom behavior. Perhaps under more realistic situations witnesses are more highly motivated to tell the truth. This criticism is valid, since all generalizations from the laboratory to the real world have to be made with caution. Nevertheless, the court cannot afford to dismiss all laboratory evidence as irrelevant.

Encouraging witnesses to speak the truth regardless of the social pressure to do otherwise still seems to fall short of the mark. In an experimental investigation designed to encourage "truth and objectivity," subjects were given three lectures stressing how science seeks the truth and how experimenters must present the facts "as they see them" without regard to personal beliefs or social influences. Following the lectures subjects were told that they would be given a quiz to test their commitment to telling the truth. In an attempt to even further strengthen their adherence to the truth ethic, half of the subjects were given specific instructions to tell the truth regardless of any subtle or overt pressures to the contrary. The quiz consisted of Asch-type judgments of lengths of lines. The results showed that in spite of all the experimental treatments to encourage truth reports, subjects still yielded to the social pressures of the group and ignored the obvious perceptual discrepancies in the situation (Luchins and Luchins, 1968).

THE OVEREAGER WITNESS

The importance of historical significance or being important in the eyes of the police often has perilous consequences for criminal justice. It appears that some people will claim to be eyewitnesses although it is proved later that they were nowhere near the incident when it occurred (Hutchins and Slesinger, 1928). Apparently, the motivation to be part of history, to be a participant in an official police case, especially one which is highly publicized, is a powerful drive which pushes some people to perjury. One example of such a motivation is the following anecdote (Buckhout, 1976). A journalist published through a newspaper wire service a fabricated human-interest story about life in a small town. Apparently, a naked woman had got herself stuck to a newly painted toilet. Following the publication of the story, several citizens came forward claiming they had been eyewitnesses to the event.

TRANKELL'S HYPOTHESIS

A sophisticated attempt to detect witness deception by testing witnesses statements against the knowledge of the reliability of evidence has been proposed by Arne Trankell (1972), a Scandinavian psychologist. Trankell starts with the assumption that evaluation of eyewitness testimony depends more upon what the witness says and the context in which the reports are made than upon the personality factors of the witness. Truth of testimony is a relative process dependent upon both the courtroom situation and the personality of the witness. Thus what an individual testifies to in court may vary over different appearances in the witness stand and between statements made outside and inside the court. It is a gross error to assume that witnesses are constantly trustworthy over time and over varied contexts and are immune to the different social pressures of these contexts.

When two witnesses give opposite or incompatible descriptions of the same event, it is possible that both are telling the truth from their perspective. Trankell argues that we should be concerned with determining which statements best fit the actual event rather than bog down in a deliberation of who speaks the truth. One way to solve this problem is to systematically study and search for "criteria of reality" in the testimonial statements presented.

True statements may be distinguished from statements which are invented or are distortions of real events by reality criteria and control criteria. Reality criteria function to test the validity of what the witness claims as truth, and control criteria function to test the probability that alternative hypotheses are false. Each type of criteria is analyzed formally through an examination of the logical structure of a witness's statements and concretely by isolation of the contents of the statements.

For example, our knowledge of memory processes leads us to expect that certain organizational and encoding changes will occur in the reconstruction of events. If, in the giving of testimony, a witness's reports are consistent with what memory theorists expect to occur in verbal recall (reality criteria), we can have confidence in the statements as "attempts to describe what happened." The greater the number of reality criteria that an investigator has to compare with a witness's statements, the greater the possible level of confidence attached. Control criteria, on the other hand, function like control treatments in any scientific investigation. Since alternative explanations should have no direct relation to the event in question, they should work to complement reality criteria through the process of relative comparisons.

NONVERBAL CUES TO LYING

A witness's reports may represent truth but not the whole truth for a number of reasons. Deceit and truth may be so intertwined in verbal communication that they are impossible to separate and differentiate. However, communication is not solely a verbal process; nonverbal communication often expresses the feelings of a communicator who is unable or unwilling to verbally state his thoughts. Over the last few years a number of empirical studies have examined the relationship between nonverbal behaviors and deceit. We know, for example, that when a person lies, he or she gesticulates less and displays fewer positive head nods. Furthermore, a deceitful communicator makes more frequent errors in speech, talks less in total number of words, and speaks at a slower rate (Rosenfeld, 1966).

Nevertheless, a word of caution is in order. In spite of the confidence that the average person has in his or her ability to detect liars by their nonverbal behaviors, there is little justification in the research literature to support such beliefs (see Hocking, Miller, and Fontes, 1978). If untrained observers, such as the typical juror, make decisions about the truth of a witness's statements solely on the basis of his stuttering or eye contact, etc., their accuracy of judgments will probably be no better than chance. As we will see, the research evidence is complex and full of ambiguities.

In an experimental study of deceitful and truthful communicators, Mehrabian (1971) showed that deceit and truth may be differentiated by the following behaviors:

1. Deceit is associated with long eye contact rather than with high frequency of eye shifts.

2. Deceit is not associated with postural relaxation, but rather with stiffness and rigidity of posture.

3. In general, deceit is related to pleasant facial expressions. However, this finding is conditional upon the anxiety level of the communicators. High-anxious communicators who are deceitful exhibit few smiles, whereas low-anxious deceitful communicators readily smile. When high-anxious communicators are being truthful, they smile more frequently than do low-anxious truthful communicators.

Deception may also be differentiated by other subtle nonverbal cues. Investigations show that facial expressions are closely monitored during verbal communication by both the speaker and the listener for suggestions of insincerity or lack of confidence. When a speaker attends closely to his own facial expressions, his feet and legs often communicate a conflicting message. The feet and legs frequently shift in agitation when deceitful messages are being controlled through facial expressions (Ekman and Friesen, 1969; Schneider and Kintz, 1977). Liars also use fewer gesticulating hand movements and have higher-pitched voices (Ekman, Friesen, and Scherer, 1976).

Eye contact also has been one of the major nonverbal clues to human deceit. Argyle and Dean (1965) found that when two people like each other, they have longer and more frequent eye contacts than when there is tension in their relationship. We assume that honest people will look us straight in the eye, and if we suspect that a person is insincere or deceitful, we quickly notice his shifty eyes. Experimental research tends to support this folklore. Subjects known to have behaved unethically make less eye contact with interviewers following a transgression than before the incident (Exline, Thibaut, Hickey, and Gumpert, 1970).

The complexity involved in making generalizations about deceit on the basis of eye contact can be seen in studies looking at sex differences and nonverbal behavior. Counter to a common belief, females do not engage in more eye gazing than do males. Females maintain longer eye contact with both males and females when lying than when telling the truth. Females gaze longer at males than other females when lying. Males gaze longer into the eyes of females when lying but show similar lengths of eye contact during truth telling and lying when looking at another male (Burns and Kintz, 1976).

An interesting question is whether verbal cues, facial cues, or paralinguistic cues are dominant in the detection of truth and lying. An experiment by Littlepage and Pineault (1977) provides evidence that facial cues are the least important source for the perception of truth. Subjects were shown videotaped segments of the television program "To Tell the Truth" and were required to judge which of the three participants being questioned was truthful. Four experimental conditions were investigated: (1) total information as shown in regular television viewing; (2) only hearing the voices of the three participants; (3) seeing the participants but hearing a dubbed-in voice which controlled for paralinguistic cues; and (4) only seeing the contestants and not hearing what they said. Results showed that only hearing the voices of the participants was almost as accurate as receiving total information. Similarly, removal of paralinguistic information by the use of dubbed voices resulted in only a slight drop in accuracy of detection. Seeing but not hearing the contestants resulted in the lowest accuracy scores of all four conditions. Thus the most important cues to the perception of truth were provided by listening to the speeches, while visual cues had little or no effect on accuracy.

It has been suggested that observers watching and listening to a speaker may suffer from a handicap of information overload. If observers are looking for deception cues, they may become distracted from listening to the verbal content of the testimony. This hypothesis has been supported by the research of Maier and Thurber (1968). Observers judged the truthfulness of a two-person role-playing situation where honest and dishonest interactions were presented in one of three conditions: watching and hearing the interviews, hearing a tape recording, or reading a written transcript. Results showed that observers simply hearing the tape or reading the transcripts of the exchanges were more accurate (77.3% and 77% respectively) at judging truth than observers who both saw and heard the testimony (58.3%). Clearly, this study and the research by Littlepage and Pineault (1977) indicate that the verbal content of testimony is more important in judging veracity than accompanying nonverbal cues.

In short, liars do behave differently than persons who are not behaving deceptively. However, naive observers are not consistently accurate in detecting deception (Kraut, 1978). Some people, for reasons not yet understood, "look like" they are lying when they are not, while others consistently give the impression that they are telling the truth. One study found that a truthful witness was judged to be lying by 74.3 percent of 715 observers, while a lying witness was considered truthful by 73.7 percent of the observers (Hocking et al., 1978). If jurors base their decisions of honesty or lying on their reading of nonverbal behaviors, justice cannot and will not be met.

Lie Detectors

The use of technical aids to uncover deception is hardly new; psychophysiological techniques have been employed for over 2,000 years (Trovillo, 1939). One of the earliest methods of detection derived by primitive witch doctors involved the eating of rice (Eysenck, 1964). People suspected of a crime were told that the guilty person would have difficulty in swallowing a bowl of rice, whereas those who were innocent would eat the rice with relative ease. The heightened use of suggestion, combined with the physiological fact that fear or any strong emotion like guilt acts to dry the mouth to make swallowing difficult, often worked to detect the villain (as well as trapping frightened but innocent victims).

POLYGRAPH

Modern techniques of lie detection do not differ much in principle from historical practices. It is assumed that the guilty person will react differently from the innocent in response to certain critical questions and his autonomic physiological reactions (e.g., heart rate, blood pressure, respiration, degree of sweating) to these questions will be detectable by a polygraph.

Until recently the courts have not accepted these types of indicators as legitimate evidence; however, some judges now permit the testimony of polygraphers to be read into the records as facts (Lykken, 1975). This decision, of course, is the court's prerogative and reflects a growing confidence in the accuracy of such "psychological assessments." Polygraph tests have become big business. This direction may be disturbing and perhaps dangerous when it is realized that very few professional polygraphers have more than a minimal training in physiological psychology and even fewer are qualified psychologists. Before we can endorse such examinations as valid and reliable diagnoses of deception, a stronger scientific foundation based upon both laboratory investigations and field investigations must be established (Podlesny and Raskin, 1977).

Contemporary lie-detection literature suggests that within certain specified limits physiological measures of deception do have scientific support. Two basic methods are usually followed in the traditional lie-detector test: deception tests and information tests. Tests of deception are based upon a series of questions relevant to the crime being investigated along with a number of irrelevant questions, such as "Are you wearing shoes?" Significant differences in physiological responses to the relevant and irrelevant items allow the examiner to make inferences of deception. The major weakness of this approach is that both the innocent parties and guilty persons know and are sensitive to the relevant questions. Consequently, the problem of stimulus saliency may be so powerful as to obviate the operations of control stimuli.

A more successful procedure is the control question technique (Barland and Raskin, 1973; Reid and Inbau, 1966). Control questions are designed specifically to have emotional connotations which are likely to arouse feelings of guilt or anxiety. For instance, a control question in an assault case would be "Have you ever hit or injured your mother?" If the subject is truthful on relevant questions, he should show more concern over the control questions and produce greater autonomic reactions to them than to the relevant items. In contrast, the deceptive subject, although attempting to control his reactions to relevant questions, should still show more physiological alarm over relevant items than over control questions. Since deception is not characterized by a distinctive physiological response, the interpretations made from polygraph results must be made with caution.

Information tests such as those using the guilty-knowledge technique (Lykken, 1959, 1960) differ from deception tests by assuming that only the guilty person knows certain answers directly associated with the crime. It is assumed that when he or she is confronted with questions touching on this knowledge, differential autonomic responding will be evoked from the guilty party. Innocent suspects, however, should not perceive a particular circumstance as critical and should show relatively equivalent reactions to each alternative offered.

The following illustration is typical of the guilty-knowledge technique. Suppose that the police learn from their investigation that the man who held up the Fast Loan Company told the manager moments before the robbery that he wanted a loan to buy a car. This information would be used then by the polygraph examiner in formulating his questions to suspects. For example, he might say, "The man we want held up a loan office. If you are the robber you will know the name of that company. I am going to read aloud the names of a few loan companies and I want you to repeat each name after me. Was it the Green Loan Company? The City Loan Company? The Easy Loan Company? The Fast Loan Company? The Future Loan Company?

"Okay, here is my second question. The bandit got into the manager's office by claiming he wanted a loan for a certain reason. If you are this man, you will know whether he said he wanted to buy some furniture, buy a car, pay off his taxes, get a stereo, or go on a vacation. I want you to repeat after me each of these possibilities as I call them out. . . ."

Only the person committing the crime would know this information and react differentially to the true statement. An innocent person would not know which alternative was critical and would have only one chance in five on each item that his strongest physiological response would be evoked by the true item. If by chance he did react more strongly to the critical item on question 1, the chances that he would repeat this reaction on ten guilty-knowledge items of this sort is only one in ten million. Provided that the police can discover enough private information about a particular crime that only the guilty person would know, this test promises to be a useful detection technique.

How accurate are these tests, and how confident should we be with the results of field testing? First of all it should be mentioned that two sorts of errors are possible. One, an innocent person who either is afraid of the test or does not believe in its validity may produce autonomic responses similar to those of a deceptive suspect. Second, it is possible that a psychopath or individual who is unusually unresponsive may go undetected although guilty. Research also indicates that results can be deliberately distorted by subjects learning how to block or inhibit their amount of sweating (Dean, Martin and Streiner, 1968) or by merely tensing their toe muscles (Smith, 1967).

One measure of the accuracy of polygraphers is the testimony of professional polygraph examiners. Not surprisingly, extremely high validities have been claimed for the conventional lie-detection methods, e.g., 92% (Bersh, 1969), 99% (Arther, 1965), and 100% (Kubis, 1950). Confidence in the worth of one's own contribution may be a virtue, but exactly how these claims can be justified is uncertain. Few polygraphers keep records to show what the correlations are between their decisions of guilt or innocence and the decisions of the courts (Inbau and Reid, 1953; Lykken, 1975). Even if we assume that a high correlation does exist, we still haven't proved the claim. That a court makes a particular decision does not in itself prove the accuracy of the polygraph examination. Professional polygraphers, to be sure, play an important role in the detection of guilty persons either through convincing suspects to confess (Thornwald, 1967) or through their skill in interpreting recordings at a much better than chance level of diagnosis. However, being better than chance is not the same as being infallible, which sometimes is claimed (see Lykken, 1975).

Although laboratory studies are not valid measures of field lie-detector tests, recent studies provide evidence that with control question techniques several indicators (e.g., differential increases in skin resistance, skin conductance and skin potential, decreases in heart rate) are valid criteria of deception (Barland and Raskin, 1975; Raskin, 1975). Unfortunately, few studies have evaluated the validity of the guilty-knowledge technique; however, those that have been conducted (Ben Shakhar, Lieblich, and Kugelmass, 1970; Davidson, 1968; Lykken, 1959, 1960) support its promise as an accurate detection technique. More recently, Lieblich, Ben Shakhar, and Kugelmass (1976) demonstrated that the guilty-knowledge technique may be efficiently employed with criminals and not just the college sophomore who is typically studied in laboratory experiments.

Expert evaluation of the validity of laboratory studies on lie-detector tests indicates that these tests are accurate about 70% to 85% of the time, which is considerably better than a chance expectancy of from 20% to 50% (Lykken, 1974). The best estimation of performance in field situations is about 90% accuracy (Lykken, 1974).

Field investigations, however, are never based solely on readings of the polygraph records. Examiners rely heavily upon their subjective assessments of other behaviors of suspects both prior to and during examinations. In addition, polygraph records of deceptive suspects and records of honest suspects differ in their ease of interpretation. One study, for example, found that field-trained evaluators making judgments only from polygraph records (and not interviewing the suspects) were more accurate, more confident, and found records more interpretable when they came from deceptive subjects than when they came from truthful suspects (Horvath, 1977).

The conclusion we can draw from these evaluations is that testimonial evidence based upon the polygrapher's diagnosis must be regarded as tentative and not as absolute. In the best of all possible situations the interpretation will be inaccurate approximately 10% of the time (Lykken, 1975).

VOICE IDENTIFICATION

In the last few years, the voiceprint method of identification has begun to interest law enforcement agencies, and promoters of this technique are putting increasing pressure on the courts to accept its validity as an identification tool (Jones, 1973). In addition, other entrepreneurs are attempting to sell the business world and the courts on a technique to detect lying through a device called the voice-stress analyzer.

The theory of voice identification by the voiceprint technique is that each person has a unique style of speaking because of the anatomy of his vocal apparatus and the manner in which he uses his teeth, tongue, and lips. By listening to the recordings of a voice and looking at the visual records of that voice on a sound spectrogram, it is claimed, trainer-operators can reliably differentiate whether two voices are those of the same person or not. The primary developer of this technique, Lawrence Kersta (1962), claims an accuracy of 99%, based upon his own laboratory studies. The scientific community of experts in acoustics, linguistics, and phonetics have not accepted these claims of reliability. In addition, the Technical Committee of the Speech Communications Section of the Acoustical Society of America has stated that "reliable machine methods for voice identification have not yet been established" (Jones, 1973).

Lie detection by the voice-stress analyzer technique is similar in many ways to the polygraph but has the advantage of being more convenient and simpler to carry out. However, critics claim that it is less reliable than the polygraph. The theory of voice-stress analysis is that a speaker's voice changes under stress. The changes are reflected in the voice by vibrations or microtremors which are collected by a tape recorder and analyzed by an electronic processor. The machine is said to detect changes in electric energy that are associated with stress in the speaker. On the basis of the machine's recordings, an operator interprets the results to indicate lying or truth.

How valid are voice analyzers? The few studies that are available indicate that the voice-stress analyzer technique ranges in accuracy scores from pure chance to manufacturers' claims of 95% to 99% accuracy (Rice, 1978). When voice analyzers were used with actual criminal suspects, who either confessed later to their guilt or were found guilty or innocent by the courts, voice analyzers were successful in only 50% to 60% of the cases, which is not much better than chance (Rice, 1978). And finally, Horvath (1978) compared evaluations made by two trained technicians on a voice-mediated lie detector, the Psychological Stress Evaluator (PSE), and a standard field polygraph instrument for analyzing galvanic skin response (GSR). Accuracy scores for the PSE analysis were no better than chance, whereas evaluations made from GSR analyzers generally exceeded chance levels. It may be concluded that the PSE is not effective in detecting deception.

Although voiceprints are easily obtained through telephone bugs and hidden recorders and the technique of voice-stress analysis is relatively simple, it is hoped that law enforcement officers and the courts are not blinded by efficiency and so sacrifice scientific accuracy, not to mention our civil liberties.

TRUTH SERUM

Any attempt to discover truth through the use of so-called truth drugs such as sodium pentothal should be discouraged, since it does not produce the desired results. Attorneys should be aware that sodium pentothal, like other anaesthetics, acts to relax and lower a person's resistance but does not guarantee truth telling, and in fact evidence shows that people can still lie while under the influence of the drug (Frank, 1966). People also may confess while under the influence of the drug but will only confess if they want to anyway (McMahon, 1977).

HYPNOSIS

On July 15, 1976, twenty-six children and their bus driver were kidnapped in Chowchilla, California, by three armed masked men. Sixteen hours later the captives escaped from an abandoned trailer truck hidden about six feet underground. Questioning of the children and driver failed to yield any significant clues about the three men. To facilitate the investigation, the FBI called in an expert on medical hypnosis, Dr. William S. Kroger. Under hypnosis the bus driver recalled all but one digit of the license plate on the kidnapper's van. This information, which was unavailable from normal questioning, assisted in the capture of the three suspects (*Time*, September 13, 1976).

Hypnosis is an important investigative tool of the police in Los Angeles and in Israel. The Israeli National Police Force has a team of trained hypnotists who reportedly solved twenty-five cases and assisted in sixty other investigations between 1972 and 1976. The Los Angeles Police Department has used hypnosis extensively since 1970 and is fully convinced of its usefulness. The police admit, however, that hypnosis is not infallible and any information uncovered has to be verified. Furthermore, it is the court that makes the ultimate decision whether or not to allow testimony of witnesses whose memories were cued through hypnosis. In the opinion of many people hypnosis is a credible instrument, particularly in its use as a clinical tool in psychiatry and medicine. Nevertheless, scientists are still undecided on what hypnosis is and what it means (see Goleman, 1977).

"Hypnosis is said to exist when suggestions from one individual seemingly alter the perceptions and memories of another" (Orne, 1971). Although the word "hypnosis" is derived from the Greek word for sleep (*hypnos*), the state of hypnosis does not resemble the brain activity (EEG recordings) of sleep or other physical measures of sleep such as respiration and heart rate. Thus hypnosis is somewhat more similar to the normal waking state. Two characteristics best typify the nature of hypnosis (see Hilgard, 1965, 1970). The first is a heightened suggestibility; the second is posthypnotic amnesia, in which the events which occurred during hypnosis are forgotten on instruction from the hypnotist.

The most interesting feature of hypnosis for our purposes is the suggestion that hypnotic age regression is possible. Reiff and Scheerer (1959) demonstrated that a deeply hypnotized person told that he is 10, 7, and 4 will show cognitive and motor behaviors appropriate to children of these ages. Furthermore, it is claimed that such regressions allow adults to accurately recover information they had stored as children and otherwise would not remember (Solomon and Goodson, 1971).

Skeptics about hypnotic age regression suggest that adults do not actually remember how they performed at these ages, but, instead, are simply play acting. According to one authority, subjects under hypnosis sometimes "remember" events which have not occurred (Orne, 1975). Experimental studies comparing a group of subjects who simulated hypnosis with a group of hypnotized subjects show that simulators also are able to show dramatic feats of memory far beyond what would normally be expected (O'Connell, Shor, and Orne, 1970).

What can we say, then, of the police use of hypnosis as an investigative tool? We can conclude that scientists are not yet sure what this phenomenon is, beyond the fact that it is a useful mechanism for altering memory states. It is possible that hypnosis assists in the recall of otherwise forgotten events, since a hypnotized person is in some kind of an altered state of consciousness which makes him receptive to posthypnotic suggestions (Schafer and Rubio, 1978). Evidence suggests that memory under hypnosis may be somewhat better than in a normal waking state especially for traumatic emotionally charged events (Goldstein and Sipprelle, 1970; Orne, 1975). This fact in itself is of vital importance for police investigations and justifies the continued use of hypnosis. However, hypnotic memory performance probably is not different in kind from other memory states, which means that it is susceptible to similar kinds of distortions and errors in recall. Furthermore, deeply hypnotized people who wish to hide information are able to fool even experienced hypnotists (Field and Dworkin, 1967). Hypnosis does not guarantee that truth will be revealed.

Personality and Deception

MACHIAVELLIANISM AND LYING

Agents of the criminal justice system from the police through to the courts and parole boards have daily contact with individuals whose goals include the manipulation and deception of others for their own personal gain. These people will not hesitate to use fraud or exploitation if their chances of success are high enough. The personality attribute which characterizes such people is called Machiavellianism, after Niccolò Machiavelli (1940), the sixteenth-century advisor to princes on the use of manipulation and control for personal and political gain.

Machiavelli advocated a view of human nature that equated man to objects. Man was meant to be rationally and unemotionally juggled as if he were a pawn on a chess board. Questions of morality were meaningless, since the goals of power and domination always justified the means, such as cheating, lying, and deceit. Guilt did not occupy a central control position in Machiavelli's philosophy, since there was no reason to experience remorse for one's actions to others. According to Machiavelli, people deserve to be manipulated since they are innately false and debased.

Whether or not anyone accepts this view of human nature, there are people who show Machiavellian tendencies. This personality trait can be isolated by a simple test devised by Christie and Geis (1970). Persons called high Machs tend to agree with statements such as "The best way to handle people is to tell them what to hear," and "Never tell anyone the real reason you did something unless it is useful to do so." In contrast, persons receiving low scores on the Mach scale are more likely to agree with statements such as "One should take action only when sure it is morally right," and "Most people are basically good and kind."

Studies of Machiavellianism reveal significant differences between high- and low-Mach scorers in a number of abilities and dispositions, some of which are relevant to our focus of concern. Researchers have found no correlation between a person's degree of Machiavellianism and intelligence or between Mach scores and years of formal education. Also, there is no relationship between Machiavellianism and the need to achieve. People scoring high on the Mach scale are not distinguishable in terms of measures of psychopathology, but they do differ from low Machs in their unflattering opinion and cynical view of people in general (see Christie and Geis, 1970).

High-Mach subjects are willing to trick, manipulate, and cheat others if given the opportunity. Their success in deception appears to come from a highly tuned ability to quickly perceive and assess the chances to manipulate others in a given situation. When caught in a dishonest act, high-Mach subjects can coolly stare down their accusers and deny cheating. In effect, high Machs show little concern for conventional morality; they will cheat if the payoff is high and if there is little chance in being caught. If high Machs see a rational justification for lying and cheating, they will do so. While opposed to deception in principle, low Machs will cheat or go along with cheating only if given strong and repeated personal persuasion.

Persuasion in the Courtroom

CREDIBILITY OF TESTIMONY

Speakers never enter the courtroom as equals. Their credibility in the first instance is tied to the prestige people award them as representatives of groups or institutions. For example, Rotter and Stein (1971) surveyed 396 college students, secretaries, and elementary school teachers for their judgments of the trustworthiness and competence of persons employed in twenty selected occupations. Table 8.1 shows the mean ratings on 4-point scales obtained from these subjects over all twenty occupations with low mean ratings indicating high truthfulness and high competence.

It is clear that professionals and more highly educated people are regarded as more trustworthy and more competent. In contrast, representatives of power groups in our society, such as executives of large corporations, U.S. Army generals, politicians, and newspaper columnists, are perceived to be low in truthfulness. Accordingly, jurors' decisions may be influenced by the prestige of witnesses giving testimony. Ludwig and Fontaine (1978) found that when testimony is held constant, simulated jurors most often

TABLE 8.1(a).   Mean ratings for twenty occupations on truthfulness*

Occupation	Mean Rating**
Physicians	1.38
Clergymen	1.40
Dentists	1.41
Judges	1.53
Psychologists	1.59
College professors	1.61
Psychiatrists	1.63
High school teachers	1.75
Lawyers	1.79
Law enforcement officials	2.07
TV news reporters	2.10
Plumbers	2.11
Executives of large corps.	2.31
U.S. Army generals	2.34
TV repairmen	2.35
Newspaper columnists	2.42
Auto repairmen	2.47
Labor union officials	2.67
Politicians	3.06
Used-car salesmen	3.23
Overall mean	2.06

(b).   Mean ratings for twenty occupations on competence*

Physicians	1.38
Dentists	1.45
Lawyers	1.56
Judges	1.83
College professors	1.85
Psychologists	1.87
Clergymen	2.05
Psychiatrists	2.10
Executives of large corps.	2.10
Plumbers	2.20
TV repairmen	2.22
High school teachers	2.23
Auto repairmen	2.34
U.S. Army generals	2.36
TV news reporters	2.39
Law enforcement officials	2.54
Newspaper columnists	2.57
Labor union officials	2.77
Politicians	2.78
Used-car salesmen	3.22
Overall mean	2.19

*(From Rotter and Stein, 1971)   **(N = 396)

decided that a defendant was guilty when incriminating testimony was given by a physician, and least often when it was given by a policeman, with the influence of a layperson (profession was not stated) being intermediate.

Other obvious variables that influence source credibility are the personal characteristics of the speaker, such as his or her physical attractiveness, race, and character. The influence of physical attractiveness and race on impression formation and on identification has been reviewed in earlier chapters and need not be repeated here. Of special interest, however, is the tendency of lawyers to cite the moral character of witnesses in an attempt to discredit testimony. In criminal cases, character evidence is usually limited to witnesses' general reputation for truthfulness. If an accused takes the witness stand in his own defense, the prosecution is allowed to inform the court of his previous convictions. In this situation, judges are required to tell the jury that such information is provided only to assist them in their evaluation of the credibility of his testimony. In addition, the jury is told not to infer from his personal history that he is morally bad and is likely to have committed the crime for which he is being tried. However, both evidence from simulated trials (Doob and Kirshenbaum, 1972; Hans, 1974) and correlational findings from actual cases (Kalven and Zeisel, 1966) show that these types of instructions generally are ignored. An accused person with a criminal record is much more likely to be convicted than a person without a record (Brooks and Doob, 1975).

Several factors are now known to be related to credibility. Observers assess credibility in terms of perceived competence, expertness, and trustworthiness (Hovland, Janis, and Kelley, 1953). More recently, Fulton (1970) demonstrated that observers are more trusting of someone rated high in agreeableness (defined in terms of disposition and manner), high in conscientiousness (dress and physical bearing), and high in culture (language and speech). Even such factors as the frequency and direction of a person's looking behavior can influence the credibility of a communicator. Hemsley and Doob (1978) found that witnesses in a simulated trial who averted their gaze from an examiner were perceived by the jury to be less credible than witnesses who looked directly at their examiner.

One of the most influential sources of witness credibility is the amount of confidence that a witness projects in giving his or her testimony. However, several investigations already cited in earlier chapters indicate that an observer's certainty of choice is not correlated to his or her correct identification of a target person. Recent studies by Clifford and Scott (1978) and by Leippe, Wells, and Ostrom (1978) add further support to the conclusion that witnesses' confidence in their ability to identify a target face or recall evidence and their actual performance are unrelated. These results should be of vital importance to defense attorneys. Jurors must be made to understand that the expressed confidence of an eyewitness does not mean that his or her identification is necessarily accurate. In fact, research indicates no relationship.

The Role of Sex and Judgments of Credibility

Who is more likely to be believed, a male witness or a female witness? Do female and male lawyers have equivalent credibility for judges and juries?

The first type of evidence we can compare is the stereotypes that men and women have about the opposite sex. Studies show that women are more positive in their evaluation of men than men are in their judgments of women (MacBrayer, 1960). Men supposedly have greater competence, rationality, and assertiveness. The stereotypes of men characterize them as independent, objective, active, competitive, adventurous, self-confident, and ambitious. Women, on the other hand, are viewed as having the opposite of each of these characteristics. And furthermore, both men and women in our culture consider the traits believed possessed by males as preferred and more desirable (Rosenkrantz, Vogel, Bee, Broverman, and Broverman, 1968).

What is the evaluation of women who display traits generally considered to be characteristic of males? Are such women evaluated positively or negatively? One recent study suggests that both male and female applicants seeking "responsible-type" jobs are more likely to be chosen if they demonstrate masculine interests over feminine interests (Spence, Helmreich, and Stapp, in press). Various interpretations can be given to these findings. It is possible that women who show masculine interests are more desired simply because masculine traits are considered more valuable. Another interpretation depends upon the physical attributes of the person being evaluated. In this study, the woman who described herself as having interests in masculine-related activities was an attractive and likable person. The physical-attractiveness stereotype may have operated to convince subjects that she was a "good" person. Finally, while this young woman claimed interests in masculine activities, she did not at the same time deny interests in more traditional female roles such as motherhood and being a wife. If she had, she probably would have been judged less favorably (Seyfried and Hendrick, 1973; Shaffer and Wegley, 1974).

Although few comparative evaluations between the sexes on verbal performance are available, studies comparing performance on written work have been completed. In one investigation, women were asked to evaluate several scholarly articles dealing with architecture, dietetics, and law and city planning. The same work when attributed to a male author was considered to be more scholarly and better written than when attributed to a female author (Goldberg, 1968). Other studies of a similar nature demonstrate that men are also prejudiced against women (e.g., Bem and Bem, 1970).

So far, the discussion strongly suggests that males usually are judged more positively than females and performance is evaluated in favor of males.

The picture is not, however, totally black (see Deaux, 1976). Women are evaluated more favorably than men when they perform unusually well in a situation where it is expected that only men would do well. To test this hypothesis, Taynor and Deaux (1973) asked subjects to evaluate the central figure in a hypothetical criminal report. In one version the key figure was a woman, in the other version a male. The story unfolds by having a holdup man rob a fellow elevator passenger, escape, and warn the passenger not to follow. The passenger is described as acting very effectively in this situation by clearly describing the physical appearance of the assailant, accurately pointing out his direction of escape, and giving the police the necessary information leading to his quick arrest. The story concludes with the police praising the witness for his or her effective actions in this emergency. Before proceeding, an important preliminary finding should be noted. Pretesting observations showed that most people thought that males but not females would be effective witnesses in such emergencies. After reading the transcript, subjects were asked to consider how deserving the witness was of a reward for his or her performance. The results showed that subjects evaluated the woman in this situation as more deserving of a reward than the man. Taynor and Deaux concluded that people do not expect women to be good witnesses in an emergency situation. When the performance of a women is clearly outstanding *and* it is confirmed by authorities, people accept its credibility.

Once a witness begins to report his or her observations, differences in the ways men and women speak also may affect credibility. Men and women speak different languages in terms of the meaning of the same words, such as "sex," "love," or "home" (Reik, 1954). Women use words which men seldom use, such as "pretty," "cute," "lovely," and "oh dear" (Jespersen, 1922). Women also tend to be more "correct" in their grammar and more likely to pronounce a word like "dancing" clearly and distinctly than men, who often slur such a word into "dancin." Attention to correct pronunciation by women may be associated with their attempt to secure social status and prestige (Trudgill, 1972).

According to one authority (Kramer, 1974), the most evident difference between the sexes occurs in the volume and pitch of speech. Since women's speech cords are generally shorter, lighter, and stretched more tightly than men's, their voice pitch is higher. Higher pitch in female voices is associated with certain negative stereotypes such as timidness (Progrebin, 1972), and frivolity, as opposed to seriousness of report (Key, 1972). Serious reports are not expected from women.

Other probable differences between men and women in speech patterns are the use by women of tag questions such as "That man is tall, isn't he?" Men are more apt to simply state, "That man is tall" (Lakoff, 1973). The use of tag questions by a speaker often suggests a lack of confidence, less assertiveness, and greater suggestibility.

The most systematic and significant investigation of the effects of spoken language in American trial courtrooms is the work currently being conducted by William O'Barr and his colleagues at Duke University. Their project began by collecting more than 150 hours of audiotape recordings of criminal courtroom trials in North Carolina. Analyses of these recordings have revealed reliable differences in speech variations between the sexes. The data support Lakoff's (1973) theory that females (particularly those with little social prestige) tend to use a less forceful language style. That is, female witnesses favor hedge words ("It seems like," "I think," etc.), intensifiers (e.g., "*very* good"), repetition, tag questions, the use of rising intonation in declarative sentences, hesitation murmurs ("uh," "um," "well," etc.) and polite phrases (i.e., "sir," "please"). However, this language style is not limited only to women witnesses. These linguistic features were also found in men of relatively low socioeconomic status such as the poor and the uneducated. O'Barr and his associates refer to this speaking style as "powerless" language.

Social psychological experiments derived from these tape-recording observations confirm the hypothesis that subject-jurors attach little credibility to female or male witnesses who speak in a powerless style. Female and male witnesses who have relatively high social status (e.g., physicians, business leaders) tend to use a straightforward style of speaking and are more highly evaluated by subject-jurors.

O'Barr and his colleagues draw a very important conclusion from these studies. When the decision making in a case revolves around the testimony of a single male or female witness, the presence or absence of powerless speech styles in that witness's testimony may be crucial. Subtle variations in styles of speech can influence the decision making of jurors and it is more likely to be women in general and low-status men who create these negative reactions (see Erickson, Lind, Johnson, and O'Barr, 1978; O'Barr and Conley, 1976; Lind and O'Barr, in press).

ANDROGYNY VS. TRADITIONAL SEX ROLES

In the last few years, Sandra Bem (1974) and others have challenged the commonly accepted assumption that masculinity and femininity represent the opposite poles of a single dimension. Such an assumption tends to lock people into rigid sex-role stereotypes of what is and what is not appropriate behavior. Bem suggests a more adaptable notion of human behavior based upon the assumption that all individuals possess both masculine- and feminine-related qualities. The androgynous person is perceived as having a balance of masculine and feminine characteristics. Thus this person could be competitive, independent, and strong and also show compassion, bashfulness, and tenderness. The advantage of such a combination of characteristics is that it frees the individual, whether male or female, from traditional, narrow stereotypes regarding sex-appropriate behavior.

The answer to our earlier question asking whether or not female lawyers have equivalent credibility with male lawyers may depend to a certain extent upon the androgynous characteristics of the individuals in question. Following Bem's argument, the androgynous female should be able to function with more assertiveness and confidence in the courtroom than her more traditional female sisters and at least as effectively as her masculine sex-typed brothers. Research is needed to determine which characteristics best typify the few but increasingly numerous successful female criminal lawyers.

PHYSIOLOGICAL CHANGES IN WOMEN AND MEN AND THEIR EFFECTS ON JUDGMENT

In 1976 Judge Vincent McEwan, 57, a provincial court judge, declared in a Toronto court that the testimony of a 48-year-old woman might be unreliable because she was at a menopausal age. Similarly, in 1972 a Maryland physician, Dr. Edgar Berman, stated that the judgment of women executives must be suspect, since their cognitive abilities are seriously impaired by the "raging hormonal influences" present in their menopausal years. In Berman's opinion, males do not go through such traumatic hormonal changes (and consequently are more credible in their judgment and other cognitive behaviors). More recently, in October 1977 a woman was convicted but given an absolute discharge in an Ontario provincial court based in part on the testimony of a psychiatrist who claimed the accused was not fully aware of her actions in a shoplifting incident because of a menopausal depression. These incidents are typical of many long-standing beliefs related to the female "change of life" period and to the female menstrual cycle.

In the last few years systematic research has begun to test many of these stereotyped conclusions. Changes in viewpoints are starting to emerge. For example, most physiological and behavioral scientists now agree that men and women between the ages of 45 and 55 are emotionally similar. Men experience hormonal changes in this period much like the changes in female menopause, although there is no known similar abrupt stoppage of reproductive ability. Instead, the male hormone testosterone drops off gradually during the middle years.

If the emotionality of middle-aged women and men is similar, the implications for the courts are clear. Testimony of women in their middle years should not be treated differently from that of their male counterparts. If women suffer defects in perception and other cognitive abilities because of changes in the menopause period, men should experience similar cognitive problems, since they also undergo physiological and psychological readjustments during this stage of life. It is also important to remember that large individual differences occur in the rates of aging and in the way that people age.

Contrary to the myths which characterize menopause (e.g., "Menopause makes women crazy"), middle-age women typically report that they feel better, are more confident and more secure, and feel freer than before menopause (Neugarten, Wood, Kraines, and Loomis, 1963). Intellectual skills do not deteriorate in middle age for men and women, but rather improve in terms of verbal and reasoning abilities provided the person is healthy (Neiswender, 1975). Mental organization of information, processing of visual information, flexibility of thinking, and memory processes all appear to be as strong as they were in early adulthood. One notable loss, however, involves tasks demanding eye-hand movement coordination: the middle-ager performs less adequately than he once did (Baltes and Schaie, 1974).

Myths also exist linking decrements in cognitive and social behavioral performances with the menstrual cycle. Supposedly, the menstrual cycle is said to contribute to female criminal behavior (Dalton, 1961) and to women's disabilities in intellectually coping with environmental stress (Abramson and Torghele, 1961; Moos, Kopell, Melges, Yalom, Lunde, Clayton, and Hamburg, 1969; Tiger, 1970).

Let us look first at the research relating mood changes and menstruation. Women's recollections of their fluctuations in mood and behavior as assessed by questionnaires (Moos, 1968) and daily self-ratings at different stages of the cycle (McCance, Luff, and Widdowson, 1937) show changes in mood and behavior over the course of their menstrual cycle. However, self-report data on mood and behavior changes are limited and must be complemented by more rigorous scientific evidence.

An experimental investigation by Zimmerman and Parlee (1973) of fourteen young adult females tested during the menstrual (days 1–4), follicular (days 6–12), luteal (days 17–21), and premenstrual (days 23–27) stages of their cycle failed to reveal any reliable changes in daily self-ratings of moods. Reports, however, did vary over the cycle in descriptions of pain, feelings of bloatedness and hunger, hours of sleep, and pressure of immediate academic work. Significant differences in behavioral changes associated with the menstrual cycle were restricted to only one measure, arm-hand steadiness. No reliable differences were found for galvanic skin response to an auditory stimulus. These results indicate that changes in mood during the menstrual cycle are not reflected in simple behavior changes. The next question is whether the affective changes influence intellectual abilities.

Intellectual performance in university women, when measured by the Watson-Glaser Critical Thinking Appraisal test and regular class examinations, has been found to be similar throughout the menstrual cycle (Sommer, 1972). No decline in intellectual performance was found in any particular phase of the cycle. Similar findings showing a lack of relationship between menstrual cycle stages and performance on complex cognitive and perceptual-motor tasks have been reported in another investigation by Sommer (1973) and by Wickham (1958).

The final question I want to consider here is whether the variability in women's self-reports of daily activities over the normal menstruation cycle is similar to or different from the variability in activities reported by men at the same times. This problem has been tackled by Alice Dan (1976). Twenty-four husband-and-wife couples were questioned about their daily activities twice weekly over a period of two months. Menstrual cycle phase was determined, using dates of menses, basal body temperature, and luteal phase progesterone assays. Analyses of reports showed a pattern of increased activity during the follicular phase (day 6 to the beginning of the ovulatory phase, i.e., 4 days before shift in basal body temperature) for normal women, which was reliably different from the activity of their husbands and from women taking oral contraceptives. Apart from this one difference, women and their husbands reported the same variability in activities over the whole two-month period. Thus the generally accepted view that women in contrast to men show a general increase or decrease in level of activity at certain critical times because of hormonal changes over the menstrual cycle was not supported. These results forcefully challenge the argument that women are emotionally and physically incapable of doing their normal activities at certain times of the month.

Any suggestion that women should be prevented from testifying during menopause or during any period of the menstrual cycle is prejudicial and scientifically invalid.

Addressing the Jury

EFFECTS OF LANGUAGE ON PERSUASION IN THE COURTROOM

Anyone who has had a will drawn up or signed a legal contract, knows first-hand that the written language of lawyers is "prolix and muddy in literary style and is given to the overuse of words" (Lavery, 1956). Nor do lawyers' oral communications appear to be any more succinct. In an attempt to be precise and conservative, lawyers often use multiple terms and phrases rather than the few words which would suffice (e.g., "annul and set aside" for "annul"). It is easy to see how this type of language style could confuse witnesses and juries. For example, lawyers sometimes use familiar words in addressing the jury or in questioning witnesses which have different meanings for the court. Technical words and specialized legal vocabulary are employed without regard for the layman audience. The use of old English (e.g., "aforesaid," "forthwith"), Latin ("corpus delicti," "mens rea"), and French ("voire dire") may add an air of nobility, but such styles also suggest pomposity and lack of clarity (see Mellinkoff, 1963).

Lawyers tend to couch their arguments either in emotional appeals or in rational presentations. Appeals to a jury's sympathy are generally on the side of the defendant in criminal cases, while rational argument and logic is the normal strategy of the prosecutor (Costopoulos, 1972). Attorneys for the defense, however, must be cautious in the extent to which they evoke emotionality. Highly emotional language in an address to a jury that already agrees with the speaker may serve to strengthen their convictions, but others, who do not agree, tend to react negatively toward intense language. Too strong an appeal may cause the jury to feel guilt, shame, or anger, which may cause a backlash onto the lawyer. Furthermore, irrelevant emotional messages cannot be a substitute for facts.

A good example showing the interdependency of psychological and courtroom persuasion is the following speech by Clarence Darrow in defense of his clients Leopold and Loeb. Because of this speech, and in spite of a strong public demand for execution, Darrow was able to obtain life sentences for these men.

1 If your Honor, in violation of all [the progress law has made] should stand
2 here in Chicago alone to hang a boy on a plea of Guilty, then we are turning
3 our faces backward toward the barbarism which once possessed the world.
4 If your Honor can hang a boy of eighteen, some other judge can hang him
5 at seventeen, or sixteen, or fourteen. Someday, if there is any such thing as
6 progress in the world, if there is any spirit of humanity that is working in
7 the hearts of men, someday men would look back upon this as a barbarous
8 age which deliberately set itself in the way of progress, humanity and sympathy,
9 and committed an unforgivable act.
10 ... Now, Your Honor, I have spoken about the war. I believed in
11 it. I don't know whether I was crazy or not. Sometimes I think perhaps I was.
12 I approved of it; I joined in the general cry of madness and despair. I urged
13 men to fight. I was safe because I was too old to go. I was like the rest. ...
14 [Killing] was taught in every school, aye in the Sunday schools. The
15 little children played at war. The toddling children on the street. ...
16 We read of killing one hundred thousand men in a day. We read
17 about it and rejoiced in it—if it was the other fellows who were killed. We
18 were fed on flesh and drank blood. ...
19 These boys were brought up in it. The tales of death were in
20 their homes, their playgrounds, their schools; they were in the newspapers that
21 they read; it was a part of the common frenzy. What was a life? It was the
22 least sacred thing in existence and these boys were trained to this cruelty. ...

23 I know it has followed every war; and I know it has influenced
24 these boys so that life was not the same to them as it would have been if
25 the world had not been made red with blood. . . . All of us have our share
26 of it . . . I have mine. I cannot tell and I shall never know how many words of
27 mine might have given birth to cruelty in place of love and kindness and
28 charity. . . .
29 Has Your Honor a right to consider the families of these two
30 defendants? I have been sorry, and I am sorry for the bereavement of Mr. and
31 Mrs. Franks [parents of the dead child], for those broken ties that cannot be
32 healed. All I can hope and wish is that some good may come from it all. But
33 as compared with the families of Leopold and Loeb [the accused], the Franks
34 are to be envied—and everyone knows it. . . .
35 Have they [the families of the accused] any rights? Is there any reason,
36 Your Honor, why their proud names and all the future generations that bear
37 them shall have this bar sinister written across them? How many boys and
38 girls, how many unborn children, will feel it? It is bad enough however it is.
39 But it's not yet death on the scaffold. It's not that. And I ask Your Honor, in
40 addition to all that I have said, to save two honorable families from a disgrace
41 that never ends, and which could be of no avail to help any human being that
42 lives. [Weinberg, 1957]

McMahon (1977), a psychologist, has analyzed this speech and shows how effective a psychologist Darrow must have been. Several techniques of persuasion can be isolated in the following line-by-line examination:

Lines 1–5. *Hyperbole* (exaggeration). Although some logic is present, the argument is nonsensical in suggesting that giving the death penalty to young men may result in a domino effect in which even young adolescents may be executed some day.

Lines 5–9. *Pride and guilt.* Darrow states that we are good men but what will future generations think of us if we allow the death penalty. He infers that we should feel guilt if we allow this to happen.

Lines 10–13. *Ambiguity.* Darrow tries in these lines to confuse the jury by drawing a connection between war and the fate of the defendants. What exactly is this connection? The more confusion Darrow can instill, the greater the likelihood that the jurors will react to their thoughts of war and not to the issue at hand.

Lines 12–13. *Reverse psychology.* By turning the tables on himself, Darrow attempts in these lines to get the sympathy of the jury.

Lines 14–25. *Scapegoating.* In this passage Darrow tells the jury that society is not blameless, that it too must shoulder the responsibility for how young boys think, feel, and act (including murder).

Lines 26–28. Another example of *reverse psychology.* Darrow admits that he accepts his share of the blame.

Lines 29–34. *Personal appeal.* Here Darrow tries to fill the listener with an emotional anguish over the bereavement of the parents of the defendants, while acknowledging that we also should feel sorry for the parents of the dead child.

Lines 32–34. *Appeal to the self-evident.* Darrow attempts to gain agreement to an obvious truth—i.e., "everyone knows it." Is it, in fact, evident to everyone?

Lines 35–42. *Symbolic appeal.* Here we see how Darrow attempts to draw the jury's attention to highly valued symbols such as "proud names," "honorable families," and "unborn children."

In summary, Darrow's success in persuasion resulted from his ability to make his audience receptive to his message. Jurors were shown that the defendants were not crazy, irresponsible young men, but were very similar to themselves. Darrow was able to use logic for his own purposes combined with appeals to emotion to promote his clients while degrading the arguments of the opposing side.

ORDER OF PRESENTATION OF OPPOSING ARGUMENTS

A basic assumption of the jury process is that jurors keep an open mind and refrain from decision making until both the prosecutor and the defense have presented their cases. An issue of importance is whether or not the side presented first or that presented second has a greater influence on persuasion.

This problem was investigated originally by F. H. Lund (1925), who found that the side presenting an issue first is more effective, suggesting the operation of a "law of primacy." Referring to civil litigation, Lund stated the following:

> Our form of jury trial, just as our procedure in debates, assumes that both sides are given an equal opportunity. But the existence of such equality is based on logical considerations, and assumes that logical factors will control the decision of the judges or jurymen as the case might be. But our beliefs are rarely if ever fashioned through such dispassionate weighings of pros and cons. While the lawyer of the plaintiff is reviewing his case and making his appeal, the belief of the jurors is already in the process of formation, and they are not to be dissuaded from their position by an equal amount of evidence or persuasive appeal on the part of the defendant's lawyer, according to the law of primacy, which appears as an indubitable factor in persuasion. . . . [p. 191]

As you would expect, few laws of psychology are as definite and as simple as Lund's proposal. Other research has often failed to support this law (see Warr and Knapper, 1968, for review). Evidence is also available showing that the second or most recent argument is more effective in persuasion, suggesting the operation of a "law of recency" (Cromwell, 1950).

It is possible that primacy effects may function under some conditions and recency under others (Hovland and Mandell, 1952). A review of primacy-recency studies shows that primacy effects are dominant if the arguments are on controversial topics (Lana, 1963a), interesting subject matter (Lana, 1963b), and highly familiar issues (Lana, 1961). In contrast, recency effects are associated with uninteresting subject matter and technical issues. However, if the arguments for one side are perceived to be stronger than the arguments for the other side, the strength of the arguments appears to outweigh the importance of who goes first or last (Rosnow, Holz, and Levin, 1966). And finally, one experiment showed that subject-jurors are not differentially influenced by the order of arguments, but are affected by whether or not they made a decision of guilt or innocence after hearing only the first speaker. Jurors tending to vote acquittal at the end of the trial are more likely to have decided that the defendant was innocent after hearing only the first speaker. Conversely, those jurors deciding he was guilty at this point are more likely to convict the defendant on the final decision making (Stone, 1969).

Primacy and recency effects are of principle importance during the closing arguments of a criminal case (Lawson, 1969). It is at this point in the trial that the art of advocacy is seen. Communications no longer need to be restricted to factual information, but instead are emotional and argumentative. If arguments from both sides of the case are inherently equal in strength, jurors in trials which are dramatic, interesting, and not too technical will tend to favor presentation made first. In criminal cases lacking in excitement and color and containing high proportions of technical information, jurors will tend to favor recent arguments.

In most jurisdictions, the prosecution in criminal cases opens first and closes last. As Lawson (1969) indicates, "... *the law has always assumed that the last word to the jury is the best word* (a law of recency), an assumption that has developed from a haphazard study of human decision-making in the judicial arena" (p. 125). In contrast to this assumption, a more accurate conclusion is that the effects of primacy and recency are not universal, but show their influences only under certain conditions (Hovland and Mandell, 1952).

Questioning the Witness

Interrogation of a witness involves the paradox of permitting clarification of testimony while at the same time increasing the probability of error. Accuracy of recall under the best of conditions is a difficult task, and recall is seldom free of error. Witnesses often are anxious and susceptible to bias which can distort memory. These influences are minimized under direct examination, since counsel is not permitted to lead his own witness. On the other hand, cross-examination permits the introduction of suggestion. The law assumes that reports are more likely to be true and accurate when witnesses are cross-examined on broad issues including counsel's presentation of alternative explanations of what was observed. Suggested answers from counsel are not considered as biasing recall, but rather are seen as tests of the veracity and validity of memory. In fact, cross-examiners seldom ask questions regarding information which is not already known by them. Furthermore, they are reasonably sure that their knowledge will be confirmed by the questioned witness. Depending upon the particular understandings and courtroom strategies the cross-examiner has formulated, he will word his questions so that his viewpoint can be verified. If a witness gives an "inappropriate" observation, meaning that it runs counter to the theory of the examiner, the witness may be accused of lying or distortion.

Witnesses themselves are not innocent of distortion resulting from interrogation. Many people hold the law in awe and officers of the court often are seen as authorities to be pleased or from whom one wishes to win approval. Consequently, witnesses unknowingly may accept the suggested answers of counsel since they "seem to fit" and are more or less accurate, especially if the witness himself isn't a hundred percent certain of his own observations.

Occasionally, a witness's poor performance in court will be due to his or her anxiety and stress. Testimony on the witness stand is comparable in some ways to other public-speaking situations which can arouse anxiety. Results of numerous studies show a strong relationship between anxiety and verbal productivity (see Murray, 1971, for a review).

Even the length of a witness's response to an attorney's questions influences the jurors' perceptions of testimony. When male witnesses (but not female) give direct and fragmented answers to a series of questions, subject-jurors judge the lawyer as exercising too much control over testimony. Subjects do not devalue the witness in this situation, but, instead, think more negatively about the lawyer. By asking a great number of questions to get answers that could have been freely narrated, the lawyer is perceived as manipulative, hostile, disrespectful, and censoring of the evidence being presented. The negative impressions generated toward the attorney because of this questioning style may have serious consequences for his client (Lind and O'Barr, in press).

Another experiment indicates that jurors' perceptions of testimony may also be influenced by interruptions in the course of questioning. Subject-jurors perceive the lawyer as being in control when no overlapping speech occurs. When both the lawyer and the witness speak at the same time, the lawyer is perceived as less in control and less credible. If the lawyer persists in talking over the voice of the witness, he is seen as less intelligent and unfair to the witness. However, when the lawyer gives in and lets the witness continue talking, the attorney is perceived positively and seen as wanting the witness to have full opportunity to present his testimony (Lind and O'Barr, in press).

Subjects testifying before a negative or disapproving audience as opposed to a receptive audience talk a significantly smaller proportion of the time (Cervin, 1956). The size of the audience also affects the amount of speech.

Children aged 10 to 12 years, for example, are much more willing to talk in front of one adult than in front of seven adults (Levin, Baldwin, Gallwey, and Paivio, 1960). The nature of the topic to be communicated also contributes to the speaker's level of anxiety. People tend to talk faster when discussing stressful topics (Kanfer, 1959, 1960). In general, high-stress situations act to reduce the amount of verbal communication, whereas moderate stress acts to increase verbal quantity. Over and above the stress factors inherent in various situations, people also differ in their dispositions to react with anxiety. Individuals defined by personality tests as high-anxiety persons show a greater tendency than low-anxious people to talk in low-stress situations. In contrast, low-anxious individuals have a greater tendency to talk in high-stress conditions.

Two final observations regarding witness communication can be mentioned here. First, speakers are perceived as more competent and more persuasive when they speak rapidly than when they speak slowly (Miller, Maruyama, Beaber, and Valone, 1976). And second, in contrast to common belief, few correlations have been found between language behavior and personality factors. One exception is the relationship between need for social approval and rate of speaking. People seeking approval tend to punctuate their speech with long pauses. This correlation suggests that such persons are overly cautious and deliberate in what they say since they are concerned with making the "correct" impression (Preston and Gardner, 1967).

EFFECTS OF TYPE OF QUESTION ON EYEWITNESS TESTIMONY

One of the first investigators to be concerned with the form of questions put to courtroom witnesses was Whipple (1909), who found decreasing accuracy in response to the following four question types:

1. Determinative question. Example: "Did the man wear gloves?"
2. Disjunctive question. Example: "Did or did not the man wear gloves?"
3. Expectative question. Example: "The man wore gloves, didn't he?"
4. Implicative question. Example: "What color were the man's gloves?"

These four questions show how a witness may be led to answer a certain way or led to assume that certain events necessarily occurred.

Suggestibility of inquiry can be manipulated by phrasing the questions with more than one negative (Muscio, 1915) or by simply changing the emotive connotation of single words. For example, Loftus and Palmer (1974) demonstrated that subjects are much more likely to make inaccurate judgments if they are asked questions containing more severe emotional words such as "smashed" as opposed to more neutral words such as "collided," "bumped," "contacted," or "hit" in connection with an automobile accident. Furthermore, subjects originally questioned with the word "smashed" in contrast to the other words are more likely to distort their recollections one week later. Initial questioning of witnesses influences their later recollections, since subjects reconstruct both their memory of the event and any interpretations given to that episode as a function of the original questions.

In another investigation, Loftus and Zanni (1975) found that questions containing a definite article (e.g., "Did you see *the* cracked windshield?") in contrast to questions having an indefinite article ("Did you see *a* cracked windshield?") produced (1) fewer uncertain, "I don't know" responses, and (2) more false recognitions of events that had not occurred. These results suggest that people are likely to infer that some event did occur when questioned with a definite article, since they assume that anything asked about in this manner by definition must have existed. In contrast, questions which include the indefinite article "a" do not necessarily presuppose the existence of some object or event.

Two other investigations by Loftus merit particular attention because of their relevance and application to practices of the police and the courts. Witnesses to an automobile accident often are examined for the completeness and accuracy of their memory of the event itself and the context in which it occurred. Experimental findings strongly suggest that questions given (for example, by the police and insurance investigators) shortly after an accident influence later recollections at the time of questioning in court (Loftus, 1975). In a test of this hypothesis, subjects viewed a film of an automobile accident and then answered a set of questions about the accident. The wording of the questions was deliberately constructed so as to introduce new information, via presuppositions, into the situation. For example, "How fast was the white sports car going when it passed the barn while traveling along the country road?" No barn, in fact, was shown in the film, yet one week later subjects who were led to believe that a barn existed were six times as likely to state that they had seen one as were subjects not given this information.

Finally, Miller and Loftus (1976) have shown that the influence of leading questions may contribute to the misidentification of one person for another who actually committed an act. Subjects were shown slides of people engaging in different activities. Afterwards some of the subjects were questioned in such a way as to suggest that a particular person had done something which actually had been done by someone else. The purpose of this study was to discover whether or not leading questions of this sort would affect the subsequent recall and testimony of subjects. The results showed that these types of questions significantly increased the likelihood that a person would be remembered as doing some action which in fact he did not do. These results support the more general hypothesis of "unconscious transference"; that is, a person seen committing one act may be confused in memory with the recall of a person seen committing a second act (see Wall, 1965). This phenomenon is not yet clearly understood. However, enough studies have now been completed to show that leading questions contribute to the inaccurate memory for complex events (see also Clifford and Scott, 1978; Loftus, 1977; Read, Barnsley, Ankers and Whishaw, 1978; Thorson and Hochhaus, 1977). Since memory is understood as a constructive and reconstructive process, it is not difficult to appreciate how the original perceived event is altered with the addition of new information given over time and at the point of remembering.

Kinds of Questions and Freedom of Response

Are witnesses more accurate in recalling their observations if permitted the freedom of free narrative, or does specific step-by-step interrogation result in more valid testimony? Early studies suggest that free narrative is more accurate whereas testimonial interrogation is more complete. If both forms of questioning are used, greater accuracy is found when spontaneous narrative precedes interrogation as opposed to the reverse order (Cady, 1924; Snee and Lush, 1941; Whitely and McGeoch, 1927). Modern investigations have supported these early findings and, in addition, have shown how testimony is related to such factors as testimonial atmosphere, immediacy of questioning, and sex of witness.

In one investigation 151 adult males, aged 21 to 64, were shown a short film involving two young men playing football, a car hitting a woman pedestrian, a scuffle between the woman's companion and the car driver, and the involvement of the players in the argument. A total of 884 scorable facts were identified from the film by the researchers. Following viewing of the film subjects were asked to give a free narrative of what they remembered. The witnesses were then divided into four subgroups and given four different types of interrogation interviews in either a supportive or challenging fashion.

In the free reports witnesses were extremely accurate (computed score of .96) in their observations but were very limited or incomplete in their accounts of what took place (score of .28). The first subgroup was asked broad questions such as "Describe the area you saw at the *very beginning of the film,* that is, to the right of the main building: what was the setting, what was the background, what objects were visible, where were they located, what color were they, and so forth." With this type of questioning the completeness index rose to .48 but accuracy fell to .90. The second subgroup was asked specific questions similar to the type of questioning involved in direct examination of witnesses in the courtroom. For example, "Tell me about the traffic and weather conditions. Mention, in detail, everything about the main building you saw. How many signs did you see, where were they, and what did they look like?" Direct examination produced a completeness score of .56 while accuracy dropped to .86. The third subgroup was given a multiple-choice test such as "Where did the incidents happen: in a vacant lot, in a street, on a sidewalk, in a parking lot, or some place else?" Multiple-choice responding raised the completeness score to .83; however, accuracy fell to .82. The fourth and final subgroup was given a forced-choice test involving leading questions similar to those used in cross-examination. Half of the questions were worded in the correct direction and the remainder were biased toward incorrect answers. For example, "The events you saw took place in a street, didn't they?" This line of questioning produced a completeness score of .84 and an accuracy index of .81. Since these scores are similar to the results with the multiple-choice questions, it may be inferred that the leading questions did not have, as expected, a negative effect on testimony.

Contrary to predictions, the supportive and challenging atmospheres failed to show any differential effects on testimony. In short, interview atmosphere had no effect on either accuracy or completeness of testimony.

In conclusion, this study shows that question form and witness's freedom of response interact to determine accuracy and completeness of testimony. The more freedom given a witness, the greater the probability that his testimony will be accurate but, at the same time, the smaller the probability that it will be complete (Marquis, Marshall, and Oskamp, 1972).

Other evidence on the psychology of eyewitness testimony indicates that the specificity of questions, the delay of interrogation, and sex of witness are related to the accuracy and completeness of reports. Using a procedure similar to that used by Marquis et al. (1972), Lipton (1977) showed forty adult males and forty adult females a filmed murder and then tested their memory of this event in a simulated courtroom situation. In contrast to the earlier study, however, each witness was given various types of questions. Results showed that testimonial accuracy dropped only 4.3% after a one-week delay while quantity of testimony fell 18% with delay. No differences were found in either accuracy or quantity of testimony if witnesses orally reported or wrote their observations. Open-ended questions such as "What did you see?" resulted in the greatest accuracy (83%) but the least complete answers (32%). Leading questions having a positive bias yielded the second highest accuracy scores (76%) while the negative-bias questions yielded only a 52% accuracy score. The quantity of testimony, however, between the two types of leading questions was not significantly different, with positive bias having a 78% and negative bias a 73% completeness index. And finally, the results showed that female witnesses were significantly more accurate in their testimony than were male witnesses, although the two sexes did not differ in their quantity of reports. However, some recent research indicated that females were significantly inferior to males when they recalled events of a violent nature. Males and females did not differ in their recall of facts from a nonviolent incident, and both sexes were able to recall more facts from a nonviolent incident than a violent event (Clifford and Scott, 1978).

Credibility and Expert Testimony

The use of experimental psychologists as expert witnesses was strongly advocated over seventy years ago by Professor Münsterberg. Münsterberg, as we know, was not without his critics, as is suggested in the following passage from Charles C. Moore (1908), an attorney:

> A former judge writes, "I have no hesitation in saying that if I were a judge I would not permit any 'experimental psychology' whatever to be practiced in my court room. I can imagine nothing better designed to confuse issues and to distract attention from real tests of credibility, etc., based on the experience of mankind. . . Would a psychological expert be allowed to supplement his tests by expressing his opinion that a witness is or is not a trustworthy observer? Not until Dr. Doyle [Sherlock Holmes] is allowed to testify to his opinion of the guilt or innocence of a defendant in a criminal case—not until then. Expert testimony has already become so scandalously degraded that in the last several years medico-legal societies, bar associations and legislators have been striving to find some means to relieve the courts from its enormities. . . . [cited in Rouke, 1957, p. 51]

In spite of this criticism, experimental psychologists, at least in Europe, were being used by the courts as expert witnesses.

The first recorded instance of a psychologist giving expert testimony concerning the reliability of other evidence presented in court involved the Belgian psychologist J. Varendonck (see Rouke, 1957; Whipple, 1913). On June 12, 1910, a 9-year-old girl named Cecile was murdered in a small town in Belgium. Police interviews that evening with two young playmates of Cecile, aged 8 and 10, revealed that a "tall, dark man with a black mustache" had taken the murdered girl away. The next day the girls were interviewed again, but on this occasion by the magistrate. Their testimony this time was very discrepant from the initial interview. After the magistrate suggested several names to the children, one of the girls stated that the man who had taken Cecile away was "Jan," and that he was the father of the other play-mate. "Jan" Amand Van Puyenbroeck was tried for murder in January 1911. The evidence against the accused rested chiefly on the testimony of the two girls. Varendonck was one of several psychologists retained by the defense to testify as to the unreliability of child witnesses. To support his testimony, Varendonck designed a set of experiments to test whether school children aged 8 to 10 years are unduly influenced by interrogation similar in form to the questions given to the two witnesses. The results of these experiments and a summary of the existing literature on the psychology of testimony were presented to the court by Varendonck. This testimony was met with resistance by court officials, who found his "expertness" to be pretentious. Nevertheless, Varendonck's testimony contributed to the jury's decision to acquit.

Today, psychologists are often called to testify as expert witnesses in courts of law, and few objections are raised to challenge their claim to expertise (see, for example, Louisell, 1955; McCary, 1956; Rice, 1961; Schofield, 1956; Silverman, 1969). According to McCormick (1954), an expert witness

> ... has something different [than the usual observer] to contribute. This is a power to draw inferences from the facts which a jury would not be competent to draw. To warrant the use of expert evidence, two elements are required. First, the subject of the inference must be so distinctively related to some art, science, profession, business, or occupation as to be beyond the ken of the average layman, and, second, the witness must have such skill, knowledge, or experience in that field or calling as to make it appear that his opinion or inference will probably aid the trier in his search for truth. . . . [p. 37]

Psychologists and psychiatrists are often asked to comment on the credibility of a witness or complainant and asked to tell the court how much weight should be given to his or her testimony. The distinctions between psychological and psychiatric testimony usually are based upon their differences in experience and training. Psychiatrists most typically understand and interpret behavior through a medical model; human disturbance is conceptualized as illness or disease. Psychologists, on the other hand, usually view disturbed behavior which does not have an organic base as a form of social maladjustment or behavior which has been learned. These differences between the two professions may result in discordant testimony on the same case.

The difficulty for the courts is further compounded when disagreements occur among expert witnesses within the same profession. Psychiatrists and psychologists often have presented conflicting testimony, which confuses the courts and the general public and generally undermines the credibility of the two professions as a whole. One explanation for these discrepancies is that testimony from experts often is designed to enhance their own self-image and give them greater public recognition. Furthermore, experts are not immune from being advocates or propagandists for their own favorite theory and explanation of criminal behavior. On occasion their testimony is clearly seen to be partial for the side which has called them to court as expert witnesses (for further discussion, see Robitscher and Williams, 1977).

Nevertheless, differences in opinion between and within professions should not necessarily be interpreted as error. These differences often reflect each expert's way of organizing information into manageable units to allow classification or diagnoses of behavior. Expert witnesses must interpret and integrate numerous bits of information into overall judgments which can be communicated to the court. It is the court's responsibility to determine through cross-examination how, when, where, and what observations were made and what inferences were required in order to arrive at final conclusions. The courts, in their evaluation of expert testimony, should determine as far as possible whether the expert has made reliable assessments over several observation periods. Opinions and conclusions presented to a court must have both descriptive and explanatory functions.

If the public understood that testimony of experts in the fields of psychiatry and psychology cannot always be judged against objective criteria, criticisms of the inexactness of these sciences and professions could be balanced with the potential insights these experts can offer to the courts. Moreover, in the final analysis, psychologists and psychiatrists do not make the ultimate decision that a complainant or witness should not be believed; that is the responsibility of the judge or jury.

This chapter has addressed the problem of truth and credibility in normal adults. In chapter 9 our focus of interest will shift to two other subjects, the child and the senior citizen. Children are not considered good witnesses because of their great suggestibility, whereas myths about the competence of senior citizens often make their testimony appear to be suspect. How valid are these beliefs?

Chapter 9

Testimony of the Young and the Aged

Most of this book has focused upon the cognitive behaviors of young and middle-aged adults. Not all eyewitnesses, however, who come in contact with the law are young adults or middle-aged. The police often have to interview young children and the elderly, some of whom, of course, will testify in court.

Psychologists interested in child development and life-span development have done extensive research in the last few years on the perception, memory, and communication skills of children as well as studies on the cognitive processes of the older adult. The major purpose of this chapter is to present some of the theoretical conceptions and empirical findings of research on how children and the aged perceive, remember, and understand their world. This discussion is relevant to the criminal justice system insofar as it clarifies what we can expect of, and accept with confidence from, the child and the aged as testifiers. To begin, we will look first at Jean Piaget's approach to cognitive development of children.

Piaget's Theory of Cognitive Development

Jean Piaget, a prominent Swiss psychologist, is considered by most child psychologists to be the prime authority on cognitive development in children. Piaget is concerned with determining the psychological origins of knowledge and with identifying the changes in development over time of man's thinking and understanding of his world. Mental development begins in infancy with the interaction between the child and his environment. As the child operates upon the environment, he learns to cope with its demands. The continuous interaction of the child operating on the environment and the environment in turn making further demands upon the child generates the growth of knowledge. The child's mental capacities develop automatically as the child acquires sets of strategies or rules to handle changing environmental conditions. The ability to adapt to the changing environment modifies the child's mental representations of the world and thereby develops his mind.

Piaget (1950) believes that all children pass through four invariant stages of cognitive development, although the age at which a particular child reaches a particular stage of development varies. The first stage is the sensorimotor period (birth to approximately 2 years), during which the child develops the ability to recognize objects. In addition, he develops his first notions of causality duurng this period. Specific actions, such as kicking, for example, result in specific consequences, such as making the bed bounce.

Stage 2 is the preoperational period (approximately 2 to 7 years), during which time the child becomes increasingly capable of thinking about his world. Children develop the ability to manipulate and verbally symbolize their environment. Thus a child can remember an object's existence by remembering its name. The development of language, the ability to understand simple concepts, and the ability to represent objects imaginally (the tree house is a "castle") are the main characteristics of this stage. Children at this stage are egocentric, or self-centered. They are unable to understand or perceive the world except from their own perspective. The young child thinks that other people see, think, and feel things exactly the same way he does. A police officer asking simple and concrete questions to a child of this age will usually get reasonable, factual responses. Nevertheless, a child seldom is able to elaborate upon his answers. As far as he or she is concerned, the answers are sufficient and fully understandable as stated. Finally, children between the ages of 2 and 7 are more likely than older children (7 to 11) to perceive only the physical or apparent characteristics of objects and not make inferences as to their "real" meaning. When parents or authorities such as the police persist in asking questions, some children, because of their early socialization training and orientations to adult authority, will want to please by giving the "correct" answer. Whatever the authority is hinting at will be accepted and confirmed as long as the child is not implicated and judged to be bad. Many children of approximately 7 years of age are afraid of authority and will defer to its power (Tapp and Kohlberg, 1971; Tapp and Levine, 1974). Fear of policemen is lessened, however, if the child has generally positive experiences with the police (Torney, 1971). Unfortunately, not many young children have much contact with the police.

Stage 3 is the period of concrete operations (approximately 7 to 11 years). In this stage the child is able to use simple logic to understand the nature of things. He knows that the sensory properties of objects such as their shape or size can change without a corresponding change in their amount, or quantity. For example, he or she understands that a pint of soda pop poured into a tall narrow glass is the same as a pint of pop poured into a short wide glass. The child's ability to understand such relationships and the ability to categorize and classify objects increase in this period. During the middle childhood years, the child is logical in dealing with concrete objects, but he has difficulty in dealing with abstract ideas. His social interactions with others are innocent and naive, he accepts surface characteristics or physical appearances and actions as true, and these characteristics make him difficult to believe as a witness. It is only at the end of this stage that the preadolescent is able to distinguish and make inferences of hidden intentions, covert meanings, and psychological attributions.

The fourth and final period is the stage of formal operations (approximately 11 to 15 years). The older child–adolescent demonstrates an understanding of abstract logic, has the ability to reason about propositions, and shows the capacity to hypothesize and solve problems in his head. In effect, the adolescent has adult-like thinking abilities with all of their assets and liabilities. Questions from the police or other authorities would be answered in the same manner as adults with the same educational level, social background, etc.

According to Piagetian theory, memory develops and improves with time, although it is not unusual even for three- and four-year-olds to remember meaningful events that happened up to a year ago. As the child grows, his memory interacts with the development of cognitive skills such as organizational strategies, rehearsal, and so on. Thus the elementary school child, in contrast to the preschooler, will recall more information, since, for example, he will tend to group materials that must be remembered into categories.

Over and above the greater use of cognitive strategies to enhance memory, the older child will show better memory with the passage of time. Piaget argues that a child's memory for an event will get better with development as he more clearly understands and comprehends what it is he originally perceived. For example, Piaget and Inhelder (1968) showed children a row of ten parallel sticks of varying lengths and asked them to remember their arrangement. One week later they were asked to draw the array of sticks from memory. After eight months the same children were asked to redraw the stimuli. The results showed that the second drawing was much more accurate than the first in reproducing the original array. Memory improved over the eight months, according to Piaget, because the children had acquired a better knowledge of or understanding of the phenomenon of seriation.

Memory in children is more than a reconstruction of what is originally stored. Instead, it is a construction of what is stored and what is understood at different stages of intellectual development. Several studies (Altemeyer, Fulton, and Berney, 1969; Dahlem, 1969; Furth, Ross, and Youniss, 1974) have confirmed the findings of Piaget and Inhelder showing later recall to improve in some children (presumably due to development). However, not all research shows this result. Samuels (1976) found that changes in recall by four-to-seven-year-old children after a five-month delay in testing were unrelated to changes in the subjects' stage of development. Nevertheless, it is likely that older children, in general, have a better sense of what should be or what is more real or true which will influence their delayed recall of events.

Attention and Memory

SELECTIVE ATTENTION

At any moment in time the child is bombarded by a multiplicity of sights, sounds, odors, and other stimuli too great in number to be perceived simultaneously. Hence a selection must be made, and the process of selection is labeled "attention." The tendency of the child to favor certain stimuli and disregard others plays a role in the young child's learning. The primary determiners of attention are certain characteristics of objects or stimuli such as size, movement, novelty, or isolation. Gradually, as the child grows, he displays greater control over his perceptual-attentional process. His attention becomes more reliable and focused on certain salient features which are relevant to his needs and purposes. For example, 8-year-old children, in contrast to 5-year-olds, can attend to two features of a stimulus when this is the more adaptive response, but can shift their attention, if necessary, to one feature when task demands change (Hale and Taweel, 1974).

One of the practical problems of a parent or teacher is that of sustaining the attention of the child. Because the child is so easily distracted by changes in the environment, sustained attention to most activities is unlikely unless the child is highly motivated. Young children will attend to certain stimuli such as a magician, clown, or circus act for a considerable amount of time, since these sorts of activities satisfy their interests and needs. It is unlikely that a young child would notice a crime in action unless it was unusually interesting or exciting. Of course, if it was too exciting, the child would probably be frightened and want to escape back to his or her mother.

Selective attention in children has been studied experimentally by comparing a child's recall performance on a central task with his or her memory for incidental information related to the task. If the child shows successful performance on the central task and poor performance on incidental memory, it is likely that his or her attention was directed to the task-relevant rather than task-irrelevant stimuli. Maccoby and Hagen (1965) tested this hypothesis in a developmental study involving 7-, 9-, 11-, and 13-year-old children. The children were told that they would have to remember the *location* of some cards that they would see. Each child was shown an array of pictures on cards depicting a familiar object like a toy train, drawn on a distinctively colored background. The experimenter then removed the row of cards from view and showed the child a cue card of the same color as one of the target cards. The child's task was to recall the location in the array of the card that matched the color of the cue card. Following fourteen trials of this sort the child was tested without warning for incidental memory involving matching each object with the background color on which it appeared. The results showed that performance on the central task improved with age but incidental recall dropped off with development. These results have been subsequently replicated by Hagen (1967) and Wheeler and Dusek (1973).

It may be concluded that selective attention is a developmental process which improves with age. If a young child is called to act as a witness, the courts should note that although a young child can attend to task-relevant information, one difference between young and older children is the greater ability with age to focus on the relevant features of situations while disregarding the irrelevant. Exactly what the relevant features in real-life situations are which should be attended to are not, of course, as simple as in experimental tasks. Nevertheless, it is probably true that the older child learns from experience which environmental stimuli he or she should seek out or be prepared for and will perceptually sample the environment in a more efficient manner (see Hale and Morgan, 1973).

DEVELOPMENT OF MEMORY IN CHILDREN

Common experience shows that most adults have superior memories to children and that older children are better in remembering than are younger children. Although memory performance becomes increasingly better with age, there are situations in which the level of retention is similar over age levels. Differences in the development of memory are the result of inequalities in the development of learning abilities (acquisition) or retrieval strategies of memory, or a combination of the two.

In order to describe and explain developmental differences in memory, our review will follow the multistore model suggested by Atkinson and Shiffrin (1968). As may be recalled from the discussion in chapter 4, this model divides memory into three structures: (1) a sensory store, (2) a short-term store, and (3) a long-term store. The structural features of the memory system are differentiated from the control processes used to operate that system. These control processes include rehearsal techniques, mnemonics, imagery, organizational strategies, and retrieval plans. Thus information moves through the memory stores as a function of the efficiency of different control processes.

Most of the research on sensory memory in children has been limited to the visual system. Experimental evidence shows that visual information held in memory for 50 milliseconds (one-twentieth of a second) is stored in a similar fashion for subjects ranging in age from 5 through 21 years (Shein-gold, 1973). In other words, the capacity of the visual sensory register is much the same for young children and young adults. However, after a 50-millisecond to 1,000-millisecond delay younger subjects show a faster rate and greater amount of information loss. These differences suggest that younger and older children have different abilities to encode information for subsequent processing in the short-term store.

The single most important characteristic of short-term memory is its limited storage capacity. Contrary to general expectations, forgetting from the short-term store is equivalent for young children and young adults (Belmont and Butterfield, 1969). Support for this conclusion has been found by several investigators. To take two examples, Hansen (1965) found that 10-year-olds retained more information, i.e., had a more efficient learning and storage system, than 5-year-olds, but their rate of forgetting was identical. In other words, the percentage of material lost over time was the same for both age groups. Similarly, Belmont (1967) compared the forgetting rates of 8-, 10-, 12-, and 20-year-old subjects and found marked forgetting over a fourteen-second retention interval for all subjects, with the rate of forgetting equivalent over the various age groups.

Adults recognize more, recall more, and reproduce more information seconds after the presentation of materials than do children. How can we explain this superiority of short-term memory with greater age when rate of forgetting does not differ? The answer lies in the unequal abilities to store information and to retrieve information from memory as a function of developmental differences.

Recall deficits often occur from a failure to actively rehearse material after it has entered the short-term store. Rehearsal is one of the principle factors that influence the movement of information through the memory system (Rundus, 1971). Several investigators have shown that individuals of different ages use dissimilar rehearsal techniques which are correlated to differences in recall from the long-term store. For example, when children of different ages are given a list of items (words or pictures of objects) to study and are asked seconds later to recall the material, the superiority in performance of older children can be attributed to a number of mediating memory processes, one of which is rehearsal.

Examination of children's verbal rehearsal shows that young children often fail to rehearse even though they are capable of doing so (Flavell,

Beach, and Chinsky, 1966). Older children, however, spontaneously rehearse verbal labels, thereby facilitating their performance (Hagen and Kingsley, 1968). As the child matures, the 11-, 13-, and 14-year-old shows active rehearsal in contrast to the 8-year-old, who rehearses relatively passively (Ornstein, Naus, and Liberty, 1975). These rehearsal procedures are directly related to developmental differences in recall. When young children are taught to actively rehearse by repeating many items together instead of attending exclusively to the most recently presented item, their recall of initially presented materials substantially improves (Ornstein, Naus, and Stone, 1977). These results suggest that developmental differences in short-term retention result from the strategies or control processes utilized, such as rehearsal, which governs the retrieval of information from the long-term memory store.

Whereas the short-term store is seen as a temporary working memory with a very limited capacity, the long-term store is conceptualized as a semipermanent repository of information. An inability to remember material in the long-term store is attributed more to a failure to retrieve stored information than to a total loss from memory (Tulving, 1962).

One reason that adults are superior to children in long-term memory is their greater efficiency in organizing information by semantic clustering, or grouping of to-be-remembered information into subcategories. Recall of items often occurs in clusters or strings of information with one item cuing the recall of another semantically related item. Studies of clustering in children reveal a definite developmental trend, with older children and adolescents benefiting more than younger children. Apparently, grouping does not facilitate recall for children 7 years and younger (Harris and Burke, 1972; McCarver, 1972). Although young children may have information available in long-term memory, they do not spontaneously use organizing activities to facilitate their recall of it (Naus and Ornstein, 1977).

The implication of this research for the criminal justice system is that questioning of children for their memory of some event will be facilitated if the questioner arranges and presents his information in a structured way. For example, questions could be organized around particular themes, time sequences, locations, and so on, without jumping to other issues before the child has been fully helped to remember each incident. In this way the child may be stimulated to search, discover, and use his own organizational processes for recall.

Poorer performance of children than adults may be attributed as well to a failure to develop systematic retrieval plans to guide recall. Effective retrieval depends primarily on successful storage in the first place, access to suitable retrieval cues, and the cleverness to use these cues to recover information from storage. Flavell (1977) in his description of retrieval strategies points out that successful and sophisticated strategies

... often involve a complex interplay between specific memory fragments, general knowledge of the world, and reasoning or reference: "I remember hearing the sound of waves outside (memory fragment), so it probably happened near an ocean (inference, general knowledge); but I've only been to the ocean once, in 1969 (memory fragment), so it must have been that summer, during vacation (inference)." [p. 204]

Information often is available in memory but not necessarily immediately accessible. What a child remembers often indicates what he can retrieve under the specific form of testing being employed rather than what he has stored in memory. Thus, to determine what a child can remember, the police officer, lawyer, or judge is advised to take a flexible approach and use different means of testing, such as free recall, cued recall, multiple-choice questions, recognition memory, and reconstructive memory.

Available research also shows that age differences in retention are partly attributable to the fact that older children make more efficient use of prompts, or retrieval cues, that are provided by a questioner. To illustrate, evidence gathered by Kobasigawa (1974) demonstrates that children of grade six, in contrast to younger children from grades one and three, are superior in recall because of their greater tendency to spontaneously use contextual cues, such as a picture of a zoo, to cue their memory of conceptually related target words—e.g., "bear," "monkey," "camel". Only when the investigator deliberately stresses a connection between the retrieval cue and the to-be-remembered words does cuing become facilitative for recall at the lower grades. Even with instructions directing the young child to make use of retrieval cues, high performance is not guaranteed at the grade-one level. Children in grade three are able to spontaneously make use of retrieval cues to recall target items. But, unlike older children, they will tend to remember only one of the sought-after words that is related to a specific retrieval cue instead of making an exhaustive search for all words related to that cue. Thus young children may have additional knowledge or have stored some relevant information but may not retrieve all of it on demand because of their tendency to abandon their memory search prematurely even though memory prompts or cues are present.

DEVELOPMENTAL DIFFERENCES IN RECOGNITION MEMORY

Recognition memory for previously seen pictures of objects is known to be extremely high for both adults (Shepard, 1967; Standing, Conezio, and Haber, 1970) and children (Brown and Campione, 1972). The ability of young children to remember visual information is much greater than many adults would suspect. To take one study as an example, Entwisle and Huggins (1973) showed a class of first-grade children 40 black-and-white slides or

40 colored slides of landscapes or cityscapes for an interval of ten seconds each. Ninety minutes later the children were given a forced-choice recognition test consisting of each target and a similar decoy slide. With black-and-white slides the children recognized an average of 31 out of the 40 slides, which is significantly better than chance. Performance was even better with colored slides. An average of 34 slides was accurately recognized. In these conditions 91% and 97% of the children correctly recognized the stimuli above chance level (20 out of 40). In order to add further credibility to these findings, a third group of children was tested with the colored slides after a one-week delay. On the average children correctly identified 32 of the 40 slides and 86% of the subjects scored above chance. This study confirms the hypothesis that young children can retain a large amount of visual information, even unremarkable or commonplace information, for a relatively long period of time.

At one time researchers did not detect developmental differences in recognition memory (e.g., Bird and Bennett, 1974; Brown, 1973), but more recently evidence has been found to show that recognition accuracy improves with age (e.g., Nelson and Kosslyn, 1976; Newcombe, Rogoff, and Kagan, 1977). Various explanations have been proposed to account for the consistent developmental trend in recognition memory. One interpretation suggests that children gradually develop planning ability or planfulness in memory tasks (Flavell, 1970). That is, they begin to show an increasing propensity to search the environment for activities which may not have immediate relevance but will facilitate performance subsequently. It is also possible that very young children, in contrast to older children and adults, do not pay attention to visual detail. Tversky and Teiffer (1976) found that although picture recognition improved with age from 5 years through 12 years, attention to visual detail was a successful search strategy only in the 12-year-old age group. Adults and children definitely search and recognize visual scenes in different ways (Mackworth and Bruner, 1970). With clear, sharp pictures adults show more complete scanning of the display and make more leaping movements of the eye to link widely separated areas of the picture than do 6-year-olds. With ambiguous, out-of-focus pictures adults are more capable of visually selecting the informative areas of the stimuli and spend 40% longer fixation times for comprehension as opposed to mere inspection.

MEMORY AND MEANING

As the child grows, his experiences increase and become more variable. Perceptual meanings of things change as he becomes more adaptable to his ever-changing environment. Thus objects that are perceived in one way and uniquely labeled from past experience may be seen as something else as language develops and discriminations become more acute. Recognition memory, however, does not necessarily involve the ability to use appropriate verbal labels. This conclusion is supported by a cross-cultural study conducted by Kagan, Klein, Haith, and Morrison (1973). Fifty-four American middle-class urban children and 54 isolated rural Guatemalan children studied sixty pictures of common objects and people taken from an American magazine. One-quarter of the pictures were completely unfamiliar (e.g., a toaster, telescope, golf clubs) to the Guatemalan children. Recognition memory was tested immediately after inspection or after a twenty-four-hour or forty-eight-hour delay. Although performance for the 5- and 8-year-old American children was superior to the Guatemalans, perhaps because of the latter having a special problem-solving deficit, the 11-year-olds in both cultures performed at an equally high level (over 82% correct) on all three test periods with both familiar and unfamiliar stimuli. The high accuracy and high similarity in performance for the two 11-year-old groups from two quite different cultures confirm the assumption that recognition memory is a fundamental human process common to all mankind (Boas, 1911).

Although children's recognition memory for pictures is not always facilitated by verbal labels, verbal descriptions can modify what is visually perceived and remembered. Bacharach, Carr, and Mehner (1976) found that verbal descriptions which focus only on part of a picture's contents, either before or after the picture is exposed for inspection, increase the recognition memory for that object in both first-grade and fifth-grade children. To put this in the context of criminal justice, the police and the courts can bias the testimony of young children if they verbally prepare the child for what he may be asked to identify.

STRESS AND RECOGNITION MEMORY IN CHILDREN

Stress is known to influence the cognitive behavior of adults, and it is not surprising to discover that stress also influences recognition performance in children. In a study which promises to have profound implications for police practices in conducting lineups with children, Dent (1977) found that children are adversely affected by the stress inherent in making identifications from live lineups in contrast to identifications made from colored slides. Children aged 10 and 11 were exposed to a workman for a period of two minutes during a regular classroom period. One week later they were asked to identify the man either from a conventional police lineup or from projected color slides of the lineup. The slides showed the full-face, profile and full-length appearance of each suspect. Although the absolute percentages of correct identifications were relatively low, significantly better performance was found with identifications made from slides, 29% accuracy compared to only 12% accuracy level in live identifications. Over and above the differences in recognition performance, striking differences were found in overt behaviors between children in the two treatment conditions. Children performing in the live situation appeared nervous, embarrassed, and frightened. Two children in this treatment refused to participate. Some of the children expressed a fear of possible repercussions in the live condition, whereas none of the children in the slide condition were frightened, were nervous, or wished to leave before carefully examining all of the slides. Clearly, the stress inherent in the live situation unduly influenced the recognition memory of these children and their willingness to participate as witnesses.

Photographic Memory and Exceptional Memory

If jurists could have one wish granted which would make their job a little easier, that witnesses have "perfect" memories would be a favorite request. As one lawyer said to me, "Where are these people claiming to have photographic memories when I examine eyewitness testimony?"

The notion of photographic memory is based on a false understanding of visual perception. Perception is not analogous to photography so that the eye acts like a camera to store and transmit pictures of the real world to the mind. Instead, perception and knowledge of the world develop from the selection and integration of stimuli hitting our sensory receptors. Consequently, the most accurate visual memories possible could only be images which reproduced the original visual integration and not the stimulus array itself. In psychological literature, the closest approximation to a literal reproduction of visual input is the eidetic image, and as we shall see, perfect reproduction is rarely or never found in eidetikers (see Neisser, 1967).

Eidetic imagery is characterized as an exceptionally vivid kind of visual image which has the clarity and definiteness of visual perception. It is often defined as "the ability, possessed by a minority of people, to 'see' an image that is an exact copy of the original sensory experience" (Kagan and Havemann, 1972, p. 588). The eidetiker experiences the image "out there" in space rather than as an idea "in the mind." He will move his eyes over the visualized scene as if it had the quality of a real perception and is able to verbally describe what he is seeing.

Eidetic imagery is usually more characteristic of children than of adults, although some aspects may be related to emotional disorders in adults and are useful to psychotherapists for the clinical insights they may provide (Ahsen, 1977). For our purposes several questions pertaining to the nature and extent of eidetic imagery merit special attention.

First of all, eidetic imagery shows its greatest frequency in early child development but beyond age 7 is almost nonexistent, at least among American children and adolescents (Giray, Altkin, Vaught, and Roodin, 1976). When strict control procedures are used to define eidetic imagery separately from the characteristics of the afterimage and the memory image, few children are classified as true eidetikers. One study of 500 school children detected only 7% as eidetic (Leask, Haber, and Haber, 1969).

Accuracy in recall of visual scenes for eidetikers is a controversial issue. At one time eidetikers were thought to have extremely accurate recall for visual displays (Klüver, 1926), but contemporary research findings are equivocal. Some evidence shows that eidetic children have greater recall accuracy for visual details than do noneidetic children (Furst, Fuld, and Pancoe, 1974; Haber and Haber, 1964; Siipola and Hayden, 1965). Other researchers have failed to find any superiority (Leask et al., 1969). It is possible that eidetic imagery per se is not related to memory and does not facilitate recall of visual details. If this is true, eidetics does not seem to have any particular usefulness, which may account for the general failure to detect its existence in adults.

Finally, eidetikers cannot generate on demand images of each and every sensory experience. Instead, imagery is developed only if the stimulus contains interesting material and a coherent structure (Jaensch, 1930). This characteristic seriously reduces potential application to criminal justice practices, particularly in light of findings by Leask et al. (1969) that a "rogues' gallery" of twenty-five cartoon faces was not conducive to the construction of eidetic images. As Gray and Gummerman (1975) pointed out in their thorough review, eidetic imagery is not equivalent to whatever laypersons mean by the term "photographic memory."

Although a belief in photographic memory is unwarranted, some people do have exceptional memories. A few of the more celebrated cases can be cited.

ROBERT A. LOVETT (CUTTS AND MOSELEY, 1969)

Lovett is a former U.S. Secretary of Defense, 1951–1953. He became aware of his unusual memory abilities in high school, where he excelled in French, Greek, and Latin and later in mathematics. One anecdote about his Harvard Law School days illustrates his superior memory. While taking a course in torts with Dean Roscoe Pound, Lovett was also involved in a moot court. One of the cases he prepared for moot court happened to be assigned on his final examination. Lovett answered the question by quoting it verbatim, including case numbers of the references. After reading his paper, Dead Pound asked Lovett to see him. Suspecting that he may have cheated, the dean said, "Mr. Lovett, you realize I must give you either an A or a zero." Lovett replied, "Would it help, Dean Pound, if I quoted the case to you now?"—which he proceeded to do, once again, line by line.

Sometimes he wonders if his mind is not cluttered with useless information. . . . his memory frequently seemed to operate involuntarily. After a drive on the crowded Long Island Expressway his children questioned him about the license numbers of cars that had passed them, and he recalled them without error. (The children had made notes.) . . . His memory is largely visual. He sees print (or a color or a picture) in "the form in which it occurred." He remembers what he has seen better than what he has heard. . . . [Cutts and Moseley, 1969, p. 9]

S. (LURIA, 1968)

Professional mnemonists have always astounded their audiences with their fantastic feats of memory. Perhaps the most famous mnemonist to be described in the psychological literature is a man called S. Luria, the late Russian neuropsychologist, found that S. could easily recall a sequence of seventy words, numbers, or letters without error. After studying a matrix of fifty digits for three minutes, S. could recall the stimuli perfectly in any order minutes, days, and even months and years later. S. performed these feats of memory by using a mnemonic imagery technique:

> When S. read through a long series of words, each word would elicit a graphic image. And since the series was fairly long, he had to find some way of distributing these images of his in a mental row or sequence. Most often (and this habit persisted throughout his life), he would "distribute" them along some roadway or street he visualized in his mind. . . . (Luria, 1968, pp. 31–32).

To recall these words, S. would make a mental walk along the roadway picking up the items as he passed. Occasionally, when an error was made, it was more an error of perception than of memory. S. would not "see" the item because it blended into the background and would go unnoticed.

Not all of his memory achievements, however, were so attractive. S. suffered from an inability to remember faces and voices. Also, he had difficulty in interpreting the meaning of simple sentences such as "The work got under way normally." It is likely that the tendency to associate images to each word produced so much visual detail that S. became confused by the imagery and lost the overall meaning of the sentence.

ALEXANDER CRAIG AITKEN (HUNTER, 1977)

In direct contrast to the mnemonic imagery technique used by S., the late Professor Aitken of the University of Edinburgh developed his powerful memory through extensive training. Hunter (1977) cites numerous examples of his astounding memory, but of more interest is the procedure Aitken used to store and retain material for months and years on end. Aitken stored information by intensively searching for patterns of meaning in the materials being studied. Memorization consisted of finding multiple patterns of meaningful properties inherent in the material and weaving these diverse properties into an elaborate conceptual map. If the materials were interesting to Aitken, their acquisition was relatively easy, and retention was extremely accurate. On the other hand, if asked to remember something which had little meaning for him, as for example, a random string of digits, he would resist. If the material was not too distasteful and he agreed to memorize it, he did not tense up and study it with extreme determination as you might expect. Rather, he would relax and "let the properties of the materials reveal themselves" (p. 158).

Aitken's memory was more developed rather than different in kind from that of other people. He was able to work creatively with general ideas, unlike S., who was a victim of his memory strategies. Whereas Aitken developed the ability to memorize by understanding the conceptual properties of the materials to be remembered, S. relied upon rich imaginal chains.

Other persons having exceptional memories have been described in the psychological literature in the last few years (see, for example, Coltheart and Glick, 1974; Gummerman and Gray, 1971; Hatakeyama, 1974; Hunt and Love, 1972). An overview of this literature suggests that two major factors determine the unique abilities of mnemonists: first, the use of imagery, and second, the construction of rich and elaborate associative networks of meanings.

Questioning Children

Parents, teachers, police officers or other persons in authority often question young children in ways which appear to be simple requests for information but from the view of the child are veiled threats or attacks. The question "Where did you go?" may not be seen as a simple inquiry, but rather may be interpreted to mean, "You weren't supposed to go out and I am angry with you." Oftentimes the child will answer the question "Where did you go?" with the evasive response "Out". He has learned through experience that straightforward answers are likely to arouse even more hostility and anger. Unfortunately, many questions put to children are a prelude to advice, orders, criticisms, censure, and so on. Questions with indirect meanings are not, of course, asked only of children. People of all ages are subjected to manipulatory techniques found in questioning. Children, however, are more susceptible to such pressures because of their greater dependency relationship with authorities.

The complexity inherent in questioning children is compounded further by their relative lack of communication skills. Young children often fail to differentiate between their own private understandings and the necessity to develop certain cognitive skills in order to communicate with others. Children aged 4 and 5, for example, are able to understand and manipulate common objects in a meaningful way, but they are unable to describe to other children or adults what the distinguishing characteristics of an object are so that it can be selected from a set of similar objects (Glucksberg and Krauss, 1967; Krauss and Glucksberg, 1969). In order to communicate meaningfully, the child must be able to judge whether the words he chooses to use best fit their referent as opposed to fitting alternative or similar objects. Research shows that young children are not deficient in perceptual abilities. Preschoolers can discriminate a novel form just as well as older children, yet they fail to communicate this information as accurately (Susswein and Smith, 1975).

One possible reason for failure in communication is a neglect to consider and describe both referents and nonreferents in messages (Asher and Parke, 1975). Another possible reason that older children such as fifth graders communicate more effectively than first graders is their greater tendency to accommodate the listener's perspective (Flavell, Botkin, Fry, Wright, and Jarvis, 1968). Younger children also fail to put adequate effort into communication. The more difficult it is to be informative, the greater the likelihood that young children will quit or fail to complete their messages (Whitehurst, 1976).

However, the most serious problem the courts face in adult-child communication is the error produced from suggestive questions (see Dale, Loftus, and Rathbun, 1978). The classic example of suggestive questioning influencing testimony of children dates back to Varendonck's experiments in 1910. As may be recalled from chapter 8, Varendonck was used in a Belgian courtroom as an expert witness to evaluate the credibility of testimony from two young witnesses in a murder trial. To show that the girls' testimony may have been encouraged by suggestive questioning, Varendonck designed a series of experiments using questions similar in kind to those originally asked of the witnesses. For instance, eighteen 7-year-old children were asked to name the color of the beard of one of their school teachers. Sixteen reported, "Black," and two did not answer. The teacher did not have a beard. Several replications of these results were found in experiments with older pupils. The most dramatic evidence showing that the original testimony could have been tainted by suggestive questions came from Varendonck's final experiment:

> Written answers were required from 8 year old pupils. "When you were standing in line in the yard, a man came up to me, didn't he? You surely know who it was. Write his name on your paper." No man had come, but 7 of 22 children gave a man's name. The experimenter continued, "Was it not Mr. M_____?" Seventeen of the twenty-two answered "yes" and in individual oral examinations gave complete descriptions of the man's appearance and dress. [Rouke, 1957, p. 54]

Moral Reasoning: An Understanding of Lies and Deception

In 1976 the U.S. Military Academy at West Point experienced one of the worst cheating scandals in its 174-year history. Approximately ninety third-year cadets were charged either with cheating on an examination or not reporting cheating they were aware of. The scandal centered around the academy's simple and inflexible honor code, which states, "A cadet will not lie, cheat or steal, or tolerate those who do." Violation of this code by cheating on an insignificant college examination may be of little importance to outsiders and even may be seen as an anachronism. However, this incident, in combination with such others as the cover-up campaigns in Vietnam—the cover-up of the My Lai massacre, the false body counts, the concealment of bombings in Cambodia—as well as the Watergate cover-up, might suggest some serious flaws in the moral fiber of Americans and their institutions.

During this same period (1970–1973), it was common practice for members of the Royal Canadian Mounted Police to engage in such illegal activities as barn burning, stealing dynamite, opening domestic mail, theft of political party membership lists, and breaking into and entering (400) homes and offices for "intelligence probes." Donald Cobb, chief superintendent for the RCMP, defended these illegal police practices on the grounds of "protecting" the country. Cobb stated, "We were used to living with certain illegalities. . . .They were so commonplace they were no longer thought of as illegal. . . .We no longer see them as illegal but as fundamental . . ." (*The Toronto Daily Star,* January 12, 1978).

If the results of a recent study (Kintz, 1977) on college students can be generalized, most people believe that lying is very common in the general population. Individuals report that they personally are opposed to lying but they consider their peers to be sympathetically inclined toward deceit. Furthermore, certain social groups such as politicians and children under 6 years are perceived as being more inclined to lie than other groups such as clergymen and elementary school teachers. To what extent lying is part of our normal social activity is unknown. But social "white lies," exaggerations, and "story telling," although not classified as outright lies, do appear to be common in our daily life.

To understand the behaviors and attitudes just described, perhaps we should look at some of the research on the development of morality. Morality is defined as a system of rules of conduct which governs peoples' beliefs about right and wrong and their behavior in social situations. The learning of morality begins early in childhood, but beliefs about right and wrong change throughout a person's life. The development of moral reasoning is assumed to reflect the sequential changes which occur in cognitive development. Piaget's (1932) studies provide the theoretical foundation for most of the current research in this area, and the most influential extension of this early theorizing is the work of Lawrence Kohlberg (1964, 1968, 1973). Kohlberg studies the way people reason about moral issues by telling his subjects a story such as the following one (which I have paraphrased):

> A woman was near death from cancer. A druggist in town had discovered a drug that might have saved her. The woman's husband tried to buy the drug but the druggist, claiming that it was expensive to make and wanting a profit, charged him ten times what it cost him to make it. The husband could not afford to pay this amount. When the druggist refused to lower the price, the desperate man stole the drug.

After hearing the story, subjects are asked what they think about the husband's action. Was it justified? Why? Kohlberg finds that people take different approaches in their moral judgments and show different attitudes depending upon their age and experience. Children progress through distinct stages of moral development, with each stage representing a more mature form of moral thinking.

Kohlberg theorizes that there are three basic levels of moral orientation: premoral, conventional role conformity, and self-accepted moral principles. Within each level there are two stages. At stage 1, the kindergarten and grade-one school-age child is primarily concerned with avoiding punishment from a superior power. He obeys rules to avoid penalties. A child at this stage would resolve the dilemma by reasoning in one or the other following ways: he would justify the theft by reasoning that people, relatives, or God would punish the husband if he let his wife die, or he would condemn the theft because it hurt the druggist.

In the second stage concern shifts to naive instrumental hedonism. Selfish needs are accepted. The child conforms to obtain rewards and to reciprocate favors. Thus stealing drugs is justified on the grounds that the husband needs a wife's companionship and assistance, or it is condemned because the druggist deserves a profit.

In stage 3 a child obeys to win approval for his social conformity. He wants to be judged for his altruistic intentions. The husband is justified in stealing the drug, according to the reasoning at this stage, since society would not think much of a man who let his wife die, or he is condemned because he would disgrace his family by being a thief.

Stage 4 generally develops between the ages of 7 and 11. This stage reflects law-and-order thinking. The law is upheld and respected because authority and social order maintain morality. People conform to avoid censure by legitimate authorities and are oriented to doing their duty. Thus a child would justify the theft because it is a husband's duty to respect his marriage vows and look after his wife. If the child did not think stealing was justified, he would encourage punishment by putting the man in jail. The man should know that he was wrong and should feel guilty for breaking the law. Most people never advance beyond stage 3 and stage 4 thinking.

Stage 5 normally does not occur before adolescence. People at this level perceive the purpose of the law to be a legal contract between society and the individual to maintain fundamental rights of the people. Individuals conform to preserve the well-being and welfare of everyone in the community. If laws are unjust, they should be changed. Rules are not absolute truths, but rather are compromises which may not work out to everyone's advantage. Theft of the drug in the illustration would be justified on the grounds that the law was wrong and was never designed to be more important than a life. On the other hand, the theft could be condemned by a person at this stage on the grounds that one does not steal under any circumstances. Alternative solutions have to be found because many people can find themselves in desperate situations. Society could not exist if everyone took the law in his own hands.

At stage 6 the individual relies on his conscience as his guide and the mutual respect and trust of others. He is oriented to abstract universal moral principles. Accordingly, the husband should steal the drug because saving a life is more justified than any of man's laws. If stealing is not seen as justified, it is rejected because of belief in a higher commitment to the abstract ideals of truth and honesty. Both choices are justifiable, and a person selects one or the other on the basis of his individual, private, unique standards.

Kohlberg finds that people tend to be consistent in their moral judgments and seldom understand the reasons to justify behavior more than one level above the one in which they are operating. Young children usually function at the premoral level, whereas most older children and adults function at the conventional level of morality. Although moral development is sequential people can backslide as a function of personal experiences and age.

It is likely that different levels of moral judgment are used by the police, the military, and the general populace to justify actions such as those taken at West Point and the illegal activities of the Royal Canadian Mounted Police. Supporters of an immediate expulsion for cadets who violate the honor code argue that the law was broken and the students deserve their consequences (stage 4). On the other hand, the Royal Canadian Mounted Police may be perceived as being justified in stealing and breaking into homes and offices since they are the lawful authority acting in the interests of the country, and know more about the situation than anyone else (stages 3 and 4). The stage 5 man sees the rigid enforcement of the West Point honor code as a violation of the individual's right to a democratic hearing and rights of due process. Stage 5 and stage 6 persons object to police violations of the law since such abuses disregard the social contracts that all people and institutions must adhere to. Violations of the law by any person including the police also violate the higher abstract laws of truth and honesty.

What can we say about the child's tendency to lie? The first major investigation of this topic was by Hartshorne and May (1928), who focused on the child's hypothesized traits of good and bad character. The two investigators failed to find any evidence of character traits or psychological dispositions which correspond to the notions of honesty and truth telling. They concluded that almost everyone lies sometimes, and if a person cheats in one situation, it does not mean that he will or will not cheat in another. Lying and cheating frequently depend on the characteristics of the specific situation such as the likelihood of being caught and the type of consequences to be received.

According to Piaget (1932) the child's understanding of what a lie is depends upon his cognitive development. Children 6 years of age equate a lie with saying naughty words and with untrue statements. For 8- or 9-year-old children a lie is any statement that departs from objective facts, and the larger the discrepancy, the greater the seriousness of the lie. Thus a child saying he saw a mouse as big as an elephant is telling a big lie because mice are never as big as elephants. Older children, about 10 and 11, interpret lies in terms of intentions to deceive. Recent evidence indicates, however, that children as young as 6 years old can understand differences in levels of intentions in making some moral judgments (Berg-Cross, 1975).

Psychology of the Aged

We often doubt the accuracy of reports from elderly persons because they speak softly and cautiously. Nevertheless, our understanding of the psychology of aging has moved in the last few years from a pessimistic view that aging necessarily involves decrement to one which recognizes changes in abilities and processes over a life span of development.

The focus of interest in this section is the elderly as a group in terms of their sensory, perceptual, memory, and intellectual abilities. It is clear that with increased age all sensory systems show a decline in functioning. Similarly, for some persons memory is not as good as it once was. Generational differences in these abilities, however, do not mean that intelligence also must decline. In fact, as we will discuss later, under certain favorable environments intellectual abilities may improve in old age. It is also helpful to differentiate among three kinds of aging: biological, psychological, and social. Biological aging refers to the genetic blueprints or maturational processes involved in growing old. The psychological age of a person reflects his adaptive capacities to cope with both internal and external changes in his environment. And social aging refers to the habits, customs, and roles of an individual relative to the expectations of his peers and society. All three components of aging are related to each other and, in part, set certain limits upon each other.

Perception

Vision and hearing have been the two most extensively studied systems of all the sensory systems, and we will restrict our attention to just these two modalities. In general, seeing and hearing in the aged require an increase in stimulus intensity, loudness of tones and brightness of lights must be greater than was once required to produce a sensation. Compensations for this sort of change are relatively easily made and routine in advanced age. However, other changes in vision and hearing such as the decrease in the diameter of the pupil, which limits the amount of light entering the eye, changes in the structure and functioning of the lens, retina, and optic nerve, and loss of auditory acuity (presbycusis) are not easily resolved by compensation.

VISUAL ACUITY

The ability to see fine details begins to decline after 40 years of age (Bischof, 1976; Hirsch, 1960). By age 70 loss in visual acuity for both distant and near objects is common. Presbyopia, the inability to focus on near objects, is gradual and begins in childhood. Most people become farsighted as they grow older, but this change is not of great practical importance in most circumstances.

DARK ADAPTATION

When an older person walks from the light into a dark room, it usually takes longer for him to adjust, and he is not as sensitive to light sources as are younger persons. Young people (16 to 19), for example, have been found to be five times more sensitive than old people (80 to 89) after two minutes of dark adaptation. By forty minutes young subjects are 240 times more sensitive than are the old (McFarland, 1968). The age–dark adaptation relationship has obvious practical significance for the courts. Older persons are definitely handicapped under such conditions. The aged, in contrast to younger persons, will have more difficulty in operating in the dark (driving, walking, etc.), since bright lights such as the headlights of an oncoming car will cost more time for the eyes to recover their sensitivity and lengthen the period of nonseeing.

COLOR VISION

By 60 years of age the tendency for the lens to yellow results in a distortion in the transmission and refraction of the shorter wavelengths of light. Consequently, blues, greens, and violets become difficult to discriminate. Although all colors are affected, the aged have less difficulty in differentiating among the reds, oranges, and yellows (Gilbert, 1957).

QUALITATIVE CHANGES

In addition to the quantitative changes that occur in aging as a result of disabilities in the sensory systems, qualitative changes in the organization of visual perceptions also are altered with age. What a person "sees" depends

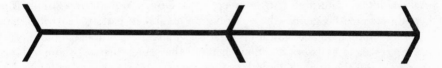

The Muller-Lyer Illusion

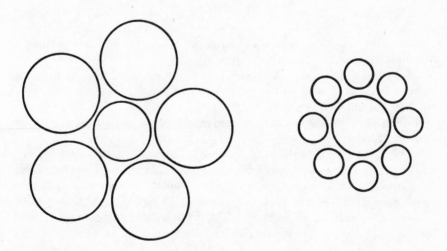

The Titchener Circles Illusion

FIGURE 9.1 Examples of the Muller–Lyer illusion and the Titchener Circles illusion (*from Wapner, Werner, and Comalli, 1960*)

upon his expectancies or hypotheses of what is "out there" and his capacity to handle this information. One question tested along this line is the relationship between susceptibility to visual illusions and age. Unfortunately, clear-cut interpretations are difficult to make in this area, since performance on one illusion task does not necessarily predict performance on another illusion task. For example, one study found that children may become more susceptible to visual illusions as they get older. From 20 to 40, susceptibility to the Muller-Lyer illusion is relatively low and constant. After age 40 susceptibility gradually increases to a high level for persons 65 to 80 (Wapner, Werner, and Comalli, 1960). However, on another illusion task, the Titchener Circles, Wapner and associates found susceptibility to the illusion relatively high and constant in 20-to-44-year-olds but lower in 45-to-49- and 65-to-80-year-old subjects. Although the results for the Muller-Lyer and Titchener Circles illusions were contradictory for the age span investigated, Wapner and his associates interpret the findings as supporting their theory regarding part-whole relationships in perception. Perception in children is hypothesized to be global (the tendency to assimilate parts to the whole), becomes more analytical and articulated in young and middle-aged adults, and regresses to global perceptions again in the senior years. Although the validity of this theory is difficult to evaluate at this time, the observation that qualitative changes in visual perception occur with increasing age is well documented, if not easily explained.

HEARING

The fact that older people do not hear as well as younger persons is common knowledge and is fully supported by scientific and clinical evidence. Decline in hearing, however, is not uniform across all frequencies of sound. Persons 66 and over have a particular problem hearing high tones with frequencies greater than 10,000 cycles per second. This difficulty begins in most persons at age 40, and men tend to show more hearing loss than women (Birren, 1964).

The practical implications of hearing loss involve among other things speech and comprehension difficulties. The ability to interpret high-frequency consonants (e.g., f, g, s, t, z, or th and sh) often is impaired in the aged. Speech perception, however, is not totally attributed to sensory difficulties, since intellectual factors and listening habits can minimize hearing deficiencies. Personality factors also contribute to impaired hearing. Senior citizens usually are more cautious in their behavior and are inclined to respond only to things which they are sure they heard. Although they may have heard something, their cautiousness may inhibit a response, which leads others to think they are hard of hearing (Botwinick, 1973).

Memory

Consistent with investigations on perception, learning and memory performance also appear to deteriorate with age, although not under all conditions. This decline can be attributed to an impairment of all memory mechanisms—attention, storage and organization, and retrieval of information. If one particular aspect can be isolated as contributing most seriously to the decline in memory function, short-term retention deteriorates most consistently with advanced age (Welford, 1958). This impairment may not seem to have serious implications for the criminal justice system, since memory is rarely tested in real-life situations only a few seconds after registration.

Since we cannot remember what we do not acquire in the first place, we will begin our review by looking first at age performances at the level of the sensory register.

SENSORY MEMORY

Information hitting the sensory system must be attended to and "read out" quickly if it is to enter the memory stores. Elderly persons find it difficult to "read out" rapidly presented material (Kinsbourne, 1973). In addition, information in the sensory register is more easily erased by new incoming information in the elderly (mean age 68 years) as opposed to the young (mean age 23 years) (Kline and Birren, 1975). Under conditions of rapid information flow, less information can pass from the sensory register to the memory stores in the aged. These results suggest that more confidence could be attached to the testimony of aged eyewitnesses if they had studied the features of a suspect's face over a period of time as opposed to testimony based upon a brief glance in the middle of rapidly changing events.

SHORT-TERM MEMORY

In general, performance on short-term memory tasks declines in advanced age (Talland, 1968). However, the decline is not due to the limited capacity of short-term stores. Under certain conditions performance shows little loss with age. On tests of memory span, subjects required to recall a list of digits that does not exceed the span of immediate memory display little age decrement (Bromley, 1958; Gilbert, 1941). Large age-related decrements are found, however, if the task exceeds the span of attention (Craik, 1968; Drachman and Leavitt, 1972). This relative decline in the elderly suggests that older persons are deficient in organizing incoming information for immediate recall. The elderly also appear to be more liable to distraction by divided attention between perceptual and memory functions at input. The presentation of distracting events or requiring the elderly to make simultaneous perceptual and motor responses reduces the attention given to encoding processes. Thus poor performance at the moment of reception may be more a function of inadequate learning from poor attention and encoding strategies than a failure in the amount of material that can be stored in short-term memory (Craik, 1971). These deficiencies would account for such limitations in the aged as relatively poor learning, faulty problem solving, and defective perceptual-motor abilities.

LONG-TERM MEMORY

We will look now at long-term memory defined in terms of minutes, hours, and days and leave the discussion of very old memories till later.

While short-term memory is understood to have a limited capacity, long-term memory is conceptualized as infinitely large. Information may be available, but if it is not easily located or retrieved from the system, it is considered forgotten rather than lost. Studies of long-term memory in the aged show that age-related differences in retrieval are evident. However, performance is more improved in the aged relative to young adults when prompts, particularly semantic cues, are available and employed to aid free recall (Hultsch, 1975; Smith, 1977).

Long-term memory is facilitated in older persons if the pace of learning is slow or self-regulated (Canestrari, 1963). Memory in the aged also shows improvement when imagery is employed to facilitate recall. Instructing older adults to generate images as they acquire information and giving them enough time to complete this action facilitates memory performance (Rowe and Schnore, 1971; Treat and Reese, 1976).

DIFFERENCES BETWEEN RECALL AND
RECOGNITION MEMORY

When memory is tested by recognition, alternatives are provided and the subject must decide which stimulus is correct. Some theorists have argued that recognition, unlike recall, does not involve a search and retrieval process, since generation of the alternatives is unnecessary. Most research either has failed to find age-related differences when recognition memory was tested (Craik, 1971; Schonfield and Robertson, 1966) or has shown smaller age differences in recognition than recall (Botwinick and Storandt, 1974; Erber, 1974). It is beyond our purposes, however, to get involved in a theoretical discussion of the aged and the processes of storage and retrieval.

In the final analysis, criminal justice workers are advised that memory can be tested in many ways. When recall tests appear to fail, recognition tests may prove more beneficial in testing the memory of the aged.

INCIDENTAL MEMORY

Very few investigations have been conducted on older subjects testing their memory for incidental recall, that is, learning without an intent to study and remember the materials presented. Two studies that have relevance to our interests, however, can be cited.

One hundred fourteen males ranging in age from 20 to 70 years were shown twenty-five silent film scenes of real-life situations such as a boy inflating a bicycle tire. Following each shot a commentator appeared on the screen and described the scene that had just been shown. Subjects were told to guess by lip reading what the speaker had said. They were not instructed to remember the scenes for a later test of memory. The results showed that the 20-to-29-year group recalled information at the fastest rate and subjects 50 to 69 displayed a constant and gradual reduction in rate of recall. The slower retrieval rate in the aged suggests that less incidental information was stored and/or accessible in this group for recall (Farrimond, 1969).

Another study by Harwood and Naylor (1969) shows that even if subjects are trained to an equal criterion of learning, retention over time declines more rapidly in the aged than in the young. Subjects aged 60 to 80 and 15 to 45 were shown a series of twenty drawings of common objects. The materials were presented as often as necessary to insure that all subjects reached the same level of learning, in this case 80% mastery. Without warning (incidental recall), a month after the learning session all subjects were tested for their memory of the drawings. Recall was significantly poorer in the older group despite their having learned the information as well as the young.

The conclusion based upon these two studies is that incidental memory and intentional memory show a similar decline in advanced age.

VERY LONG-TERM MEMORY

It is a common belief that the aged have excellent memory for old experiences of their early life but have difficulty in remembering recent events. An early theory known as Ribot's (1882) law of forgetting states that the loss of memory strength for any event is inversely related to the remoteness of the event. Thus memory is said to grow stronger over time so that the oldest memories are the most resistant to decay. The question is, how accurate are these old memories? We know that the ability to remember new information declines with age, since we can easily test subjects under controlled laboratory conditions. But in the case of old memories, much of our evidence is based on anecdotal and retrospective data. Evidence gathered from informal interviews is difficult to assess, since it is impossible to distinguish whether or not our remote memories are accurate reconstructions or refabrications. However, if the aim of interviewing the elderly for their remote memories is to ascertain their beliefs rather than a concern for authenticity and accuracy of remote experiences, then retrospective reports are quite legitimate (Yarmey and Bull, 1978).

In light of experimental evidence, Ribot's law of forgetting most likely refers to the confidence and belief that the elderly hold in the accuracy of old memories rather than to detailed accuracy of reports per se. Objective examinations of remote memories for former postage-stamp values (Speakman, 1954), memory for past public events (Squire, 1974; Warrington and Sanders, 1971), and names and faces of former schoolmates (Bahrick, Bahrick, and Wittlinger, 1975) significantly declined in each case for elderly subjects. These results show that remote and recent memory for these types of information are equally influenced by aging. It is likely that old memories which are accurately recalled have high personal value and are often rehearsed over the years because of their emotional relevance. However, vivid memory for highly meaningful materials in the aged does not prove that all old information is retained more readily than recently acquired information. The belief that memory is inversely related to the remoteness of the event in the aged is more myth than fact.

Intelligence and Aging

If the criminal justice system is typical of most social institutions, then the police and courts operate with the belief that intelligence normally declines in old age. Apart from certain exceptions such as Einstein, Churchill, or Golda Meir, who are classified as very special, most people, and especially the mass media, perceive the senior citizen as slow in reasoning, comprehension, and general intelligence.

At one time this view was supported by the research literature. Early studies did show intelligence dropping with age starting around 21 years (Jones and Conrad, 1933; Wechsler, 1944). However, by the 1950s these results, which were gathered by cross-sectional research (testing of different age levels at the same time), were challenged by the findings of longitudinal studies. In this type of investigation, a single group of subjects is tested several times over a period of years. Longitudinal studies reveal that adult intelligence does not necessarily decline in old age as the authorities had once accepted.

In the practical sense, what does intelligence in the aged mean for the police and the courts? The answer, I think, is a general one. Criminal justice workers seek to find credibility and trust in the reports of all their witnesses. If senior citizens display logical reasoning and good vocabulary skills, then their abilities as witnesses from an intellectual point of view should not be questioned.

Intelligence does not refer to a single dimension, but rather refers to how adequately an individual adapts to his environment. In describing adult intelligence, four different kinds of intellectual abilities emerge (Baltes and Schaie, 1974): (1) *crystallized intelligence*, skills acquired through formal education and through culture, such as verbal understanding, numerical skills, logically reasoning, and social and cultural awareness; (2) *cognitive flexibility*, the ability to shift from one way of thinking to another, as in providing either an antonym or synonym to a word when cued in one way or another; (3) *visuomotor flexibility*, the skill involved in shifting from familiar to unfamiliar patterns on visual perceptual-motor tasks, as when one must copy words while interchanging capitals and lowercase letters; (4) *visualization*, the ability to organize and process visual materials, for example, finding a simple figure which is embedded in a complex pattern or identifying a picture that is incomplete.

Baltes and Schaie (1974) found that as people age, their performance declines on only one of the four intellectual abilities, visuomotor flexibility. Cognitive flexibility does not show age-related changes, whereas crystallized intelligence and visualization improve with age, even in people 70 years and over.

These findings deserve emphasis because of their practical significance for the courts. Performance on intelligence tests declines only on visual-motor tasks, which require speed for high scores. But performance on the most important dimension of intelligence, crystallized intelligence, and on visualization systematically increases in scores right into the 70s and 80s. However, regardless of age, for men and women between the ages of 55 and 75, intelligence scores do decline on the average over the five years preceding natural death (Riegel and Riegel, 1972). A tentative interpretation of this "terminal drop" in intellectual abilities is the possibility of neurophysiological deterioration as death approaches.

It is also important to remember the variance of individual differences in intellectual functioning. Many aged persons in their 70s, 80s, and even 90s may be much brighter and quicker in intellectual abilities than middle-aged and younger persons. If the elderly are of average health, there is no reason why they should show any decline in intelligence until near the end of life.

As a rule of thumb, the educational level of a person is more important than his age in predicting his mental ability (Birren and Morrison, 1961). In addition, if intellectual abilities do decline in later life, the major impairment is due to loss in memory and attention abilities (Horn, 1975). Both of these cognitive factors are, of course, of vital importance to the courts.

Cautious Behavior

Many areas of research on adult aging such as motivation, personality, and health could be examined in depth and included in this chapter. The decision not to focus on these topics should not be interpreted as suggesting they have little significance for eyewitness testimony. One concept, however, that touches on each of these areas is the cautious behavior usually found in older men and women.

Most older persons react slowly, especially if their responses involve complex decision making. Psychomotor coordination and speed of response will be particularly impaired if their physical health has declined. But even apart from this problem, there is a greater tendency for older people to be more cautious about responding than younger persons, particularly in "life situations" (Wallach and Kogan, 1961). One possible reason for their caution is the high value they give to accuracy at the expense of speed (Botwinick and Shock, 1952). Older persons often choose not to respond on a decision-making task if they are uncertain. The motivation to avoid mistakes and embarrassment, the high need for certainty before committing oneself, and less confidence about personal judgments rather than defects in attention and memory may be responsible for cautious behavior (Elias, Elias, and Elias, 1977). These factors are not divorced from the chicken-and-the-egg dilemma. Without knowing about the past experiences of success and failure for a particular individual, it is difficult to know if the elderly person performs slowly and poorly because he is afraid of being embarrassed or is unwilling to risk embarrassment because he has made poor decisions in the past and fears that he will perform inadequately in the present. Eyewitness testimony is never a simple process. The aged have the same problems that face the young in attentional and memorial processes, but in addition, they have to cope with stereotyped thinking about what they can and cannot do.

Chapter 10

Toward Integration of Psychology and the Law

In 1908 Münsterberg laid the foundations for the application of experimental psychology to the evaluation and assessment of courtroom testimony. Over the years several lawyers and psychologists including Burtt (1931), Hutchins and Slesinger (1928), McCarty (1929), Toch (1961), among others, have attempted to bridge the gap between the study of human behavior and its application to law. Critics are probably correct in their observation that although "psychologists and lawyers still confront the problems of eyewitness evidence, . . . most law classrooms remain unaffected by the accrued knowledge on mediating psychological processes" (Tapp, 1976, p. 387). To a large extent this separation may be valid. Experimental psychology is a relatively young science, and its insights into the workings of the law are at best partial. However, the issue of failure in influencing the practices of the police and the courts may be a pseudo-issue (Fishman, 1957). Applications of psychological theories and findings have a tendency to be adopted in due time in spite of the law's lack of awareness or resistance to accept, to utilize, or even to credit psychology for its contributions. What one generation of lawyers prefer to understand as "common sense" often depends upon the theory and findings of the previous generation of investigators.

If the research activity of both social scientists and legal scholars is an indicator of a supporting zeitgeist, the time is now ripe for an integration of psychological theories, methodologies, and findings with the law. Several areas of research interest—legal socialization, courtroom procedures, jury selection, decision processes in juries, prison behavior and prison reform, parole decisions, crime and mental illness, and so on—are currently being pursued by both psychologists and lawyers. Interdisciplinary inquiry into legal problems affecting society has begun, but only just begun. It is my view that the future of scientific psychology depends to a large extent upon what it can contribute to the individual and to our society and culture as a whole. It is the responsibility of experimental and social psychologists to develop models, theories, and programs of research that can test the fundamental assumptions of human behavior that affect the legal process.

Perhaps the one area in which we are most advanced and most able to make a significant contribution to the legal system is in the psychology of eyewitness identification and testimony (Bermant, Nemeth, and Vidmar, 1976). In the foregoing pages I have presented a summary and critique of the literature on eyewitness testimony and its relevance and implications for the law. However, a few points need to be emphasized. Societies' trust in the accuracy of eyewitness testimony has to be challenged on several counts. First, the police and the courts have placed unwarranted confidence in eyewitness accounts of crimes and suspects. Second, the biases or errors that are presently found in the police practices of artist's drawings, Identi-Kit, and Photo-Fit representations of suspect's faces, as well as the conducting of lineups, may be subtle but are profound in their possible distortion of justice and the consequences to the individual and society as a whole.

This book and others that have recently been published on the psychology of the law (e.g., Bermant et al., 1976; Sales, 1977a, 1977b; Tapp and Levine, 1977) have attempted each in its own way to show the relevance of psychological theories to criminal justice practices and courtroom procedures. Nevertheless, in spite of the plea for integration of disciplines, involvement in new research directions, and new understandings, there still remains the need for caution, especially from those who work in the discipline of psychology. Ultimately, we have to answer the charge "What good does psychology do?" Unless the legal community can make some use of our theories and findings, our contributions can have little influence. We have to translate our technical phrases into workable, understandable language which can be adopted by nonpsychologists. Furthermore, we have to start applying our theories in socially relevant situations instead of remaining in our laboratories in search of grander models, more elegant theories, and the ever-elusive "decisive" experiment. We must question the importance of simply demonstrating statistically significant differences among age groups, or between males and females, in abilities without going further in our inquiry. The courts may be interested in knowing about differences in perceptual abilities or memory abilities between 50-year-olds and college sophomores but more important is information which tells them whether or not they can have confidence in testimony of particular witnesses. In short, one of our challenges is to design studies which will allow us to apply our theories and our research methods in such a way that we will be able to contribute scientific findings and not mere professional guesses and commonsense notions to the legal process.

The contributions of perceptual and memory theorists (chapters 3 and 4) have been impressively ambitious in scope but meager in detail, especially in explaining everyday behaviors outside of laboratory settings. We know a great deal about the processes of selective attention and how stimulus variables such as intensity, novelty, and complexity affect perception. Explaining why we have difficulty in remembering lists of words in laboratory experiments is a relatively easy task. But explanations are not so readily available to account for the difficulty people have in remembering such common things as birth dates, appointments, or shopping lists. Why, for example, does my son bring home a package of cigarettes when he was sent to the corner store for cottage cheese? In terms of criminal justice, we know very little about the environmental characteristics or observer variables which determine our attending to and remembering crimes in action. Again, why do people (apparently) forget one criminal incident but remember another? Why are some faces more easily remembered than others? Why do some people look more like criminals than do others? We simply do not have enough hard evidence on such questions.

A more complete science of the psychology of law will only be achieved if enough researchers are willing to make the effort to combine hard science with practical applications. This book has only begun to consider some of the very difficult factors which influence eyewitness testimony. The next step for experimental and social psychologists and criminal justice researchers is to provide the imagination, the ingenuity, and the effort to develop models, theories, and methodologies to further our understanding and explanation in this vitally important area.

In closing, I want to repeat an observation that was made over twenty-five years ago by Riesman (1951): "psychology has as much to gain from studying the operation of law as law has to gain from greater appreciation of psychology." Psychologists have to appreciate that law has its own unique purposes and value orientations, even its own logic (Jones, 1966). When psychologists deal with lawyers, they must understand that good lawyers are inquisitive, prying, perhaps even meddlesome, and not content to accept generalities and mean averages as support of a position. At the same time, psychologists must be aware of the danger of overrating the infallibility of their own scientific evidence, forgetting that science is an artificial construction which is not to be equated with ultimate reality.

Provided that psychologists accept their responsibility both to science and to the application of scientific findings and lawyers accept their responsibility to show the inventive thinking necessary for the adoption of psychological evidence for testimonial uses, progress will occur. If the current literature in both law and psychology is an accurate reflection of a growing respect for each other's contributions, there is reason to be optimistic.

References

ABRAMSON, M., & TORGHELE, J. R. Weight, temperature changes, and psychosomatic symptomology in relation to the menstrual cycle. *American Journal of Obstetrics and Gynecology*, 1961, *81*, 223–232.

ADAMS, J. A. *Learning and memory: An introduction.* Homewood, Ill.: Dorsey Press, 1976.

ADCOCK, C. J., & WEBBERLEY, M. Primary mental abilities. *Journal of General Psychology*, 1971, *84*, 229–243.

ADLER, F. The rise of the female crook. *Psychology Today*, 1975, 9, 42, 46, 48, 112, 114.

AHSEN, A. Eidetics: An overview. *Journal of Mental Imagery*, 1977, *1*, 5–38.

ALLISON, H. C. *Personal identification.* Boston: Holbrook Press, 1973.

ALLPORT, G. *Pattern and growth in personality.* New York: Holt, Rinehart and Winston, 1961.

ALLPORT, G. W., & KRAMER, B. M. Some roots of prejudice. *Journal of Psychology*, 1946, *22*, 9–39.

ALLPORT, G. W., & POSTMAN, L. F. The basic psychology of rumor. *Transactions of the New York Academy of Sciences, Series 11*, 1945, *8*, 61–81.

ALPER, A., BUCKHOUT, R., CHERN, S., HARWOOD, R., & SLOMOVITS, M. Eyewitness identification: Accuracy of individual vs. composite recollections of a crime. *Bulletin of the Psychonomic Society*, 1976, *8*, 147–149.

ALTEMEYER, R. A., FULTON, D., & BERNEY, K. M. Long-term memory improvement: Confirmation of a finding by Piaget. *Child Development*, 1969, *40*, 845–857.

AMES, A. Visual perception and the rotating trapezoidal window. *Psychological Monographs*, 1951, *65*, No. 7, Whole No. 324.

ANDERSON, N. H. Adding versus averaging as a stimulus combination rule in impression formation. *Journal of Experimental Psychology*, 1965, *70*, 394–400.

ANDERSON, N. H., & HUBERT, S. Effects of concomitant verbal recall on order effects in personality impression formation. *Journal of Verbal Learning and Verbal Behavior*, 1963, *2*, 379–391.

ANDERSON, R. C., & PICHERT, J. W. Recall of previously unrecallable information following a shift in perspective. *Journal of Verbal Learning and Verbal Behavior*, 1978, *17*, 1–12.

ANDREOFF, G. R., & YARMEY, A. D. Bizarre imagery and associative learning: A confirmation. *Perceptual and Motor Skills*, 1976, *43*, 143–148.

ARGYLE, M. *The psychology of interpersonal behaviour.* London: Cox & Wyman, 1967.

ARGYLE, M., & DEAN, J. Eye contact, distance and affiliation. *Sociometry*, 1965, *28*, 289–304.

ARNHEIM, R. Words in their place. *The Journal of Typographic Research*, 1970, *4*, 199–212.

ARTHER, R. O. *The scientific investigator.* Springfield, Ill.: Charles C Thomas, 1965.

ASCH, S. E. Forming impressions of personality. *Journal of Abnormal and Social Psychology*, 1946, *41*, 258–290.

ASCH, S. E. Studies of independence and conformity: 1. A minority of one against a unanimous majority. *Psychological Monographs*, 1956, *70*, No. 9, Whole No. 416.

ASHER, S. R., & PARKE, R. D. Influence of sampling and comparison processes on the development of communication effectiveness. *Journal of Educational Psychology*, 1975, *67*, 64–75.

ATKINSON, J. W., & Walker, E. L. The affiliation motive and perceptual sensitivity to faces. *Journal of Abnormal and Social Psychology*, 1956, *53*, 38–41.

ATKINSON, R. C., & SHIFFRIN, R. M. Human memory: A proposed system and its control processes. In K. W. Spence & J. T. Spence (Eds.), *The psychology of learning and motivation: Advances in research and theory*, Vol. 2. New York: Academic Press, 1968.

ATTNEAVE, F. Transfer of experience with a class-schema to identification-learning of patterns and shapes. *Journal of Experimental Psychology*, 1957, *54*, 81–88.

ATTNEAVE, F. How do you know? *American Psychologist*, 1974, *29*, 493–499.

BACHARACH, V. R., CARR, T. H., & Mehner, D. S. Interactive and independent contributions of verbal descriptions to children's picture memory. *Journal of Experimental Child Psychology*, 1976, *22*, 492–498.

BADDELEY, A. D. Closure and response bias in short-term memory for form. *British Journal of Psychology*, 1968, *59*, 139–145.

BADDELEY, A. D. *The psychology of memory.* New York: Basic Books, 1976.

BAHRICK, H. P., BÁHRICK, P. O., & WITTLINGER, R. P. Fifty years of memory for names and faces: A cross-sectional approach. *Journal of Experimental Psychology: General*, 1975, *104*, 54–75.

BAHRICK, H. P., & BOUCHER, B. Retention of visual and verbal codes of the same stimuli. *Journal of Experimental Psychology*, 1968, *78*, 417–422.

BAKAN, D. *On method.* San Francisco: Jossey-Bass, 1967.

BAKER, E. Perceiver variables involved in the recognition of faces. Unpublished doctoral dissertation, University of London, 1967.

BALTES, P. B., & SCHAIE, K. W. Aging and I.Q.: The myth of the twilight years. *Psychology Today,* 1974, *7,* 35–40.

BARLAND, G. H., & RASKIN, D. C. Detection of deception. In W. F. Prokasy and D. C. Raskin (Eds.), *Electrodermal activity in psychological research.* New York: Academic Press, 1973.

BARLAND, G. H., & RASKIN, D. C. An evaluation of field techniques in detection of deception. *Psychophysiology,* 1975, *12,* 321–330.

BARTLETT, F. C. *Remembering.* London: Cambridge University Press, 1932.

BASSILI, J. N. Facial motion in the perception of faces and of emotional expression. *Journal of Experimental Psychology: Human Perception and Performance,* 1978, *4,* 373–379.

BAUMRIN, J. M. Aristotle's empirical nativism. *American Psychologist,* 1975, *30,* 486–494.

BAY, E. Disturbances of visual perception and their examination. *Brain,* 1953, *76,* 515–550.

BEIER, E. G. The effect of induced anxiety on flexibility of intellectual functioning. *Psychological Monographs: General and Applied,* 1951, *65,* No. 9, Whole No. 326.

BEIJK-DOCTER, M. A., & ELSHOUT, J. J. Veldafhankelijkheid en geheugen met betrekking tot sociaal relevant en sociaal niet-relevant materiaal. *Nederlands Tijdschrift voor de Psychologie en haar Grensgebieden,* 1969, *24,* 267–279.

BELLI, M. M. *Modern trials,* Vols. 1, 2 and 3. Indianapolis: Bobbs-Merrill, 1954.

BELMONT, J. M. Short-term memory in mental retardates, normal children and normal adults. *Journal of Experimental Child Psychology,* 1967, *5,* 114–122.

BELMONT, J. M., & BUTTERFIELD, E. C. The relations of short-term memory to development and intelligence. In L. P. Lipsitt and H. W. Reese (Eds.), *Advances in child development and behavior,* Vol. 4. New York: Academic Press, 1969, pp. 29–82.

BEM, D. J. Self-perception: An alternative interpretation of cognitive dissonance phenomena. *Psychological Review,* 1967, *74,* 183–200.

BEM, S. L. The measurement of psychological androgyny. *Journal of Consulting and Clinical Psychology,* 1974, *42,* 155–162.

BEM, S. L., & BEM, D. J. Case study of a non-conscious ideology: Training the woman to know her place. In D. J. Bem (Ed.), *Beliefs, attitudes, and human affairs.* Monterey, Calif.: Brooks/Cole, 1970.

BEN SHAKHAR, G., LIEBLICH, I., & KUGELMASS, S. Guilty knowledge technique: Application of signal detection measures. *Journal of Applied Psychology,* 1970, *54,* 409–418.

BENTON, A. L., & VAN ALLEN, M. W. Impairment of facial recognition in patients with cerebral disease. *Cortex,* 1968, *4,* 344–358.

BERELSON, B., & SALTER, P. J. Majority and minority Americans: An analysis of magazine fiction. *Public Opinion Quarterly*, 1946, *10*, 168–190.

BERG, K. S., & VIDMAR, N. Authoritarianism and recall of evidence about criminal behavior. *Journal of Research in Personality*, 1975, *9*, 147–157.

BERG-CROSS, L. G. Intentionality, degree of damage, and moral judgments. *Child Development*, 1975, *46*, 970–974.

BERMANT, G., NEMETH, C., & VIDMAR, N. (Eds.) *Psychology and the law.* Lexington, Mass.: Lexington Books, 1976.

BERSCHEID, E., & WALSTER, E. Physical attractiveness. In L. Berkowitz (Ed.), *Advances in experimental social psychology*, Vol. 7. New York: Academic Press, 1974. (a)

BERSCHEID, E., & WALSTER, E. A little bit about love. In T. L. Huston (Ed.), *Foundations of interpersonal attraction.* New York: Academic Press, 1974. (b)

BERSH, P. J. A validation of polygraph examiner judgments. *Journal of Applied Psychology*, 1969, *53*, 399–403.

BERSOFF, D. N., & PRASSE, D. Applied psychology and judicial decision making: Corporal punishment as a case in point. *Professional Psychology*, August 1978, 400–411.

BERTILLON, A. *Signaletic instructions: The theory and practice of anthropometrical identification.* Ed. and trans. R. W. McCloughry. Chicago: The Werner Co., 1896.

BEYN, E. S., & KNYAZEVA, G. R. The problem of prosopagnosia. *Journal of Neurology, Neurosurgery, and Psychiatry*, 1962, *25*, 154–158.

BIRD, J. E., & BENNETT, A. F. A developmental study of recognition of pictures and nouns. *Journal of Experimental Child Psychology*, 1974, *18*, 117–126.

BIRREN, J. E. *The psychology of aging.* Englewood Cliffs, N.J.: Prentice-Hall, 1964.

BIRREN, J. E., & MORRISON, D. F. Analysis of the WAIS subtests in relation to age and education. *Journal of Gerontology*, 1961, *16*, 363–369.

BISCHOF, L. J. *Adult psychology.* New York: Harper & Row, 1976.

BLANEY, R. L., & WINOGRAD, E. Developmental differences in children's recognition memory for faces. *Developmental Psychology*, 1978, *14*, 441–442.

BLOM-COOPER, L., & WEGNER, J. Psychological selectivity in the courtroom. *Medicine, Science and the Law*, 1968, *8*, 31–37.

BOAS, F. *The mind of primitive man.* New York: Macmillan, 1911.

BOEHM, V. Mr. Prejudice, Miss Sympathy and the authoritarian personality. *Wisconsin Law Review*, 1968, 734–750.

BORCHARD, E. M. *Convicting the innocent.* Hamden, Conn.: Archon, 1961.

BOTWINICK, J. *Aging and behavior.* New York: Springer, 1973.

BOTWINICK, J., & SHOCK, N. W. Age differences in performance decrement with continuous work. *Journal of Gerontology*, 1952, *7*, 41–46.

BOTWINICK, J., & STORANDT, M. *Memory, related functions, and age.* Springfield, Ill.: Charles C Thomas, 1974.

BOUSFIELD, W. A. The occurrence of clustering in the recall of randomly arranged associates. *Journal of General Psychology*, 1953, *49*, 229–240.

BOWER, G. H. Analysis of a mnemonic device. *American Scientist*, 1970, *58*, 496–510.

BOWER, G. H., & CLARK, M. C. Narrative stories as mediators for serial learning. *Psychonomic Science*, 1969, *14*, 181–182.

BOWER, G. H., & KARLIN, M. B. Depth of processing pictures of faces and recognition memory. *Journal of Experimental Psychology*, 1974, *103*, 751–757.

BRADSHAW, J. L., & WALLACE, G. Models for the processing and identification of faces. *Perception and Psychophysics*, 1971, *9*, 443–448.

BROMLEY, D. B. Some effects of age on short term learning and remembering. *Journal of Gerontology*, 1958, *13*, 398–406.

BROOKS, R. M., & GOLDSTEIN, A. G. Recognition by children of inverted photographs of faces. *Child Development*, 1963, *34*, 1033–1040.

BROOKS, W. N., & DOOB, A. N. Justice and the jury. *Journal of Social Issues*, 1975, *31*, 171–182.

BROWN, A. L. Judgments of recency for long sequences of pictures: The absence of a development trend. *Journal of Experimental Child Psychology*, 1973, *15*, 473–480.

BROWN, A. L., & CAMPIONE, J. C. Recognition memory for perceptually similar pictures in preschool children. *Journal of Experimental Psychology*, 1972, *95*, 55–62.

BROWN, A. L., & SCOTT, M. S. Recognition memory for pictures in preschool children. *Journal of Experimental Child Psychology*, 1971, *11*, 401–412.

BROWN, J. Distortions in immediate memory. *Quarterly Journal of Experimental Psychology*, 1956, *8*, 134–139.

BROWN, R., & McNEILL, D. The "tip-of-the-tongue" phenomenon. *Journal of Verbal Learning and Verbal Behavior*, 1966, *5*, 325–337.

BROWN, R. W., & LENNEBERG, E. H. A study in language and cognition. *Journal of Abnormal and Social Psychology*, 1954, *49*, 454–462.

BRUNER, J. S. On perceptual readiness. *Psychological Review*, 1957, *64*, 123–152.

BRUNER, J. S., & GOODMAN, C. D. Value and need as organizing factors in perception. *Journal of Abnormal and Social Psychology*, 1947, *42*, 33–34.

BRUNER, J. S., GOODNOW, J. J., & AUSTIN, G. A. *A study of thinking.* New York: Wiley, 1956.

BRUNER, J. S., & TAGIURI, R. The perception of people. In G. Lindzey (Ed.), *Handbook of Social Psychology*, Vol. 2. Reading, Mass.: Addison-Wesley, 1954, pp. 601–633.

BRUNING, J. L. The effects of connotative meaning on the learning of names. *Journal of Social Psychology*, 1972, *86*, 105–110.

BRUNING, J. L., & ALBOTT, W. Funny, you don't look Cecil. *Human Behavior*, July 1974. Reprinted in D. Krebs (Ed.), *Readings in Social Psychology: Contemporary Perspectives*. New York: Harper & Row, 1976.

BRUNSWIK, E. *Perception and the representative design of psychological experiments.* Berkeley: University of California Press, 1956.

BUCK, R. Nonverbal communication of affect in children. *Journal of Personality and Social Psychology*, 1975, *31*, 644–653.

BUCK, R., MILLER, R. E., & CAUL, W. F. Sex, personality, and physiological variables in the communication of emotion via facial expression. *Journal of Personality and Social Psychology*, 1974, *30*, 587–596.

BUCKHOUT, R. Eyewitness testimony. *Scientific American*, 1974, *231*, No. 6, 23–31.

BUCKHOUT, R. Guilt by fabrication: Psychology and the eyewitness. In M. H. Siegel & H. P. Zeigler (Eds.), *Psychological research: The inside story*. New York: Harper & Row, 1976.

BUCKHOUT, R., ALPER, A., CHERN, S., SILVERBERG, G., & SLOMOVITS, M. Determinants of eyewitness performance on a lineup. *Bulletin of the Psychonomic Society*, 1974, *4*, 191–192.

BUCKHOUT, R., FIGUEROA, D., & HOFF, E. Eyewitness identification: Effects of suggestion and bias in identification from photographs. *Bulletin of the Psychonomic Society*, 1975, *6*, 71–74.

BUGELSKI, B. R. Images as mediators in one-trial paired-associate learning: II. Self-timing in successive lists. *Journal of Experimental Psychology*, 1968, *77*, 328–334.

BUGELSKI, B. R., KIDD, E., & SEGMEN, J. Image as a mediator in one-trial paired-associate learning. *Journal of Experimental Psychology*, 1968, *76*, 69–73.

BUGENTAL, D. E., KASWAN, J. W., & LOVE, L. R. Perception of contradictory meanings conveyed by verbal and nonverbal channels. *Journal of Personality and Social Psychology*, 1970, *16*, 647–655.

BULL, R. H. C., & REID, R. L. Recall after briefing: Television versus face-to-face presentation. *Journal of Occupational Psychology*, 1975, *48*, 73–78.

BURNS, J. A., & KINTZ, B. L. Eye contact while lying during an interview. *Bulletin of the Psychonomic Society*, 1976, *7*, 87–89.

BURTT, H. *Legal psychology*. New York: Prentice-Hall, 1931.

BUTTER, M. Differential recall of paired associates as a function of arousal and concreteness-imagery levels. *Journal of Experimental Psychology*, 1970, *84*, 252–256.

CADY, H. M. On the psychology of testimony. *American Journal of Psychology*, 1924, *35*, 110–112.

CAMPBELL, C. Detectives of the mind? Portrait of a mass killer. *Psychology Today*, May 1976, 110–119.

CANESTRARI, R. E., Jr. Paced and self-paced learning in young and elderly adults. *Journal of Gerontology*, 1963, *18*, 165–168.

CANNAVALE, F. J., Jr., & FALCON, W. D. *Witness cooperation*, Lexington, Mass.: Heath, 1976.

CARDNO, J. A. Imagination: Some early American approaches evaluated. *Psychological Record*, 1967, *17*, 65–76.

CAREY, S., & DIAMOND, R. From piecemeal to configurational representation of faces. *Science*, 1977, *195*, 312–314.

CARMICHAEL, L. L., HOGAN, H. P., & WALTER, A. A. An experimental study of the effect of language on the reproduction of visually perceived form. *Journal of Experimental Psychology*, 1932, *15*, 73–86.

CARTER, L. J. The identification of racial membership. *Journal of Abnormal and Social Psychology*, 1948, *43*, 279–286.

CAVIOR, H. E., HAYES, S. C., & CAVIOR, N. Physical attractiveness of female offenders: Effects on institutional performance. *Criminal Justice and Behavior*, 1974, *1*, 321–331.

CERVIN, V. Individual behavior in social situations: Its relation to anxiety, neuroticism, and group solidarity. *Journal of Experimental Psychology*, 1956, *51*, 161–168.

CHANCE, J., & GOLDSTEIN, A. G. Recognition of faces and verbal labels. *Bulletin of the Psychonomic Society*, 1976, *7*, 384–386.

CHANCE, J., GOLDSTEIN, A. G., & MCBRIDE, L. Differential experience and recognition memory for faces. *Journal of Social Psychology*, 1975, *97*, 243–253.

CHRISTIE, R., & GEIS, F. *Studies in Machiavellianism*. New York: Academic Press, 1970.

CLARKE, H. M. Recall and recognition for faces and names. *Journal of Applied Psychology*, 1934, *18*, 757–763.

CLIFFORD, B. Police as eyewitnesses. *New Society*, 1976, *22*, 176–177.

CLIFFORD, B. R., & SCOTT, J. Individual and situational factors in eyewitness testimony. *Journal of Applied Psychology*, 1978, *63*, 352–359.

CLINE, V. B. Interpersonal perception. In B. A. Maher (Ed.), *Progress in experimental personality research*, Vol. 1. New York: Academic Press, 1964.

CLORE, G. L., WIGGINS, N. H., & ITKIN, S. Gain and loss in attraction: Attributions from nonverbal behavior. *Journal of Personality and Social Psychology*, 1975, *31*, 706–712.

COCOZZA, J. J., & STEADMAN, H. J. Prediction in psychiatry: An example of misplaced confidence in experts. *Social Problems*, 1978, *25*, 265–276.

COHEN, A. A. Number of features, and alternatives per feature, in reconstructing faces with the Identi-Kit. *Journal of Police Science and Administration*, 1973, *1*, 349–354.

COHEN, J. Psychological time. *Scientific American*, 1964, *211*, 116–124.

COHEN, M. E., & CARR, W. J. Facial recognition and the von Restorff effect. *Bulletin of the Psychonomic Society*, 1975, *6*, 383–384.

COHEN, R. L., & GRANSTRÖM, K. The role of verbalizing in the memorizing of conventional figures. *Journal of Verbal Learning and Verbal Behavior*, 1968, *7*, 380–383.

COLE, M., & PEREZ-CRUET, J. Prosopagnosia. *Neuropsychologia*, 1964, *2*, 237–246.

COLLINS, A. M., & QUILLIAN, M. R. Retrieval time from semantic memory. *Journal of Verbal Learning and Verbal Behavior*, 1969, *8*, 240–247.

COLTHEART, M., & GLICK, M. J. Visual imagery: A case study. *Quarterly Journal of Experimental Psychology*, 1974, *26*, 438–453.

COOK, M., & MCHENRY, R. *Sexual attraction*. Toronto: Pergamon Press, 1978.

COSTOPOULOS, W. C. Commentaries: Persuasion in the courtroom. *Duquesne Law Review*, 1972, *10*, 384–409.

CRAIK, F. I. M. Short-term memory and the aging process. In G. A. Talland (Ed.), *Human aging and behavior*. New York: Academic Press, 1968.

CRAIK, F. I. M. Age differences in recognition memory. *Quarterly Journal of Experimental Psychology*, 1971, *23*, 316–323.

CRAIK, F. I. M., & LOCKHART, R. S. Levels of processing: A framework for memory research. *Journal of Verbal Learning and Verbal Behavior*, 1972, *11*, 671–684.

CROMWELL, H. The relative effect on audience attitude of the first versus the second argumentative speech of a series. *Speech Monographs*, 1950, *17*, 105–122.

CRONBACH, L. J. Processes affecting scores on "understanding of others" and "assumed similarity". *Psychological Bulletin*, 1955, *52*, 177–193.

CROSS, J. F., CROSS, J., & DALY, J. Sex, race, age, and beauty as factors in recognition of faces. *Perception and Psychophysics*, 1971, *10*, 393–396.

CRUMBAUGH, J. C. Temporal changes in the memory of visually perceived form. *American Journal of Psychology*, 1954, *67*, 647–658.

CRUTCHFIELD, R. S., WOODWORTH, D. G., & ALBRECHT, R. E. *Perceptual performance and the effective person* [WADC–TN–58–60]. Lackland Air Force Base, Tex.: Personnel Laboratory, Wright Air Development Center, Air Research and Development Command, April, 1958. [ASTIA No. AD–151 039]

CULLITON, B. J. Edelin trial: Jury not persuaded by scientists for the defense. *Science*, 1975, *187*, 814–816.

CURTIS, C. P. The advocate. In W. H. Davenport (Ed.), *Voices in court*. New York: Macmillan, 1958.

CUTTS, N. E., & MOSELEY, N. Notes on photographic memory. *Journal of Psychology*, 1969, *71*, 3–15.

DAHLEM, N. W. Reconstitutive memory in kindergarten children revisited. *Psychonomic Science*, 1969, *17*, 101–102.

DALE, P. S., LOFTUS, E. F., & RATHBUN, L. The influence of the form of the question on the eyewitness testimony of preschool children. *Journal of Psycholinguistic Research*, 1978, *7*, 269–277.

DALTON, K. Menstruation and crime. *British Medical Journal*, 1961, *2*, 1752–1753.

DAN, A. J. Behavioral variability and the menstrual cycle. Paper presented at the annual meeting of the American Psychological Association, Washington, D.C., 1976.

DANNENMAIER, W. D., & THUMIN, F. J. Authority status as a factor in perceptual distortion of size. *Journal of Social Psychology*, 1964, *63*, 361–365.

DARWIN, C. *The expression of the emotions in man and animals*. London: J. Murray, 1872.

DAVIDSON, H. A. Appraisal of the witness. *American Journal of Psychiatry*, 1954, *110*, 481–486.

DAVIDSON, P. O. Validity of the guilty knowledge technique: The effects of motivation. *Journal of Applied Psychology*, 1968, *52*, 62–65.

DAVIES, G., ELLIS, H., & SHEPHERD, J. Cue saliency in faces as assessed by the 'Photofit' technique. *Perception*, 1977, *6*, 263–269.

DAVIES, G., ELLIS, H., & SHEPHERD, J. Face recognition accuracy as a function of mode of representation. *Journal of Applied Psychology*, 1978, *63*, 180–187.

DAVIES, G. M. Recognition memory for pictured and named objects. *Journal of Experimental Child Psychology*, 1969, *7*, 448–458.

DAVIES, G. M. The influence of verbal labeling on the retention of pictured stimuli: An alternative viewpoint. *Journal of Special Education*, 1971, *5*, 323–336.

DAVIS, H. On the names of animal behaviorists. *Worm Runner's Digest*, 1974, *16*, 73–76.

DEAN, S. J., MARTIN, R. B., & STREINER, D. Mediational control of the GSR. *Journal of Experimental Research in Personality*, 1968, *3*, 71–76.

DEAUX, K. *The behavior of women and men.* Monterey, Calif.: Brooks/Cole, 1976.

DEESE, J. *Psychology as science and art.* New York: Harcourt Brace Jovanovich, 1972.

DEFFENBACHER, K., BROWN, E., & STURGILL, W. Memory for faces and the circumstances of their encounter. Report from the Department of Criminal Justice, The University of Nebraska at Omaha, 1975.

DEFFENBACHER, K. A., PLATT, G. J., & WILLIAMS, M. A. Differential recall as a function of socially induced arousal and retention interval. *Journal of Experimental Psychology*, 1974, *103*, 809–811.

DENT, H. R. Stress as a factor influencing person recognition in identification parades. *Bulletin of the British Psychological Society*, 1977, *30*, 339–340.

DE RENZI, E., & SPINNLER, H. Facial recognition in brain-damaged patients. *Neurology*, 1966, *16*, 145–152.

DETTERMAN, D. K., & ELLIS, N. R. Determinants of induced amnesia in short-term memory. *Journal of Experimental Psychology*, 1972, *95*, 308–316.

DIAMOND, R., & CAREY, S. Developmental changes in the representation of faces. *Journal of Experimental Child Psychology*, 1977, *23*, 1–22.

DION, K. K. Physical attractiveness and evaluation of children's transgressions. *Journal of Personality and Social Psychology*, 1972, *24*, 207–213.

DION, K. K., BERSCHEID, E., & WALSTER, E. What is beautiful is good. *Journal of Personality and Social Psychology*, 1972, *24*, 285–290.

DIRKS, J., & NEISSER, U. Memory for objects in real scenes: The development of recognition and recall. *Journal of Experimental Child Psychology*, 1977, *23*, 315–328.

DOOB, A. N., & KIRSHENBAUM, H. M. Some empirical evidence on the effect of S.12 of the Canada Evidence Act on an accused. *Criminal Law Quarterly*, 1972, *15*, 88–96.

DOOB, A. N., & KIRSHENBAUM, H. M. Bias in police lineups—partial remembering. *Journal of Police Science and Administration*, 1973, *1*, 287–293.

DORNBUSCH, S., HASTORF, A. H., RICHARDSON, S. A., MUZZY, R. E., & VREELAND, R. S. The perceiver and the perceived: Their relative influence on the categories of interpersonal cognition. *Journal of Personality and Social Psychology*, 1965, *1*, 434–441.

DOWDLE, M. D., & SETTLER, J. M. Recognition memory and prejudice. Paper presented at the annual meeting of the Midwestern Psychological Association, Cincinnati, 1970.

DRACHMAN, D. A., & LEAVITT, J. Memory impairment in the aged: Storage versus retrieval deficit. *Journal of Experimental Psychology*, 1972, *93*, 302–308.

DUDA, P. D. Issues in visual laterality research. Colloquium presented to the Department of Psychology, University of Guelph, Guelph, Ontario, 1978.

DUNCAN, C. P., SECHREST, L., & MELTON, A. W. (Eds.) *Human memory: Festschrift for Benton J. Underwood*. New York: Appleton-Century-Crofts, 1972.

EBBINGHAUS, H. *Memory: A contribution to experimental psychology*. New York: Dover, 1964. (Originally published at Leipzig: Duncker and Humblot, 1885.)

EFRAN, M. G. The effect of physical appearance on the judgment of guilt, interpersonal attraction, and severity of recommended punishment in a simulated jury task. *Journal of Research in Personality*, 1974, *8*, 45–54.

EIDLIN, F. Symposium on the meaning of science in the social sciences. College of Social Science, University of Guelph, Guelph, Ontario, February, 1975.

EKMAN, P. Universals and cultural differences in facial expression of emotion. In J. K. Cole (Ed.), *Nebraska Symposium on Motivation*. Lincoln: University of Nebraska Press, 1972.

EKMAN, P., & FRIESEN, W. Nonverbal leakage and clues to deception. *Psychiatry*, 1969, *32*, 88–106.

EKMAN, P., & FRIESEN, W. V. Constants across cultures in the face and emotion. *Journal of Personality and Social Psychology*, 1971, *17*, 124–129.

EKMAN, P., FRIESEN, W. V., & ELLSWORH, P. *Emotion in the human face*. New York: Pergamon Press, 1972.

EKMAN, P., FRIESEN, W. V., & SCHERER, K. R. Body movement and voice pitch in deceptive interaction. *Semiotica*, 1976, *16*, 23–27.

EKMAN, P., SORENSEN, E. R., & FRIESEN, W. V. Pan-cultural elements in facial displays of emotions. *Science*, April 4, 1969, *164* (3875), 86–88.

EKSTRAND, B. R. To sleep, perchance to dream (about why we forget). In C. P. Duncan, L. Sechrest, & A. W. Melton (Eds.), *Human memory: Festschrift for Benton J. Underwood*. New York: Appleton-Century-Crofts, 1972.

ELIAS, M. F., ELIAS, P. K., & ELIAS, J. W. *Basic processes in adult developmental psychology*. St. Louis: C. V. Mosby, 1977.

ELLIOTT, E. S., WILLS, E. J., & GOLDSTEIN, A. G. The effects of discrimination training on the recognition of white and oriental faces. *Bulletin of the Psychonomic Society*, 1973, *2*, 71–73.

ELLIOTT, D. N., & WITTENBERG, D. H. Accuracy of identification of Jewish and non-Jewish photographs. *Journal of Abnormal and Social Psychology*, 1955, *51*, 339–341.

ELLIS, H., SHEPHERD, J., & BRUCE, A. The effects of age and sex upon adolescents' recognition of faces. *Journal of Genetic Psychology*, 1973, *123*, 173–174.

ELLIS, H., SHEPHERD, J., & DAVIES, G. An investigation of the use of the Photo-Fit technique for recalling faces. *British Journal of Psychology*, 1975, *66*, 29–37.

ELLIS, H. C. Transfer of stimulus predifferentiation to shape recognition and identification learning: Role of properties of verbal labels. *Journal of Experimental Psychology*, 1968, *78*, 401–409.

ELLIS, H. C., & DANIEL, T. C. Verbal processes in long-term stimulus-recognition memory. *Journal of Experimental Psychology*, 1971, *90*, 18–26.

ELLIS, H. C., & MULLER, D. G. Transfer in perceptual learning following stimulus predifferentiation. *Journal of Experimental Psychology*, 1964, *68*, 388–395.

ELLIS, H. D. Recognizing faces. *British Journal of Psychology*, 1975, *66*, 409–426.

ELLIS, H. D., DAVIES, G. M., & SHEPHERD, J. W. A critical examination of the Photofit system for recalling faces. *Egonomics*, 1978, *21*, 297–307.

ELLIS, H. D., DEREGOWSKI, J. B., & SHEPHERD J. W. Descriptions of white and black faces by white and black subjects. *International Journal of Psychology*, 1975, *10*, 119–123.

ELLIS, N. R., DETTERMAN, D. K., RUNCIE, D., McCARVER R. B., & CRAIG, E. M. Amnesic effects in short-term memory. *Journal of Experimental Psychology*, 1971, *89*, 357–361.

ELLSWORTH, P. C., CARLSMITH, J. M., & HENSON, A. Staring as a stimulus to flight in humans: A series of field studies. *Journal of Personality and Social Psychology*, 1972, *21*, 302–311.

ELWORK, A., SALES, B. D., & ALFINI, J. J. Juridic decisions: In ignorance of the law or in light of it? *Law and Human Behavior*, in press.

ENTWISLE, D. R., & HUGGINS, W. H. Iconic memory in children. *Child Development*, 1973, *44*, 392–394.

ERBER, J. T. Age differences in recognition memory. *Journal of Gerontology*, 1974, *29*, 177–181.

ERDELYI, M. H. A new look at the new look. *Psychological Review*, 1974, *81*, 1–25.

ERDELYI, M. H., & BECKER, J. Hypermnesia for pictures: Incremental memory for pictures but not words in multiple recall trials. *Cognitive Psychology*, 1974, *6*, 159–171.

ERDELYI, M. H., & KLEINBARD, J. Has Ebbinghaus decayed with time? The growth of recall (hypermnesia) over days. *Journal of Experimental Psychology: Human Learning and Memory*, 1978, *4*, 275–289.

ERICKSON, B., LIND, E. A., JOHNSON, B. C., & O'BARR, W. M. Speech style and impression formation in a court setting: The effects of "power" and "powerless" speech. *Journal of Experimental Social Psychology*, 1978, *14*, 266–279.

ERVIN, F. R., & ANDERS, T. R. Normal and pathological memory: Data and conceptual scheme. In *The neurosciences second study program*. New York: Rockefeller University Press, 1970.

EXLINE, R., THIBAUT, J., HICKEY, C., & GUMPERT, P. Visual interaction in relation to Machiavellianism and an unethical act. In R. Christie and Florence Geis (Eds.), *Studies in Machiavellianism*. New York: Academic Press, 1970.

EXLINE, R. V. Visual interaction. In J. Cole (Ed.), *Nebraska symposium on motivation*. Lincoln: University of Nebraska Press, 1971.

EYSENCK, H. J. *Sense and nonsense in psychology*. Harmondsworth, England: Penguin, 1964.

FAGAN, J. F., III. Memory in the infant. *Journal of Experimental Child Psychology*, 1970, *9*, 217–226.

FAGAN, J. F., III. Infants' recognition memory for faces. *Journal of Experimental Child Psychology*, 1972, *14*, 453–476.

FAGAN, J. F., III. Infants' delayed recognition memory for faces. *Journal of Experimental Child Psychology*, 1973, *16*, 424–450.

FAGAN, J. F., III. Infant recognition of faces. Paper read at the annual meeting of the Midwestern Psychological Association, Chicago, 1975.

FANTZ, R. L. A method for studying early visual development. *Perceptual and Motor Skills*, 1956, *18*, 13–15.

FANTZ, R. L. Visual experience in infants: Decreased attention to familiar patterns relative to novel ones. *Science*, 1964, *146*, 668–670.

FANTZ, R. L. Pattern discrimination and selective attention as determinants of perceptual development after birth. In Aline Kidd & Jeanne L. Rivoire (Eds.), *Perceptual development in children*. New York: International Universities Press, 1966.

FANTZ, R. L., & NEVIS, S. The predictive value of changes in visual preferences in early infancy. In J. Hellmuth (Ed.), *The exceptional infant*, Vol. 1. Seattle: Special Child Publications, 1967.

FARRIMOND, T. Age differences in speed of retrieval from memory store. *Australian Journal of Psychology*, 1969, *21*, 79–83.

FAUST, C. Partielle Seelenblindheit nach Occipitalverletzung mit besonderer Beeinträchtigung des Physiognomieerkennens. *Nervenarzt*, 1947, *18*, 294–297.

FEINMAN, S., & ENTWISLE, D. R. Children's ability to recognize other children's faces. *Child Development*, 1976, *47*, 506–510.

FELDMAN-SUMMERS, S., & LINDNER, K. Perceptions of victims and defendants in criminal assault cases. *Criminal Justice and Behavior*, 1976, *3*, 135–150.

FIELD, P. B., & DWORKIN, S. F. Strategies of hypnotic interrogation. *Journal of Psychology*, 1967, *67*, 47–58.

FILLENBAUM, S. Prior deception and subsequent experimental performance: The "faithful" subject. *Journal of Personality and Social Psychology*. 1966, *4*, 532–537.

FINKELSTEIN, M. O., & FAIRLEY, W. B. A Bayesian approach to identification evidence. *Harvard Law Review*, 1970, *83*, 489–517.

FISCHER, R. The biological fabric of time. In *Interdisciplinary perspectives of time*. Annals New York Academy of Sciences, 1967, *138*, Article 2.

FISCHHOFF, B. Hindsight ≠ foresight: The effect of outcome knowledge on judgment under uncertainty. *Journal of Experimental Psychology: Human Perception and Performance*, 1975, *1*, 288–299.

FISHER, G., & COX, R. Recognising human faces. *Applied Ergonomics*, 1975, *6*, 104–109.

FISHMAN, J. A. Some current research needs in the psychology of testimony. *Journal of Social Issues*, 1957, *13*, 60–67.

FITZSIMONS, J. Science and law—a lawyer's viewpoint. *Journal of Forensic Science Society*, 1975, *13*, 261–267.

FLAVELL, J. H. Developmental studies of mediated memory. In H. W. Reese & L. P. Lipsitt (Eds.), *Advances in child development and behavior,* Vol. 5. New York: Academic Press, 1970.

FLAVELL, J. H. *Cognitive development.* Englewood Cliffs, N.J.: Prentice-Hall, 1977.

FLAVELL, J. H., BEACH, D. H., & CHINSKY, J. M. Spontaneous verbal rehearsal in a memory task as a function of age. *Child Development,* 1966, *37,* 283–299.

FLAVELL, J. H., BOTKIN, P. T., FRY, C. L., WRIGHT, J. W., & JARVIS, P. E. *The development of role-taking and communication skills in children.* New York: Wiley, 1968.

FLOROVSKY, G. The study of the past. In R. H. Nash (Ed.), *Ideas of history,* Vol. 2. New York: Dutton, 1969.

FORBES, D. D. S. Interference effects in facial memory. Paper presented at the annual meeting of the British Psychological Society, Exeter, 1977.

FORSTON, R. F. Judge's instructions: A quantitative analysis of juror's listening comprehension. *Today's Speech,* 1970, *18,* 34–38.

FOX, M. W. Social dynamics of three captive wolf packs. *Behavior,* 1973, *47,* 290–301

FRAISSE, P. *The psychology of time.* New York: Harper & Row, 1963.

FRANK, G. *The Boston strangler.* New York: New American Library, 1966.

FRANK, J. Say it with music. *Harvard Law Review,* 1948, *61,* 934–947.

FRANK, J. *Courts on trial.* Princeton, N.J.: Princeton University Press, 1949.

FREEDMAN, J., & HABER, R. N. One reason why we rarely forget a face. *Bulletin of the Psychonomic Society,* 1974, *3,* 107–109.

FREEDMAN, J. L., CARLSMITH, J. M., & SEARS, D. O. *Social psychology,* second edition. Englewood Cliffs, N.J.: Prentice-Hall, 1974.

FREUD, S. Totem and taboo. In A. A. Brill (Ed.), *The basic writings of Sigmund Freud.* New York: Random House, 1938.

FREUD, S. Psycho-analysis and the ascertaining of truth in courts of law, 1906. In *Clinical Papers and Papers on Technique, Collected Papers,* Vol. 2. New York: Basic Books, 1959, pp. 13–24. Five volumes.

FREUD, S. *The psychopathology of everyday life.* London: Hogarth Press, 1960. (First published in German, 1900.)

FRIEDMAN, M. P., REID, S. R., & CARTERETTE, E. C. Feature saliency and recognition memory for schematic faces. *Perception and Psychophysics,* 1971, *10,* 47–50.

FRIJDA, N., & VAN DE GEER, J. P. Codability and recognition. *Acta Psychologica,* 1961, *18,* 360–367.

FRIJDA, N. H. Recognition of emotion. In L. Berkowitz (Ed.), *Advances in experimental social psychology,* Vol. 4. New York: Academic Press, 1969.

FROST, N. Clustering by visual shape in the free recall of pictorial stimuli. *Journal of Experimental Psychology,* 1971, *88,* 409–413.

FROST, N. Encoding and retrieval in visual memory tasks. *Journal of Experimental Psychology*, 1972, *95*, 317–326.

FULTON, R. B. The measurement of speaker credibility. *Journal of Communication*, 1970, *20*, 270–279.

FURST, C. J., FULD, K., & PANCOE, M. Recall accuracy of eidetikers. *Journal of Experimental Psychology*, 1974, *102*, 1133–1135.

FURTH, H. G., ROSS, B. M., & YOUNISS, J. Operative understanding in reproductions of drawings. *Child Development*, 1974, *45*, 63–70.

GALANTER, E. Contemporary psychophysics. In R. Brown, E. Galanter, E. H. Hess, & G. Mandler (Eds.), *New directions in psychology*. New York: Holt, Rinehart and Winston, 1962.

GALPER, R. E. Recognition of faces in photographic negative. *Psychonomic Science*, 1970, *19*, 207–208.

GALPER, R. E. Functional race membership and recognition of faces. *Perceptual and Motor Skills*, 1973, *37*, 455–462.

GALPER, R. E., & HOCHBERG, J. Recognition memory for photographs of faces. *American Journal of Psychology*, 1971, *84*, 351–354.

GALTON, F. *Inquiries into human faculty*. London: Dent, 1883.

GARCIA, L., & GRIFFITT, W. Evaluation and recall of evidence: Authoritarianism and the Patty Hearst Case. *Journal of Research in Personality*, 1978, *12*, 57–67.

GARCIA, L. T., & GRIFFITT, W. Impact of testimonial evidence as a function of witness characteristics. *Bulletin of the Psychonomic Society*, 1978, *11*, 37–40.

GARDNER, D. S. The perception and memory of witnesses. *Cornell Law Quarterly*, 1933, *18*, 391–409.

GEEN, R. G. Effects of being observed on short- and long-term recall. *Journal of Experimental Psychology*, 1973, *100*, 395–398.

GEIDT, F. H. Comparison of visual, content, and auditory cues in interviewing. *Journal of Consulting Psychology*, 1955, *19*, 407–416.

GIBSON, E. J. *Principles of perceptual learning and development*. New York: Appleton-Century-Crofts, 1969.

GIBSON, J. J. *The perception of the visual world*. Boston: Houghton Mifflin, 1950.

GILBERT, C., & BAKAN, P. Visual asymmetry in perception of faces. *Neuropsychologia*, 1973, *11*, 355–362.

GILBERT, J. G. Memory loss in senescence. *Journal of Abnormal and Social Psychology*, 1941, *36*, 73–86.

GILBERT, J. G. Age changes in color matching. *Journal of Gerontology*, 1957, *12*, 210–215.

GILLIGAN, F. Comments: Eyewitness identification. *Military Law Review*, 1972, *58*, 183–207.

GIRAY, E. F., ALTKIN, W. M., VAUGHT, G. M., & ROODIN, P. A. The incidence of eidetic imagery as a function of age. *Child Development*, 1976, *47*, 1207–1210.

GLANZER, M., & CLARK, W. H. Accuracy of perceptual recall: An analysis of organization. *Journal of Verbal Learning and Verbal Behavior*, 1963, *1*, 289–299. (a)

GLANZER, M., & CLARK, W. H. The verbal loop hypothesis: Binary numbers. *Journal of Verbal Learning and Verbal Behavior*, 1963, 2, 301–309. (b)

GLANZER, M., & CLARK, W. H. The verbal-loop hypothesis: Conventional figures. *American Journal of Psychology*, 1964, 77, 621–626.

GLUCKSBERG, S., & KRAUSS, R. M. What do people say after they have learned how to talk? Studies of the development of referential communication. *Merrill-Palmer Quarterly*, 1967, 13, 309–316.

GODDEN, D. R., & BADDELEY, A. D. Context-dependent memory in two natural environments: On land and underwater. *British Journal of Psychology*, 1975, 66, 325–332.

GOING, M., & READ, J. D. Effects of uniqueness, sex of subject, and sex of photograph on facial recognition. *Perceptual and Motor Skills*, 1974, 39, 109–110.

GOLDBERG, P. Are women prejudiced against women? *Transaction*, 1968, 6, 28–30.

GOLDSTEIN, A. G. Learning of inverted and normally oriented faces in children and adults. *Psychonomic Science*, 1965, 3, 447–448.

GOLDSTEIN, A. G. Recognition of inverted photographs of faces by children and adults. *Journal of Genetic Psychology*, 1975, 127, 109–123.

GOLDSTEIN, A. G. The fallibility of the eyewitness: Psychological evidence. In B. D. Sales (Ed.), *Psychology in the legal process*. New York: Spectrum, 1977, pp. 223–247.

GOLDSTEIN, A. G., & CHANCE, J. E. Recognition of children's faces. *Child Development*, 1964, 35, 129–136.

GOLDSTEIN, A. G., & CHANCE, J. E. Visual recognition memory for complex configurations. *Perception and Psychophysics*, 1970, 9, 237–241.

GOLDSTEIN, A. G., & CHANCE, J. Measuring psychological similarity of faces. *Bulletin of the Psychonomic Society*, 1976, 7, 407–408.

GOLDSTEIN, A. G., & CHANCE, J. Intra-individual consistency in visual recognition memory. Paper presented at the annual meeting of the American Psychological Association, Toronto, 1978. (a)

GOLDSTEIN, A. G., & CHANCE, J. Judging face similarity in own and other races. *Journal of Psychology*, 1978, 98, 185–193. (b)

GOLDSTEIN, A. G., JOHNSON, K. S., & CHANCE, J. Face recognition and verbal description of faces from memory. Paper presented at the annual meeting of the Psychonomic Society, Washington, D.C., 1977.

GOLDSTEIN, A. G. & MACKENBERG, E. J. Recognition of human faces from isolated facial features: A developmental study. *Psychonomic Science*, 1966, 6, 149–150.

GOLDSTEIN, A. G., STEPHENSON, B., & CHANCE, J. Face recognition memory: Distribution of false alarms. *Bulletin of the Psychonomic Society*, 1977, 9, 416–418.

GOLDSTEIN, M. S., & SIPPRELLE, C. N. Hypnotically induced amnesia versus ablation of memory. *International Journal of Clinical and Experimental Hypnosis*, 1970, 18, 211–216.

GOLDSTONE, S., BOARDMAN, W. K., & LHAMON, W. T. Effects of quinal barbitone, dextro-amphetamine and placebo on apparent time. *British Journal of Psychology*, 1958, 49, 324–328.

GOLEMAN, D. Hypnosis comes of age. *Psychology Today*, July 1977, 54–60.

GOLLIN, E. S. Organizational characteristics of social judgment: A developmental investigation. *Journal of Personality*, 1958, *26*, 139–154.

GOODWIN, G. W., POWELL, B., BREMER, D., HOINE, H., & STERN, J. Alcohol and recall: State dependent effects in man. *Science*, 1969, *163*, 1358.

GORDON, I.E., & HAYWARD, S. Second-order isomorphism of internal representations of familiar faces. *Perception and Psychophysics*, 1973, *14*, 334–336.

GRAHAM, M. H. The confrontation clause, the hearsay rule, and the forgetful witness. *Texas Law Review*, 1978, *56*, 151–205.

GRAY, C. R., & GUMMERMAN, K. The enigmatic eidetic image: A critical examination of methods, data, and theories. *Psychological Bulletin*, 1975, *82*, 383–407.

GREEN, D. M., & SWETS, J. A. *Signal detection theory and psychophysics*. New York: Wiley, 1966.

GREENSPOON, J., & RANYARD, R. Stimulus conditions and retroactive inhibition. *Journal of Experimental Psychology*, 1957, *53*, 55–59.

GUMMERMAN, K., & GRAY, C. R. Recall of visually presented material: An unwanted case and a bibliography for eidetic imagery. *Psychonomic Monograph Supplements*, 1971, *4*, No. 10, Whole No. 58.

HAAF, R. A. Complexity and facial resemblance as determinants of response to facelike stimuli by 5- and 10-week-old infants. *Journal of Experimental Child Psychology*, 1974, *18*, 480–487.

HABER, R. N., & HABER, R. B. Eidetic imagery: 1. Frequency. *Perceptual and Motor Skills*, 1964, *19*, 131–138.

HAGEN, J. W. The effect of distraction on selective attention. *Child Development*, 1967, *38*, 685–694.

HAGEN, J. W., & KINGSLEY, P. R. Labeling effects in STM. *Child Development*, 1968, *39*, 113–121.

HALE, G. A., & MORGAN, J. S. Developmental trends in children's component selection. *Journal of Experimental Child Psychology*, 1973, *15*, 302–314.

HALE, G. A., & TAWEEL, S. S. Age differences in children's performance on measures of component selection and incidental learning. *Journal of Experimental Child Psychology*, 1974, *18*, 107–116.

HALL, D. F., & OSTROM, T. M. Accuracy of eyewitness identification after biasing or unbiased instructions. Paper presented at the annual meeting of the American Psychological Association, Chicago, 1975.

HANS, V. P. The effect of criminal record on individual and group judgments of guilt in a jury simulation paradigm. Unpublished master's thesis, University of Toronto, 1974.

HANSEN, D. N. Short-term memory and presentation rates with young children. *Psychonomic Science*, 1965, *3*, 253–254.

HARARI, H., & McDAVID, J. W. Name stereotypes and teachers' expectations. *Journal of Educational Psychology*, 1973, *65*, 222–225.

HARMON, L. D. The recognition of faces. *Scientific American*, November, 1973, 71–82.

HARRIS, G. J., & BURKE, D. The effects of grouping on short-term serial recall of digits by children: Developmental trends. *Child Development*, 1972, *43*, 710–716.

HARRIS, R. J., TESKE, R. R., & GINNS, M. J. Memory for pragmatic implications from courtroom testimony. *Bulletin of the Psychonomic Society*, 1975, *6*, 494–496.

HARTSHORNE, H., & MAY, M. A. Studies in deceit. In Columbia University, Teachers College, *Studies in the Nature of Character*, Vol. 1. New York: Macmillan, 1928.

HARVEY, O. J. System structure, flexibility and creativity. In O. J. Harvey (Ed.), *Experience, structure and adaptability*. New York: Springer, 1966.

HARVEY, O. J., HUNT, D. E., & SCHRODER, H. M. *Conceptual systems and personality organization*. New York: Wiley, 1961.

HARVEY, O. J., & SCHRODER, H. M. Cognitive aspects of self and motivation. In O. J. Harvey (Ed.), *Motivation and social interaction: Cognitive determinants*. New York: Ronald, 1963.

HARWOOD, E., & NAYLOR, G. F. K. Recall and recognition in elderly and young subjects. *Australian Journal of Psychology*, 1969, *21*, 251–257.

HASTORF, A. H., SCHNEIDER, D. J., & POLEFKA, J. *Person perception*. London: Addison-Wesley, 1970.

HATAKEYAMA, T. The process of having identified an adult eidetic person and her eidetic experiences in daily life. *Tohoku Psychologica Folia*, 1974, *33*, 102–118.

HEBB, D. O. *Organization of behavior*. New York: Wiley, 1949.

HÉCAEN, H., & ANGELERGUES, R. Agnosia for faces (prosopagnosia). *Archives of Neurology*, 1962, *7*, 92–100.

HEIDER, F. *The psychology of interpersonal relations*. New York: Wiley, 1958.

HEISENBERG, W. *Physics and philosophy*. New York: Harper and Row, 1958.

HEMSLEY, G. D., & DOOB, A. N. The effect of looking behavior on perceptions of a communicator's credibility. *Journal of Applied Social Psychology*, 1978, *8*, 136–144.

HESS, E. H. Attitude and pupil size. *Scientific American*, 1965, *212*, 46–54.

HILGARD, E. R. *Hypnotic susceptibility*. New York: Harcourt Brace Jovanovich, 1965.

HILGARD, E. R. *Personality and hypnosis: A study of imaginative involvement*. Chicago: University of Chicago Press, 1970.

HILL, M. K., & LANDO, H. A. Physical attractiveness and sex-role stereotypes in impression formation. Paper presented at the annual meeting of the Midwestern Psychological Association, Chicago, 1975.

HILLIARD, R. D. Hemispheric laterality effects on a facial recognition task in normal subjects. *Cortex*, 1973, *9*, 246–258.

HIMMELFARB, S. Studies in the perception of ethnic group members: 1. Accuracy, response bias, and anti-Semitism. *Journal of Personality and Social Psychology*, 1966, *4*, 347–355.

HIRSCH, M. J. Effect of age on visual acuity. In M. J. Hirsch & R. F. Wick (Eds.), *Vision of the aging patient*. Philadelphia: Chilton, 1960.

HOAGLAND, H. The physiological control of judgments of duration: Evidence for a chemical clock. *Journal of General Psychology*, 1933, 9, 267–287.

HOCHBERG, J., & GALPER, R. E. Recognition of faces: 1. An exploratory study. *Psychonomic Science*, 1967, 9, 619–620.

HOCHBERG, J., & GALPER, R. E. Attribution of intention as a function of physiognomy. *Memory and Cognition*, 1974, 2, 39–42.

HOCKING, J. E., MILLER, G. R., & FONTES, N. E. Videotape in the courtroom: Witness deception. *Trial*, 1978, 14, 52–55.

HOFFMAN, C., & KAGAN, S. Field dependence and facial recognition. *Perceptual and Motor Skills*, 1977, 44, 119–124.

HOLMES, D. S. Investigations of repression: Differential recall of material experimentally or naturally associated with ego threat. *Psychological Bulletin*, 1974, 81, 632–653.

HORN, J. L. Psychometric studies of aging and intelligence. In S. Gershon & A. Raskind (Eds.), *Aging*, Vol. 2, *Genesis and treatment of psychologic disorders in the elderly*. New York: Raven Press, 1975.

HORTON, D. L., & TURNAGE, T. W. *Human learning*. Englewood Cliffs, N.J.: Prentice-Hall, 1976.

HORVATH, F. The effect of selected variables on interpretation of polygraph records. *Journal of Applied Psychology*, 1977, 62, 127–136.

HORVATH, F. An experimental comparison of the psychological stress evaluator and the galvanic skin response in detection of deception. *Journal of Applied Psychology*, 1978, 63, 338–344.

HOVLAND, C. I., JANIS, I. L., & KELLEY, H. H. *Communication and persuasion*. New Haven, Conn.: Yale University Press, 1953.

HOVLAND, C. I., & MANDELL, W. An experimental comparison of conclusion drawing by the communicator and by the audience. *Journal of Abnormal and Social Psychology*, 1952, 47, 581–588.

HOWELLS, T. H. A study of ability to recognize faces. *Journal of Abnormal and Social Psychology*, 1938, 33, 124–127.

HOWES, D. H., & SOLOMON, R. L. A note on McGinnies' "emotionality and perceptual defense." *Psychological Review*, 1950, 57, 229–234.

HULTSCH, D. F. Adult age differences in retrieval: Trace-dependent and cue-dependent forgetting. *Developmental Psychology*, 1975, 11, 197–201.

HUNT, E., & LOVE, T. How good can memory be? In A. W. Melton & E. Martin (Eds.), *Coding processes in human memory*. Washington, D.C.: Winston/Wiley, 1972.

HUNTER, I. M. L. An exceptional memory. *British Journal of Psychology*, 1977, 68, 155–164.

HUTCHINS, R. M., & SLESINGER, D. Some observations on the law of evidence-memory. *Harvard Law Review*, 1928, 41, 860–873.

HUTT, C. *Males and females.* Harmondsworth, England: Penguin, 1972.

IMMERGLUCK, L. Determinism-freedom in contemporary psychology: An ancient problem revisited. *American Psychologist,* 1964, *19,* 270–281.

INBAU, F. E., & REID, J. E. *Lie detection and criminal interrogation,* third edition. Baltimore: Williams & Wilkins, 1953.

IRWIN, F. W., & SEIDENFELD, M. A. The application of the method of comparison to the problem of memory change. *Journal of Experimental Psychology,* 1937, *21,* 363–381.

ITTELSON, W. H., & KILPATRICK, F. P. Experiments in perception. *Scientific American,* 1951, *185,* No. 2.

IZARD, C. E. *The face of emotion.* New York: Appleton, 1971.

JAENSCH, E. R. *Eidetic imagery.* Trans. O. Oeser. New York: Harcourt, Brace, 1930.

JAMES, W. *The principles of psychology.* New York: Dover, 1950.

JENKINS, J. R., NEALE, D. C., & DENO, S. L. Differential memory for picture and word stimuli. *Journal of Educational Psychology,* 1967, *58,* 303–307.

JESPERSEN, O. *Language: Its nature, development, and origin.* London: Allen & Unwin, 1922.

JOHNSON, J. H. Memory and personality: An information processing approach. *Journal of Research in Personality,* 1974, *8,* 1–32.

JONES, C., & ARONSON, E. Attribution of fault to a rape victim as a function of respectability of the victim. *Journal of Personality and Social Psychology,* 1973, *26,* 415–419.

JONES, E. E. How do people perceive the causes of behavior? *American Scientist,* 1976, *64,* 300–305.

JONES, E. E., & NISBETT, R. E. The actor and the observer: Divergent perceptions of the causes of behavior. In E. E. Jones, D. E. Kanouse, H. H. Kelley, R. E. Nisbett, S. Valins, & B. Weiner (Eds.), *Attribution: Perceiving the causes of behavior.* Morristown, N.J.: General Learning, 1972.

JONES, H. E., & CONRAD, H. S. The growth and decline of intelligence: A study of a homogeneous group between the ages of ten and sixty. *Genetic Psychology Monographs,* 1933, *13,* 223–294.

JONES, H. W. Legal inquiry and the methods of science. In H. W. Jones (Ed.), *Law and the social role of science.* New York: Rockefeller University Press, 1966, pp. 120–131.

JONES, W. R. Danger—voiceprints ahead. *American Criminal Law Review,* 1973, *11,* 549–573.

KAESS, W. A., & WITRYOL, S. L. Memory for names and faces: A characteristic of social intelligence. *Journal of Applied Psychology,* 1955, *39,* 457–462.

KAGAN, J., & HAVEMANN, E. *Psychology: An introduction,* second edition. New York: Harcourt Brace Jovanovich, 1972.

KAGAN, J., HENKER, B. A., HEN-TOV, M., LEVINE, J., & LEWIS, M. Infants' differential reactions to familiar and distorted faces. *Child Development,* 1966, *37,* 519–532.

KAGAN, J., KLEIN, R. E., HAITH, M. M., & MORRISON, F. J. Memory and meaning in two cultures. *Child Development,* 1973, *44,* 221–223.

KALVEN, H., & ZEISEL, H. *The American jury.* Boston: Little, Brown, 1966.

KANFER, F. H. Verbal rate, content, and adjustment ratings in experimentally structured interviews. *Journal of Abnormal and Social Psychology*, 1959, *58*, 305–311.

KANFER, F. H. Verbal rate, eyeblink, and content in structured interviews. *Journal of Abnormal and Social Psychology*, 1960, *61*, 341–347.

KAPLAN, R. M. Is beauty talent? Sex interaction in the attractiveness halo effect. *Sex Roles*, 1978, *4*, 195–204.

KASSARJIAN, H. H. Voting intentions and political perception. *Journal of Psychology*, 1963, *56*, 85–88.

KAUSLER, D. H. *Psychology of verbal learning and memory.* New York: Academic Press, 1976.

KELLEY, H. H. The warm-cold variable in the first impressions of persons. *Journal of Personality*, 1950, *18*, 431–439.

KEMENY, J. G. A philosopher looks at science, 1959. In M. S. Gazzaniga & E. P. Lovejoy (Eds.), *Good readings in psychology.* Englewood Cliffs, N.J.: Prentice-Hall, 1971, pp. 90–104.

KERSTA, L. Voiceprint identification. *Nature*, 1962, *1253*, 1256–1257.

KEY, M. R. Linguistic behavior of male and female. *Linguistics*, 1972, *88*, 19.

KIMURA, D., & DURNFORD, M. Normal studies on the function of the right hemisphere in vision. In S. J. Dimond & J. G. Beaumont (Eds.), *Hemisphere function in the human brain.* London: Paul Elek, 1974.

KING, D. The use of the Photo-fit 1970–1971: A progress report. *Police Research Bulletin*, 1971, *18*, 40–44.

KINGSTON, C. R. Probability and legal proceedings. *Journal of Criminal Law, Criminology and Police Science*, 1966, *57*, 93–98.

KINGSTON, C. R., & KIRK, P. L. The use of statistics in criminalistics. *Journal of Criminal Law, Criminology and Police Science*, 1964, *55*, 514–521.

KINSBOURNE, M. Age effects on letter span related to rate of sequential dependency. *Journal of Gerontology*, 1973, *28*, 317–319.

KINTZ, B. L. College student attitudes about telling lies. *Bulletin of the Psychonomic Society*, 1977, *10*, 490–492.

KINTZ, B. L., DELPRADO, D. J., METTEE, D. R., PERSONS, C. E., & SCHAPEE, R. H. The experimenter effect. *Psychological Bulletin*, 1965, *63*, 223–232.

KIRBY, D. M., & GARDNER, R. C. Ethnic stereotypes: Norms of 208 words typically used in their assessment. *Canadian Journal of Psychology*, 1972, *26*, 140–154.

KIRKHAM, G. L. From professor to patrolman: A fresh perspective on the police. *Journal of Police Science and Administration*, 1974, *2*, 127–137.

KLATZKY, R. L. *Human memory.* San Francisco: W. H. Freeman, 1975.

KLEINSMITH, L. J., & KAPLAN, S. Paired-associates learning as a function of arousal and interpolated interval. *Journal of Experimental Psychology*, 1963, *65*, 190–193.

KLINE, D. W., & BIRREN, J. E. Age differences in dichoptic masking. *Experimental Aging Research*, 1975, *1*, 17–25.

KLÜVER, H. An experimental study of the eidetic type. *Genetic Psychology Monographs*, 1926, *1*, 71–230.

KNAPP, M. L. *Nonverbal communication in human interaction*. New York: Holt, Rinehart and Winston, 1972.

KOBASIGAWA, A. Utilization of retrieval cues by children in recall. *Child Development*, 1974, *45*, 127–134.

KOHLBERG, L. Development of moral character and moral ideology. In M. L. Hoffman & L. W. Hoffman (Eds.), *Review of child development research*, Vol. 1. New York: Russell Sage Foundation, 1964.

KOHLBERG, L. The child as a moral philosopher. *Psychology Today*, 1968, *2*, 25–30.

KOHLBERG, L. Continuities in childhood and adult moral development. In P. B. Baltes & K. W. Schaie (Eds.), *Life-span developmental psychology: Personality and socialization*. New York: Academic Press, 1973.

KÖHLER, W. *Dynamics in psychology*. New York: Liveright, 1940.

KRAMER, C. Women's speech: Separate but unequal? *Quarterly Journal of Speech*, 1974, *60*, 14–24.

KRAUSS, R. M., & GLUCKSBERG, S. The development of communication: Competence as a function of age. *Child Development*, 1969, *40*, 255–266.

KRAUT, R. E. Verbal and nonverbal cues in the perception of lying. *Journal of Personality and Social Psychology*, 1978, *36*, 380–391.

KUBIS, J. F. Experimental and statistical factors in the diagnosis of consciously suppressed affective experience. *Journal of Clinical Psychology*, 1950, *6*, 12–16.

KUEHN, L. L. Looking down a gun barrel: Person perception and violent crime. *Perceptual and Motor Skills*, 1974, *39*, 1159–1164.

KURTZ, D. L. Physical appearance and stature: Important variables in sales recruiting. *Personnel Journal*, December, 1969.

KURTZ, K. H., & HOVLAND, C. I. The effect of verbalization during observation of stimulus objects upon accuracy of recognition and recall. *Journal of Experimental Psychology*, 1953, *45*, 157–164.

LAFAVE, L. Psychological methodology: Should it differ from that of natural science? *Canadian Psychologist*, 1971, *12*, 513–525.

LAKOFF, R. Language and woman's place. *Language in Society*, 1973, *2*, 45–79.

LANA, R. E. Familiarity and the order of presentation of persuasive communications. *Journal of Abnormal and Social Psychology*, 1961, *62*, 573–577.

LANA, R. E. Controversy of the topic and the order of presentation in persuasive communications. *Psychological Reports*, 1963, *12*, 163–170. (a)

LANA, R. E. Interest, media, and order effects in persuasive communications. *Journal of Psychology*, 1963, *56*, 9–13. (b)

LANDY, D., & ARONSON, E. The influence of the character of the criminal and his victim on the decisions of simulated jurors. *Journal of Experimental Social Psychology*, 1969, *5*, 141–152.

LANGER, J., WAPNER, S., & WERNER, H. The effect of danger upon the experience of time. *American Journal of Psychology*, 1961, *74*, 94–97.

LANTZ, D., & STEFFLRE, V. Language and cognition revisited. *Journal of Abnormal and Social Psychology*, 1964, *69*, 472–481.

LAUGHERY, K. R., ALEXANDER, J. F., & LANE, A. B. Recognition of human faces: Effects of target exposure time, target position, pose position, and type of photograph. *Journal of Applied Psychology*, 1971, *55*, 477–483.

LAUGHERY, K. R., DUVAL, G. C., & FOWLER, R. H. An analysis of procedures for generating facial images. University of Houston Mug File Project, Report No. UHMUG-2, 1977.

LAUGHERY, K. R., FESSLER, P. K., LENOROVITZ, D. R., & YOBLICK, D. A. Time delay and similarity effects in facial recognition. *Journal of Applied Psychology*, 1974, *59*, 490–496.

LAUGHERY, K. R., & FOWLER, R. H. Factors affecting facial recognition. University of Houston Mug File Project, Report No. UHMUG-3, 1977.

LAUGHERY, K. R., & FOWLER, R. H. Analysis of procedures for generating facial images. Paper presented at the annual meeting of the American Psychological Association, Toronto, 1978.

LAVERY, U. A. The language of the law. In E. C. Gerhart (Ed.), *The lawyer's treasury*. Indianapolis: Bobbs-Merrill, 1956, pp. 376–394.

LAVRAKAS, P. J., & BICKMAN, L. What makes a good witness? Paper presented at the annual meeting of the American Psychological Association, Chicago, 1975.

LAVRAKAS, P. J., BURI, J. R., & MAYZNER, M. S. A perspective on the recognition of other-race faces. *Perception and Psychophysics*, 1976, *20*, 475–481.

LAWSON, R. G. The law of primacy in the criminal courtroom. *Journal of Social Psychology*, 1969, *77*, 121–131.

LEASK, J., HABER, R. N., & HABER, R. B. Eidetic imagery in children: II. Longitudinal and experimental results. *Psychonomic Monograph Supplements*, 1969, *3*, No. 3, Whole No. 35.

LEIPPE, M. R., WELLS, G. L., & OSTROM, T. M. Crime seriousness as a determinant of accuracy in eyewitness identification. *Journal of Applied Psychology*, 1978, *63*, 345–351.

LERNER, M. J., & SIMMONS, C. H. Observer's reaction to the "innocent victim": Compassion or rejection? *Journal of Personality and Social Psychology*, 1966, *4*, 203–210.

LEVIN, H., BALDWIN, A. L., GALLWEY, M., & PAIVIO, A. Audience stress, personality and speech. *Journal of Abnormal and Social Psychology*, 1960, *61*, 469–473.

LEVINE, F. J., & TAPP, J. L. The psychology of criminal identification: The gap from Wade to Kirby. *University of Pennsylvania Law Review*, 1973, *121*, 1079–1131.

LEVINE, M. Scientific method and the adversary model: Some preliminary thoughts. *American Psychologist*, 1974, *29*, 661–677.

LEVINE, R. I., CHEIN, I., & MURPHY, G. The relation of the intensity of a need to the amount of perceptual distortion. *Journal of Psychology*, 1942, *13*, 283–293.

LEWIS, M. Infants' responses to facial stimuli during the first year of life. *Developmental Psychology*, 1969, *1*, 75–86.

LIEBLICH, I., BEN SHAKHAR, G., & KUGELMASS, S. Validity of the guilty knowledge technique in a prisoners' sample. *Journal of Applied Psychology*, 1976, *61*, 89–93.

LIGGETT, J. *The human face*. London: Constable, 1974.

LIGHT, L. L. Homonyms and synonyms as retrieval cues. *Journal of Experimental Psychology*, 1972, *96*, 255–262.

LIND, E. A., & O'BARR, W. M. The social significance of speech in the courtroom. In H. Giles & R. St. Clair (Eds.), *Language and Social Psychology*, Rowley, Mass.: Newbury, in press.

LINDZEY, G., & ROGOLSKY, S. Prejudice and identification of a minority group membership. *Journal of Abnormal and Social Psychology*, 1950, *45*, 37–53.

LIPTON, J. P. On the psychology of eyewitness testimony. *Journal of Applied Psychology*, 1977, *62*, 90–95.

LITTLEPAGE, G. E., & PINEAULT, T. Verbal, facial, and paralinguistic cues to detection of truth and lying. Paper presented at the annual meeting of the American Psychological Association, San Francisco, 1977.

LOCKHART, R. S., CRAIK, F. I. M., & JACOBY, L. Depth of processing, recognition and recall. In J. Brown (Ed.), *Recall and recognition*. London: Wiley, 1976.

LOFTUS, E. F. Leading questions and the eyewitness report. *Cognitive Psychology*, 1975, *7*, 560–572.

LOFTUS, E. F. Shifting human color memory. *Memory and Cognition*, 1977, *5*, 696–699.

LOFTUS, E. F., & PALMER, J. C. Reconstruction of automobile destruction: An example of the interaction between language and memory. *Journal of Verbal Learning and Verbal Behavior*, 1974, *13*, 585–589.

LOFTUS, E. F., & ZANNI, G. Eyewitness testimony: The influence of the wording of a question. *Bulletin of the Psychonomic Society*, 1975, *5*, 86–88.

LOFTUS, G. R., & LOFTUS, E. F. *Human memory: The processing of information*. Hillsdale, N.J.: Lawrence Erlbaum, 1976.

LORAYNE, H., & LUCAS, J. *The memory book*. London: Allen, 1976.

LOUISELL, D. W. The psychologist in today's legal world. *Minnesota Law Review*, 1955, *39*, 235–272.

LUCE, T. S. The role of experience in inter-racial recognition. Paper presented at the annual meeting of the American Psychological Association, New Orleans, 1974.

LUCHINS, A. S. Experimental attempts to minimize the impact of first impressions. In C. Hovland (Ed.), *The order of presentation in persuasion*. New Haven, Conn.: Yale University Press, 1957.

LUCHINS, A. S., & LUCHINS, E. H. Motivation to tell the truth vs. social influences. *Journal of Social Psychology*, 1968, *76*, 97–105.

LUDWIG, K., & FONTAINE, G. Effect of witnesses' expertness and manner of delivery of testimony on verdicts of simulated jurors. *Psychological Reports*, 1978, *42*, 955–961.

LUND, F. H. The psychology of belief: IV. The law of primacy in persuasion. *Journal of Abnormal and Social Psychology*, 1925, *20*, 183–191.

LURIA, A. R. *Speech and the regulation of behaviour*. London: Pergamon, 1961.

LURIA, A. R. *The mind of a mnemonist*. New York: Basic Books, 1968.

LYKKEN, D. T. The GSR in the detection of guilt. *Journal of Applied Psychology*, 1959, *43*, 385–388.

LYKKEN, D. T. The validity of the guilty knowledge technique: The effect of faking. *Journal of Applied Psychology*, 1960, *44*, 258-262.

LYKKEN, D. T. Psychology and the lie detector industry. *American Psychologist*, 1974, *29*, 725-739.

LYKKEN, D. T. The right way to use a lie detector. *Psychology Today*, 1975, *8*, 56-60.

MACBRAYER, C. T. Differences in perception of the opposite sex by males and females. *Journal of Social Psychology*, 1960, *52*, 309-314.

MACCOBY, E. E., & HAGEN, J. W. Effects of distraction upon central versus incidental recall: Developmental trends. *Journal of Experimental Child Psychology*, 1965, *2*, 280-289.

MACCOBY, E. E., & JACKLIN, C. N. *The psychology of sex differences*. Stanford, Calif.: Stanford University Press, 1974.

MACDOUGALL, R. Recognition and recall. *Journal of Philosophy*, 1904, *1*, 299-333.

MACHIAVELLI, N. *The prince*. New York: Modern Library, 1940.

MACKWORTH, N. H., & BRUNER, J. S. How adults and children search and recognize pictures. *Human Development*, 1970, *13*, 149-177.

MACRAE, D., & TROLLE, E. The defect of function in visual agnosia. *Brain*, 1956, *79*, 94-110.

MAIER, N. R., & THURBER, J. A. Accuracy of judgments of deception when an interview is watched, heard, and read. *Personnel Psychology*, 1968, *21*, 23-30.

MALPASS, R. S. Racial bias in eyewitness identification. *Personality and Social Psychology Bulletin*, 1974, *1*, 42-44.

MALPASS, R. S. Towards a theoretical basis for understanding differential face recognition. Paper presented at the annual meeting of the Midwestern Psychological Association, Chicago, 1975.

MALPASS, R. S., & KRAVITZ, J. Recognition for faces of own and other race. *Journal of Personality and Social Psychology*, 1969, *13*, 330-334.

MALPASS, R. S., LAVIGUEUR, H., & WELDON, D. E. Verbal and visual training in face recognition. *Perception and Psychophysics*, 1973, *14*, 285-292.

MANDLER, J. M., & STEIN, N. L. Recall and recognition of pictures by children as a function of organization and distractor similarity. *Journal of Experimental Psychology*, 1974, *102*, 657-669.

MANDLER, J. M., & STEIN, N. L. The myth of perceptual defect: Sources and evidence. *Psychological Bulletin*, 1977, *84*, 173-192.

MARQUIS, K. H., MARSHALL, J., & OSKAMP, S. Testimony validity as a function of question form, atmosphere, and item difficulty. *Journal of Applied Social Psychology*, 1972, *2*, 167-186.

MARSHALL, J. *Law and psychology in conflict*. Indianapolis: Bobbs-Merrill, 1966,

MATTHEWS, M. L. Discrimination of Identi-kit constructions of faces: Evidence for a dual processing strategy. *Perception and Psychophysics*, 1978, *29*, 153-161.

MAZANEC, N., & McCALL, G. J. Sex, cognitive categories, and observational accuracy. *Psychological Reports*, 1975, *37*, 987-990.

MAZANEC, N., & McCALL, G. J. Sex factors and allocation of attention in observing persons. *Journal of Psychology*, 1976, 93, 175–180.

McCALL, G. J., MAZANEC, N., ERICKSON, W. L., & SMITH, H. W. Same-sex recall effects in tests of observational accuracy. *Perceptual and Motor Skills*, 1974, 38, 830.

McCANCE, R. A., LUFF, M. C., & WIDDOWSON, E. E. Physical and emotional periodicity in women. *Journal of Hygiene*, 1937, 37, 571–605.

McCARTY, D. G. *Psychology for the lawyer.* New York: Prentice-Hall, 1929.

McCARTY, D. G. *Psychology and the law.* Englewood Cliffs, N.J.: Prentice-Hall, 1960.

McCARVER, R. B. A developmental study of the effect of organizational cues on short-term memory. *Child Development*, 1972, 43, 1317–1325.

McCARY, J. L. The psychologist as expert witness in court. *American Psychologist*, 1956, 11, 8–13.

McCORMICK, C. T. *Handbook of law of evidence.* St. Paul, Minn.: West, 1954.

McDAVID, J. W., & HARARI, H. Stereotyping of names and popularity of grade-school children. *Child Development*, 1966, 37, 453–459.

McFARLAND, R. A. The sensory and perceptual processes in aging. In K. W. Schaie (Ed.), *Theory and methods of research on aging.* Morgantown: West Virginia University Press, 1968.

McGINNIES, E. Emotionality and perceptual defense. *Psychological Review*, 1949, 56, 244–251.

McKELLAR, P. *Experience and behaviour.* Harmondsworth, England: Penguin, 1968.

McKELVIE, S. J. The meaningfulness and meaning of schematic faces. *Perception and Psychophysics*, 1973, 14, 343–348.

McKELVIE, S. J. The role of eyes and mouth in recognition memory for faces. *American Journal of Psychology*, 1976, 89, 311–323.

McKELVIE, S. J. The effects of verbal labelling on recognition memory for schematic faces. *Quarterly Journal of Experimental Psychology*, in press.

McMAHON, F. B. *Psychology: The hybrid science,* third edition. Englewood Cliffs, N.J.: Prentice-Hall, 1977.

MEEHL, P. E. Psychology and the criminal law. *University of Richmond Law Review*, 1970, 5, 1–30.

MEEHL, P. E. Law and the fireside inductions: Some reflections of a clinical psychologist. *Journal of Social Issues*, 1971, 27, 65–100.

MEHRABIAN, A. Communication without words. *Psychology Today*, September 1968, 53–55.

MEHRABIAN, A. Nonverbal betrayal of feeling. *Journal of Experimental Research in Personality*, 1971, 5, 64–73.

MEHRABIAN, A. *Nonverbal communication.* New York: Aldine-Atherton, 1972.

MELLINKOFF, D. *The language of the law.* Boston: Little, Brown, 1963.

MESSICK, S., & DAMARIN, F. Cognitive style and memory for faces. *Journal of Abnormal and Social Psychology*, 1964, 69, 313–318.

MICHOTTE, A. *The perception of causality*. Trans. T. R. Miles and E. Miles. London: Methuen, 1963.

MILLER, A. G. Role of physical attractiveness in impression formation. *Psychonomic Science*, 1970, *19*, 241–243.

MILLER, D. G., & LOFTUS, E. F. Influencing memory for people and their actions. *Bulletin of the Psychonomic Society*, 1976, *7*, 9–11.

MILLER, N., MARUYAMA, G., BEABER, R. J., & VALONE, K. Speed of speech and persuasion. *Journal of Personality and Social Psychology*, 1976, *34*, 615–624.

MILNER, B. Visual recognition and recall after right temporal lobe excision in man. *Neuropsychologia*, 1968, *6*, 191–209.

MILNER, B. Interhemispheric differences and psychological processes. *British Medical Bulletin*, 1971, *27*, 272–277.

MOENSSENS, A. A. The origin of legal photography. *Finger Print and Identification Magazine*, January 1962, pp. 3–7, 11–17.

MOENSSENS, A. A., MOSES, R. E., & INBAU, F. E. *Scientific evidence in criminal cases*. New York: Foundation Press, 1973.

MONAHAN, F. *Women in crime*. New York: Washburn, 1941.

MOORE, C. C. Psychology in the courts. *Law Notes*, 1908, *11*, 186–187.

MOOS, R. H. The development of a menstrual distress questionnaire. *Psychosomatic Medicine*, 1968, *30*, 853–867.

MOOS, R. H., KOPELL, B. S., MELGES, F. T., YALOM, I. D., LUNDE, D. T., CLAYTON, R. B., & HAMBURG, D. A. Fluctuations in symptoms and moods during the menstrual cycle. *Journal of Psychosomatic Research*, 1969, *13*, 37–44.

MORRIS, P. E., JONES, S., & HAMPSON, P. An imagery mnemonic for the learning of people's names. *British Journal of Psychology*, 1978, *69*, 335–336.

MORSE, S. J. Law and mental health professionals: The limits of expertise. *Professional Psychology*, August 1978, 389–399.

MUELLER, J. H. Levels of processing and facial recognition. Paper presented at the annual meeting of the American Psychological Association, Toronto, 1978.

MUELLER, J. H., BAILIS, K. L., & GOLDSTEIN, A. G. Depth of processing and anxiety in facial recognition. *British Journal of Psychology*, in press.

MUELLER, J. H., CARLOMUSTO, M., & MARLER, M. Recall as a function of method of presentation and individual differences in test anxiety. *Bulletin of the Psychonomic Society*, 1977, *10*, 447–450.

MUELLER, J. H., & GOULET, L. R. The effects of anxiety on human learning and memory. Paper presented at the annual meeting of the American Psychological Association, Montreal, 1973.

MUNN, N. L. The effect of knowledge of the situation upon judgment of emotion from facial expressions. *Journal of Abnormal and Social Psychology*, 1940, *35*, 324–338.

MÜNSTERBERG, H. *On the witness stand: Essays on psychology and crime*. New York: Clark, Boardman, 1908.

MURRAY, D. C. Talk, silence, and anxiety. *Psychological Bulletin*, 1971, *75*, 244–260.

MURRAY, J. The criminal lineup at home and abroad. *Utah Law Review,* 1966, *610,* 621–627.

MUSCIO, B. The influence of the form of question. *British Journal of Psychology,* 1915, *8,* 351–386.

NAGEL, E. *The structure of science: Problems in the logic of scientific explanation.* New York: Harcourt, Brace & World, 1961.

NAUS, M. J., & ORNSTEIN, P. A. Developmental differences in the memory search of categorized lists. *Developmental Psychology,* 1977, *13,* 60–68.

NEISSER, U. *Cognitive psychology.* New York: Appleton, 1967.

NEISWENDER, M. Middle adulthood: Making the most of it. In *Developmental Psychology Today,* second edition. New York: Random House, 1975.

NELSON, K. E. Memory development in children: Evidence from nonverbal tasks. *Psychonomic Science,* 1971, *25,* 346–348.

NELSON, K. E., & KOSSLYN, S. M. Recognition of previously labeled or unlabeled pictures by 5-year-olds and adults. *Journal of Experimental Child Psychology,* 1976, *21,* 40–45.

NEUGARTEN, B. L., WOOD, V., KRAINES, R. J., & LOOMIS, B. Women's attitudes toward the menopause. *Vita Humana,* 1963, *6,* 140–151.

NEWCOMBE, N., ROGOFF, B., & KAGAN, J. Developmental changes in recognition memory for pictures of objects and scenes. *Developmental Psychology,* 1977, *13,* 337–341.

NISBETT, R. E., CAPUTO, C., LEGANT, P., & MARACEK, J. Behavior as seen by the actor and as seen by the observer. *Journal of Personality and Social Psychology,* 1973, *27,* 154–164.

NISBETT, R. E., & VALINS, S. Perceiving the causes of one's own behavior. In E. E. Jones, D. E. Kanouse, H. H. Kelley, R. E. Nisbett, S. Valins, & B. Weiner (Eds.), *Attribution: Perceiving the causes of behavior.* Morristown, N.J.: General Learning, 1972.

NORMAN, D. *Memory and attention,* second edition. New York: Wiley, 1976.

O'BARR, W. M. The language of the law—vehicle or obstacle? Paper prepared for a volume on language and law, East-West Center Learning Institute, Honolulu, August 1976.

O'BARR, W. M., & CONLEY, J. M. When a juror watches a lawyer. *Barrister,* 1976, *3,* 8–11, 33.

O'CONNELL, D. N., SHOR, R. E., & ORNE, M. T. Hypnotic age regression: An empirical and methodological analysis. *Journal of Abnormal Psychology Monograph,* 1970, *76,* No. 3, Part 2.

O'HARA, C. E. *Fundamentals of criminal investigation.* Springfield, Ill.: Charles C Thomas, 1970.

OLIVER, E., & GRIFFITT, W. Emotional arousal and "objective" judgment. *Bulletin of the Psychonomic Society,* 1976, *8,* 399–400.

OLTMAN, P. K., GOODENOUGH, D. R., WITKIN, H. A., FREEDMAN, N., & FRIEDMAN, F. Psychological differentiation as a factor in conflict resolution. *Journal of Personality and Social Psychology,* 1975, *32,* 730–736.

OPPENHEIMER, R. Analogy in science. *American Psychologist,* 1956, *11,* 127–135.

ORNE, M. T. On the social psychology of the psychological experiment: With particular reference to demand characteristics and their implications. *American Psychologist,* 1962, *17,* 776–783.

ORNE, M. T. The simulation of hypnosis: Why, how, and what it means. *International Journal of Clinical and Experimental Hypnosis,* 1971, *19,* 183–210.

ORNE, M. T. Hypnosis. In G. Lindzey, C. Hall, & R. F. Thompson (Eds.), *Psychology.* New York: Worth Publishers, 1975, pp. 150–153.

ORNSTEIN, P. A., NAUS, M. J., & LIBERTY, C. Rehearsal and organizational processes in children's memory. *Child Development,* 1975, *46,* 818–830.

ORNSTEIN, P. A., NAUS, M. J., & STONE, B. P. Rehearsal training and developmental differences in memory. *Developmental Psychology,* 1977, *13,* 15–24.

PAIVIO, A. Effects of imagery instructions and concreteness of memory pegs in a mnemonic system. *Proceedings, 76th Annual Convention, American Psychological Association,* 1968, pp. 77–78.

PAIVIO, A. Mental imagery in associative learning and memory. *Psychological Review,* 1969, *76,* 241–263.

PAIVIO, A. *Imagery and verbal processes.* New York: Holt, Rinehart and Winston, 1971. (a)

PAIVIO, A. Imagery and language. In S. J. Segal (Ed.), *Imagery: Current cognitive approaches.* New York: Academic Press, 1971. (b)

PALLIS, C. A. Impaired identification of faces and places with agnosia for colours. *Journal of Neurology, Neurosurgery, and Psychiatry,* 1955, *18,* 218–224.

PATTERSON, K. E., & BADDELEY, A. D. When face recognition fails. *Journal of Experimental Psychology: Human Learning and Memory,* 1977, *3,* 406–417.

PIAGET, J. *The language and thought of the child.* New York: Harcourt, Brace, 1926.

PIAGET, J. *The child's conception of physical causality.* New York: Harcourt Brace Jovanovich, 1930.

PIAGET, J. *The moral judgment of the child.* London: Routledge & Kegan Paul, 1932.

PIAGET, J. *The psychology of intelligence.* London: Routledge & Kegan Paul, 1950.

PIAGET, J., & INHELDER, B. *Mémoire et intelligence.* Paris: Presses Universitaires de France, 1968.

PLATO. *The dialogues of Plato,* Vol. 4, third edition. Trans. B. Jowett. Oxford: Clarendon Press, 1892.

PODLESNY, J. A., & RASKIN, D. C. Physiological measures and the detection of deception. *Psychological Bulletin,* 1977, *84,* 782–799.

POLANYI, M. *Personal knowledge: Towards a post-critical philosophy,* revised edition. New York: Harper Torchbooks, 1964.

POLANYI, M. Logic and psychology. *American Psychologist,* 1968, *23,* 27–43.

POPPER, K. R. *The logic of scientific discovery.* London: Hutchinson, 1959.

POPPER, K. R. *Conjectures and refutations.* London: Routledge & Kegan Paul, 1963.

POPPER, K. R. *Objective knowledge.* London: Oxford University Press, 1972.

POSTMAN, L. Choice behavior and the process of recognition. *American Journal of Psychology,* 1950, *63,* 443–447.

POSTMAN, L. Short-term memory and incidental learning. In A. W. Melton (Ed.), *Categories of human learning*. New York: Academic Press, 1964.

POSTMAN, L., & BRUNER, J. S. Perception under stress. *Psychological Review*, 1948, 55, 314–323.

PRESTON, J. M., & GARDNER, R. C. Dimensions of oral and written language fluency. *Journal of Verbal Learning and Verbal Behavior*, 1967, 6, 936–945.

PROGREBIN, L. D. Down with sexist upbringing. *Ms*, Spring 1972.

PULOS, L., & SPILKA, B. Perceptual selectivity, memory and anti-Semitism. *Journal of Abnormal and Social Psychology*, 1961, 62, 690–693.

RAMIREZ, M., & CASTENADA, A. *Cultural democracy, bicognitive development, and education*. New York: Academic Press, 1974.

RASKIN, D. C. Psychopathy and detection of deception in a prison population. Report No. 75-1, Contract No. 75-N1-99-0001, U.S. Department of Justice. Salt Lake City, Utah: University of Utah, Department of Psychology, June 1975.

READ, J. D., BARNSLEY, R. H., ANKERS, K., & WHISHAW, I. Q. Variations in severity of verbs and eyewitnesses' testimony: An alternative interpretation. *Perceptual and Motor Skills*, 1978, 46, 795–800.

READ, J. D., & PETERSON, R. H. Individual differences in the ease of imagining the faces of others. *Bulletin of the Psychonomic Society*, 1975, 5, 347–349.

REDMOUNT, R. S. The psychological basis of evidence practices: Memory. *Journal of Criminal Law, Criminology, and Police Science*, 1959, 50, 249–264.

REED, J. A. You are what you wear. *Human Behavior*, 1974, July.

REID, J. E., & INBAU, F. E. *Truth and deception: The polygraph ("lie detector") technique*. Baltimore: Williams & Wilkins, 1966.

REIFF, R., & SCHEERER, M. *Memory and hypnotic age regression: Developmental aspects of cognitive function explored through hypnosis*. New York: International Universities Press, 1959.

REIK, T. Men and women speak different languages. *Psychoanalysis*, 1954, 2 (Spring-Summer), 15.

RIBOT, T. *Diseases of memory*. New York: Appleton, 1882.

RICE, B. The new truth machines. *Psychology Today*, June 1978, 61–64, 67, 72, 74, 77–78.

RICE, G. P. The psychologist as expert witness. *American Psychologist*, 1961, 16, 691–692.

RIECKEN, H. W. A program for research on experiments in social psychology. In N. F. Washburne (Ed.), *Decisions, values and groups*, Vol. 2. New York: Pergamon Press, 1962.

RIEGEL, K. F., & RIEGEL, R. M. Development, drop and death. *Developmental Psychology*, 1972, 6, 306–319.

RIESMAN, D. Some observations on law and psychology. *University of Chicago Law Review*, 1951, 19, 30–44.

RILEY, D. A. Memory for form. In L. Postman (Ed.), *Psychology in the making*. New York: Knopf, 1962.

RIZZOLATTI, G., UMILTA, C., & BERLUCCHI, G. Opposite superiorities of the right and left cerebral hemispheres in discriminative reaction time to physiognomical and alphabetical material. *Brain*, 1971, *94*, 431–442.

ROBITSCHER, J., & WILLIAMS, R. Should psychiatrists get out of the courtroom? *Psychology Today*, December 1977, 85–86, 91–92, 138, 140.

ROGOFF, B., NEWCOMBE, N., & KAGAN, J. Planfulness and recognition memory. *Child Development*, 1974, *45*, 972–977.

ROSENBERG, S., NELSON, C., & VIVEKANANTHAN, P. S. A multidimensional approach to the structure of personality impression. *Journal of Personality and Social Psychology*, 1968, *9*, 283–294.

ROSENFELD, H. M. Approval-seeking and approval-inducing functions of verbal and nonverbal responses in the dyad. *Journal of Personality and Social Psychology*, 1966, *4*, 597–605.

ROSENHAN, D. L. On being sane in insane places. *Science*, 1973, *179*, 250–258.

ROSENKRANTZ, P. S., VOGEL, S. R., BEE, H., BROVERMAN, I. K., & BROVERMAN, D. M. Sex-role stereotypes and self-concepts in college students. *Journal of Consulting and Clinical Psychology*, 1968, *32*, 287–295.

ROSENTHAL, R. *Experimenter effects in behavioral research*. New York: Appleton Century Crofts, 1966.

ROSENTHAL, R., ARCHER, D., DiMATTEO, M. R., KOIVUMAKI, J. H., & ROGERS, P. L. Measuring sensitivity to nonverbal communication: The PONS test. Paper presented at the International Conference on Non-Verbal Behavior, Toronto, 1976.

ROSENTHAL, R., & JACOBSON, L. *Pygmalion in the classroom: Teacher expectation and pupils' intellectual development*. New York: Holt, 1968.

ROSNOW, R., HOLZ, R., & LEVIN, J. Differential effects of complimentary and competing variables in primacy-recency. *Journal of Social Psychology*, 1966, *69*, 135–147.

ROTTER, J. B., & STEIN, D. K. Public attitudes toward the trustworthiness, competence, and altruism of twenty selected occupations. *Journal of Applied Social Psychology*, 1971, *1*, 334–343.

ROUKE, F. L. Psychological research on problems of testimony. *Journal of Social Issues*, 1957, *13*, 50–59.

ROWE, E. J., & SCHNORE, M. M. Item concreteness and reported strategies in paired-associate learning as a function of age. *Journal of Gerontology*, 1971, *26*, 470–475.

RUNDUS, D. Analysis of rehearsal processes in free recall. *Journal of Experimental Psychology*, 1971, *89*, 63–77.

RUPP, A., WARMBRAND, A., KARASH, A., & BUCKHOUT, R. Effects of group interaction on eyewitness reports. Paper presented at the annual meeting of the Eastern Psychological Association, New York, 1976.

RUSSELL, W. R., & NATHAN, P. W. Traumatic amnesia. *Brain*, 1946, *69*, 280–301.

SAAYMAN, G., AMES, E. W., & MOFFETT, A. Response to novelty as an indicator of visual discrimination in the human infant. *Journal of Experimental Child Psychology*, 1964, *1*, 189–198.

SALES, B. D. (Ed.) *Psychology in the legal process*. New York: Spectrum, 1977. (a)

SALES, B. D. (Ed.) *Perspectives in law and psychology*, Vol. 1, *The Criminal Justice System*. New York: Plenum, 1977. (b)

SALES, B. D., ELWORK, A., & ALFINI, J. J. Improving comprehension for jury instructions. In B. D. Sales (Ed.), *Perspectives in law and psychology*, Vol. 1, *The Criminal Justice System*. New York: Plenum, 1977.

SAMUELS, M. Scheme influences on long-term event recall in children. *Child Development*, 1976, *47*, 824–830.

SANDERS, H. I., & WARRINGTON, E. K. Memory for remote events in amnesic patients. *Brain*, 1971, *94*, 661–668.

SANDERS, W. B. The detective: Qualitative methodologist. Paper presented at the annual meeting of the American Sociological Associatio:., San Francisco, 1975.

SANDERS, W. B. *Detective work: A study of criminal investigations*. New York: Free Press, 1977.

SANTA, J. L., & RANKEN, H. B. Effects of verbal coding on recognition memory. *Journal of Experimental Psychology*, 1972, *93*, 268–278.

SAUFLEY, W. H., Jr., & WINOGRAD, E. Retrograde amnesia and priority instructions in free recall. *Journal of Experimental Psychology*, 1970, *85*, 150–152.

SAVITSKY, J. C., IZARD, C. E., KOTSCH, W. E., & CHRISTY, L. Aggressor's response to the victim's facial expression of emotion. *Journal of Research in Personality*, 1974, *7*, 346–357.

SCAPINELLO, K. F., & YARMEY, A. D. The role of familiarity and orientation in immediate and delayed recognition of pictorial stimuli. *Psychonomic Science*, 1970, *21*, 329–330.

SCHACTER, S., & SINGER, J. E. Cognitive, social and physiological determinants of emotional state. *Psychological Review*, 1962, *69*, 379–399.

SCHAFER, D. W., & RUBIO, R. Hypnosis to aid the recall of witnesses. *International Journal of Clinical and Experimental Hypnosis*, 1978, *26*, 81–91.

SCHILL, T. R. Effects of approval motivation and varying conditions of verbal reinforcement on incidental memory for faces. *Psychological Reports*, 1966, *19*, 55–60.

SCHOFIELD, W. Psychology, law, and the expert witness. *American Psychologist*, 1956, *11*, 1–7.

SCHONFIELD, D., & ROBERTSON, B. A. Memory storage and aging. *Canadian Journal of Psychology*, 1966, *20*, 228–236.

SCHNEIDER, S. M., & KINTZ, B. L. The effect of lying upon foot and leg movement. *Bulletin of the Psychonomic Society*, 1977, *10*, 451–453.

SCHULZ, L. S., & STRAUB, R. B. Effects of high-priority events on recognition of adjacent items. *Journal of Experimental Psychology*, 1972, *95*, 467–469.

SECORD, P. F. The role of facial features in interpersonal perception. In R. Tagiuri & L. Petrullo (Eds.), *Person perception and interpersonal behavior*. Stanford, Calif.: Stanford University Press, 1958, pp. 300–315.

Secord, P. F., & Backman, C. W. *Social psychology*, second edition. New York: McGraw-Hill, 1974.

Secord, P. F., Dukes, W. F., & Bevan, W. Personalities in faces: 1. An experiment in social perceiving. *Genetic Psychology Monographs*, 1954, *49*, 231–279.

Seeleman, V. The influence of attitude upon the remembering of pictorial material. *Archives of Psychology*, 1940, *36*, 1–64.

Seyfried, B. A., & Hendrick, C. When do opposites attract? When they are opposite in sex and sex-role attitudes. *Journal of Personality and Social Psychology*, 1973, *25*, 15–20.

Shaffer, D. R., & Wegley, C. Success orientation and sex-role congruence as determinants of the attractiveness of competent women. *Journal of Personality*, 1974, *42*, 586–600.

Shaffer, J. P. Social and personality correlates of children's estimates of height. *Genetic Psychological Monographs*, 1964, *70*, 97–134.

Shapiro, S., & Erdelyi, M. H. Hypermnesia for pictures but not words. *Journal of Experimental Psychology*, 1974, *103*, 1218–1219.

Shaver, K. G. Defensive attribution: Effects of severity and relevance on the responsibility assigned for an accident. *Journal of Personality and Social Psychology*, 1970, *14*, 101–113.

Sheingold, K. Developmental differences in intake and storage of visual information. *Journal of Experimental Child Psychology*, 1973, *16*, 1–11.

Sheldon, W. H. *The varieties of temperament*. New York: Harper & Row, 1942.

Shepard, R. N. Recognition memory for words, sentences, and pictures. *Journal of Verbal Learning and Verbal Behavior*, 1967, *6*, 156–163.

Shepherd, J. W., Deregowski, J. B., & Ellis, H. D. A cross-cultural study of recognition memory for faces. *International Journal of Psychology*, 1974, *9*, 205–211.

Shepherd, J. W., & Ellis, H. D. The effect of attractiveness on recognition memory for faces. *American Journal of Psychology*, 1973, *86*, 627–633.

Shepherd, J. W., Ellis, H. D., McMurran, M., & Davies, G. M. Effect of character attribution on Photofit construction of a face. *European Journal of Social Psychology*, 1978, *8*, 263–268.

Sherif, M. A study of some social factors in perception. *Archives of Psychology*, 1935, *27*, No. 187.

Shoemaker, D. J., South, D. R., & Lowe, J. Facial stereotypes of deviants and judgments of guilt or innocence. *Social Forces*, 1973, *51*, 427–433.

Sigall, H., & Ostrove, N. Beautiful but dangerous: Effects of offender attractiveness and nature of the crime on juridic judgment. *Journal of Personality and Social Psychology*, 1975, *31*, 410–414.

Siipola, E. M., & Hayden, S. D. Exploring eidetic imagery among the retarded. *Perceptual and Motor Skills*, 1965, *21*, 275–286.

Silverman, H. Determinism, choice, responsibility and the psychologist's role as an expert witness. *American Psychologist*, 1969, *24*, 5–9.

Simmonds, D. C. V., Poulton, E. C., & Tickner, A. H. Identifying people in a videotape recording made at night. *Ergonomics*, 1975, *18*, 607–618.

SMITH, A. D. Adult age differences in cued recall. *Developmental Psychology*, 1977, *13*, 326–331.

SMITH, A. D., & WINOGRAD, E. Adult age differences in remembering faces. *Developmental Psychology*, 1978, *14*, 443–444.

SMITH, B. M. The polygraph. *Scientific American*, 1967, *216*, No. 1.

SMITH, G. H. Size-distance judgments of human faces. *Journal of General Psychology*, 1953, *49*, 46–64.

SMITH, H. C. *Sensitivity to people.* New York: McGraw-Hill, 1966.

SNEE, T. J., & LUSH, D. E. Interaction of the narrative and interrogatory methods of obtaining testimony. *Journal of Psychology*, 1941, *11*, 229–236.

SOLOMON, D., & GOODSON, D. F. Hypnotic age regression evaluated against a criterion of prior performance. *International Journal of Clinical and Experimental Hypnosis*, 1971, *19*, 243–259.

SOMMER, B. Menstrual cycle changes and intellectual performance. *Psychosomatic Medicine*, 1972, *34*, 263–269.

SOMMER, B. The effect of menstruation on cognitive and perceptual-motor behavior: A review. *Psychosomatic Medicine*, 1973, *35*, 515–534.

SORCE, J. F., & CAMPOS, J. J. The role of expression in the recognition of a face. *American Journal of Psychology*, 1974, *87*, 71–82.

SPEAKMAN, D. The effect of age on the incidental relearning of stamp values. *Journal of Gerontology*, 1954, *9*, 162–167.

SPENCE, J. T., HELMREICH, R., & STAPP, J. Likability, sex-role congruence of interest, and competence: It all depends on how you act. *Journal of Applied Social Psychology*, in press.

SQUIRE, L. R. Remote memory as affected by aging. *Neuropsychologia*, 1974, *12*, 429–435.

SQUIRE, L. R. A stable impairment in remote memory following electroconvulsive therapy. *Neuropsychologia*, 1975, *13*, 51–58.

SQUIRES, P. C. The law as a major field for psychological research. *Journal of Abnormal and Social Psychology*, 1931, *26*, 314–323.

STANDING, L. Learning 10,000 pictures. *Quarterly Journal of Experimental Psychology*. 1973, *25*, 207–222.

STANDING, L., CONEZIO, J., & HABER, R. N. Perception and memory for pictures: Single-trial learning of 2,500 visual stimuli. *Psychonomic Science*, 1970, *19*, 73–74.

STECHLER, G. Newborn attention as affected by medication during labor. *Science*, 1964, *144*, 315–317.

STEIN, N. L., & MANDLER, J. M. Development of detection and recognition orientation of geometric and real figures. *Child Development*, 1975, *46*, 379–388.

STONE, V. A. A primacy effect in decision-making by jurors. *Journal of Communication*, 1969, *19*, 239–247.

STRNAD, B. N., & MUELLER, J. H. Levels of processing in facial recognition memory. *Bulletin of the Psychonomic Society*, 1977, *9*, 17–18.

SUEDFELD, P., ERDELYI, M. H., & CORCORAN, C. R. Rejection of input in the processing of an emotional film. *Bulletin of the Psychonomic Society*, 1975, *5*, 30–32.

SUSSWEIN, B. J., & SMITH, R. F. Perceptual discriminability and communication performance in preschool children. *Child Development*, 1975, *46*, 954–957.

SWORD, S. B. Identification of names and faces as a function of cognitive style, incidental learning, and imagery instructions. Unpublished M.A. thesis, University of Guelph, Guelph, Ontario, 1970.

TAGIURI, R. Person perception. In G. Lindzey & E. Aronson (Eds.), *Handbook of social psychology*, Vol. 3, second edition. Reading, Mass.: Addison-Wesley, 1969, pp. 395–449.

TALLAND, G. A. Age and the span of immediate recall. In G. A. Talland (Ed.), *Human aging and behavior*. New York: Academic Press, 1968.

TAPP, J. L. Psychology and the law: An overture. *Annual Review of Psychology*, 1976, *27*, 359–404.

TAPP, J. L., & KOHLBERG, L. Developing senses of law and legal justice. *Journal of Social Issues*, 1971, *27*, 65–92.

TAPP, J. L., & LEVINE, F. J. Legal socialization: Strategies for an ethical legality. *Stanford Law Review*, 1974, *27*, 1–72.

TAPP, J. L., & LEVINE, F. J. (Eds.) *Law, justice, and the individual in society*. New York: Holt, Rinehart and Winston, 1977.

TAYNOR, J., & DEAUX, K. When women are more deserving than men: Equity, attribution, and perceived sex differences. *Journal of Personality and Social Psychology*, 1973, *28*, 360–367.

THOMAS, E. I. Cross-examination and rehabilitation of witnesses. *Defense Law Journal*, 1965, *15*, 247–263.

THOMPSON, D. F., & MELTZER, L. Communication of emotional intent by facial expression. *Journal of Abnormal and Social Psychology*, 1964, *68*, 129–135.

THORNWALD, J. *Crime and science: The new frontier in criminology*. New York: Harcourt Brace Jovanovich, 1967.

THORSON, G., & HOCHHAUS, L. The trained observer: Effects of prior information on eyewitness reports. *Bulletin of the Psychonomic Society*, 1977, *10*, 454–456.

TICKNER, A. H., & POULTON, E. C. Watching for people and actions. *Ergonomics*, 1975, *18*, 35–51.

TIFFANY, L. P., McINTYRE, D. M., & ROTENBERG, D. L. *Detection of crime*. Toronto: Little, Brown, 1967.

TIGER, L. The possible biological origins of sexual discrimination. *Impact of Science on Society*, 1970, *20*, 29–44.

TOCH, H. *Legal and criminal psychology*. New York: Holt, Rinehart and Winston, 1961.

TORNEY, J. V. Socialization of attitudes toward the legal system. *Journal of Social Issues*, 1971, *27*, 137–154.

TOYAMA, J. S. The effect of orientation on the recognition of faces: A reply to Yin. Unpublished doctoral dissertation, University of Waterloo, Waterloo, Ontario, 1975.

TRANKELL, A. *Reliability of evidence: Methods for analyzing and assessing witness statements.* Stockholm: Beckman, 1972.

TREAT, N. J., & REESE, H. W. Age, pacing, and imagery in paired-associate learning. *Developmental Psychology,* 1976, *12,* 119–124.

TRIBE, L. H. Trial by mathematics: Precision and ritual in the legal process. *Harvard Law Review,* 1971, *84,* 1329–1393.

TROVILLO, P. V. A history in lie detection. *Journal of Criminal Law and Criminology,* 1939, *29,* 848–881.

TRUDGILL, P. Sex, covert prestige, and linguistic change in the urban British English of Norwich. *Language in Society,* 1972, *1,* 179–195.

TULVING, E. Subjective organization in free-recall of "unrelated" words. *Psychological Review,* 1962, *69,* 344–354.

TULVING, E. Retrograde amnesia in free recall. *Science,* 1969, *164,* 88–90.

TULVING, E., & PEARLSTONE, Z. Availability versus accessibility of information in memory for words. *Journal of Verbal Learning and Verbal Behavior,* 1966, *5,* 381–391.

TULVING, E., & THOMSON, D. M. Encoding specificity and retrieval processes in episodic memory. *Psychological Review,* 1973, *80,* 352–373.

TURNER, W. W. *Invisible witness: The use and abuse of the new technology of crime investigation.* New York: Bobbs-Merrill, 1968.

TVERSKY, B. Eye fixations in prediction of recognition and recall. *Memory and Cognition,* 1974, *2,* 275–278.

TVERSKY, B., & TEIFFER, E. Development of strategies for recall and recognition. *Developmental Psychology,* 1976, *12,* 406–410.

TYLER, L. E. *The psychology of human difference,* second edition. New York: Appleton-Century-Crofts, 1956.

VAN CAMP, J. Preparing the criminal defense case. *Trial,* 1978, *14,* 38–41.

VERINIS, J. S., & WALKER, V. Policemen and the recall of criminal details. *Journal of Social Psychology,* 1970, *81,* 217–221.

VIDMAR, N., & CRINKLAW, L. D. Attributing responsibility for an accident. *Canadian Journal of Behavioral Science,* 1974, *6,* 112–130.

WALL, P. M. *Eyewitness identification in criminal cases.* Springfield, Ill.: Charles C Thomas, 1965.

WALLS, H. J. What is "reasonable doubt?" A forensic scientist looks at the law. *Criminal Law Review,* August 1971, 458–470.

WALLACE, G., COLTHEART, M., & FORSTER, K. I. Reminiscence in recognition memory for faces. *Psychonomic Science,* 1970, *18,* 335–336.

WALLACH, M. A., & KOGAN, N. Aspects of judgment and decisionmaking: Interrelationships and changes with age. *Behavioral Science,* 1961, *6,* 23–36.

WALSTER, E. Assignment of responsibility for an accident. *Journal of Personality and Social Psychology,* 1966, *3,* 73–79.

WALSTER, E., ARONSON, E., ABRAHAMS, D., & ROTTMAN, L. Importance of physical attractiveness in dating behavior. *Journal of Personality and Social Psychology,* 1966, *4,* 508–516.

WAPNER, S., WERNER, H., & COMALLI, P. E. Perception of part-whole relationships in middle and old age. *Journal of Gerontology*, 1960, *15*, 413–418.

WARD, C. D. Own height, sex, and liking in the judgment of others. *Journal of Personality*, 1967, *35*, 381–401.

WARE, R., & HARVEY, O. J. A cognitive determinant of impression formation. *Journal of Personality and Social Psychology*, 1967, *5*, 38–44.

WARR, P. B., & KNAPPER, C. *The perception of people and events.* Toronto: Wiley, 1968.

WARRINGTON, E. K., & ACKROYD, C. The effect of orienting tasks on recognition memory. *Memory and Cognition*, 1975, *3*, 140–142.

WARRINGTON, E. K., & JAMES, M. An experimental investigation of facial recognition in patients with unilateral cerebral lesions. *Cortex*, 1967, *3*, 317–326.

WARRINGTON, E. K., & SANDERS, H. The fate of old memories. *Quarterly Journal of Experimental Psychology*, 1971, *23*, 432–442.

WARRINGTON, E. K., & TAYLOR, A. M. Immediate memory for faces: Long- or short-term memory? *Quarterly Journal of Experimental Psychology*, 1973, *25*, 316–322.

WATSON, A. (Ed.) *Adolf Beck's Trial*, in Notable British Trials Series. Glasgow: Hodge, 1924.

WATSON, J. B. Psychology as the behaviorist views it. *Psychological Review*, 1913, *20*, 158–177.

WECHSLER, D. *The measurement of adult intelligence.* Baltimore: Williams & Wilkins, 1944.

WEIMER, W. B. Psycholinguistics and Plato's paradoxes of the Meno. *American Psychologist*, 1973, *28*, 15–33.

WEINBERG, A. *Attorney for the damned.* New York: Simon & Schuster, 1957.

WELFORD, A. T. *Ageing and human skill.* London: Oxford University Press, 1958.

WELLMAN, F. L. The manner of cross-examination. In W. H. Davenport (Ed.), *Voices in court.* New York: Macmillan, 1958.

WERNER, H., & WAPNER, S. Changes in psychological distance under conditions of danger. *Journal of Personality*, 1955, *24*, 153–167.

WEST, S. G., & SHULTS, T. Liking for common and uncommon first names. *Personality and Social Psychology Bulletin*, 1976, *2*, 299–302.

WHEELER, R. J., & DUSEK, J. B. The effects of attentional and cognitive factors on children's incidental learning. *Child Development*, 1973, *44*, 253–258.

WHIPPLE, G. M. The observer as reporter: A survey on the "psychology of testimony." *Psychological Bulletin*, 1909, *6*, 753–770.

WHIPPLE, G. M. Review: Les tesmoignages d'enfants dans us proces rententissant, by J. Varendonck. *Journal of Criminal Law and Criminology*, 1913, *4*, 150–154.

WHITEHURST, G. J. The development of communication: Changes with age and modeling. *Child Development*, 1976, *47*, 473–482.

WHITELY, P. L., & MCGEOCH, J. A. The effect of one form of report upon another. *American Journal of Psychology*, 1927, *38*, 280–284.

WHORF, B. L. *Language, thought, and reality.* ed. J. B. Carroll, Cambridge, Mass.: M.I.T. Press, 1956.

WICKELGREN, W. A. *Learning and memory.* Englewood Cliffs, N.J.: Prentice-Hall, 1977.

WICKHAM, M. The effects of the menstrual cycle on test performance. *British Journal of Psychology,* 1958, *49,* 34–41.

WIGGELSWORTH, V. B. *The life of insects.* London: Weidenfeld & Nicolson, 1964.

WIGMORE, J. H. Professor Münsterberg and the psychology of testimony. *Illinois Law Review,* 1909, *3,* 399–445.

WIGMORE, J. H. *Evidence,* second edition. Boston: Little, Brown, 1923.

WIGMORE, J. H. *Principles of judicial proof.* Boston: Little, Brown, 1931.

WILLIAMS, G. *The proof of guilt.* London: Stevens & Sons, 1958.

WILLIAMS, G., & HAMMELMAN, B. Identification parades, part 1. *Criminal Law Review,* 1963, 479, 487.

WILLIAMS, M. Retrograde amnesia. In Alan Kennedy & Alan Wilkes (Eds.), *Studies in long term memory.* London: Wiley, 1975.

WINOGRAD, E. Recognition memory for faces following nine different judgments. *Bulletin of the Psychonomic Society,* 1976, *8,* 419–421.

WISEMAN, S., & NEISSER, U. Perceptual organization as a determinant of visual recognition memory. *American Journal of Psychology,* 1974, *87,* 675–681.

WITKIN, H. A., DYK, R. B., FATERSON, H. F., GOODENOUGH, D. R., & KARP, S. A. *Psychological differentiation.* New York: Wiley, 1962.

WITKIN, H. A., & GOODENOUGH, D. R. Field dependence and interpersonal behavior. *Psychological Bulletin,* 1977, *84,* 661–689.

WITKIN, H. A., LEWIS, H. B., HERTZMAN, M., MACHOVER, K., MEISSNER, P. B., & Wapner, S. *Personality through perception.* New York: Harper, 1954.

WITRYOL, S. L., & KAESS, W. A. Sex differences in social memory tasks. *Journal of Abnormal and Social Psychology,* 1957, *54,* 343–346.

WOLFE, J. B. Effectiveness of token-records for chimpanzees. *Comparative Psychological Monographs,* 1936, *12,* 5.

WOODWORTH, R. S. *Experimental psychology.* New York: Holt, 1938.

YARMEY, A. D. The effect of mnemonic instructions on paired-associate recognition memory for faces or names. *Canadian Journal of Behavioral Science,* 1970, *2,* 181–190.

YARMEY, A. D. Recognition memory for familiar "public" faces: Effects of orientation and delay. *Psychonomic Science,* 1971, *24,* 286–288.

YARMEY, A. D. I recognize your face but I can't remember your name: Further evidence on the tip-of-the-tongue phenomenon. *Memory and Cognition,* 1973, *1,* 287–290.

YARMEY, A. D. Proactive interference in short-term retention of human faces. *Canadian Journal of Psychology,* 1974, *28,* 333–338.

YARMEY, A. D. Introspection and imagery reports of human faces. *Perceptual and Motor Skills,* 1975, *41,* 711–719. (a)

YARMEY, A. D. Social-emotional factors in recall and recognition of human faces. Paper presented at the annual meeting of the Midwestern Psychological Association. Chicago, 1975. (b)

YARMEY, A. D. Hypermnesia for pictures but not for concrete or abstract words. *Bulletin of the Psychonomic Society,* 1976, *8,* 115–117.

YARMEY, A. D. The effects of attractiveness, feature saliency, and liking on memory for faces. In M. Cook & G. Wilson (Eds.), *Love and attraction: An international conference.* Toronto: Pergamon Press, 1978, pp. 51–53. (a)

YARMEY, A. D. Recognition memory for male and female faces. Paper presented at the annual meeting of the American Psychological Association, Toronto, 1978. (b)

YARMEY, A. D., & BEIHL, H. The influence of attitudes and recall of impressions on memory for faces. Paper presented at the annual meeting of the Psychonomic Society, Washington, D.C., 1977.

YARMEY, A. D., & BOWEN, N. V. The role of imagery in incidental learning of educable retarded and normal children. *Journal of Experimental Child Psychology,* 1972, *14,* 303–312.

YARMEY, A. D., & BULL, M. P., III. Where were you when President Kennedy was assassinated? *Bulletin of the Psychonomic Society,* 1978, *11,* 133–135.

YARMEY, A. D., & URE, G. Incidental learning, noun imagery-concreteness and direction of associations in paired-associate learning. *Canadian Journal of Psychology,* 1971, *25,* 91–102.

YIN, R. K. Looking at upside-down faces. *Journal of Experimental Psychology,* 1969, *81,* 141–145.

YIN, R. K. Face recognition by brain-injured patients: A dissociable ability? *Neuropsychologia,* 1970, *8,* 395–402.

ZAJONC, R. B. Attitudinal effects of mere exposure. *Journal of Personality and Social Psychology Monographs,* 1968, *9,* (2, Part 2), 1–27.

ZIMBARDO, P. G., & RUCH, F. L. *Psychology and life,* ninth edition. Glenview, Ill.: Scott, Foresman, 1977.

ZIMMERMAN, E., & PARLEE, M. B. Behavioral changes associated with the menstrual cycle: An experimental investigation. *Journal of Applied Social Psychology,* 1973, *3,* 335–344.

ZUCKERMAN, M., HALL, J. A., DeFRANK, R. S., & ROSENTHAL, R. Encoding and decoding of spontaneous and posed facial expressions. *Journal of Personality and Social Psychology,* 1976, *34,* 966–977.

Name Index

Subject Index